D1542937

A Concise Bibliography of
French Literature

For Roger Parant

(

A Concise Bibliography of
French Literature

DENIS MAHAFFEY

1975
BOWKER
LONDON & NEW YORK

ISBN 0 85935 008 8   LC 75–7801

First published in 1975 by the Bowker Publishing Company,
Epping, Essex, England.

Printed and bound in Great Britain by
REDWOOD BURN LIMITED
Trowbridge & Esher

Typeset by Amos Typesetters, Hockley, Essex.

Preface

This book attempts to supply basic bibliographical information on the outstanding features of French literature and scholarship, with details of English translations.

In selecting the contents, I have tried to avoid personal choice and value judgements, and simply include what most people would expect to find in such a book. It begins with the *Serments de Strasbourg* of A.D. 842, the earliest extant text in French, and ends with authors whose reputations were established by 1960. The aim is to cover all major French authors and works, and a considerable number of the best minor ones, with only occasional figures of more purely literary-historical interest. Writers from outside France have been included only if in the main stream of French literature. This means leaving out Canadian, Belgian, African and other writers of distinction. Provençal literature has been excluded: this rich and lively vein deserves more than the cursory treatment it could have been given here.

The book is divided into six period sections, containing individual entries in alphabetical order. There is also an introductory section, which begins with a list of general bibliographies, critical and other background works, and anthologies in French and in English translation, followed by similar lists for each period.

Authors are listed under the second element of their name, not counting "de" or "d' " (Agrippa d'AUBIGNÉ, Jean de LA FONTAINE). This also applies to the Mediaeval period (Jean LE BEL), even when the second element is geographical (Charles d'ORLEANS). Cross-references are given in the text for any exceptions, and the index at the end takes account of other conventional ways of listing early names. Anonymous and collective works, and a few of known authorship better known by their title, are located by the initial letter of the first main word of the title (*La CHÂTELAINE de Vergi*), except where this defines a *genre* (*Roman de RENART*). This exception does not apply to entries for *genres* as such (*CHANSONS de geste*).

Each entry is set out as follows:

> Author's name and dates (or title and date of composition of anonymous and collective works).

v

Individual bibliographies and references to works containing useful bibliographical material.*

Collected and selected works, and collected and selected English translations.

A selection from the canon in order of publication (unless otherwise noted), except that related works (series, sequels, etc) are grouped together.

Journals and correspondence.

Selected critical studies and biographies, with the emphasis on recent scholarship, and on books rather than articles.

Information on works consists of the short title as it appears in the first known edition, unless otherwise noted, but with capitals kept to a minimum, punctuation simplified, modern accentuation added where necessary, and modern usage adopted for u, v, i and j. The title is followed by the number of volumes, if more than one, place (if not Paris) and year of publication in volume form (except for some Mediaeval works available only in periodicals); year of any significant revisions (usually confined to the one taken to reflect the author's final intentions); details of any subsequent editions of special interest, and of scholarly and reliable modern editions. Reprints are never included. For editions after the first, and for translations, place of publication is given only when it changes. Details of any translations are given next in the same way, beginning with the earliest.

Much of the final stage of work on this book was done with the help of Michael de Sainte-Croix. Máire Neligan was responsible for tracking down most of the bibliographies and translations; and Carsten Jensen did a lot of thankless work at the start. I am also grateful to Ian Laurie, who recognized the need for such a book, and to Derek French, for preparing the manuscript for publication. Only with their assistance, advice from others, and reliance on earlier scholarship have I been able even to approach fulfilment of the aims of this book.

Paris, March 1975

---

*Standard general bibliographies, such as those by Cioranesco/u and Talvart & Place, often give by far the fullest coverage available, and should also be consulted where appropriate.

Contents

Abbreviations

abr.	abridged
adapt.	adaptation, adapted
anon.	anonymous
bibl.	bibliography
bk	book
c.	*circa*
ch.	chapter
cntg	containing
collab.	collaboration
ed.	edited by, edition, editor
enl.	enlarged
facs.	facsimile
fl.	*floruit*
incl.	including
introd.	introduced by
ms.(s)	manuscript(s)
n.d.	no date of publication given
n.p.	no place of publication given
pbd	published
pbn	publication
pt	part
ptd	printed
revd	revised
rpt(d)	reprint(ed)
sel.	selection
tr.	translated by, translation
unpbd	unpublished
vol	volume

General Bibliographies and Background

GENERAL WORKS

Bibliographies

British Museum general catalogue of printed books, 263 vols, London 1965–6
(to 1955; plus *Ten-year supplement*, 50 vols, 1968, and *Five-year supplement*, 36 vols, 1972).

BRUNET, J. C., *Manuel du libraire et de l'amateur de livres*, 3 vols, 1810; 6 vols, 1860–5.

Catalogue général des livres imprimés de la Bibliothèque nationale, 1897 onwards
(to 1959; 221 vols pbd, to 'Wetz').

   Catalogue général, 1960–1969, 1972 onwards (12 vols pbd, to 'Laf').

CLAUDIN, A., *Bibliographie des éditions originales d'écrivains français du 15e au 18e siècles*, 1888.

CORDIÉ, C., *Avviamento allo studio della lingua e della letteratura francese*, Milan 1955.

French language and literature, in *Proceedings of the Modern Language Association*, New York 1921–69.

   French literature, in *International bibliography*, New York 1969 onwards.

French studies, in *The year's work in modern languages*, Oxford and London 1930 onwards.

GOLDEN, H. H. and SIMCHES, S. O., *Modern French literature and language: a bibliography of homage studies*, Cambridge (Mass) 1953.

KLAPP, O., *Bibliographie der französischen Literaturwissenschaft*, Frankfurt-am-Main 1960 onwards.

LANGLOIS P., and MAREUIL, A., *Guide bibliographique des études littéraires*, 1958; 1965 (enl.).

LANSON, G., *Manuel bibliographique de la littérature française moderne, 1500–1900*, 5 vols, 1909–12; 2 vols, 1921 (enl.).

   GIRAUD, J., *Manuel de bibliographie littéraire pour les 16e, 17e et 18e siècles français, 1921–1935*, 1939 (plus supplements *1936–1945*, 1956, and *1946–1955*, 1970).

OSBURN, C. B., *Research and reference guide to French studies*, Metuchen (NJ) 1968 (and *Supplement*, 1972).

   The present state of French studies, Metuchen (NJ) 1971.

PARKS, G. B. and TEMPLE, R. Z., *The romance literatures*, 2 vols, New York 1970 (vol 3, pts 1–2 of *The literatures of the world in English translation*).

QUÉRARD, J. N., *La France littéraire, ou dictionnaire bibliographique*, 12 vols, 1827–64.

RANCOEUR, R., *Bibliographie littéraire*, 1953 onwards.

Répertoire analytique de littérature française, Bordeaux 1970 onwards.

SIMONE, F. et al., *Dizionario critico della letteratura francese*, 2 vols, Turin 1972.

TCHEMERZINE, A., *Bibliographie d'éditions originales et rares d'auteurs français des 15e, 16e, 17e et 18e siècles*, 10 vols, 1927–33.

TOUGAS, G., *A check list of printed materials relating to French Canadian literature*, Vancouver 1958; 1973 (updated to 1968).

Reference books

BOUVIER, E. and JOURDA, P., *Guide de l'étudiant en littérature française*, 1936; 1968.

BRAUN, S. D., *Dictionary of French literature*, New York 1958.

GRENTE, G. et al., *Dictionnaire des lettres françaises*, 7 vols, 1951–72.

HARVEY, P. and HESELTINE, J. E., *The Oxford companion to French literature*, Oxford 1959.

NATHAN, J., NATHAN, C. and BASCH, R., *Encyclopédie de la littérature française*, 1952.

Background and literary criticism

ABRAHAM, P. and DESNE, E., *Manuel d'histoire littératire de la France*, 1973.

ABRY, E., AUDIC, C. and CROUZET, P., *Histoire illustrée de la littérature française*, 1912; 1929.

ADAM, A., LERMINIER, G. and MOROT-SIR, E., *Littérature française*, 2 vols, 1967–8; 2 vols, 1972.

BÉDIER, J. and HAZARD, P., *Histoire de la littérature française illustrée*, 2 vols, 1923–4; 2 vols, 1948–9.

BORNECQUE, P. and J. H., *La France et sa littérature*, 2 vols, Lyon 1957.

BRAUNSCHVIG, M., *Notre littérature étudiée dans les textes*, 2 vols, 1921.

BREMOND, H., *Histoire littéraire du sentiment religieux en France*, 12 vols, 1916–36. Tr. K. L. Montgomery. *A literary history of religious thought in France*, 3 vols, London 1928–36 (incomplete).

BRERETON, G., *A short history of French literature*, Baltimore (Md) 1954.

An introduction to the French poets, London 1956.

BRUNETIÈRE, F., *Manuel de l'histoire de la littérature française*, 1898. Tr. R. Derechef, *Manual of the history of French literature*, London 1898.

CAZAMIAN, L. F., *A history of French literature*, Oxford 1955.

CHARLTON, D. G. (ed.), *France: a companion to French studies*, London 1972; 1974 (enl., as 5 separate books, incl. *French literature from 1600 to the present*, by W. D. Howarth, H. M. Peyre and J. Cruickshank).

CHARVET, P. E. et al., *Literary history of France*, 5 vols, London 1967–70.

CRUICKSHANK, J. (ed.), *French literature and its background*, 6 vols, London 1969–70.

DUBY, G. and MANDROU, R., *Histoire de la civilisation française*, 2 vols, 1958. Tr. J. B. Atkinson, *A history of French civilization*, New York 1964.

FAGUET, E., *Histoire de la littérature française*, 2 vols, 1901.

FONTAINE, A., *Les doctrines d'art en France*, 1909.

HANOTAUX, G., ed., *Histoire de la nation française*, 15 vols, 1920–9. Tr. E. F. Buckley, 3 vols, London and New York 1928–30 (part tr.).

HÉMON, F., *Cours de littérature*, 9 vols, 1889–1906.

Histoire littéraire de la France, 1733 onwards (40 vols pbd).

JASINSKI, R., *Histoire de la littérature française*, 2 vols, 1947.

LANSON, G., *Histoire de la littérature française*, 1895–1906.

LEGGE, J. G., *Chanticleer: a study of the French Muse*, London 1935.

LEGOUIS, E., *Défense de la poésie française, à l'usage des lecteurs anglais*, London 1912.

MORNET, D., *Histoire générale de la littérature française*, 2 vols, 1939.

NITZE, W. A. and DARGAN, E. P., *A history of French literature*, New York 1923; 1938.

PETIT DE JULLEVILLE, L. et al., *Histoire de la langue et de la littérature française*, 8 vols, 1896–9.

Le théâtre en France: histoire de la littérature dramatique depuis ses origines jusqu'à nos jours, 1889.

PICHOIS, C. (ed.), *Littérature française*, 1968 onwards (6 vols pbd).

QUENEAU, R. (ed.), *Littératures françaises*, 1958 (vol. 3 of *Histoire des littératures*).

RAGON, M., *Histoire de la littérature prolétarienne*, 1974.

RITCHIE, R. L. G., *France: a companion to French studies*, London 1907.

SABATIER, R., *Histoire de la poésie française*, 1975 onwards (2 vols pbd).

SAINTSBURY, G., *A short history of French literature*, London 1882.

History of the French novel, 2 vols, London 1917–19.

STRACHEY, L., *Landmarks in French literature*, London 1912.

SUCHIER, H. and BIRSCH-HIRSCHFELD, A., *Geschichte der französischen Literatur*, Leipzig 1900.

VIER, J., *Histoire de la littérature française*, 3 vols, 1959–71.

WRIGHT, C. H. C., *A history of French literature*, New York 1912; 1925.

Anthologies in French

Anthologie de la correspondance française, ed. A. Maison, 7 vols, Lausanne 1969.

Anthologie des écrivains belges, ed. L. Dumont-Wilden, 2 vols, 1917.

Anthologie des écrivains catholiques, ed. H. Bremond and C. Grolleau, 1919.

Anthologie des écrivains français, ed. L. Gauthier-Ferrières, 10 vols, 1908–13.

Anthologie de la poésie française, ed. M. Arland, 1941.

Anthologie de la poésie française, ed. A. Gide, 1949.

Anthologie de la poésie française, ed. R. Kanters, M. Nadeau and G. Sigaux, 12 vols, Lausanne n.d.

Anthologie de la poésie française, ed. G. Pompidou, 1961.

Anthologie poétique française, ed. M. Allem, 5 vols, 1914–19 (16th–18th centuries).

Life and letters in France, ed. R. Fargher, A. Gill and W. D. Howarth, 3 vols, London 1965–70.

Le livre d'or de la poésie française, ed. P. Seghers, 1961.

The Oxford book of French prose, Oxford 1972.

The Oxford book of French verse, Oxford 1908.

The Penguin book of French verse, 4 vols, Harmondsworth 1958–61 (with English trs).

La poésie française, ed. M. P. Fouchet, 1963.

The poetry of France, ed. A. M. Boase, 4 vols, London 1952–69.

Three centuries of French verse, 1511–1819, ed. A. J. Steele, Edinburgh 1961.

Trésors du pastiche, ed. F. Cardec, 1971.

Anthologies in translation

Anthology of French poetry, 10th to 19th centuries, tr. H. Carrington, London 1900.

Cassell's anthology of French poetry, tr. A. Conder, London 1950 (New York 1951, as *A treasury of French poetry*).

Fleurs-de-lys, a book of French poetry, tr. A. Thorley, Boston (Mass) 1920.

Flowers of France, tr. J. Payne, 6 vols, London 1906–13.

French lyrics, tr. W. F. Giese, Madison (Wis) 1946.

Invitation to French poetry, tr. S. Appelbaum, New York 1969.

The Penguin book of French verse: see anthologies in French above.

Poems, tr. T. S. Moore, 2 vols, London 1932.

THE MIDDLE AGES

See also separate general entries for *CHANSONS de geste* (page 6) and *MATIÈRE DE BRETAGNE* (page 21).

Bibliographies

BOSSUAT, R., *Manuel bibliographique de la littérature française du Moyen Age*, Melun 1951 (plus *Supplément, 1949–1953*, 1955, and *Second supplément, 1954–1960*, 1961).

DE JONGH, W. F. J., *A bibliography of the novel and short story in French from the beginning of printing till 1600*, Albuquerque (NMex) 1944.

HOLMES, U. T. et al. (ed. D. C. Cabeen), *A critical bibliography of French literature: the mediaeval period*, Syracuse (NY) 1947; 1952.

RAYNAUD, G., *Bibliographie des chansonniers français des 13e et 14e siècle*, 2 vols, 1884.

> JEANROY, A., *Bibliographie sommaire des chansonniers français du Moyen Age*, 1918.

STRATMAN, C. J., in his *Bibliography of mediaeval drama*, Berkeley (Calif) 1954; 2 vols, 1972 (enl.).

THOMAS, H. et al., *Short-title catalogue of books printed in France and of French books printed in other countries from 1470 to 1600, now in the British Museum*, London 1924.

WOLEDGE, B., *Bibliographie des romans et nouvelles en prose française antérieurs à 1500*, Geneva 1954.

WOLEDGE, B. and CLIVE, H. P., *Répertoire des plus anciens textes en prose française depuis 842 jusqu'aux premières années du 13e siècle*, Geneva 1964.

Background and literary criticism

BEZZOLA, R., *Les origines et la formation de la littérature courtoise en Occident*, 5 vols, 1944–63.

BRUYNE, E. de, *Etudes d'esthétique médiévale*, 3 vols, Bruges 1946.

BURGER, M., *Recherches sur la structure et l'origine des vers romans*, Geneva 1957.

CHAILLEY, J., *Histoire musicale du Moyen Age*, 1950.

CHAMARD, H., *Les origines de la poésie française de la Renaissance*, 1920.

CHAMPION, P., *Histoire poétique du 15e siècle*, 2 vols, 1923.

CHATELAIN, H., *Recherches sur le vers français au 15e siècle*, 1908.

COHEN, G., *Le théâtre en France au Moyen Age*, 2 vols, 1928–31.

> *Etudes d'histoire du théâtre en France au Moyen Age et à la Renaissance*, 1956.

DRAGONETTI, R., *La technique poétique des trouvères dans la chanson courtoise*, Bruges 1960.

EVANS, J., *Life in mediaeval France*, Oxford 1925.

FOURRIER, A. et al., *L'humanisme médiéval dans les littératures romanes du 12e au 14e siècle*, 1964.

FRANK, G., *The Medieval French drama*, Oxford 1954.

GÉNICOT, L., *Les lignes de faîte du Moyen Age*, 1951.

HOLMES, U. T., *A history of Old French literature from the origins to 1300*, New York 1937.

JEANROY, A., *Les origines de la poésie lyrique en France au Moyen Age*, 1925.

KUKENHEIM, L. and ROUSSEL, H., *Guide de la littérature française du Moyen Age*, Leiden 1957.

LEGGE, M. D., *Anglo-Norman literature and its background*, Oxford 1963.

LOTE, G., *Histoire du vers français*, 3 vols, 1949–55.

OLSCHKI, L., in his *Die romanischen Literaturen des Mittelalters*, Potsdam 1928.

PARIS, G., *La littérature française au Moyen Age, 11e au 14e siècle*, 1888. Tr. H. Lynch, *Mediaeval French literature*, London 1903.

PETIT DE JULLEVILLE, L., *Histoire du théâtre en France*, 5 vols, 1880–6.

RASMUSSEN, J., *La prose narrative française du 15e siècle*, Copenhagen 1958.

Romania, ed. P. Meyer, G. Paris and M. Roques, 1872 onwards.

RYCHNER, J., *La littérature et les moeurs chevaleresques à la cour de Bourgogne*, Neufchâtel 1950.

SÖDERHJELM, W., *La nouvelle française au 15e siècle*, 1910.

TIEMANN, H., *Die Entstehung der mittelalterlichen Novelle in Frankreich*, Hamburg 1961.

TILLEY, A. A. (ed.), *Medieval France, a companion to French studies*, Cambridge 1922.

VORETZSCH, C., *Einführung in des Studium der altfranzösischen Literatur*, Halle 1905. Tr. F. M. Dumont, *Introduction to the study of Old French literature*, New York 1931.

YOUNG, K., *The drama of the medieval church*, Oxford 1933.

ZUMTHOR, P., *Histoire littéraire de la France médiévale, 6e–14e siècles*, 1954.

Anthologies in French

Anthologie de la littérature française du Moyen Age, ed. G. Cohen, 1946.

Chrestomathie de la littérature en ancien français, Berne 1954.

La fleur de la poésie française, ed. A. Mary, 1951; 2 vols, 1967 (as *Anthologie poétique française, Moyen Age*.

Anthologies in translation

Aucassin and Nicolette and other mediaeval romances and legends, tr. E. Mason, London 1910.

The early French novella, an anthology of 15th and 16th century tales, tr. P. F. and R. C. Cholakian, Albany (NY) 1972.

Formal spring, tr. R. N. Currey, New York and London 1950.

Lays of courtly love, tr. P. Terry, New York 1963.

Medieval literature in translation, ed. C. W. Jones, New York and London 1950.

Medieval song, tr. J. J. Wilhelm, London 1972.

Romances of love: early French romances in verse, tr. E. Rickert, London 1908.

Tales from the Old French, tr. I. Butler, Boston (Mass) 1910.

THE SIXTEENTH CENTURY

Bibliographies

CIORANESCO, A., *Bibliographie de la littérature française du 16e siècle*, 1959.

LACHÈVRE, F., *Bibliographie des recueils collectifs de poésies du 16e siècle*, 1922.

SCHUTZ, A. H. (ed. D. C. Cabeen), *A critical bibliography of French literature: 2, The 16th century*, Syracuse (NY) 1956.

THOMAS, H. et al., *Short-title catalogue of books printed in France and of French books printed in other countries from 1470 to 1600, now in the British Museum*, London 1924.

Background and literary criticism

ATKINSON, G., *Les nouveaux horizons de la Renaissance française*, 1935.

BELLOC, H., *Avril, being essays on the poetry of the French Renaissance*, London 1904.

BRERETON, G., *French tragic drama in the 16th and 17th centuries*, London 1973.

BUSSON, H., *Les sources et le développement du rationalisme dans la littérature française de la Renaissance*, 1922.

CHAMARD, H., *Histoire de la Pléiade*, 4 vols, 1939–40.

DAINVILLE, F. de, *La naissance de l'humanisme moderne*, 1940.

DELUMEAU, J., *Naissance et affirmation de la Réforme*, 1965.

FEBVRE, L., *Au cœur religieux du 16e siècle*, 1957.

    In his *Le problème de l'incroyance au 16e siècle: la religion de Rabelais*, 1942.

FEBVRE, L. and MARTIN, H. J., *L'apparition du livre*, 1958.

GUY, H., *Histoire de la poésie française au 16e siècle, l'école des rhétoriqueurs*, 1910.

HAUSER, H., *Les sources de l'histoire de France, 16e siècle*, 4 vols, 1906–15.

IMBART DE LA TOUR, P., *Les origines de la Réforme*, 4 vols, 1905–35.

LANCASTER, H. C., *The French tragicomedy, its origin and development from 1552 to 1628*, Baltimore (Md) 1907.

LEBÈGUE, R., *La tragédie religieuse en France*, 1929.

    La tragédie française de la Renaissance, Brussels 1944.

LECLER, J., *Histoire de la tolérance au siècle de la Réforme*, 2 vols, 1955.

LEFRANC, A., *La vie quotidienne au temps de la Renaissance*, 1938.

MARSAN, J., *La pastorale dramatique en France à la fin du 16e et au commencement du 17e siècle*, 1905.

MÉNAGER, D., *Introduction à la vie littéraire du 16e siècle*, 1968.

RAYMOND, M. and STEELE, A. J., ed., *La poésie française et le maniérisme, 1546–1610*, Geneva 1971.

REDENBACHER, F., *Die Novellistik der französischen Hochrenaissance*, Munich 1926.

SAINTE-BEUVE, C. A. de, *Tableau historique et critique de la poésie française et du théâtre français au 16e siècle*, 1828.

SCHMIDT, A. M., *La poésie scientifique en France au 16e siècle*, 1939.

SIMONE, F., *Il Rinascimento francese*, Turin 1961.

STONE, D., *France in the 16th century: a medieval society transformed*, Englewood Cliffs (NJ) and Hemel Hempstead 1969.

TILLEY, A. A., *The literature of the French Renaissance*, 2 vols, Cambridge 1904.

    The dawn of the French Renaissance, Cambridge 1918.

WEBER, H., *La création au 16e siècle en France, de Maurice Scève à Agrippa d'Aubigné*, 2 vols, 1956.

WILSON, D. B., *Descriptive poetry in France from Blason to Baroque*, Manchester and New York 1967.

Anthologies in French

Anthologie du 16e siècle, ed. J. Plattard, 1927.
La langue française au 16e siècle, ed. P. Rickard, Cambridge 1968.
Poètes du 16e siècle, ed. A. M. Schmidt, 1953.
Seizième siècle, ed. P. Bennezon et al., 1963.

Anthologies in translation

The early French novella, an anthology of 15th and 16th century tales, tr. P. F. and R. C. Cholakian, Albany (NY) 1972.
The early French poets, tr. H. F. Cary, London 1846.
European metaphysical poetry, tr. F. Warnke, New Haven (Conn) 1961.
Renaissance and Baroque lyrics, an anthology, ed. H. M. Priest, Evanston (Ill) 1962.

THE SEVENTEENTH CENTURY

Bibliographies

Bibliography of French 17th-century studies (French III bibliography), Bloomington (Ind) 1953 onwards.

CIORANESCU, A., *Bibliographie de la littérature française du 17e siècle*, 3 vols, 1965–7.

CONLON, P. M., *Prélude au siècle des lumières en France; répertoire chronologique de 1680 à 1715*, 4 vols, Geneva 1969–73 (vols 1–2: 1680–99).

EDELMAN, N. et al. (ed. D. C. Cabeen), *A critical bibliography of French literature: 3, The 17th century*, Syracuse (NY) 1961.

GOLDSMITH, V. F., *A short-title catalogue of French books, 1601–1700, in the library of the British Museum*, 7 pts, Folkestone and London 1969–73.

LACHÈVRE, F., *Bibliographie des recueils collectifs de poésies publiés de 1597 à 1700*, 4 vols, 1901–5.

WILLIAMS, R. C., *Bibliography of the 17th century novel in France*, New York 1931.

    BALDNER, R. W., *Bibliography of 17th century French prose fiction*, New York 1967.

Background and literary criticism

ADAM, A., *Histoire de la littérature française au 17e siècle*, 5 vols, 1948–56.

BORGERHOFF, E. B. O., *The freedom of French classicism*, Princeton (NJ) 1950.

BRAY, R., *La formation de la doctrine classique en France*, Paris 1927.

BRERETON, G., *French tragic drama in the 16th and 17th centuries*, London 1973.

BRODY, J., ed., *French classicism, a critical miscellany*, Englewood Cliffs (NJ) 1966.

CLERCX, S., *Le Baroque et la musique*, Brussels 1948.

DALLAS, D., *Le roman français de 1660 à 1680*, 1932.

DEIERKAUF-HOLSBOER, S. W., *L'histoire de la mise en scène dans le théâtre français à Paris de 1600 à 1673*, 1960.

DELOFFRE, F., *La nouvelle en France à l'âge classique*, 1967.

FIDAO-JUSTINIANI, J. E., *L'esprit classique et la préciosité au 17e siècle*, 1954.

FUKUI YOSHIO, *Raffinement précieux dans la poésie française du 17e siècle*, 1964.

GILLOT, H., *La querelle des anciens et des modernes en France*, 1914.

KOHLER, P., *Autour de Molière: l'esprit classique et la comédie*, 1925.

LANCASTER, H. C., *A history of French dramatic literature in the 17th century*, 9 vols, Baltimore (Md) and Paris 1929–42.

LANSON, G., *Esquisse d'une histoire de la tragédie française*, New York 1920; Paris 1927.

LE BRETON, A., *Le roman au 17e siècle*, 1890; 1912.

LITMAN, T. A., *Le sublime en France, 1660–1714*, 1971.

LOCKERT, C. L., *Studies in French classical tragedy*, Nashville (Tenn) 1958.

MAGENDIE, M., *Le roman français au 17e siècle, de l'Astrée au Grand Cyrus*, 1932.

MARSAN J., *La pastorale dramatique en France*, 1905.

MONGRÉDIEN, G., *La vie littéraire au 17e siècle*, 1947.

    La vie quotidienne sous Louis XIV, 1948.

    (ed.), *Les précieux et les précieuses*, 1963.

MORÇAY, R. and SAGE, P., *Le préclassicisme*, 1962.

MORNET, D., *Histoire de la littérature française classique, 1660–1700*, 1940.

MOORE, W. G., *French classical literature: an essay*, Oxford 1962.

    The classical drama in France, Oxford 1971.

PEYRE, H., *Qu'est-ce que le classicisme? essai de mise au point*, 1942; 1964.

PINTARD, R., *Le libertinage érudit dans la première moitié du 17e siècle*, 2 vols, 1943.

RAYMOND, M., *Baroque et renaissance poétique*, 1955.

REYNOLD, G. de, *Synthèse du 17e siècle: France classique et Europe baroque*, 1962.

RIGAULT, H., *Histoire de la querelle des anciens et des modernes*, 1856.

ROUSSET, J., *La littérature de l'âge baroque en France*, 1954.
    L'intérieur et l'extérieur, 1968.

SCHERER, J., *La dramaturgie classique en France*, 1950.

SHOWALTER, E., *The evolution of the French novel, 1641–1782*, Princeton (NJ) 1972.

TAPIÉ, V. L., *Baroque et classicisme*, 1957.

TILLEY, A. A., *The decline of the age of Louis XIV, or French literature 1687–1715*, Cambridge 1929.

TOURNAND, J. C., *Introduction à la vie littéraire du 17e siècle*, 1970.

WILEY, W. L., *The early public theatre in France*, Cambridge (Mass) 1960.

Anthologies in French

Anthologie de la poésie baroque française, ed. J. Rousset, 2 vols, 1961.

An anthology of French 17th century lyric poetry, ed. O. de Mourgues, Oxford 1966.

Dix-septième siècle, ed. P. Bennezon et al., 1962.

La poésie française de 1640 à 1680, ed. R. Picard, 1964.

Poésie du 17e siècle, ed. T. Maulnier, 1945.

Les satires françaises du 17e siècle, ed. F. Fleuret and L. Perceau, 2 vols, 1923.

Anthologies in translation

The chief rivals of Corneille and Racine, tr. C. L. Lockert, Nashville (Tenn) 1956.
    More plays by the rivals of Corneille and Racine, tr. C. L. Lockert, Nashville (Tenn) 1968.

Renaissance and Baroque lyrics, an anthology, ed. H. M. Priest, Evanston (Ill) 1962.

THE EIGHTEENTH CENTURY

Bibliographies

BRENNER, C. D., *A bibliographical list of plays in the French language, 1700–1789*, Berkeley (Calif) 1947.

CIORANESCU, A., *Bibliographie de la littérature française du 18e siècle*, 3 vols, 1969.

CONLON, P. M., *Prélude au siècle des Lumières en France: répertoire chronologique de 1680 à 1715*, 4 vols, Geneva 1969–73 (vols 3–4: 1700–1715).

HAVENS, G. R., BOND, D. F. et al. (ed. D. C. Cabeen), *A critical bibliography of French literature: 4, The 18th century*, Syracuse (NY) 1951 (plus *Supplement* 1968).

JONES, S. P., *A list of French prose fiction from 1700 to 1750*, New York 1939.

Background and literary criticism

AGHION, M., *Le théâtre à Paris au 18e siècle*, 1926.

ANCHOR, R., *The Enlightenment tradition*, New York, 1967

ATKINSON, G. and KELLER, A. C., *Prelude to the Enlightenment*, London 1971.

BERLIN, I., *The 18th century philosophers, the Age of Enlightenment*, London and New York 1956.

BROOKS, P., *The novel of worldliness*, Princeton (NJ) 1969.

CHINARD, G., *L'Amérique et le rêve exotique dans la littérature française au 17e et au 18e siècle*, 1934.

EHRARD, J., *L'idée de nature en France dans la première moitié du 18e siècle*, 2 vols, 1963.

ESTÈVE, E., *Etudes de littérature préromantique*, 1923.

FINCH, M. B. and PEERS, E. A., *The origins of French romanticism*, London 1920.

FINCH, R., *The sixth sense: individualism in French poetry, 1686–1760*, Toronto 1966.

GAIFFE F., *Le drame en France au 18e siècle*, 1910.

GAY, P., *The Enlightenment: an interpretation*, 2 vols, New York 1966–9.

GILMAN, M., *The idea of poetry in France from Houdar de La Mothe to Baudelaire*, Cambridge (Mass) 1958.

GREEN, F. C., *Minuet: a critical survey of English and French literary ideas in the 18th century*, London 1935.

HAVENS, G. R., *The age of ideas*, New York 1955.

HAZARD, P., *La crise de la conscience européenne, 1680–1715*, 1935. Tr. J. L. May, *The European mind: the critical years*, New Haven (Conn) 1953.
La pensée européenne au 18e siècle, de Montesquieu à Lessing, 1946. Tr. J. L. May, *European thought in the 18th century*, New Haven (Conn) 1954.

HEARNSHAW, F. J. C. (ed.), *The social and political ideas of some great thinkers of the Age of Reason*, New York 1930.

JAUFFRET, E., *Le théâtre révolutionnaire, 1788–1799*, 1869.

KELLENBERGER, R. K., *La décade philosophique: a study in literary history and criticism*, Princeton (NJ) 1947.

LANCASTER, H. C., *French tragedy in the time of Louis XV and Voltaire*, 2 vols, Baltimore (Md) 1950.

LAUNAY, M. and MAILHOS, G., *Introduction à la vie littéraire du 18e siècle*, 1969.

LE BRETON, A., *Le roman au 18e siècle*, 1898.

MAUZI, R., *L'idée du bonheur dans la littérature et la pensée françaises au 18e siècle*, 1960.

MAY, G., *Le dilemme du roman au 18e siècle: étude sur les rapports du roman et de la critique, 1715–1761*, New Haven (Conn) and Paris 1963.

MONGLOND, A., *Histoire intérieure du préromantisme français*, 2 vols, Grenoble 1929.

MOREL, J., *La tragédie*, 1964.

MORNET, D., *Les origines intellectuelles de la Révolution française*, 1934.

MYLNE, V., *The 18th century French novel: techniques of illusion*, Manchester and New York 1965.

POMEAU, R., *L'Europe des lumières*, 1966.

ROGER, J., *Les sciences de la vie dans la pensée française du 18e siècle*, 1963.

SHOWALTER, E., *The evolution of the French novel, 1641–1782*, Princeton (NJ) 1972.

STEWART, P., *Imitation and make-believe in the French memoir-novel, 1700–1750*, New Haven (Conn) 1969.

TRAHARD, P., *Les maîtres de la sensibilité française au 18e siècle*, 4 vols, 1931–3.

VAN TIEGHEM, P., *Le préromantisme*, 3 vols, 1948.

Anthologies in French

Anthologie du 18e siècle romantique, ed. J. Bousquet, 1972.
Chefs d'oeuvre des poètes galants du 18e siècle, 1921.
Dix-huitième siècle, ed. P. Bennezon and R. Virolle, 1966.
Le 18e siècle: goût, lumières, nature, ed. R. Saisselin, Englewood Cliffs (NJ) 1973.
Lettres du 18e siècle, ed. A. Cahen, 1894.
La philosophie des lumières dans sa dimension européenne, ed. A. Biedermann, 1973.

Anthologies in translation

The Age of Enlightenment, an anthology of 18th-century French literature, ed. O. E. Fellows and N. L. Torrey, New York 1942.
French comedies of the 18th century, tr. R. Aldington, London 1923.

THE NINETEENTH CENTURY

Bibliographies

ASSELINEAU, C., *Bibliographie romantique*, 1874.

BRAY, R., *Chronologie du romantisme, 1804–30*, 1932.

CHÉRON, P. A., *Catalogue général de la librairie française au 19e siècle*, 2 vols, 1856–59.

ESCOFFIER, M., *Le mouvement romantique 1788–1850: essai de bibliographie synchronique et méthodique*, 1934.

HAYNE, D. M., and TIROL, M., *Bibliographie critique du roman canadien-français, 1837–1900,* Toronto 1968.

STARR, W. T. (ed.), *Critical and biographical references for the study of 19th century French literature (French VI bibliography),* New York 1956 onwards.

TALVART, H. and PLACE, J., *Bibliographie des auteurs modernes de langue française,* 1928 onwards (20 vols pbd, to 'Montherlant').

THIÈME, H. P., *Bibliographie de la littérature française de 1800 à 1930,* 3 vols, 1933.

DREHER, S. and ROLLI, M., *Bibliographie de la littérature française, 1930–1939,* Lille and Geneva 1948.

DREVET, M. L., *Bibliographie de la littérature française, 1940–1949,* Lille and Geneva 1955.

VICAIRE, G., *Manuel de l'amateur de livres du 19e siècle,* 8 vols, 1894–1920.

Background and literary criticism

ABRAMS, M. H., *The mirror and the lamp; romantic theory and the critical tradition,* New York, 1953

ALLARD, L., *La comédie de moeurs en France au 19e siècle,* 2 vols, 1923–33.

BÉGUIN, A., *L'âme romantique et le rêve,* Marseille 1937.

BEUCHAT, C., *Histoire du naturalisme français,* 2 vols, 1949.

BOUSQUET, J., *Les thèmes du rêve dans la littérature romantique,* 1964.

CARTER, A. E., *The idea of decadence in French literature,* Toronto 1958.

CLANCIER, G. E., *De Rimbaud au surréalisme, panorama critique,* 1966.

CLOUARD, H., *Histoire de la littérature française du symbolisme à nos jours,* 2 vols, 1947–50 (vol 1: 1885–1914).

DESCOTES, M., *Le drame romantique et ses grands créateurs, 1827–1839,* 1955.

DUMESNIL, R., *Le réalisme et le naturalisme,* 1955.

EGGLI, E., *Le débat romantique en France,* 1933.

EMERY, L., *L'âge romantique,* 2 vols, Lyon 1960.

EVANS, D. O., *Le théâtre pendant la période romantique,* 1925.

GINISTY, P., *France d'antan: le théâtre romantique,* 1922.

GUICHARD, L., *La musique et les lettres au temps du romantisme,* 1955.

GUIRAL, P. et al, *La société française 1815–1914, vue par les romanciers,* 1969.

HENDERSON, J. A., *The first avant-garde, 1887–1894: sources of the modern French theatre,* London 1971.

JOURDA, P., *L'exotisme dans la littérature française depuis Chateaubriand, le romantisme,* 1938.

LE BRETON, A., *Le roman français au 19e siècle avant Balzac,* 1901.

LEHMANN, A. G., *The symbolist aesthetic in France, 1885–1895,* Oxford 1950.

MARSAN, J., *La bataille romantique,* 2 vols, 1912–n.d.

MARTINO, P., *Le roman réaliste sous le Second Empire,* 1913.

Le naturalisme français, 1923.

L'époque romantique en France, 1945.

MICHAUD, G., *La doctrine symboliste*, 1947.
  Message poétique du symbolisme, 2 vols, 1947.
MOREAU, P., *Le romantisme*, 1958.
PETER, R., *Le théâtre et la vie sous la 3e République*, 2 vols, 1946–8.
RICHARD, J. P., *Etudes sur le romantisme*, 1970.
RIFFATERRE, H., *L'orphisme dans la poésie romantique*, 1970.
SHATTUCK, R., *The banquet years: the arts in France, 1885–1918*, London 1958; New York 1965.
SOURIAU, M., *Histoire du romantisme en France*, 3 vols, 1927–8.
  Histoire du Parnasse, 1930.
TADIÉ, J. Y., *Introduction à la vie littéraire du 19e siècle*, 1970.
TISON-BRAUN, M., *La crise de l'humanisme*, 2 vols, 1958–67 (vol 1: 1860–1914).
TURNELL, M., *The art of French fiction*, London 1951.
VIATTE, A., *Les sources occultes du romantisme*, 1928.
WEINBERG, B., *French realism: the critical reaction, 1830–1870*, New York 1937.

Anthologies in French

Anthologie du conte fantastique français, ed. P. G. Castex, 1963.
Anthologie des poètes français contemporains; le Parnasse et les écoles postérieures au Parnasse, ed. G. Walch, 3 vols, 1906.
A book of French verse, Lamartine to Eluard, ed. P. Mansell Jones and G. Richardson, Oxford 1964.
Dix-neuvième siècle, ed. P. Bennezon, P. Albouy and J. Lac, 1968.

Anthologies in translation

An anthology of French poetry from Nerval to Valéry, ed. A. Flores, New York 1958.
French short stories of the 19th and 20th centuries, tr. M. B. Green, London 1961.
French stories and tales, ed. S. Geist, New York 1954.
Pastels in prose, tr. S. Merrill, New York 1890.
The Penguin book of French short stories, tr. E. Marielle, Harmondsworth 1968.
The Symbolist poem, ed. E. Engelberg, New York 1967.

THE TWENTIETH CENTURY

Bibliographies

ALDEN, D. W. et al., *Bibliography of critical and biographical references for the study of contemporary French literature, 1940–1948*, New York 1949.
  French VII bibliography, 1949 onwards.

ARNAUD, J. et al., *Bibliographie de la littérature nord-africaine d'expression française, 1945–1962*, Paris and The Hague 1965.

BARATTE-ENO BELINGA, T., *Bibliographie d'auteurs africains et malgaches de langue française*, 1972.

CULOT, J. M., BRUCHER, R. et al., *Bibliographie des écrivains français de Belgique, 1881–1950*, Brussels 1958 onwards (4 vols pbd, to 'N').

DROLET, A., *Bibliographie du roman canadien-français, 1900–1950*, Quebec 1955.

TALVART, H. and PLACE, J., *Bibliographie des auteurs modernes de langue française*, 1928 onwards (20 vols pbd, to 'Montherlant').

THIÈME, H. P., *Bibliographie de la littérature française de 1800 à 1930*, 3 vols, 1933.

> DREHER, S. and ROLLI, M., *Bibliographie de la littérature française, 1930–1939*, Lille and Geneva 1948.

> DREVET, M. L., *Bibliographie de la littérature française, 1940–1949*, Lille and Geneva 1955.

Reference books

ALBÉRÈS, R. M. et al., *Dictionnaire de littérature contemporaine, 1900–1962*, 1963.

PINGAUD, E., *Ecrivains d'aujourd'hui, 1940–1960, dictionnaire anthologique et critique*, 1960.

Background and literary criticism

ALBÉRÈS, R. M., *L'aventure intellectuelle du 20e siècle, 1900–1950*, 1950.

ALQUIÉ, F., *Philosophie du surréalisme*, 1955.

BALAKIAN, A., *Surrealism, the road to the absolute*, New York 1959.

BALDENSPERGER, F., *La littérature française entre les deux guerres*, Los Angeles (Calif) 1941.

BARRAULT, J. L., *Réflexions sur le théâtre*, 1949.

BÉHAR, H., *Etude sur le théâtre dada et surréaliste*, 1967.

BLOCH-MICHEL, J., *Le présent de l'indicatif*, 1963.

BOISDEFFRE, P. de, *Métamorphose de la littérature*, 2 vols, 1963.

BRÉE, G. and GUITON, M., *An age of fiction*, London 1957.

BRISSON, P., *Le théâtre des années folles*, Geneva 1943.

BROMBERT, V., *The intellectual hero: studies in the French novel, 1880–1955*, Philadelphia (Pa) and New York 1961.

CRU, J. N., *Témoins*, 1929.

CRUICKSHANK, J. (ed.), *The novelist as philosopher: studies in French fiction, 1935–1960*, London 1962.

DÉCAUDIN, M., *La crise des valeurs symbolistes: vingt ans de poésie française, 1895–1914*, Toulouse 1960.

ESSLIN, M., *The theatre of the absurd*, New York 1961. Tr. M. Buchet et al., *Le théâtre de l'absurde*, Paris 1963.

FOULQUIÉ, P., *L'existentialisme*, 1949.

FOWLIE, W., *A guide to contemporary French literature, from Valéry to Sartre*, New York 1957.
   Climate of violence: the French literary tradition from Baudelaire to the present, New York 1967.

GOLDMANN, L., *Pour une sociologie du roman*, 1964.

GRIMSLEY, R., *Existentialist thought*, Cardiff 1955.

GROSSVOGEL, D. I., *The self-conscious stage*, New York 1958; 1961 (renamed *20th century French drama*).

GUICHARNAUD, J., *Modern French theatre*, New Haven (Conn) 1961; 1967.

JANVIER, L., *Une parole exigeante: le nouveau roman*, 1964.

KNOWLES, D., *French drama of the inter-war years, 1918–1939*, London 1967.

MAGNY, C. E., *Histoire du roman français depuis 1918*, 1950.

MICHEL, H., *Les courants de pensée de la Résistance*, 1962.

NADEAU, M., *Histoire du surréalisme*, 2 vols, 1945–7. Tr. R. Howard, *The history of Surrealism*, New York 1965.

NATHAN, J., *Histoire de la littérature contemporaine*, 1954.

PEYRE, H., *The contemporary French novel*, New York 1955; 1967 (renamed *French novelists of today*).

PICON, G., *Panorama de la nouvelle littérature française*, 1950.

PRONKO, L. C., *Avant-garde: the experimental theater in France*, Berkeley (Calif) 1962.

RICHARD, J. P., *Onze études sur la poésie moderne*, 1964.

ROUSSELOT, J., *Panorama critique des nouveaux poètes français*, 1953.

SÉRANT, P., *Le romantisme fasciste*, 1959.

SERREAU, G., *Histoire du nouveau théâtre*, 1966.

SIMON, P. H., *Histoire de la littérature française au 20e siècle*, 2 vols, 1956.

STURROCK, J., *The French new novel*, London 1969.

SURER, P., *Le théâtre français contemporain*, 1964.

TISON-BRAUN, M., *La crise de l'humanisme*, 2 vols, 1958–67 (vol 2: 1914–39).

WELLWARTH, G. E., *The theater of protest and paradox*, New York 1964.

Anthologies in French

Anthologie de la nouvelle poésie nègre et malgache, ed. L. S. Senghor, 1948; 1969.

Une anthologie vivante de la littérature d'aujourd'hui, 1945–1965, ed. P. de Boisdeffre, 1965.

An anthology of French poetry, ed. C. A. Hackett, Oxford 1952.

Anthologies in translation

Absurd drama, ed. M. Esslin, Harmondsworth 1965.

An anthology of French poetry from Nerval to Valéry, ed. A. Flores, New York 1958.

Apollinaire to Aragon, thirty modern French poets, tr. W. J. Strachan, London 1948.

Contemporary French poetry, ed. A. Aspel and D. Justice, Ann Arbor (Mich) 1965.

French poetry from Baudelaire to the present, ed. E. Marks, New York 1962.

French writing today, ed. S. W. Taylor, Harmondsworth 1966.

Masterpieces of the modern French theatre, ed. R. W. Corrigan, New York 1967.

Mid-century French poets, tr. W. Fowlie, New York 1955.

A mirror for French poetry, 1840–1940, ed. C. Mackworth, London 1947.

Modern French theatre: the avant-garde, Dada and Surrealism, an anthology of plays, tr. M. Benedikt and G. E. Wellwarth, New York 1964.

Modern one-act plays from the French, tr. V. and F. Vernon, New York 1933.

The Penguin book of French short stories, tr. E. Marielle, Harmondsworth 1965.

1
The Middle Ages

ADAM, Jeu d' (*or Mystère d'*)   c. 1150–70

Adam, ed. V. Luzarche, Tours 1854; ed. K. Grass, Halle 1891 (revd 1907); ed. P. Studer, Manchester 1918 (revd 1928); ed. P. Äbischer, Geneva 1963; ed. W. Noomen, Paris 1971. Modern French version, G. Cohen, Paris 1936. English tr. S. F. Barrow and W. H. Hulme, Ohio 1925 (in *Antichrist and Adam*); tr. E. N. Stone, Seattle (Wash.) 1926; tr. R. Axton and J. Stevens, Oxford 1971 (in *Medieval French plays*).

AXELSEN, A., *Studie til en litterær og sproglig vurdering af Jeu d'Adam*, Copenhagen 1920.
FRANK, G., in her *The medieval French drama*, Oxford 1954.

ALEXANDRE, Romans d'   12th–14th centuries

BERZUNGA, J., *A tentative classification of books, pamphlets and pictures concerning Alexander the Great and the Alexander romances*, Durham (NC) 1939.

The medieval French Roman d'Alexandre, ed. E. C. Armstrong, A. Foulet et al., 7 vols, Princeton (NJ) 1937–55. Comprising:
1   *L'Alexandre décasyllabique* and *Alixandre en Orient* (Lambert le Tort's continuation), ed. M. S. La Du, 1937.
2   Alexandre de Paris' version (4 branches), ed. E. C. Armstrong, D. L. Buffum, B. Edwards and L. F. H. Lowe, 1937.
3   Albéric's fragment (and notes on branch 1 of Alexandre de Paris).
4   *Le roman du Fuerre de Gadres*, ed. E. C. Armstrong and A. Foulet, 1942.
5–7   Notes on branches 2–4.

Li romans d'Alexandre par Lambert li Tors et Alexandre de Bernay, ed. H. Michelant, Stuttgart 1846.
Alexandre (Alberic's fragment), ed. K. Bartsch, Vienna 1856 (in *Germania*, vol 2); ed. P. Meyer, 1886 (in his *Alexandre le Grand* below, vol 1).
Die vengeance Alixandre von Jehan le Nevelon, ed. O. Schultz-Gora, Berlin 1902; ed. E. W. Ham, Princeton (NJ) 1931.
Der altfranzösische Prosa-Alexanderroman, ed. A. Hilka, Halle 1920.

Voeux du paon (by Jacques de Longuyon), ed. R. L. Graeme, Edinburgh and London 1921–9 (in his ed. of John Barbour's *The buik of Alexander*, Scots adapt. of *Le fuerres de Guadres* and *Voeux du paon*, vols 2–4).

Le vengement Alixandre (by Gui de Cambrai), ed. B. Edwards, Princeton (NJ) 1928.

La prise de Defur and *Le voyage d'Alexandre au paradis terrestre*, ed. L. P. G. Peckham and M. S. La Du, Princeton (NJ) 1935.

CARY, G., *The medieval Alexander*, Cambridge 1956.

MAGOUN Jr, F. P., *The gestes of King Alexander of Macedon*, Cambridge (Mass) 1929.

MEYER, P., *Alexandre le Grand dans la littérature française du moyen âge*, 2 vols, 1886.

ROSS, D. J. A., *Alexander historiatus, a guide to medieval illustrated Alexander literature*, London 1963.

ALISCANS, Les   c 1180?
(later version of *Chanson de GUILLAUME*)

For general bibliographies and studies, see *CHANSONS DE GESTE*.

Les Aliscans, ed. W. J. A. Jonckbloet, 2 vols, The Hague 1854 (in *Guillaume d'Orange*); ed. F. Guessard and A. de Montaiglon, Paris 1870; ed. G. Rolin, Leipzig 1894; ed. E. Wienbeck, W. Hartnacke and P. Rasch, Halle 1903. Modern French version C. Chacornac, Paris 1933.

FRAPPIER, J., in his *Les chansons de geste du cycle de Guillaume d'Orange*, vol 1, 1955.

ANDELI, Henri d'   13th century

Oeuvres, ed. A. Héron, Rouen 1881.

Le lay d'Aristote, ed. E. Barbazan, 1756 (in *Fabliaux et contes*; revd D. M. Méon, 1808); ed. A. Héron, Rouen 1901; ed. M. Delbouille, Paris 1951.

La bataille des VII arts, ed. A. Jubinal, 1838. Tr. and ed. L. F. Paetow, *The battle of the seven arts*, Berkeley (Calif) 1914 (in *Memoirs of the University of California*, vol 4, *History* vol 1).

La bataille des vins, ed. D. M. Méon, 1808 (in *Fabliaux et contes*, vol 1); ed. F. Augustin, Marburg 1886 (in *Ausgaben und Abhandlungen aus dem Gebiets der Romanischen Philologie*, vol 44).

ARRAS, Gautier d'   fl. 1161–1166

Oeuvres, ed. E. Löseth, 1890.

Eracles, ed. H. P. Massmann, Leipzig 1842.

Ille et Galeron, 1890 (in *Oeuvres* above); ed. W. Förster, Halle 1891; ed. F. A. G. Cowper, Paris 1956.

ARTHURIAN LEGENDS

See *MATIÈRE DE BRETAGNE*.

AUCASSIN ET NICOLETTE c. 1200

Bibl. See Roques ed. below.

Aucassin et Nicolette, ed. D. M. Méon, 1808 (in *Fabliaux et contes*, vol 1); ed. H. and W. Suchier, Paderborn 1921 (revd 1932); ed. M. Roques, Paris 1925 (revd 1955; incl. bibl.). Modern French versions, M. Coulon, Nîmes 1933; G. Cohen, Paris 1954. English tr. A. R. Macdonough, New York 1880; tr. A. Lang, London 1887; tr. N. L. Goodrich, Boston (Mass) 1964 (in *The ways of love*); tr. P. Matarasso, Harmondsworth 1971.

FRANK, G., in her *The medieval French drama*, Oxford 1954.
PAUPHILET, A., in his *Le legs du moyen âge*, Melun 1950.
SAUTER, H., *Wortgut und Dichtung; eine lexicographisch-literargeschichtliche Studie über den Verfasser der altfranzösischen Cantefable Aucassin et Nicolette*, Münster and Paris 1934.

AYMERI DE NARBONNE c. 1217?
(by Bertrand de Bar-sur-Aube; belonging to the *Geste de Guillaume*).

For general bibliographies and studies, see *CHANSONS DE GESTE*.

Aymeri de Narbonne, ed. F. de Reiffenberg, Brussels 1836 (fragment, in the introduction to Philippe Mouskés' *Chronique*); ed. L. Demaison, 2 vols, 1887. Modern French version, C. Chacornac, 1931.

BARLAAM ET JOSAPHAT 13th century
(three versions, one ascribed to Gui de Cambrai)

Barlaam et Josaphat, ed. H. Zotenberg and P. Meyer, Stuttgart 1864 (Gui de Cambrai's version and an anon. version); ed. C. Appel, Halle 1907 (Gui de Cambrai's version); ed. E. C. Armstrong, Princeton (NJ) 1922 (all 3 versions); ed. J. Sonet, 3 vols, Namur and Paris 1949–52 (anon. version); ed. L. R. Mills, Geneva 1973 (anon. version).

BEAUMANOIR, Philippe de c. 1250–1296

Oeuvres poétiques, ed. H. L. Bordier, 1869 (in *Philippe de Remi, sire de Beaumanoir* below); ed. H. Suchier, 2 vols, 1884–5 (incl. *La manekine, Jehan et Blonde* and *Salut d'amour*).

3

Coustumes de Beauvoisis, ed. G. Thaumas, 1690; ed. A. Salmon, 2 vols, 1899–1900.

Roman de la manekine, ed. F. Michel, 1840.

The romance of Blonde of Oxford and Jehan of Dammartin, ed. A. J. V. Le Roux de Lincy, London 1858 (French text with summary in English).

BORDIER, H. L., *Philippe de Remi, sire de Beaumanoir*, 2 vols, 1869–73.

LANGLOIS, C. V., in his *La vie en France au moyen âge d'après les romans mondains du temps*, 1924.

LYONS, F., in her *Les éléments descriptifs dans le roman d'aventure au 13e siècle*, Geneva and Paris 1965.

BERTHE AU GRAND PIED   c. 1273

(by Adenet le Roi; belonging to the *Geste du roi*)

For bibliographies and general studies, see *CHANSONS DE GESTE*.

Li romans de Berte aus grans piés, ed. A. Scheler, Brussels 1874; ed. U. T. Holmes, Chapel Hill (NC) 1946. Modern French versions, R. Perié, Paris 1901; L. Brandin, 1924.

MEMMER, A., *Die altfranzösische Bertasage und das Volksmärchen*, Halle 1935.

BÉTHUNE, Conon de   c. 1150–c. 1219

Les chansons, ed. A. Wallensköld, Helsinki 1891 (revd Paris 1921).

BODEL, Jean   c. 1165–c. 1210

Bibl. See Jeanroy ed. of *Li jus saint Nicolai* below.

NARDIN, P., *Lexique comparé des fabliaux de Jean Bodel*, 1942.

Che sont li congié Jehan Bodel d'Aras, ed. D. M. Méon 1808 (in *Fabliaux et contes*, vol 1); ed. G. Raynaud, 1880 (in *Romania*, vol 9); ed. P. Ruelle, Brussels 1965 (in *Les congés d'Arras*).

Li jus saint Nicolai, ed. L. J. N. Monmerqué, 1832; ed. A. Jeanroy, 1925 (revd M. Ruffini, Turin 1949; incl. bibl.); ed. F. J. Warne, Oxford 1951 (revd 1963); ed. A. Henry, Brussels and Paris 1962 (with modern French version). Tr. R. Axton and J. Stevens, Oxford 1971 (in *Medieval French plays*).

La chanson des Saxons, ed. F. Michel, 2 vols, 1839; ed. F. Menzel and E. Stengel, Marburg 1906–9 (in *Ausgaben und Abhandlungen aus dem Gebiete der Romanischen Philologie*, vols 99 and 107).

Fabliaux, ed. A. de Montaiglon and G. Raynaud, 1872–90 (in *Recueil général et complet des fabliaux*, vols 1, 4 and 5); ed. P. Nardin, Dakar 1959.

FOULON, C., *L'oeuvre de Jean Bodel*, 1958.
ROHNSTRÖM, O., *Etude sur Jehan Bodel*, Uppsala 1900.

BORON, Robert de   end of 12th century

Verse romances:
> *Le roman du saint Graal* (known as *Joseph d'Arimathie*), ed. F. Michel,
> Bordeaux 1841; ed. F. Furnivall, London 1861 (as appendix to *Seynt
> Graal*, vol 1); ed. W. A. Nitze, Paris 1927.
> *Merlin* (fragment), ed. F. Michel, Bordeaux 1841 (with *Le roman du
> saint Graal* above); ed. W. A. Nitze, Paris 1927 (with *Le roman du
> saint Graal* above).

Petit saint Graal (prose adaptations, ascribed to Robert de Boron, of *Joseph
d'Arimathie* above, *Merlin* above, and his hypothetical *Perceval*):
> *Le saint Graal, ou le Joseph d'Arimathie*, ed. E. Hucher, Le Mans 1875;
> ed. G. Weidner, Oppeln 1881.
> *Merlin*, ed. G. Paris and J. Ulrich, 2 vols, 1886 (with '*Suite Huth*'); ed.
> H. O. Sommer, London 1894 (*LANCELOT-GRAAL* version).
> *Trèsplaisante et récréative hystoire de trèspreulx et vaillant chevallier
> Perceval le Galloys* (known as the *Didot-Perceval*), 1530; ed. E. Hucher,
> Le Mans 1875 (with *Le saint Graal* above); ed. J. L. Weston, London
> 1909 (in her *The legend of Sir Perceval*, vol 2); ed. W. Roach, Phila-
> delphia (Pa) 1941.

BRULÉ, Gace   fl. 1180–1200

Bibl. See Petersen Dyggve ed. below.

Chansons, ed. G. Huet, 1902; ed. H. Petersen Dyggve, Helsinki 1951 (enl.;
incl. bibl.).

CENT NOUVELLES NOUVELLES, Les   1462
(Sometimes ascribed to Antoine de LA SALE)

Les cent nouvelles nouvelles, 1486 (untitled; text begins '*S'ensuyt la table de ce
présent livre intitulé des Cent nouvelles nouvelles*'); ed. A. J. V. Le Roux de
Lincy, 2 vols, 1841; ed. P. Champion, 3 vols, 1928; ed. P. Jourda, 1965 (in
Conteurs français du 16e siècle); ed. F. P. Sweetser, 1966. Tr. R. H. Robbins,
The hundred tales, New York 1960.

DUBUIS, R., *Les cent nouvelles nouvelles et la tradition de la nouvelle en France
au moyen âge*, Grenoble 1973.
FERRIER, J. M., in his *Forerunners of the French novel*, Manchester 1954.
HAAG, K., *Ein altfranzösisches Novellenbuch*, Stuttgart 1903.

CHAMPAGNE, Thibaut de, (Roi de Navarre) 1201–1253

Les poésies, ed. P. A. Levesque de La Ravalière, 2 vols, 1762 (poems in vol 2); ed. P. Tarbé, 1851; ed. A. Wallensköld, 1925; ed. B. Woledge, Harmondsworth 1961 (selection, in *The Penguin book of French verse*).

CHANSONS DE GESTE late 11th–early 14th century

See also separate entries for *Les ALISCANS, AYMERI DE NARBONNE, BERTHE AU GRAND PIED,* Jean BODEL (*La chanson des Saxons*), *DOON DE MAYENCE, GARIN DE MONGLANE, GIRART DE ROUSSILLON, GORMONT ET ISEMBART, Chanson de GUILLAUME, RAOUL DE CAMBRAI, RENAUT DE MONTAUBAN* (or *Les quatre fils Aymon*), *Chanson de ROLAND.*

GAUTIER, L., *Bibliographie des chansons de geste*, 1897.
Bulletin bibliographique de la Société rencesvals, 1958 onwards.
See also NYROP below.
LANGLOIS, E., *Table des noms propres de toute nature compris dans les chansons de geste imprimées*, 1904.

BÉDIER, J., *Les légendes épiques, recherches sur la formation des chansons de geste*, 4 vols, 1908–13; 4 vols, 1926–9.
Colloquios de Roncesvalles, Zaragoza 1956 (critical articles).
CROSLAND, J., *The old French epic*, Oxford 1951.
DICKMAN, A. J., *Le role du surnaturel dans les chansons de geste*, 1926.
DOUTREPONT, G., *Les mises en prose des épopées et des romans chevaleresques du 14e au 16e siècle*, Brussels 1939.
GAUTIER, L., *Les épopées françaises*, 3 vols, 1865–8; 4 vols, 1878–94.
KÜRTH, G., *L'histoire poétique des Mérovingiens*, 1893.
LOT, F., *Etudes sur les légendes épiques françaises*, 1958.
MANDACH, A. de, *Naissance et développement de la chanson de geste en Europe*, Geneva 1961.
NYROP, K., *Den oldfranske heltedigtning*, Copenhagen 1883 (incl. bibl.). Italian tr. E. Gorra, *Storia dell'epopea francese nel medio evo*, Florence.
PARIS, G., *Chansons de geste*, 1852 (in *Histoire littéraire de la France*, vol. 14).
    Histoire poétique de Charlemagne, 1865; 1905.
SICILIANO, I., *Le origini delle canzoni di gesta*, Padua and Milan 1940. French tr. P. Antonetti, *Les chansons de geste et l'épopée, les origins des chansons de geste*, Paris 1951.

CHARTIER, Alain c. 1390–c. 1440

Bibl. See CHAMPION below; also HOFFMAN below.

Les fais, 1489 (collected works).

Les oeuvres, ed. A. Du Chesne, 1617 (with *Histoire de Charles VII,* wrongly ascribed to Chartier); 2 vols, Boston (Mass) 1929.

Le quadrilogue invectif, Bruges 1477 (untitled; text ends '*Cy finist le qdrilogue* [. . .]); ed. E. Droz, Paris 1923; ed. R. Bouvier, 1944. Tr. anon., ed. R. A. Dwyer, Los Angeles (Calif) 1965 (2 late 15th century trs).

Le breviaire des nobles, Bréhat-Lodéac 1484; ed. W. H. Rice, Paris 1951 (in *Romania,* vol 72).

Le lay de paix, 1489 (in *Les fais* above); Lyon 1500.

Rondeaux et ballades, 1489 (in *Les fais* above); ed. P. de Chennevières, Caen 1846.

Livre des quatre dames, 1485 (in *Les fais* above); ed. Vallet de Vivirille, 1858; ed. G. Hirschel, Brunswick 1929 (in *Archiv für das Studium der neueren Sprachen und Literaturen,* vol 159).

Lay de plaisance, 1489 (in *Les fais* above); ed. L. E. Kastner, Cambridge (Mass) 1917 (in *Modern Language Review,* vol 12).

Tractatus de vita curiali, 1489 (in *Les fais* above; in Latin). French tr. anon., ed. F. Heuckenkamp, *Le curial,* Halle 1899. English tr. W. Caxton, London 1484 (untitled; text ends '*Thus endeth the Curial* [. . .]); ed. P. Meyer and F. J. Furnivall, London 1888.

La belle dame sans merci, 1489 (in *Les fais* above); ed. L. Charpennes, 1901; ed. A. Pagès, 1937; ed. A. Piaget and R. L. Wagner, Lille and Geneva 1949 (with *poésies lyriques*). Tr. R. Ros, London 1526; tr. G. Chaucer?, *La bele dame saun mercy,* 1526 (in untitled text, beginning '*Here begynneth the boke of fame*'; ed. W. Thynne, 1532; revd W. W. Skeat 1897 in *Complete works of Chaucer,* vol 7).

Le débat des deux amants and *La complainte du prisonnier d'amours,* c. 1502, (in *Le jardin de plaisance et fleur de rhétorique;* ed. E. Droz. and A. Piaget, 2 vols, 1910–25).

CHAMPION, P., in his *Histoire poétique du 15e siècle,* vol. 1, 1923 (incl. bibl.).

HOFFMAN, E. J., *Alain Chartier, his work and reputation,* 1942 (incl. bibl.).

PIAGET, A., *La belle dame sans merci et ses imitations,* 1901–5 (in *Romania,* vols 30–1, 33–4).

WALRAVENS, C. J. H., *Alain Chartier, études biographiques,* Amsterdam 1971.

CHASTELLAIN, Georges 1415–1474

Bibl. See MOLINIER below; also URWIN below.

Oeuvres, ed. J. M. Kervyn de Lettenhove, 8 vols, Brussels 1863–6.

Chroniques des choses de ce temps, 5 vols, Brussels 1863–6 (in *Oeuvres,* vols 1–5 above). Contains surviving fragments for the following years, first pbd as follows:

    1464–1470, ed. J. A. Buchon, 1827 (in *Collection de chroniques,* vols 42–3).

1418–1422, ed. J. A. Buchon, 1827 (in *Choix de chroniques*, vol 6).
1451–2, 1454–8, ed. B. Renard, 1843 (in *Trésor national*, vols 1 and 3).
1431–1432, ed. J. Quicherat, 1843 (in *Bibliothèque de l'Ecole des Chartes*, vol 4).

Les douze dames de rhétorique, ed. L. Batissier, Moulins 1838.

Le miroir de mort, 3 vols, Brussels 1863–6 (in *Oeuvres* above, vols 6–8); ed. E. Droz and C. Dalbanne, Mainz 1928 (in *Gutenberg Jahrbuch*).

HOMMEL, L., *Chastellain*, Brussels 1945.

MOLINIER, A., in his *Les sources de l'histoire de France*, vol 4, 1904 (incl. bibl.).

PEROUSE, G., *Georges Chastellain*, Brussels and Paris 1910.

URWIN, K., *Georges Chastellain, la vie, les oeuvres*, 1937 (incl. bibl.).

CHÂTELAINE DE VERGI, La c. 1288

Ci commence de la chastelaine de Vergi, ed. D. M. Méon, 1808 (in *Fabliaux et contes*, vol 4); ed. G. Raynaud and L. Foulet, 1921; ed. J. Bédier, 1927 (with modern French version); ed. F. Whitehead, Manchester 1944. Tr. A. Kemp-Welch, *The châtelaine of Vergi*, Paris and London 1903; tr. P. Terry, New York 1963 (in *Lays of courtly love*); tr. P. Matarasso, Harmondsworth 1971.

RAYNAUD, G., *La chastelaine de Vergi*, 1892 (in *Romania*, vol 21).

CLARI, Robert de   1170?–1216

Li estoires de chiaus qui conquisent Constantinoble, ed. P. Riant, 1868; ed. K. Hopf, Berlin 1873 (ed. corrected A. Jeanroy, Paris 1927, in *Romania*, vol 53); ed. P. Lauer, 1924; ed. A. Pauphilet and E. Pognon, 1952 (in *Historiens et chroniqueurs du moyen âge*). Tr. E. McNeal, *The conquest of Constantinople*, New York 1936.

PAUPHILET, A., *Sur Robert de Clari*, 1931 (in *Romania*, vol 57).

QUIGNON, G. H., *Un historien picard de la quatrième croisade*, Cayeux-sur-Mer 1908.

CLOPINEL DE MEUNG, Jean

See *Roman de la ROSE*.

COINCY, Gautier de   1177–1236

Bibl. See DUCROT-GRANDERYE below.

Complete miracles, ed. V. F. Koenig, 4 vols, Lille and Geneva 1955–70.

Miracles de Nostre Dame, ed. E. Barbazan, 1756 (extracts, in *Fabliaux et contes*; revd and enl. D. M. Méon, 1808); ed. A. Poquet, Soissons 1857 (13 miracles); ed. J. Ulrich, Halle 1882 (miracles 20, 22, 45, in *Zeitschrift für romanische Philologie*, vol 6); ed. C. Samaran, Paris 1925 (fragments of 11 and 60, in *Romania*, vol 51); ed. A. P. Ducrot-Granderye, Helsinki 1932 (30 and 63, in her *Etudes* below); ed. E. Boman, Gothenburg 1935 (miracles 62 and 66); ed. A. Långfors, Helsinki 1937 (extracts of miracles in Hermitage ms.); ed. G. Lozinski, Helsinki 1938 (*De Saint Bon*); ed. E. von Krämer, Helsinki 1950 (*Du clerc qui feme espousa*); ed. V. Väänänen, 1951 (*D'une feme de Laon*); ed. E. von Krämer, 1953 (*De la bonne espereris*); ed. E. Rankka, Uppsala 1955 (*Les 150 ave* and *Le sacristain noyé*); ed. R. Hakamies, Helsinki 1958 (*D'un vilain qui fut sauvé* and *Du cierge de Nostre Dame de Rochemadour*); ed. P. Jonas, 1959 (*C'est d'un moine*).

DUCROT-GRANDERYE, A. P., *Etudes sur les miracles Nostre-Dame de Gautier de Coincy*, Helsinki 1932 (incl. bibl.).

LANGFORS, A., *Gautier de Coincy*, 1927–30 (in *Romania*, vols 53 and 56).

SZAROTA, E. M., *Studien zu Gautier de Coincy*, Limburg 1934.

COMMYNES (or COMMINES), Philippe de   c. 1445–1511

Bibl. See Calmette–Durville ed. below.

Cronique et hystoire, 1524 (pt 1 of *Mémoires*);
   Croniques du Roy Charles huytiesme, 1528 (pt 2 of *Mémoires*);
   ed. B. de Mandrot, 2 vols, 1901–3; ed. J. Calmette and G. Durville, 3 vols, 1924–5 (incl. bibl.); ed. A. Pauphilet and E. Pognon 1952 (in *Historiens et chroniqueurs du moyen âge*); ed. J. Bastin, Brussels 1945 (selection). Tr. T. Danett, *The historie of Philip de Commines*, London 1596 (ed. C. Whibley, 2 vols, 1897); tr. anon., *The memoirs*, 1674 (ed. A. R. Scoble, 2 vols, 1855–6); tr. I. Caseaux, Columbia 1969.

CHARLIER, G., *Commynes*, Brussels 1945.

SAINTE-BEUVE, C. A. de, in his *Causeries du lundi*, vol 1, 1851.

COUCY, Gui de (identified with the Châtelain de Coucy)   ?–1203

Chansons, ed. J. B. de Labrode, 2 vols, 1781 (in his *Mémoires historiques sur Raoul de Coucy*); ed. F. Michel, 1830; ed. F. Fath, Heidelberg 1883; ed. A. Lerond, Paris 1964.

DESCHAMPS, Eustache   1346–c. 1406

Oeuvres, ed. A. H. E. Queux de Saint-Hilaire and G. Raynaud, 11 vols, 1878–1903.

Some *ballades* translated in anthologies.

Miroir de mariage (unfinished), ed. P. Tarbé, Rheims 1865.

HOEPFFNER, E., *Eustache Deschamps Leben und Werke*, Strasbourg 1904.

RAYNAUD, G., *Eustache Deschamps, sa vie, son oeuvre, son temps*, 1903 (as vol 11 of *Oeuvres* above); 1904.

SARRADIN, A., *Etude sur Eustache des Champs, sa vie et ses oeuvres*, Versailles 1878.

DOON DE MAYENCE   end of 12th century
(belonging to the *Geste des vassaux révoltés*)

For bibliographies and general studies, see *CHANSONS DE GESTE*.

Doon de Mayence, ed. A. Vérard, 1501 (as *La fleur des batailles Doolin de Mayence*); ed. A. Peÿ, 1859; ed. J. Mauclere, 1937 (pt 1).

ENEAS, Roman d'   c. 1160

Bibl. See 1925–31 Salverda de Grave ed. below.

Eneas, ed. J. J. Salverda de Grave, Halle 1891; ed. J. J. Salverda de Grave, 2 vols, Paris 1925–31 (incl. bibl.).

FARAL, E., in his *Recherches sur les sources latines des contes et romans courtois du moyen âge*, 1913.

FABLIAUX   12th–14th centuries

See also Henri d'ANDELI (*Lay d'Aristote, Bataille des VII arts, Bataille des vins*) and RUTEBEUF (in his *Oeuvres complètes*).

Fabliaux et contes des poètes françois (incl. items not now regarded as *fabliaux*), ed. E. Barbazan, 3 vols, 1756; revd D. M. Méon, 4 vols, 1808 (enl.).
　　Nouveaux recueil de fabliaux et contes inédits, ed. D. M. Méon, 2 vols, 1823.
Fabliaux ou contes (modern French versions), ed. P. J. B. Legrand-d'Aussy, 4 vols, 1779; revd A. A. Renouard, 1829.
Nouveau recueil de contes, dits, fabliaux et autres pièces inédites, ed. A. Jubinal, 2 vols, 1839–42.
Recueil général et complet des fabliaux, ed. A. de Montaiglon and G. Raynaud, 6 vols, 1872–90.
Sechs altfranzösische Fabeln, ed. G. Rohlfs, Halle 1925 (cntg 6 *fabliaux* from Berlin ms.).
Lais et fabliaux, ed. L. Brandin, 1932 (modern French versions).
Fabliaux, ed. R. C. Johnston and D. D. R. Owen, Oxford 1957 (selection).

Twelve fabliaux, ed. T. B. W. Reid, Manchester 1958 (from Bibliothèque nationale ms. 19152).

Tr. R. Hellman and R. O'Gorman, *Ribald tales*, New York and London 1965.

De Constant Duhamel, 1756 (in *Fabliaux et contes*, vol 2 above); ed. J. Bolte, 1915 (in *Zeitschrift für Volkskunde*, vol 25).

La male honte, 1756 (Huon de Cambrai's version and Guillaume's version, in *Fabliaux et contes*, vol 2 above); ed. A. Långfors, 1912 (both versions; revd 1927).

Ci du vilain mire, 1756 (in *Fabliaux et contes*, vol 1 above); ed. C. Zipperling, Halle 1912.

Le castoiement ou instruction d'un père à son fils (adapt. from Pierre Alphonse's *Disciplina clericalis*), ed. E. Barbazan, Paris and Lausanne 1760; ed. A. Hilka and W. Söderhjelm, Helsinki.

Des trois avugles de Compiengne, ed. D. M. Méon, 1808 (in *Fabliaux et contes*, vol 3 above); ed. G. Gougenheim 1932.

Du vair palefroi (by Huon le Roi), ed. D. M. Méon, 1808 (in *Fabliaux et contes*, vol 1 above); ed. A. Långfors, 1912 (with *La male honte* above; revd 1927). Tr. P. Matarasso, Harmondsworth 1971 (with *Aucassin et Nicolette*).

La housse partie, ed. D. M. Méon, 1808 (in *Fabliaux et contes*, vol 4 above); ed. K. Bartsch, Leipzig 1913 (in *Chrestomathie de l'ancien français*).

Richeut, 1872 (in *Recueil général* above, vol 1); ed. J. Bédier, 1891 (in *Etudes romanes dédiées à Gaston Paris*); ed. I. C. Lecompte, New York 1913 (in *Romanic Review*, vol 4).

Le tombeur de Notre Dame, ed. H. Waechter, Erlangen 1901 (as *Der Springer unserer lieben Frau*, in *Romanische Forschungen*, vol 11); ed. E. Lommatzsch, Berlin 1920. Tr. P. H. Wicksteed, *Our Lady's tumbler*, London 1894; tr. I. Butler, Boston (Mass) 1898; tr. G. Cormack, London 1907; tr. A. Lang, New York and London 1950 (in *Medieval literature in translation*).

BÉDIER, J., *Les fabliaux*, 1893; 1928.

NYKROG, P., *Les fabliaux, étude d'histoire littéraire et de stylistique médiévale*, Copenhagen 1957

RYCHNER, J., *Contribution à l'étude des fabliaux*, 2 vols, Neuchâtel and Geneva 1960.

SUDRE, L., *Les fables*, 1896 (in L. Petit de Julleville's *Histoire de la langue et de la littérature française*, vol 2).

FLOIRE ET BLANCHEFLEUR   c. 1160 (version 1), c. 1200 (version 2)

Bibl. See Krüger ed. below.

Li romanz de Floire et Blancheflor, ed. E. Du Méril, 1856 (both versions); ed. M. Pelan, 1937 (version 1; revd 1956); ed. F. Krüger, Berlin 1938 (both versions; incl. bibl.). Tr. and adapt. anon., ed. J. R. Lumby, *Floris and Blancheflour*, 1866 (13th century tr. of version 1; ed. A. B. Taylor, Oxford 1927); tr. Mrs. Leighton, *The tale of Fleur and Blanchefleur*, London 1922; tr. M. J. Hubert, *The romance of Floire and Blanchefleur*, Chapel Hill (NC) 1967.

REINHOLD, J., *Floire et Blanchefleur; étude de littérature comparée*, 1906.

FOURNIVAL, Richard de   1201–not later than 1260

Le bestiaire d'amours, ed. C. Hippeau, 1860; ed. A. Långfors, Helsinki 1925; ed. C. Segre, Milan and Naples 1957.
Lieder, ed. P. Zarifopol, Halle 1904 (chansons).
Consaus d'amours, ed. W. M. McLeod, Chapel Hill (NC) 1935 (in *Studies in Philology*, vol 32).

LANGLOIS, E., *Quelques oeuvres de Richard de Fournival*, 1904 (in *Bibliothèque de l'Ecole des Chartes*, vol 65).
Lai d'Eliduc, 1820 (in *Poésies*, vol 1 above); ed. E. Levi, Florence 1924.

FRANCE, Marie de   fl. late 12th century

Poésies, ed. B. de Roquefort, 2 vols 1820.
Lais, ed. K. Warnke, Halle 1885 (revd R. Köhler, 1925); ed. E. Hoepffner, Strasbourg 1921; ed. A. Ewert, Oxford 1944; ed. J. Rychner, Paris 1971. Modern French version, P. Jonin 1972. English tr. J. L. Weston, *Four lais*, London and New York 1900; tr. E. Rickert, *Seven of her lays*, 1901; tr. E. Mason, London 1911 (12 lays, in *French medieval romances*).
Fables, ed. K. Warnke, Halle 1898; ed. E. Faral, Paris 1934 (in his *Le manuscrit 19152*); ed. A. Ewert and R. C. Johnston, Oxford 1942.

Lai de Lanval, 1820 (in *Poésies*, vol 1 above); ed. J. Harris, New York 1930 (with *Gugemar* and part of *Yonec*); ed. J. Rychner and P. Äbischer, Geneva and Paris 1958 (with modern French version).
Lai de Chèvrefeuille, 1820 (in *Poésies*, vol 1 above).
Le purgatoire saint Patrice, 1820 (in *Poésies*, vol 2 above); ed. T. A. Jenkins, Philadelphia (Pa) 1894; ed. K. Warnke, Halle 1908.

FOULET, L., *Marie de France et les lais bretons*, Halle 1905 (in *Zeitschrift für romanische Philologie*).
   Marie de France et la légende de Tristan, Halle 1908 (in *Zeitschrift für romanische Philologie*).
HOEPFFNER, E., *Les lais de Marie de France*, 1935.

FROIDMONT, Hélinand de   c. 1160–after 1229

Vers de la mort, ed. A. L'Oisel, n.p., n.d.; ed. F. Wulff and E. Walberg, Paris 1905. Modern French version, J. Coppin, 1930.

FROISSART, Jean 1337–c. 1404

Bibl. See MOLINIER below; also SHEARS below.

Le premier [second, tiers, quart] volume de Froissart, des croniques, (4 vols), 1495; ed. J. M. Kervyn de Lettenhove, 26 vols, Brussels 1867–77; ed. S. Luce, G. Raymond, and A. and L. Mirot, Paris 1869 onwards (14 vols pbd); ed. A. Pauphilet and E. Pognon 1952 (in *Historiens et chroniqueurs du moyen âge*); ed. A. H. Diverre, Manchester 1953 (ed. of section *Voyage en Béarn*); ed. G. T. Diller, Geneva 1972 (ed. of bk 1). Tr. J. Bourchier, Lord Berners, London 1523–5 (untitled; begins '*Here begynneth the first [second, thirde, fourthe] bok of Sir John Froissart of the cronycles*'; ed. W. P. Ker, 6 vols, London 1901–3); tr. T. Johnes, 5 vols, Hafod (Wales) 1803–10; tr. and ed. J. Jolliffe, *Chronicles*, London 1967 (abr.); tr. G. Brereton, Harmondsworth 1968 (abr.).

Poésies, ed. J. A. Buchon, 1829; ed. A. Scheler, 3 vols, Brussels 1870–2.

Pastourelles, ed. K. Bartsch, Leipzig 1870 (in *Altfranzösischen Romanzen und Pastourellen*).

Méliador, ed. A. Longnon, 3 vols, 1895–9.

L'espinette amoureuse, 1829 (in *Poésies* above); ed. A. Fourrier, 1962.

DARMESTETER, M., *Froissart*, 1894.

MOLINIER, A., in his *Les sources de l'histoire de France*, vol 4, 1904 (incl. bibl.).

SHEARS, F. S., *Froissart, chronicler and poet*, London 1930 (incl. bibl.).

GARIN DE MONGLANE 13th century
(belonging to the *Geste de Guillaume*)

For bibliographies and general studies, see *CHANSONS DE GESTE.*

Garin de Monglane, ed. J. Trepperel, n.d. (untitled; text begins '*S'ensuyt la très plaisante histoire du preux et vaillant Guérin de Monglane*'; incomplete); ed. H. Menn, Greifswald 1913 (pt 3); ed. M. Müller, 1913 (pt 2); ed. V. Jeran, 1913 (*Enfances Garin, Prologue*).

FRAPPIER, J., in his *Les chansons de geste du cycle de Guillaume d'Orange*, vol 1, 1955.

HOYER, R., *Das Auftreten der Geste Garin de Monglane, in der Chansons der anderen Gesten*, Halle 1900.

GERSON, Jean (or Jean Le Charlier) 1363–1429

Opera omnia, ed. L. E. Du Pin, 4 vols, Antwerp 1706 (Latin works, and French works in Latin tr.).

Tr. S. Evans, *Poems*, London 1875 (in *The studio*).
Tr. H. Austin, *Practical guide to spiritual prayer*, London 1884.

Le traité contre le Roman de la rose, ed. E. Langlois, 1918–19 (in *Romania,* vol 45).

Six sermons français, ed. L. Mourin, 1946.

COMBES, A., *Jean Gerson commentateur dionysien,* 1940.
CONNOLLY, J. L., *John Gerson, reformer and mystic,* Louvain 1928.
MOURIN, L., *Jean Gerson, prédicateur français,* Bruges 1952.
SCHWAB, J. B., *Johannes Gerson,* Würzburg 1858.

GIÉLÉE, Jacquemart   1174–1205

See *Roman de RENART (Renart le nouvel).*

GIRART DE ROUSSILLON   c. 1150
(belonging to the *Geste des vassaux révoltés*)

For general bibliographies and studies, see *CHANSONS DE GESTE.*

Gérard de Roussillon, ed. F. Michel, 1856 (incomplete); ed. C. A. F. Mahn, Berlin 1863 (in his *Gedichte der Troubadours,* vol 1); ed. W. Förster et al., Halle 1880; ed. W. M. Hackett, 3 vols, Paris 1953–5. Modern French versions, P. Meyer, 1884; H. Berthaut, 1929.

GORMONT ET ISEMBART   c. 1080
(belonging to the *Geste des vassaux révoltés*)

For general bibliographies and studies, see *CHANSONS DE GESTE.*

La mort du roi Gormond (only surviving fragment), ed. F. de Reiffenberg, Brussels 1837 (in *Bulletin de la Commission Royale d'Histoire,* vol 1); ed. F. de Reiffenberg, 1838 (in his ed. of Philippe Mouskés' *Chronique,* vol 2); ed. A. Scheler, 1875 (in *Bibliophile Belge,* vol 10); ed. R. Heiligbrodt, Strasbourg 1878 (in *Romanische Studien,* vol 3); ed. A. Bayot, Paris 1914 (revd 1931).

CALIN, W. C., *The old French epic of revolt,* Geneva 1962.

GRÉBAN, Arnoul   early 15th century

Le mystère de la Passion, ed. G. Paris and G. Raynaud, 1878; ed. O. Jodogne, 1965 onwards (1 vol pbd). Modern French version, A. Pauphilet, 1941 (in *Jeux et sapience du moyen âge*). Tr. J. Kirkup, *The true mistery of the passion,* New York 1962.

CHAMPION, P., in his *Histoire poétique du 15e siècle,* vol 2, 1923.
FRANK, G., in her *The medieval French drama,* Oxford 1954.

GRISÉLIDIS   c. 1390

Le mystère de Grisélidis, ed. J. Bonfons, 1548–50; ed. H. Gröneveld, Marburg 1888; ed. B. Craig, Lawrence (Kan) 1953; ed. M. Roques, Geneva and Paris 1957. Tr. H. Chettle, T. Dekker and W. Haughton, *The pleasant comödie of patient Grissill,* London 1603.

GOLENISTCHEFF-KOUTOUZOFF, E., *L'histoire de Griseldis en France au 14e et au 15e siècle,* 1933.
PETIT DE JULLEVILLE, L., in his *Les mystères,* 2 vols, 1880.

GUILLAUME, *Chanson de*   early 12th century
(belonging to the *Geste de Guillaume*)

Bibl. See ISELEY ed. below.
For general bibliographies and studies, see *CHANSONS DE GESTE.*

La chançun de Willame, ed. G. Dunn, London 1903; ed. G. Baist, Freiburg 1904; ed. H. Suchier, Halle 1911; ed. E. S. Tyler, New York 1919; ed. D. McMillan, 2 vols, Paris 1949–50; ed. N. V. Iseley, Chapel Hill (NC) 1961 (incl. bibl.). Tr. E. N. Stone, *The song of William,* Seattle (Wash) 1951 (to line 1980).

FRAPPIER, J. in his *Les chansons de geste du cycle de Guillaume d'Orange,* vol 1, 1955.

ISOPETS (or *FABLES ÉSOPIQUES*)   late 12th–14th century

See also Marie de FRANCE (*Fables*).

KEIDEL, G. C., *A manual of Aesopic fable literature,* Baltimore (Md) 1896.

Fables inédites, ed. A. C. M. Robert, 2 vols, 1825.
Recueil général des Isopets, ed. J. Bastin, 2 vols, 1929–30 (incl. *Romulus en vers,* or *Anonyme de Nevelet,* first pbd 1610).

HERVIEUX, M., *Les fabulistes latins depuis le siècle d'Auguste jusqu'à la fin du moyen âge,* 5 vols, 1884; 5 vols, 1893–9.
JACOBS, J., *The fables of Aesop,* London 1889.
WIENERT, W., *Die Typen der griechisch-römischen Fabel,* Helsinki 1925.

JOINVILLE, Jean de   1225–1317

Bibl. See MOLINIER below.

L'histoire & chronique du tréschrestien roy S. Loys, IX du nom, ed. A. P. De Rieux, Poitiers 1547; ed. C. Menard, Paris 1617; ed. C. Capperonnier

1761 (first ed. to be based on original ms.); ed. Natalis de Wailly, 1874; ed. A. Pauphilet and E. Pognon, 1952 (in *Historiens et chroniqueurs du moyen âge*). Tr. T. Johnes, *Memoirs of John, Lord de Joinville*, 2 vols, Hafod, (Wales) 1807; tr. J. Hutton, *Saint Louis, King of France*, London 1868; tr. J. Evans, *The history of St Louis*, London and New York 1938; tr. M. R. B. Shaw, Harmondsworth 1963 (in *Chronicles of the crusades*).

DELABORDE, H. F., *Jean de Joinville et les seigneurs de Joinville*, 1894.

MOLINIER, A., in his *Les sources de l'histoire de France*, vol 4, 1904 (incl. bibl.).

JOURNAL D'UN BOURGEOIS DE PARIS 1405–1449

Journal d'un bourgeois de Paris 1405–1449, ed. E. Pasquier, 1596 (fragments, in *Recherches de la France*); ed. D. Godefroy, 1653 (extracts, in *Histoire de Charles VI*); ed. La Barre, 1729; ed. J. F. Michaud, 1837 (in *Nouvelle collection des mémoires*, vol 3); ed. J. A. C. Buchon, 1838 (in *Choix de chroniques et mémoires sur l'histoire de France*, vol 7); ed. A. Tuetey, 1881 (revd and abr. A. Mary, 1929). Modern French version, J. Mégret, 1944. Tr. J. Shirley, *A Parisian journal*, Oxford and New York 1968.

LA HALLE, Adam de   c. 1240–c. 1288

Bibl. See GUY below.

Oeuvres complètes, ed. E. de Coussemaker, 1872.

C'est li congiés d'Adam d'Aras, ed. D. M. Méon, 1808 (in *Fabliaux et contes*, vol 1); ed. P. Ruelle, Brussels 1965 (in *Les congés d'Arras*).

Li gieus de Robin et de Marion, ed. L. J. N. Monmerqué, 1822; ed. E. Langlois, 1895 (revd 1924); ed. K. Varty, 1962. Modern French version, G. Cohen, 1935. Tr. J. M. Gibbon, *The play of Robin and Marion*, Boston (Mass) and New York 1928; tr. R. Axton and J. Stevens, Oxford 1971 (in *Medieval French plays*).

Li jus Adam ou de la Feuillée, ed. L. J. N. Monmerqué, 1828; ed. E. Langlois, 1917 (revd 1923). Modern French version, E. Langlois, 1923. Tr. R. Axton and J. Stevens, Oxford 1971 (in *Medieval French plays*).

Dit d'amours, 1872 (in *Oeuvres complètes* above); ed. A. Jeanroy, 1893 (in *Romania*, vol 22).

Canchons et Partures, 1872 (in *Oeuvres complètes* above); ed. R. Berger, Halle 1900 (36 *chansons*); ed. J. H. Marshall, Manchester 1971.

Les partures d'Adan, 1872 (in *Oeuvres complètes* above); ed. L. Nicot, 1917.

CHAILLY, J., in his *Histoire musicale du moyen âge*, 1950.

GUY, H., *Le trouvère Adam de le Hale, essai sur sa vie et ses oeuvres littéraires*, 1898 (incl. bibl.).

LA MARCHE, Olivier de   c. 1426–1502

Le chevalier délibéré, Gouda c. 1486; Paris 1488; ed. F. Lippmann, London 1898.

Les mémoires, ed. D. Sauvage, Lyon 1562; ed. H. Beaune and J. d'Arbaumont, 4 vols, Paris 1883–8.

Le livre de l'advis de gaige de bataille, 1586 (in *Traitez et advis de quelques gentils hommes françois sur les duels et gages de bataille*); ed. B. Prost, 1872 (in *Traités du duel judiciaire*).

Le parement et triumphe des dames, 1510; ed. J. Kalbfleisch-Benas, Rostock 1901.

STEIN, H., *Olivier de La Marche, poète et diplomate bourguignon*, Brussels and Paris 1888.

LANCELOT-GRAAL (or *THE VULGATE CYCLE OF THE ARTHURIAN ROMANCES*)   early 13th century

For general bibliographies and studies, see *MATIÈRE DE BRETAGNE*.

The vulgate version of the Arthurian romances, ed. H. O. Sommer, 8 vols, Washington (DC) 1909–16. Comprising:
1   *L'estoire del saint Graal* (*branche 1*), 1909.
2   *L'estoire de Merlin* (*branche 2*, ascribed to Robert de BORON).
3–5   *Le livre de Lancelot del lac* (*branche 3*, or '*Lancelot propre*'), 1910–12.
6   *Les aventures ou la queste del saint Graal* (*branche 4*), and *La mort le roi Artus* (*branche 5*), 1913.
7   *Le livre d'Artus* (another version of the Merlin legend), 1913.
8   Index, 1916.

Individual works below are listed in the order of their position in the Cycle.

Lhystoire du sainct Greaal, 2 vols, 1516 (with *PERLESVAUS* and abr. *Queste* below); ed. E. Hucher, Le Mans 1875–8 (in *Le saint Graal*, vols 2–3); ed. F. Furnivall, 2 vols, London 1861–3 (in *Seynt Graal, or the Sank Ryal*).

L'estoire de Merlin, 3 vols, 1498 (untitled; text begins '*Le premie volume de Merlin*'; with *Les prophécies de Merlin* in vol 3); ed. H. O. Sommer, London 1894 (rptd Washington 1908, as vol 2 of *The vulgate version* above).

Lancelot du lac, 2 vols, Rouen and Paris 1488 (untitled; text begins '*Cy commence la table et registre des rubriches du premier volume ou rômât fait et côposé à la perpétuation de mémoire des vertueux fais et gestes de plusieurs nobles et excellês chevaliers qui furêt au têps du trèsnoble et puissât roy Art' côpagnôs de la table rôde, spécialemêt à la louêge du trèsvaillât chevalier Lancelot du lac*'; with *Queste* and *Mort le roi Artus* below); 3 vols, 1533; ed. W. J. A. Yonckbloet, The Hague 1850 (*Charete* section, with Chrétien de TROYES' *Lancelot*); ed. G. Brauner, H. Becker, H. Bubinger and A. Zimmerman, 4 vols, Marburg 1911–17 (1st section); ed. G. Hutchings, Paris 1938 (2nd section).

La queste del saint Graal, 1488 (with *Lancelot du lac* above); 1516 (abr., with *Lhystoire du sainct Graal* above, and *PERLESVAUS*); ed. F. Furnivall, London 1864; ed. A. Pauphilet, Paris 1923. Modern French versions A. Pauphilet, 1925 (revd 1949); A. Béguin, 1945.

La mort le roi Artus, 1488 (with *Lancelot du lac* above); ed. J. D. Bruce, Halle 1910; ed. J. Frappier, Paris 1936 (concise ed. Geneva and Lille 1954).

Modern French versions: J. Boulenger, *Les romans de la Table ronde*, 4 vols, 1922–3; G. Sneyers, Brussels 1941 (without *L'estoire del saint Graal*). See also Thomas Malory's *Le morte Darthur* (adapted from the *Lancelot-Graal* and prose *TRISTAN*), ed. W. Caxton, London 1485; ed. A. W. Pollard, 2 vols, 1900.

BRIEL, H. de and HERRMANN, M., *King Arthur's knights and the myths of the Round Table: a new approach to the French Lancelot en prose*, 1972.

FRAPPIER, J., *Etude sur la Mort de roi Artu*, 1936; 1961 (incl. bibl.).

LOT, F., *Etude sur le Lancelot en prose*, 1918; 1954.

LOT-BORODINE, M., *Trois essais sur le roman de Lancelot du lac et la Queste du saint Graal*, 1919.

PARIS, P., *Les romans de la Table ronde*, 5 vols, 1868–77 (incl. modern French versions of major episodes).

PAUPHILET, A., *Etudes sur la Queste del saint Graal attribuée à Gautier Map*, 1921.

PICKFORD, C. E., *L'évolution du roman arthurien en prose vers la fin du moyen âge*, 1960.

VINAVER, E., *Malory*, Oxford 1929.

WESTON, J. L., *The legend of Sir Lancelot du Lac*, London 1901.
   The quest of the Holy Grail, London 1913.

ZUMTHOR, P., *Merlin le prophète*, Lausanne 1943.

LA SALE, Antoine de   1385–after 1461

See separate entries for *Les CENT NOUVELLES NOUVELLES* and *Les QUINZE JOYES DU MARIAGE*, sometimes ascribed to La Sale.

Oeuvres complètes, ed. F. Desonay, 2 vols, Liège and Paris 1935–41 (incomplete; not incl. *Jehan Saintré*, *Réconfort*, *Traité des tournois*).

Lhystoire et plaisante cronicque du petit Jehan de Saintre de la jeune dame des Belles Cousines, 1517; ed. Tressan, 1780; ed. J. M. Guichard, 1843; ed. P. Champion and F. Desonay, 1926; ed. J. Misrahi and C. A. Knudson, Geneva 1965. Tr. A. Vance, *The history and pleasant chronicle of Little*

Jehan de Saintré, and of the Lady of the Fair Cousins, 2 vols, London 1862; tr. I. Gray, *Little John of Saintré*, London 1931.

La Salade, 1521.

Paradis de la reine Sybille, 1521 (as episode in *La Salade* above); ed. W. Söderhjelm, Helsinki 1897 (in *Mémoires de la Société néophilologique*, vol 2); ed. J. Nève, Brussels 1903 (in his *Antoine de La Salle* below); ed. F. Desonay, Paris 1930.

Traicté des anciens tournois et faictz d'armes, ed. B. Prost, 1872 (in *Traités du duel judiciaire*).

Du réconfort de Madame Du Fresne, ed. J. Nève, Brussels 1881; ed. J. Nève, Paris 1903 (in his *Antoine de la Salle* below).

COVILLE, A., *Le petit Jean de Saintré, recherches complémentaires*, 1937.

DESONAY, F., *Le petit Jehan de Saintré*, 1927 (in *Revue du 16e siècle*, vol 14).

GOSSART, E., *Antoine de La Salle, sa vie et ses oeuvres*, Brussels 1871 (in *Bibliophile belge*, vol 6); 1902.

NÈVE, J., *Antoine de La Salle, sa vie et ses ouvrages*, Brussels 1903.

RASMUSSEN, J., in his *La prose narrative française du 15e siècle*, 1958.

SÖDERHJELM, W., *Notes sur Antoine de La Sale et ses oeuvres*, Helsinki 1904. In his *La nouvelle française*, 1910.

LATINI, Brunetto (or Brunet Latin)   c. 1220–1294

Li livre dou tresor, ed. P. Chabaille, 1863; ed. F. Carmody, Berkeley (Calif) 1948.

PEZARD, A., *Dante sous la pluie de feu (Enfer, chant 15)*, 1950.

SUNDBY, T., *Brunetto Latinos levnet og skrifter*, Copenhagen 1869. Italian tr. R. Renier, *Delle vita e delle opere di Brunetto Latini*, Florence 1884.

LE BEL, Jean   c. 1290–1370

Bibl. See COVILLE below.

Les vrayes chroniques, ed. M. L. Polain, Mons 1850 (fragments recorded in Jean d'Outremeuse's *Le myreur des histors*); ed. M. L. Polain, 2 vols, Brussels 1863 (complete text); ed. J. Viard and E. Déprez, 2 vols, 1904–5.

Li ars d'amour, de vertu et de boneurté, ed. J. Petit, 2 vols, Brussels 1867–9.

COVILLE, A., *Jean Le Bel, chroniqueur*, 1941 (in *Histoire littéraire de la France*), vol 38; incl. bibl.); 1949.

LORRIS, Guillaume de

See *Roman de la ROSE*.

MACHAULT, Guillaume de   c. 1300–1377

Oeuvres, ed. P. Tarbé, Rheims 1849 (selection, as vol 3 of *Collection des poètes de Champagne*); ed. E. Hoepffner, 3 vols, 1908–21 (not incl. *Voir dit* or *Prise d'Alexandrie*).
Poésies lyriques, ed. V. F. Chichmaref, 2 vols, 1909.
Musikalische Werke, ed. F. Ludwig, 3 vols, Leipzig 1926–30.

Translated in anthologies.

Le livre du voir dit, ed. P. Paris, 1875.
La prise d'Alexandrie, ed. M. L. de Mas Latrie, Geneva 1877.
Le dit du hardi cheval, ed. G. Raynaud, 1903 (in *Romania*, vol 32).
Dit de la harpe, ed. K. Young, New Haven (Conn) 1943 (in *Essays in honor of Albert Feuillerat*).

CHAILLEY, J., in his *Histoire musicale du moyen âge*, 1950.
MACHABEY, A., *Guillaume de Machault, la vie et l'oeuvre musicale*, 2 vols, 1955.

MAILLART, Jean   fl. c. 1316

Le roman du Comte d'Anjou, ed. B. Schumacher and E. Zubke, Greifswald 1920 (as *La Contesse d'Anjou*); ed. M. Roques, Paris 1931.

LANGLOIS, C. V., in his *La vie en France au moyen âge d'après les romans mondains du temps*, 1924.

MAISTRE PIERRE PATHELIN, La Farce de   15th century

Bibl. See Picot ed. below; also Holbrook ed. below; also HOLBROOK below.

Maistre Pierre Pathelin, ed. G. Le Roy, 1485 or 1486; ed. P. Levet 1489; c. 1500; ed. F. Génin, 1854; ed. E. Picot, 1904 (incl. bibl. of early eds); ed. R. T. Holbrook, 1924 (revd Oxford 1943; incl. bibl.); ed. J. Hasselmann, Paris 1958 (with modern French version). Tr. R. T. Holbrook, *Master Pierre Pathelin*, Boston (Mass) 1905 (revd 1914); tr. M. Relonde, 1917.

FRANK, G., in her *The medieval French drama*, Oxford 1954.
HOLBROOK, R. T., *Etude sur Pathelin, essai de bibliographie et d'interprétation*, Princeton (NJ) 1917.
　　Etudes et aventures patheliniennes, 1925.

MARCADÉ (or MERCADÉ), Eustache   late 14th century–1440?

La vengeance nostre Seigneur (possibly later version of text in Arras ms. below), ed. A. Vérard, 1491.

Le mystère de la Passion (based on text in Arras ms., which also contains *La vengeance de Jésus Christ*), ed. J. M. Richard, Arras 1893.

CHAMPION, P., in his *Histoire poétique du 15e siècle*, vol 2, 1929.

MATIÈRE DE BRETAGNE (or *ARTHURIAN LEGENDS*)

See separate entries for Robert de BORON, *LANCELOT-GRAAL* (or *The Vulgate Cycle of the Arthurian Romances*), *PERCEFOREST*, *PERLESVAUS* and *TRISTAN LEGEND*. See also Marie de FRANCE (*Lais*), Jean FROISSART (*Méliador*), Chrétien de TROYES (*Romans arthuriens*) and WACE (*Roman de Brut*).

PARRY, J. J. and SCHLAUCH, M., *A bibliography of critical Arthurian literature*, 2 vols, 1931–6 (for 1922–35; supplemented annually in *Modern Language Quarterly*).
Bulletin bibliographique de la Société internationale arthurienne, 1949 onwards.
See also BRUCE below; also LOOMIS below.

BARBER, R, *The figure of Arthur*, London 1972.
BOGDANOW, F., *The romance of the grail, a study of the structure and genesis of a 13th century Arthurian prose romance*, Manchester 1966.
BRUCE, J. D., *Evolution of the Arthurian romance*, 2 vols, Göttingen 1923; 2 vols, Baltimore (Md) 1928 (incl. critical bibl.).
CHAMBERS, E. K., *Arthur of Britain*, London 1927.
FARAL, E., *La légende arthurienne, études et documents*, 3 vols, 1929.
LOOMIS, R. S. and LOOMIS, L. H., *Arthurian legends in medieval art*, Oxford and New York 1938.
LOOMIS, R. S. et al., *Arthurian literature in the middle ages*, Oxford 1959 (incl. bibl.).
 Nouvelles recherches sur la littérature arthurienne, 1965 (incl. bibl. for 1952–63).
OWEN, D. D. R. (ed.), *Arthurian romance, seven essays*, Edinburgh 1970.
PARIS, P., *Les romans de la Table ronde*, 5 vols, 1868–77 (with modern French versions of major episodes).
RYDING, W. W., *Structure of the medieval romance*, The Hague 1971.
VINAVER, E., *The rise of romance*, Oxford 1971.

MIRACLES DE NOSTRE DAME PAR PERSONNAGES
14th century

Bibl. See GLUTZ below.

Miracles de Nostre Dame par personnages, ed. L. J. N. Monmerqué and F. Michel, 1842 (in their *Théâtre français au moyen âge*); ed. G. Paris, U. Robert and F. Bonnardot, 8 vols, 1876–93.

GLUTZ, R., *Miracles de Nostre Dame par personnages: kritische Bibliographie und neue Studien zum Text*, Berlin 1954.

PETIT DE JULLEVILLE, L., in his *Les Mystères*, vol 2, 1880.

ROY, E., in his *Etude sur le théâtre français du 14e et du 15e siècle*, 1903.

MOLINET, Jean   1435–1507

DUPIRE, N., *Étude critique des manuscrits et de toutes les éditions, intégrales ou partielles, de 1476 à 1926*, 1932.
See also DUPIRE below.

Le Temple de Mars, c. 1499.

Lart et science de rhethorique, ed. A. Vérard, 1493; ed. E. Langlois, 1902 (as *L'art de rhétorique vulgaire*, in *Recueil d'arts de seconde rhétorique*).

Les faictz et dictz, 1531 (certain poems first pbd separately from c. 1476); ed. N. Dupire, 3 vols, 1926–9.

Chroniques, ed. J. A. Buchon, 5 vols, 1827–8; ed. G. Doutrepont and O. Jodogne, 3 vols, Brussels 1935–7.

Le mistere de saint Quentin (ascribed to Molinet), ed. H. Chatelain, 1908.

CHAMPION, P., in his *Histoire poétique du 15e siècle*, vol 2, 1929.

DUPIRE, N., *Jean Molinet; la vie, les oeuvres*, 1932 (incl. bibl.).

MONIOT D'ARRAS, Pierre   fl. 1225–1250
MONIOT DE PARIS, Jean   fl. 1225–1250

Chansons, ed. H. Petersen Dyggve, Helsinki 1938 (in *Mémoires de la Société néo-philologique*, vol. 13).

MUSET, Colin   fl. 1230–50

Chansons, ed. J. Bédier, 1893 (revd and enl. 1912; revd 1938); ed. A. Jeanroy and A. Långfors, 1921 (in *Chansons satiriques et bachiques du 13e siècle*).

ORESME, Nicole   c. 1325–1382

MENUT, A. D., *A provisional bibliography of Oresme's writings*, Stockholm 1966 (in *Moderna Språk*, vol 28).
See also MEUNIER below.

Traictié de la première invention des monnoies (Oresme's tr. of his Latin treatise *De origine, jure et mutationibus monetarum*, first pbd 1511), Bruges c. 1477; ed. C. Johnson, London 1956 (Latin text, with English tr.).

Les éthiques (tr. from Aristotle), ed. A. Vérard, 1488; ed. A. D. Menut, New York 1940.

Le livre de politiques (tr. from Aristotle), ed. A. Vérard, 1489.

Le livre de yconomique d'Aristote, ed. A. Vérard, 1489; ed. A. D. Menut, Philadelphia (Pa) 1957 (with English tr.).

Le livre du ciel et du monde (tr. from Aristotle's *De caelo et mundo*), ed. A. D. Menut and A. J. Denomy, New York 1940.

Traictié de l'espere, ed. L. M. McCarthy, Toronto 1957.

COOPLAND, G. W., *Nicole Oresme and the astrologers, a study of his Livre des divinacions*, Cambridge (Mass) 1952.

MEUNIER, F., *Essai sur la vie et les ouvrages de Nicole Oresme*, 1857 (incl. bibl. of works).

ORLÉANS, Charles d'   1394–1465

CHAMPION, P., *La librairie de Charles d'Orléans*, 1911.
    Un inventaire des papiers de Charles d'Orléans, 1912.
Bibl. See Cigada ed. of *Poésies* below; also Steele–Day ed. of *The English poems* below.

Poésies, ed. C. Sallier, 1740 (extracts, in *Mémoires de l'Académie des belles lettres et des inscriptions*, vol 13); ed. V. Chalvet, Grenoble 1803 (incomplete); ed. C. d'Héricault, 2 vols, Paris 1874; ed. P. Champion, 2 vols, 1923–7; ed. J. Charpier, 1958 (selection); ed. S. Cigada, Milan 1960 (incl. bibl.). Tr. C. Wallis, *Rondels*, London 1951 (tr. of *Rondeaux*); tr. S. Purcell, 1973. Also tr. in anthologies, incl. *Formal spring*, ed. and tr. R. N. Currey, London and New York 1950; *The Penguin book of French verse*, vol 1, tr. B. Woledge, Harmondsworth 1961.

The English poems, ed. G. W. Taylor, London 1827; ed. R. Steele and M. Day, 1941 (reissued 1970, incl. critical bibl. 1945–69 by C. Clark).

CHAMPION, P., La *Vie de Charles d'Orléans*, 1911.

FOX, J., *The lyric poetry of Charles d'Orléans*, Oxford 1969.

GOODRICH, N. L., *Charles of Orleans, a study of themes in his French and in his English poetry*, Geneva 1967.

MCLEOD, E., *Charles of Orleans, prince and poet*, London 1969.

POIRION, D., in his *Le poète et le prince*, 1965.

PASSION, La (known as *La Passion de Clermont-Ferrand*)
                                    2nd half of 10th century

La Passion, ed. G. Paris, 1873 (in *Romania*, vol 2); ed. W. Förster and E. Koschwitz, Heilbronn 1884 (in their *Altfranzösisches Übungsbuch*; revd A. Hilka 1932); ed. S. d'Arco Avalle, Milan and Naples 1962. Tr. anon, *The Passion of Christ*, Oxford 1912 (in *The oldest monuments of the French language*).

KOSCHWITZ, E., *Commentar zu den ältesten französischen Denkmälern*, Heilbronn 1886.

PERCEFOREST c. 1340
(prose romance linking the *Romans d'ALEXANDRE* and *LANCELOT GRAAL*).

For general studies and bibliographies, see *MATIÈRE DE BRETAGNE*.

La trèsélégante délicieuse melliflue et trèsplaisante hystoire du trèsnoble victorieux et excellentissime roy Perceforest, 6 vols, 1528; ed. G. Paris, 1894 (episode *Le lai de la rose à la Dame Léal*, in *Romania*, vol 23); ed. H. Vaganay, Mâcon 1907 (*Prologue*); ed. J. Lods, Paris 1953 (lyrics).

LODS, J., *Le roman de Perceforest*, Geneva and Lille 1951.

PERLESVAUS before 1212
(prose romance continuation of *Perceval* by Chrétien de TROYES)

For general studies and bibliographies, see *MATIÈRE DE BRETAGNE*.

Perlesvaus, 1516 (untitled, in *Lhystoire du sainct Greaal*, vol 2; text begins '*Le second volume du sainct Greaal*'); ed. C. Potvin, Mons 1866 (as *Le roman en prose*, in *Perceval le Gallois*, vol 1); ed. W. A. Nitze et al., 2 vols, Chicago 1932–7. Tr. S. Evans, *The high history of the Holy Grail*, 2 vols, London 1898.

PISAN, Christine de   c. 1365–c. 1431

Oeuvres poétiques, ed. M. Roy, 3 vols, 1886–96 (incomplete).
In *Collection des meilleurs ouvrages françois composés par des femmes françoises*, ed. G. de Kéralio, vols 2 and 3, 1786 (cntg extracts from *Ballades*, *Epistre au dieu d'amours* and *Livre des trois vertus*).

Le livre des fais d'armes et de chevalerie, 1488 (as *L'art de chevalerie selon Vegece*). Tr. W. Caxton, London 1489 (untitled; text begins '*Here begynneth the book of fayttes of arms and of chyvalrye*'; ed. A. T. P. Byles, 1932).
Le trésor de la cité des dames, 1497. Tr. B. Anslay, London 1521 (untitled; text begins '*Here begynneth the boke of the Cyte of ladyes*').
Les cent histoires of Troye; Lépistre de Othea déesse de prudence envoyée à lesperit chevalereux Hector de Troye, c. 1500. Tr. S. Scrope, *The epistle of Othea to Hector*, c. 1440 (ed. G. F. Warner, 1904); tr. R. Wyer, *The C. hystoryes of Troye*, London 1540?.
Livre des fais et bonnes meurs du sage roi Charles, ed. J. Lebeuf, 1743 (in *Dissertations sur l'histoire écclésiastique et civile de Paris*; incomplete); ed. C. B. Petitot, 1835 (in *Panthéon littéraire*, vols 5 and 6); ed. S. Solente, 2 vols, 1936–41.

Le livre des trois vertus, 1787 (extracts, in *Collection des meilleurs ouvrages above*); ed. M. Laigle, 1912.

Dittié sur Jeanne d'Arc, ed. A. Jubinal, 1838 (in his *Rapport au Ministre*); ed. J. Quicherat, 1841–9 (in *Procès de condemnation et de réhabilitation de Jeanne d'Arc*, vol 5).

Le chemin de long estude, ed. R. Püschel, Berlin and Paris 1881 (prose adapt. by Jean Chaperon pbd Paris 1549).

Ballades, rondeaux and virelais, 1886 (in *Oeuvres poétiques*, vol 1 above); ed. K. Varty, 1965.

Le dit de la rose, 1891 (in *Oeuvres poétiques*, vol 2 above); ed. F. Heuckenkamp, Halle 1891.

Epître au dieu d'amours, 1891 (in *Oeuvres poétiques*, vol 2 above). Tr. T. Occleve, *The letter of Cupid*, London 1721 (ed. J. Urry, 1801, in *Chaucer's works*).

Le livre du duc des vrais amans, 1896 (in *Oeuvres poétiques*, vol 3 above). Tr. A. Kemp-Welch, L. Binyon and E. R. D. Maclagan, *The book of the Duke of true lovers*, London 1908.

Oraisons, enseignements et proverbes moraux, 1896 (in *Oeuvres poétiques*, vol 3 above). Tr. A. Wideville, ed. Dibden, *The morale proverbes*, London 1477 (*Biblioteca Spenceriana*, vol 4); tr. Earl Rivers, Westminster, 1478; tr. J. Misrahi and M. Marks, *Prayer to Our Lady*, New York 1953 (tr. of *L'oroyson nostre dame*).

La vision Christine, ed. M. L. Towner, Washington (DC) 1932.

Livre de la paix, ed. C. C. Willard, 1958.

Livre du corps de policie, ed. R. H. Lucas, 1967. Tr. anon., London 1521 (untitled; text begins '*Here begynneth the booke which is called the body of polycye*').

Le livre de mutacion de fortune, ed. S. Solente, 4 vols, 1959–66.

DU CASTEL, F., *Damoiselle Christine de Pisan*, 1972.

PINET, M. J., *Christine de Pisan, étude biographique et littéraire*, 1927.

PONT-SAINTE-MAXENCE, Garnier (or Guernes) de   12th century

La vie de saint Thomas le martyr, ed. I. Bekker, Berlin 1838; ed. E. Walberg, Lund 1922 (concise ed. Paris 1936).

WALBERG, E., in his *La tradition hagiographique de saint Thomas Beckett avant la fin du 12e siècle*, 1929.

PROVINS, Guiot de   late 12th century

Bibl. See Orr ed. of *Oeuvres* below.

Oeuvres, ed. A. Baudler, Halle 1902 (in his *Guiot de Provins* below; cntg extracts from *Bible, Suite de la Bible,* and 5 lyrics); ed. J. Orr, Manchester 1915 (complete works; incl. bibl.).

Bible, ed. D. M. Méon, 1808 (in *Fabliaux et contes,* vol 2).

BAUDLER, A., *Guiot de Provins,* Halle 1902.

QUINZE JOYES DE MARIAGE, Les early 15th century
(Sometimes ascribed to Antoine de LA SALE)

Bibl. See Fleuret ed. below.

Les quinze joyes de mariage, ed. G. Leroy, Lyons c. 1480–90 (untitled; text ends '*Cy finist ce présent livre qui est dit les Quinze joyes de mariage*'); ed. J. Le Duchat, The Hague 1726; ed. P. Jannet, Paris 1853 (revd 1857); ed. F. Fleuret, 1936 (incl. bibl.). Modern French version M. L. Simon, 1929. Tr. anon. *The fifteen joys of marriage,* London 1509; tr. and adapt. T. Dekker?, *The batchelars banquet,* 1603; tr. anon., *Fifteen comforts of rash and inconsiderate marriage,* 1682; tr. R. Aldington, *The fifteen joys of marriage,* London and New York 1926; tr. E. Abbot, London 1959.

SODERHJELM, W., in his *La nouvelle française au 15e siècle,* Helsinki 1910.

RAOUL DE CAMBRAI c. 1180
(belonging to the *Geste des vassaux révoltés*)

For general bibliographies and studies, see *CHANSONS DE GESTE.*

Li romans de Raoul de Cambrai et de Bernier, ed. E. Le Glay, 1840; ed. P. Meyer and A. Longnon, 1882. Modern French version, P. Tuffrau, 1924. English tr. J. Crosland, London 1926.

CALIN, W. C., *The old French epic of revolt,* Geneva 1962.

RÉGNIER, Jean 1390?–1467

Les fortunes et adversitez, 1526; ed. P. Lacroix, Geneva 1867; ed. E. Droz, Paris 1923.

CHAMPION, P., in his *Histoire poétique du 15e siècle,* vol 1, 1923.
PETIT, E., *Le poète Jean Régnier,* Auxerre 1904.

RENART, Jean fl. 1200–1230

Lai de l'ombre, ed. F. Michel, 1846 (in *Lais inédits des 12e et 13e siècles*); ed. J. Bédier, 1913; ed. J. Orr, Edinburgh 1948. Tr. N. L. Goodrich, *The lay of a shadow,* Boston (Mass) 1964 (in *The ways of love*); tr. P. Matarasso, Harmondsworth 1971 (with *Aucassin et Nicolette*).

Le roman de Galeran (by Renaut, sometimes identified with Jean Renart), ed. A. Boucherie, Montpellier and Paris 1888; ed. L. Foulet, Paris 1925.

Le roman de la rose ou de Guillaume de Dôle, ed. G. Servois, 1893; ed. R. Lejeune-Dehousse, 1936; ed. F. Lecoy, 1972.

L'escoufle, ed. H. Michelant and P. Meyer, 1894. Modern French version, A. Mary, 1925.

De Renart et de Piaudoue and *Plaid de Renart de Dammartin*, ed. R. Lejeune-Dehousse, Paris and Liège 1935 (in her *L'oeuvre de Jean Renart* below).

CREMONESI, C., *Jean Renart, romanziere del 13 secolo*, Milan 1950.

LANGLOIS, C. V., in his *La vie en France au moyen âge d'après les romans mondains du temps*, 1924.

LEJEUNE-DEHOUSSE, R., *L' oeuvre de Jean Renart*, Paris and Liège 1935.

RENART, Roman de   late 12th–14th centuries

See also RUTEBEUF (*Renart le bestourné*).
Bibl. See FLINN below.
TILANDER, G., *Lexique du Roman de Renart*, Gothenburg 1924.

Le roman de Renart, ed. D. M. Méon, 4 vols, 1828 (revd and enl. P. Chabaille, 5 vols, 1835); ed. E. Martin, 4 vols, 1882–7 (revd. J. Dufournet, 1970); ed. H. Breuer, Halle 1929 (2 episodes of *Branche 2*, and *Branches* 8 and 25); ed. M. Roques, 6 vols, Paris 1948–63 (*Branches* 1–19). Modern French versions, P. Paris 1861 (revd J. de Foucaut, 1949); L. Chauveau, 1925; B. A. Jeanroy, 1926; R. L. Busquet, 1936.

Le jugement de Renart, 1828 (in *Le roman de Renart* above, vol 4); ed. M. Roques, 1948 (in *Branche 1* above, with *Le siège de Maupertuis* and *Renart teinturier*).

Renart le nouvel (by Jacquemart Giélée), 1828 (in *Roman de Renart* above, vol 4); ed. J. Houdoy, 1874; ed. H. Roussel, 1960.

Le couronnement Renart, 1828 (in *Roman de Renart* above, vol 4); ed. A. Foulet, Princeton (NJ) and Paris 1929.

Le roman de Renart le contrefait, ed. G. Raynaud and H. Lemaître, 2 vols, 1914.

BOSSUAT, R., *Le roman de Renart*, 1957.

BÜTTNER, H., *Studien zu dem Roman de Renart und dem Reinhart Fuchs*, 2 vols, Strasbourg 1891.

DAHNHARDT, O. (ed.), *Natursagen*, vols 3 and 4, Leipzig and Berlin 1907–12.

FLINN, J., *Le roman de Renart dans la littérature française et dans les littératures étrangères du moyen âge*, Toronto 1963 (incl. bibl.).

FOULET, L., *Le roman de Renart*, 1914.

NIVARD, *Ysengrimus* (main source for Renart), ed. E. Voigt, Halle 1884.

RENAUT DE MONTAUBAN (or *Les Quatre Fils Aymon*) c. 1200
(belonging to the *Geste des vassaux révoltés*)

For bibliographies and general studies, see *CHANSONS DE GESTE.*

Renaut de Montauban, ed. H. Michelant, Stuttgart 1862 (in *Bibliothek des literarischen vereins,* vol 67); ed. F. Castets, Montpellier 1909. Tr. W. Hazlitt, *The four sons of Aymon,* London 1851.

CALIN, W. C., *The old French epic of revolt,* Geneva 1962.

ROLAND, Chanson de   late 11th century
(belonging to the *Geste du roi*)

For general bibliographies and studies, see *CHANSONS DE GESTE.*

SEELMANN, E. P., *Bibliographie des altfranzösischen Rolandsliedes,* Heilbronn 1888.
See also FARAL below.

La chanson de Roland ou de Roncesvaux, ed. F. Michel, 1837 (revd 1869); ed. L. Gautier, 2 vols, Tours 1872 (with modern French version); ed. T. Müller, Gottingen 1851 (revd 1878); ed. E. Stengel, Leipzig 1900; ed. J. Bédier, Paris 1922 (revd 1937); ed. T. A. Jenkins, Boston 1924; ed. A. Hilka, Halle 1926 (revd Baden-Baden 1952); ed. G. Bertoni, Florence 1935 (enl. 1936); ed. F. Whitehead, Oxford 1947; ed. G. Gasca-Queirazza, Turin 1955; ed. C. Segre, Milan 1971. Modern French versions, C. Voile, Paris 1925; M. Tessier, 1948; G. Moignet, 1970; G. F. Jones and A. Denaitre, Englewood Cliffs (NJ) 1972. Tr. Mrs Marsh, *The Song of Roland,* London 1854; tr. J. O'Hagan, 1880; tr. J. Crosland, 1907; tr. R. Hague, 1937; tr. D. L. Sayers, 1937; tr. W. A. Merwin, New York 1963 (in *Medieval epics*); tr. P. Terry, Indianapolis (Ind) 1965.

BÉDIER, J., *La chanson de Roland,* 1927.

FARAL, E., *La chanson de Roland. Etude et analyse,* 1934 (incl. bibl.).

HORRENT, J., *La chanson de Roland dans les littératures française et espagnole du moyen âge,* 1951.

LE GENTIL, P., *La chanson de Roland,* 1955; 1967.

MENENDEZ-PIDAL, R., *La Chanson de Roland y el neotradicionalismo,* Madrid 1959. French tr. I. M. Cluzel, *La Chanson de Roland et la tradition épique des Francs,* Paris 1960 (revd ed.).

MORTIER, R., *La Chanson de Roland, essai d'interprétation du problème des origines,* 1939.

OWEN, D. D. R., *The legend of Roland,* London 1972.

PAUPHILET, A., in his *Le legs du moyen âge,* Melun 1950.

ROSE, Roman de la
First part by Guillaume de Lorris   ?–c. 1240
Second part by Jean Clopinel de Meung   mid-13th century–c. 1318

BOURDILLON, F. W., *The early editions*, London 1906.
DUPIRE, N., *Bibliographie des travaux de Ernest Langlois*, 1929.

Le roman de la rose, Lyon c. 1481 (untitled; text begins 'Cȳ commēce le romāt de la rose, Ou tout lart damours est enclose'); ed. C. Marot, Paris 1526; ed. N. Lenglet du Fresnoy, 3 vols, Amsterdam 1735 (with Jean de Meung's *Testament* and *Codicille*; revd 1798); ed. D. M. Méon, 4 vols, Paris 1813 (with *Sept articles de la foi, Testament* and *Codicille*); ed. E. Langlois, 5 vols, 1914–24; ed. S. F. Baridon and A. Viscardi, Geneva and Paris 1957; ed. F. Lecoy, Paris, 3 vols, 1965–70. Modern French version, A. Mary, 1928. Tr. Chaucer?, ed. W. Thynne, *The romaunt of the rose*, London 1532 (tr. of pt 1 and some of pt 2; ed. R. Sutherland, below); tr. F. S. Ellis, *The romance of the rose*, 3 vols, London, 1900; tr. H. W. Robbins, New York 1962; tr. C. Dahlberg, Princeton (NJ) 1971.

FLEMING, J., *The Roman de la rose: a study in allegory and iconography*, Princeton (NJ) 1969.
GUNN, A. M. F., *The mirror of love, a reinterpretation of the romance of the rose*, Lubbock (Tex) 1951.
JORET, C., *La rose dans l'antiquité et au moyen âge*, 1892.
LEWIS, C. S., *The allegory of love*, Oxford 1936.
SUTHERLAND, R., *The romaunt of the rose and Le roman de la rose*, Oxford 1967.
WARD, C.F., *The epistles on Romance of the rose, and other dreamers in the debate*, Montreal 1911 (in *Transactions of the Royal Society of Canada*).

RUTEBEUF   fl. 1250–1280

Bibl. See Frank ed. of *Miracle de Théophile* below.

Oeuvres complètes, ed. A. Jubinal, 2 vols, 1839 (revd, 3 vols, 1874–5); ed. A. Kressner, Wolfenbüttel 1885; ed. H. Lucas, Paris 1938 (7 'personal poems', incl. *Mariage Rutebeuf, Complainte* and *Pauvreté Rutebeuf*); ed. H. Lucas, Manchester 1952 (*Poèmes concernant l'Université de Paris*); ed. E. Faral and J. Bastin, 2 vols, 1959–60.

La vie de sainte Marie l'Egyptienne, 1839 (in *Oeuvres complètes* above, vol 2); ed. B. A. Bujila, Ann Arbor (Mich) 1949.
Miracle de Théophile, 1839 (in *Oeuvres complètes* above, vol 2); ed. G. Frank, 1925 (incl. bibl.). Modern French versions, A. Jeanroy, 1932; G. Cohen, 1934. Tr. R. Axton and J. Stevens, Oxford 1971 (in *Medieval French plays*).

Renart le bestourné, 1839 (in *Oeuvres complètes* above). Tr. and ed. E. B. Ham, Ann Arbor (Mich) 1947.

CLÉDAT, L., *Rutebeuf*, 1891; 1898.

FARAL, E., in his *La vie quotidienne au temps de saint Louis*, 1942.

REGELADO, N. F., *Poetic patterns in Rutebeuf*, Newhaven (Conn) 1971.

SAINT ALEXIS, La Vie de   c. 1050

La vie de saint Alexis, ed. G. Paris and L. Pannier, 1872 (revd M. Roques, 1908); ed. G. Paris, 1911; ed. M. Rösler, Halle 1928; ed. V. L. Dedeck-Héry, New York 1931; ed. C. Storey, Paris 1934; ed. G. Rohlfs, Halle 1950 (revd Tübingen 1958). Tr. anon., *The life of Saint Alexis*, Oxford 1912 (in *The oldest monuments of the French language*).

SAINTE EULALIE, La Cantilène (or Séquence) de   c. 880

La cantilène de sainte Eulalie, ed. K. Bartsch, Leipzig 1866 (in his *Chrestomathie de l'ancien français*, revd L. Wiese, 1908); ed. W. Förster and E. Koschwitz, Heilbronn 1884 (in their *Altfranzösisches Übungsbuch*, revd A. Hilka, 1932). Tr. anon., *The prose of Saint Eulalie*, Oxford 1912 (in *The oldest monuments of the French language*).

KOSCHWITZ, E., in his *Commentar zu den ältesten französischen Denkmälern*, Heilbronn 1886.

LECLERQ, H., Cantilène, 1910 (in *Dictionnaire d'archéologie chrétienne et de liturgie*, vol 2, pt 2).

SAINTE-MAURE, Benoît de   fl. c. 1150

Bibl. See Joly ed. of *Le roman de Troie* below.

Chronique des ducs de Normandie, ed. F. Michel, 3 vols, 1836–44; ed. C. Fahlin, 2 vols, Uppsala 1951–4.

[. . .] *Le roman de Troie*, ed. A. Joly, 2 vols, 1870–1 (incl. bibl.); ed. L. Constans, 6 vols, 1904–12. Tr. R. K. Gordon, in his *The story of Troilus*, London 1934 (Troilus episodes).

SAINT LÉGER, La Vie de   second half of 10th century

La vie de saint Léger, ed. G. Paris, 1872 (in *Romania*, vol 1); ed. J. Linskill, 1937. Tr. anon., *The life of Saint Leger*, Oxford 1912 (in *The oldest monuments of the French language*).

KOSCHWITZ, E., *Commentar zu den ältesten französischen Denkmälern*, Heilbronn 1886.

SERMENTS DE STRASBOURG   842

Bibl. See EWERT below.

Serments de Strasbourg, ed. M. Bouquet, 1738 (in his ed. of Nithard's *Historiarum libri IV*, in *Recueil des historiens des Gaules et de la France*, vol 1; ed. P. Lauer, 1926 (in his French tr. of Nithard); ed. R. L. Wagner, Lille and Geneva 1949 (in *Textes d'études*); ed. W. D. Elcock, London 1960 (in *The Romance languages*). Tr. anon., *The Strasbourg oaths*, Oxford 1912 (in *The oldest monuments of the French language*).

EWERT, A., *The Strasbourg oaths*, London 1935 (in *Transactions of the Philological Society*; incl. bibl.).
WALLENSKÖLD, A., *Strassburger ederna*, Helsinki 1921.

SPONSUS (or *Le Drame de l'époux*)   c. 1100

Bibl. See Young ed. below; also Thomas ed. below.

Sponsus, ed. W. Cloetta, 1893 (in *Romania*, vol 22); ed. K. Young, Oxford 1933 (in his *The drama of the medieval church*; incl. bibl.); ed. L. P. Thomas, Paris 1951 (incl. bibl.). Tr. R. T. Hill, New Haven (Conn) 1936.

THAON (or THAUN), Philippe de   early 12th century

Le comput, ed. T. Wright, London 1841 (as *Li livre des créatures*; with English tr.); ed. E. Mall, Strasbourg 1873.
Le bestiaire, ed. T. Wright, London 1841 (with *Le comput* above; also with English tr., *The bestiary*); ed. E. Walberg, Paris and Lund 1900.

LANGLOIS, C. V., in his *La connaissance de la nature et du monde au moyen âge*, 1911; 1927.

THÈBES, *Roman de*   c. 1150

Le roman de Thèbes, ed. L. Constans, 2 vols, 1890.

FARAL, E., in his *Recherches sur les sources latines des contes et romans courtois du moyen âge*, 1913.

TRISTAN LEGEND

See also Marie de FRANCE (*Lai de Chèvrefeuille*).

For general bibliographies and studies, see *MATIÈRE DE BRETAGNE*.

KÜPPER, H., *Bibliographie zur Tristansage*, Jena 1941 (for years 1739–1941).

See also Curtis ed. of *Roman de Tristan en prose* below; also SCHOEPPERLE below; also VINAVER below.

The works below are listed in order of composition.

Tristan ('version courtoise', by Thomas), ed. F. Michel, London and Paris 1838 (in *Tristan*, vol 2); ed. J. Bédier, 2 vols, Paris 1902–5; ed. B. H. Wind, Leiden 1950. Tr. R. S. Loomis, *The romance of Tristran and Ysolt*, New York 1923 (revd 1951); tr. A. T. Hatto, Harmondsworth 1960.

Tristan ('version commune', fragment by Béroul), ed. H. von der Hagen, Breslau 1823 (in Gottfried von Strassburg's *Werke*, vol 2); ed. F. Michel, London and Paris 1835–8 (in *Tristan*, vols 1–2); ed. E. Muret, Paris 1903 (revd 1913; revd M. L. Defourques, 1947); ed. A. Ewert, Oxford 1939.

La folie Tristan, ed. F. Michel, London and Paris 1835–8 (Berne ms. version in *Tristan*, vol 1; Oxford ms. version in vol 2); ed. H. Mort, Paris 1886 (Berne ms. version, in *Romania*, vol 15); ed. J. Bédier, 1907 (both versions); ed. E. Hoepffner, 2 vols, 1934–8 (Berne ms. version, vol 1; Oxford ms. version, vol 2; revd, 2 vols, 1943–9). Modern French version, G. Lély, 1954 (Oxford ms. version).

Roman de Tristan en prose, Rouen 1489 (untitled; text ends *'Cy fine la secôde et derroîne partie de ce présent livre fait et cômposé en lhonneur et mémoire de très vaillant noble et excellent chevalier Tristâ, fils du noble roy Mésiachus de Léonois, lequel regna au têps du roy Art' et du roy Marc de Cornouaille, et de la belle Yseulde fille d. roy dirlâde et fême du roy Marc'*); Paris before 1533; ed. R. L. Curtis, Munich 1963 onwards (1 vol pbd; incl. list of mss and early eds). Modern French version, P. Champion, Paris 1947.

Other versions of the Tristan legend:

    Le morte Darthur (by Thomas Malory; Middle English adapt. of the prose *Tristan* and *LANCELOT-GRAAL*), ed. W. Caxton, London 1485; ed. A. W. Pollard, 2 vols, 1900.

    Sir Tristrem (Middle English version, based on Thomas' version), ed. W. Scott, Edinburgh 1804.

    Tristrans saga (Icelandic version, based on Thomas' version), ed. E. Koelbing, Heilbronn 1878 (with *Sir Tristrem* above, and German tr.).

    Tristan und Isolde (German version by Gottfried von Strassburg, based on Thomas' version), ed. W. Golther, Berlin and Stuttgart 1888. Tr. E. R. Zeydel, *Tristan and Isolde*, Princeton (NJ) 1948 (abr.); tr. A. T. Hatto, Harmondsworth 1960 (with tr. of Thomas' *Tristan* above).

    Eilhart von Oberge (closely related to Béroul's version), ed. F. Lichtenstein, Strasbourg 1877; ed. K. Wagner, Bonn and Leipzig 1924.

    Le roman de Tristan et Iseut (by Joseph Bédier, based mainly on Béroul's version), 1900. Tr. H. Belloc, *The romance of Tristan and Iseult*, London 1903; tr. D. L. Sayers, *Tristan in Brittany*, 1929.

BARTEAU, F., *Les romans de Tristan et Iseut*, 1972.

GOLTHER, W., *Die Sage von Tristan und Isolde*, Munich 1887.

LÖSETH, E., *Le roman en prose de Tristan*, 1891.

REID, T. B. W., *The Tristram of Béroul, a textual commentary*, Oxford 1972.

SCHOEPPERLE, G., *Tristan and Isolt, a study of the sources of the romance*, 2 vols, Frankfurt 1913; 2 vols, New York 1963 (with *A survey of Tristan scholarship after 1911*, by R. S. Loomis, in vol 2).

VAN DAM, J., *Tristanprobleme*, Groningen and Leipzig 1930 (in *Neophilologus*, vol 15).

VETTER, F., *La légende de Tristan d'après le poème français de Thomas et les versions principales qui s'y rattachent*, Marburg 1882.

VINAVER, E., *Etudes sur le Tristan en prose*, 1925 (incl. critical bibl.).

TROYES, Chrétien de   c. 1135–c. 1190

POTVIN C., *Bibliographie*, Brussels 1863.

REINHARD, J. R., *A bibliographical essay*, Ann Arbor (Mich) 1932.

See also Comfort tr. of *Romans arthuriens* below; BRUCE below; also FRAPPIER below. Also:

FÖRSTER, W. and BREUER, H., *Wörterbuch zu Kristian von Troyes sämtlichen Werken*, Halle 1933.

Sämtliche erhaltene Werke, ed. W. Förster, 4 vols, Halle 1884–9 (complete works, except for *Perceval* and *Philomena*).

Romans arthuriens (composed c. 1170–c. 1190). Tr. W. W. Comfort, *Arthurian romances*, London 1913 (incl. bibl.). Comprising:

Yvain or Le chevalier au lion, ed. C. Guest, London 1838 (in her *The Mabinogion from the Llyfr Coch and Hergest*, vol 1); ed. W. L. Holland, Hanover 1862 (revd A. Schulze, Berlin 1902); ed. W. Förster, Halle 1891 (concise version of ed. in *Werke* above; revd A. Hilka, 1926); ed. T. B. W. Reid, Manchester 1942; ed. M. Roques, Paris 1961. Modern French version, S. Hannedouche, 1960; C. Buridant and J. Trotin, 1971. Tr. anon., ed. J. Ribon, London 1802 (in *Ancient medieval metrical romances*); tr. R. W. Ackerman and F. W. Locke, *The knight of the lion*, New York 1957.

Roman van Lancelot, ed. W. J. A. Jonckbloet, 2 vols, s'Gravenhage 1846–9; ed. P. Tarbé, Rheims 1849; ed. M. Roques, Paris 1958. Modern French version J. Frappier, 1962.

Eric et Enide, ed. J. Bekker, Leipzig 1856 (in *Zeitschrift für deutsches Altertum*, vol 10); ed. W. Förster, Halle 1896 (concise version of ed. in *Werke* above; revd 1932); ed. M. Roques, Paris 1952. Modern French version R. Louis, 1954.

Cligès, Halle 1884 (in *Werke* above; concise version 1910, revd A. Hilka, 1921). Modern French version and ed. A. Micha, Paris 1957. Tr. L. J. Gardiner, London and New York 1912.

Perceval le Gallois ou le conte du Graal, ed. C. Potvin, 6 vols, Mons 1866–71 (with *PERLESVAUS* and *Continuations* below); ed. G. Baist, Fribourg 1909; ed. A. Hilka, Halle 1932; ed. W. Roach, Geneva and Lille 1956; ed. F. J. Carmody, Berkeley (Calif) 1970; ed. F. Lecoy, 1973 onwards (1 vol pbd). Modern French versions, L. Foulet, 1947; S. Hannedouche, 1960. Tr. and adapt. anon., *Sir Percyvelle de Galles,* ed. J. O. Halliwell, London 1844 (late 14th cent. version, in *Thornton romances;* re-ed. J. L. Weston, Boston (Mass) 1914, in *Chief medieval poets);* tr. R. W. Linker, *The story of the grail,* Chapel Hill (NC) 1952.

Continuations (by other writers, 1190–1235), ed. C. Potvin, Mons 1867–71 (with *Perceval le Gallois* above; vol 3, *Première continuation,* or *Continuation Gauvain,* or pseudo-Wauchier *continuation;* vols 4–5, Wauchier's *continuation;* vols 5–6, Manessier's *continuation;* vol 6, extracts from Gerbert de Montreuil's *continuation);* ed. M. Williams, 2 vols, Paris 1922–5 (Gerbert de Montreuil's *continuation);* ed. W. Roach, Philadelphia (Pa) 1949 onwards (5 vols pbd, cntg *Première* and Wauchier *continuations).*

Guillaume d'Angleterre, ed. F. Michel, 1840 (in *Chroniques anglo-normandes,* vol 3); ed. W. Förster, Halle 1911 (concise version of ed. in *Werke* above); ed. M. Wilmotte, Paris 1927. Tr. W. G. Collingwood, *King William the wanderer,* London 1904.

Chansons, ed. W. L. Holland, Tübingen 1854 (4 poems in his *Crestien de Troies, eine literaturgeschichtliche Untersuchung);* ed. W. Förster, Halle 1914 (2 poems, in 1st ed. of his *Wörterbuch* above).

Philomena (adapt. from Ovid; ascribed to Chrétien de Troyes), ed. C. de Boer, 1909.

BEZZOLA, R., *Le sens de l'aventure et de l'amour,* 1947.

BRAND, W., *Chrétien de Troyes, zur Dichtungstechnik seiner Romane,* Munich 1972.

BRUCE, J. D., in his *The evolution of Arthurian romance,* 2 vols, Göttingen 1923 (incl. bibl.).

COHEN, G., *Chrétien de Troyes et son oeuvre,* 1931.

FRAPPIER, J., *Chrétien de Troyes l'homme et l'oeuvre,* 1957.

HOFER, S., *Chrétien de Troyes, Leben und Werke,* Graz and Cologne 1954.

LAURIE, H. C. R., *Two studies of Chrétien de Troyes,* Geneva 1972.

LOOMIS, R. S., *Arthurian tradition and Chrétien de Troyes,* New York 1949.

PARIS, G., *Cligès,* 1902 (in *Journal des Savants);* ed. M. Roques, 1910 (in *Mélanges de littérature française,* vol 1).

ZADDY, Z. P., *Chrétien studies,* Glasgow 1973.

VILLEHARDOUIN, Geoffroi de   1152–c. 1212

Bibl. See Faral ed. below.

L'histoire [. . .] *de la conqueste de Constantinople*, 1585 (partial ed. possibly first pbd Venice 1573); Lyon 1601; ed. Du Cange, Paris 1657; ed. C. B. Petitot, 1819 (in *Collection complète des mémoires relatifs à l'histoire de France*, vol 1); ed. P. Paris, 1838; ed. N. de Wailly, 1872 (with Henri de Valenciennes' continuation, and modern French version); ed. E. Faral, 1938–9 (incl. bibl.); ed. A. Pauphilet and E. Pognon, 1952 (in *Historiens et chroniqueurs du moyen âge*). Tr. T. Smith, *The chronicle* [. . .] *concerning the conquest of Constantinople*, London 1829; tr. M. R. B. Shaw, Harmondsworth 1963 (in *Chronicles of the Crusades*).

LONGNON, J., *Recherches sur la vie de Geoffroy de Villehardouin*, 1939.

MOSER, H., *Gottfried von Villehardouin und der Lateinerzug gegen Byzanz*, Breslau 1897.

SAINTE-BEUVE, C. A. de, in his *Causeries du lundi*, vol 9, 1856.

VILLON, François   1431–after 1463

CONS, L., *Etat présent des études sur Villon*, 1936.
See also Longnon ed. below; also Neri ed. below; also BRUNELLI below.

Le grant testament Villon et le petit. Son codicille. Le jargon & ses balades, ed. P. Levet 1489; ed. G. Nyverd, c. 1520 (with *Repues franches*, wrongly ascribed to Villon); ed. Clément Marot, 1533 (as *Les Oeuvres*); ed. E. de Laurière and J. A. Du Cerceau, 1723; ed. J. H. Prompsault, Paris 1832; ed. La Monnoye and P. Jannet, 1867 (ed. prepared by La Monnoye 1723–8); ed. W. G. C. Bijvanck, Leiden 1882 (ed. of *Petit testament*); ed. A. Longnon, 1892 (incl. bibl. to 1892; concise version 1911; revd L. Foulet, 1914); ed. W. von Wurzbach, Erlangen 1903; ed. L. Thuasne, Paris 1923; ed. F. Neri, Turin 1923 (incl. Italian critical bibl.); ed. A. Jeanroy, Paris 1934 (based on Marot ed.); ed. A. Mary, 1951 (revd 1957); ed. R. Guiette, 1959; ed. A. Lanly, 2 vols, 1969. Tr. J. Payne, *The poems of Master Francis Villon of Paris*, London 1878; tr. H. de Vere Stacpoole, *The poems*, 1913; tr. A. C. Swinburne, 1916 (selection); tr. G. Atkinson, *The works*, 1930; tr. E. F. Chaney, Oxford 1940; tr. H. B. McCaskie, *The poems*, London 1946; tr. A. Bonner, *The complete works*, New York, 1960; tr. B. Saklatvala, *Complete poems*, London 1968. Various poems also translated by D. G. Rossetti (notably *Ballade des dames du temps jadis*), Synge, Henley and Gosse.

BRUNELLI, G. A., *François Villon*, Milan 1960 (incl. bibl.).

CAMPAUX, A. F., *François Villon, sa vie et ses oeuvres*, 1859.

CHAMPION, P., *François Villon, sa vie et son temps*, 2 vols, 1913.

In his *Histoire poétique du 15e siècle*, vol 2, 1929.

CHARPENTIER, L., *François Villon, le personnage*, 1933.

CORTI, A., *François Villon, su vid y su obra*, Buenos Aires 1931.

DUFOURNET, J., *Villon et sa fortune littéraire*, 1970.

FOX, J., *The poetry of Villon*, London and Edinburgh 1962.

LEWIS, D. B. Wyndham, *François Villon, a documented survey*, New York and Hartford (Conn), 1928.

NAGEL, S., *François Villon, Versuch einer kritischen Darstellung seines Lebens nach seinen Gedichten*, Mülheim an der Ruhr 1856.

PARIS, G., *François Villon*, 1901.

SICILIANO, I., *François Villon et les thèmes poétiques du moyen âge*, 1934.
Mésaventures posthumes de Maître Françoys Villon, 1973.

WACE   c. 1110–c. 1175

Roman de Rou et des ducs de Normandie, ed. F. Pluquet, Caen 1825 (as *Chronique ascendante des ducs de Normandie*, in *Mémoires de la Société des antiquaires de Normandie*, vol. 1); 2 vols, Rouen 1827; ed. H. Andresen, 2 vols, Heilbronn 1877–9; ed. A. J. Holden, 3 vols, Paris 1970–3. Tr. E. Taylor, *Chronicle of the Norman conquest, from the Roman de Rou*, London 1837; tr. A. Malet, *The conquest of England, from Wace's poem of the Roman de Rou*, 1860.

De sancto Nichalae, alias li livres de Saint Nicolay, ed. L. J. N. Monmerqué and A. de la Borderie, Paris 1834; ed. M. S. Crawford, Philadelphia (Pa) 1923; ed. E. Ronsjö, Lund 1942.

Le roman de Brut, ed. A. J. V. Le Roux de Lincy, 2 vols, Rouen 1836–8; ed. I. Arnold, 2 vols, Paris 1938–40; ed. I. Arnold and M. Pelan, 1962 (Arthurian sections). Tr. and adapt. Lazamon, ed. F. Madden, *Brut, or chronicle of Britain* (11th century adapt.), London 1847.

La vie de Sainte Marguerite, ed. A. Joly, 1879 (incomplete); ed. E. A. Francis, 1932.

L'établissement de la fête de la conception Nostre Dame, ed. G. Mancel and G. S. Trébutien, Caen 1842; ed. W. R. Ashford, Chicago (Ill) 1933.

FLETCHER, R. H., in his *Arthurian material in the chronicles*, Boston (Mass) 1906.

PHILPOT, J. H., *Maistre Wace, a pioneer in two literatures*, London 1925 (incl. translated extracts).

2
The Sixteenth Century

AMYOT, Jacques   1513–1593

Bibl. See CIORANESCU below.

L'histoire aethiopique (tr. of Heliodorus' *Aethiopica*), 1547; ed. P. L. Courier,
    2 vols, 1822–3.
Sept livres des histoires de Diodore Sicilien (tr. from Diodorus), 1554.
Les vies des hommes illustres (tr. of Plutarch's *Parallel lives*), 2 vols, 1559;
    6 vols, 1567; ed. G. Walter, 2 vols, 1937; ed. J. Massin, 2 vols, 1967.
Les amours pastorales de Daphnis et de Chloe (tr. of Longus' *Daphnis and
    Chloe*), 1559; ed. P. L. Courier, Florence 1810 (revd Paris 1821).
Les oeuvres morales et meslées de Plutarque (tr. of Plutarch's *Moralia*), 2 vols,
    1572; 1618.

AULOTTE, R., *Amyot et Plutarque: la tradition des Moralia au 16e siècle*,
    Geneva 1965.
CIORANESCU, A., *Vie de Jacques Amyot*, 1941 (incl. bibl.).
STUREL, R., *Jacques Amyot, traducteur des Vies parallèles*, 1908.

AUBIGNÉ, Agrippa d'   1552–1630

Bibl. See GARNIER below.

Oeuvres complètes, ed. E. Réaume, F. de Caussade and A. Legouëz, 6 vols,
    1873–92 (not incl. *Histoire universelle*).

Confession catholique du sieur de Sancy, n.p. 1600?; Cologne 1660 (in *Recueil
    de diverses pièces servans à l'histoire de Henry III*). Tr. anon., *Hell illumin-
    ated, or Sancy's Roman Catholic confession*, London 1679.
Les tragiques, Maillé 1616; n.p. 1620; ed. A. Garnier and J. Plattard, 4 vols,
    Paris 1932–3. Tr. J. Zeldan, New York 1953 (tr. of bks 1–3).
L'histoire universelle, 3 vols, Maillé 1616–20; ed. A. de Ruble, 10 vols, Paris
    1886–1909 (incomplete); ed. J. Plattard, 1925 (remainder).
Les avantures du baron de Faeneste, Maillé 1617 (pts 1–2); 1619 (pt 3); 1630
    (complete); ed. J. Le Duchat, Cologne 1729.
Histoire secrète, ed. J. Le Duchat, Cologne 1729 (with *Les avantures du baron
    de Faeneste* above); ed. J. Prévost, Paris 1928 (as *Sa vie à ses enfants*).

Le printemps, ed. C. Read, 1874; ed. B. Gagnebin and F. Desonay, 2 vols, Lille and Geneva 1948–52; ed. H. Wéber, Paris 1960.

BAILBÉ, J., *Agrippa d'Aubigné, poète des Tragiques*, Caen 1968.
GARNIER, A., *Agrippa d'Aubigné et le parti protestant*, 3 vols, 1928 (incl. bibl. in vol. 3).
LEBOIS, A., *La fortune littéraire des Tragiques d'Aubigné*, 1957.
PLATTARD, J., *Une figure de premier plan dans nos lettres de la Renaissance*, 1931.

BELLEAU, Remi   1528–1577

Les oeuvres poétiques, 2 vols, 1578; 2 vols, 1585; ed. C. Marty-Laveaux, 2 vols, 1877–8.

Translated in anthologies, incl. *Flowers of France, the Renaissance*, tr. J. Payne, London 1907.

Les odes d'Anacréon Teien [. . .] *ensemble quelques petites hymnes*, 1556; 1574.
La bergerie, 1565; 2 vols, 1572.
Les amours et nouveaux eschanges des pierres précieuses, 1576; ed. A. van Bever, 1909; ed. M. Verdier, Geneva 1973.

ECKHARDT, A., *Remi Belleau, sa vie, sa Bergerie*, Budapest 1917.

BÈZE, Théodore de   1519–1605

GARDY, F. and DUFOUR, A., *Bibliographie des oeuvres*, Geneva 1960.
See also GEISENDORF below.

Abraham sacrifiant, Geneva, 1550; ed. K. Cameron, K. M. Hall and F. Higman, 1967. Tr. A. Golding, *A tragedie of Abraham's sacrifice*, London 1577 (ed. M. W. Wallace, Toronto 1906).
L'histoire de la vie & mort de [*Jean Calvin*], Geneva 1564 (as preface to Calvin's *Commentaires sur Josué*); 1565 (enl.); ed. A. Franklin, Paris 1864. Tr. J. Stockwood, *A discourse* [. . .] *conteyning in briefe the life and death of Maister John Calvin*, London 1564; tr. H. Beveridge, Edinburgh 1844 (in *Tracts relating to the Reformation, by John Calvin*, vol 1).
Histoire ecclésiastique des églises reformées au royaume de France (First third by Bèze, remainder compiled by Jean des Gallards), 3 vols, Antwerp 1580; ed. G. Baum, E. Cunitz and R. Reuss, 3 vols, Paris 1883–9.
Chrestienne méditations sur huict pseaumes, Geneva 1582; ed. M. Richter, 1964. Tr. J. Stockwood, *Christian meditations upon eight psalmes*, London 1582.

Also wrote many works in Latin.

Correspondance, ed. H. Aubert et al., 5 vols, Geneva 1960–8.

GEISENDORF, P. F., *Théodore de Bèze*, Geneva 1949 (incl. bibl.).
JEANNERET, M., in his *Poésie et tradition biblique au 16e siècle*, 1969.

BODIN, Jean   1530–1596

Bibl. See CHAUVIRÉ below.

Oeuvres philosophiques, ed. P. Mesnard, 1951.

Reponse aux paradoxes de M. de Malestroit, 1568. Tr. G. A. Moore, *The response of Jean Bodin to the paradoxes of Malestroit, and the paradoxes*, Washington (DC) 1946.
Les six livres de la republique, 1576; 2 vols, London 1775 (abr.). Tr. R. Knolles, *The six books of a commonweale*, London 1606 (ed. K. D. McRae, Cambridge (Mass) 1962); tr. and abr. M. J. Tooley, *Six books of the Commonwealth*, Oxford 1955.
De la démonomanie des sorciers, 1560; Antwerp 1593.

Also published works in Latin, notably *Methodus ad facilem historiarum cognitionem* (1566).

CHAUVIRÉ, R., *Jean Bodin, auteur de la République*, 1914 (incl. bibl.).
FRANKLIN, J. L., *Jean Bodin and the 16th century revolution in the methodology of law and history*, London and New York 1963.

BRANTÔME, Pierre de   c. 1540–1614

Oeuvres, ed. J. Le Duchat et al., 15 vols, The Hague 1740; ed. L. J. N. Monmerqué, 8 vols, Paris 1822–4; ed. P. Mérimée and L. Lacour, 13 vols, 1858–95; ed. L. Lalanne, 11 vols, 1864–82.

Mémoires, 8 vols, Leiden 1665–6 (vol 1, *Vies des dames illustres*; vols 2–3, *Vies des dames galantes*; vols 4–7, *Vies des hommes illustres et grands capitaines*; vol 8, *Vies des hommes illustres et grands capitaines étrangers*). Tr. K. P. Wormeley, *The book of the ladies: illustrious dames of the court of the Valois kings*, London 1899; tr. A. Brown, *The lives of gallant ladies*, 1962.

COTTRELL, R., *Brantôme, the writer as portraitist of his age*, Geneva 1970.
CRUCY, F., *Brantôme*, 1934.
LALANNE, L., *Brantôme, sa vie et ses écrits*, 1896.

CALVIN, Jean   1509–1564

ERICHSON, A., *Bibliographia Calvinana*, Berlin 1900.
NIESEL, W., *Bibliographie 1900–1959*, Munich 1961.

Opera omnia (works in Latin), 9 vols, Amsterdam 1671; ed. J. W. Baum et al., 58 vols, Brunswick 1863–1900.

Oeuvres françoises, ed. P. L. Jacob, 1842.

Tr. H. Beveridge et al., *Calvin translations*, 48 vols, Edinburgh 1843–55.

Tr. J. K. S. Reid, *Theological treatises*, London 1954.

Institution de la religion chrestienne, 4 vols, Geneva 1541 (first pbd in Latin, Basle 1539); n.p. 1562; ed. A. Lefranc, H. Châtelain and J. Pannier, 2 vols, Paris 1911; ed. J. Pannier, 1936–9; ed. J. D. Benoît, 5 vols, 1957–63. Tr. T. Norton, *The institute of the Christian religion*, London 1561.

Traité de la prédestination, Geneva 1560 (first pbd in Latin, Geneva 1550). Tr. J. K. S. Reid, *Concerning the eternal predestination of God*, London 1961.

BÈZE, Théodore de, *Discours* [. . .] *contenant en bref l'histoire de la vie et mort de maistre Jean Calvin*, Geneva 1565; ed. A. Franklin, Paris 1864. Tr. H. Beveridge, *Life of John Calvin*, Edinburgh 1844 (in *Tracts relating to the Reformation, by John Calvin*, vol 1).

DOUMERGUE, E., *Jean Calvin, les hommes et les choses de son temps*, 7 vols, Lausanne 1899–1927.

DOWEY Jr., E. A., *The knowledge of God in Calvin's theology*, New York 1952.

HIGMAN, F., *The style of John Calvin in his French polemical treatises*, Oxford 1967.

HUNT, R. N. C., *Calvin*, London 1933.

PANNIER, J., *Calvin écrivain, sa place et son rôle dans l'histoire de la langue et de la littérature française*, 1930 (shorter ed. first pbd 1909).

CHARRON, Pierre   1541–1603

Bibl. See SABRIÉ below.

Toutes les oeuvres, 1635 (incomplete).

Les trois veritez, Bordeaux 1593; 1595 (enl.).

De la sagesse, livres trois, Bordeaux 1601; Paris 1604 (enl.); ed. A. Duval, 3 vols, 1820–4. Tr. S. Lennard, *Of wisdome three bookes*, London 1608; tr. and adapt. M. H. N. Daly, *A treatise on wisdom*, New York and London 1891.

CHARRON, J. D., *The Wisdom of Pierre Charron, an original and orthodox code of morality*, Chapel Hill (NC) 1960.

SABRIÉ, J. B., *De l'humanisme au rationalisme: Pierre Charron*, 1913 (incl. bibl.).

CRENNE, Hélisenne de   fl. c. 1540

Les oeuvres, 1560.

Les angoysses douloureuses qui procèdent d'amours, 1538; ed. P. Demats, 1968 onwards (1 vol pbd).
Les épistres familières et invectives, 1539; 1540.
Le songe de ma dame Hélisenne, 1540.

REYNIER, G., in his *Le roman sentimental avant l'Astrée*, 1908.

DES MASURES, Louis   c. 1515–1574

Tragédies sainctes: David combattant; David triomphant; David fugitif, Geneva 1566; ed. C. Comte, Paris 1907.

LEBÈGUE, R., in his *La tragédie religieuse en France*, 1929.

DES PÉRIERS, Bonaventure   c. 1510–1544

Recueil des oeuvres, Lyons 1544; ed. L. Lacour, 2 vols, 1856.

Cymbalum mundi, 1538; ed. F. Frank, 1873; ed. P. H. Nurse, Manchester 1958. Tr. P. Marchand, London 1712; tr. B. L. Knapp, New York 1965.
Les nouvelles récréations et joyeux devis, Lyons 1558; ed. P. L. Jacob, Paris 1843; ed. L. Lacour, 2 vols, 1874. Tr. 'T. D.', *The mirrour of mirth and pleasant conceits*, London 1583 (ed. J. W. Hassell, Columbia 1959).

BECKER, P. A., *Bonaventure Des Périers als Dichter und Erzähler*, Vienna 1924.
FEBVRE, L., *Origène et Des Périers*, 1942.
SOZZI, L., *Les contes de Bonaventure Des Périers*, Turin 1965.

DESPORTES, Philippe   1546–1606

Bibl. See LAVAUD below.

Oeuvres, ed. A. Michiels, 1858; ed. V. E. Graham, 7 vols, Geneva and Paris 1958–63 (secular poems).

Tr. in anthologies, incl. *Flowers of France, the Renaissance*, tr. J. Payne, London 1907.

Imitations de quelques chans de l'Arioste (incl. poems by Mellin de SAINT-GELAIS et al.), 1572; ed. J. Lavaud, 1936 (with other poems).
La mort de Rodomont, 1572 (in *Imitations* above). Tr. G. Markham, *Rodomonth's infernall, or the Divel conquered*, London 1607.
Premières oeuvres, 1573; ed. T. Desportes, 1611.
Soixantes pseaumes (tr.), Rouen 1591; 1598 (*Cent pseaumes*); 1603 (*Les cent cinquante psaumes*).
Prières et autres oeuvres chrestiennes, Rouen 1594; ed. H. Vaganay, Lyon 1925.

LAVAUD, J., *Un poète de cour au temps des derniers Valois*, 1936 (incl. bibl.).

DU BARTAS, Guillaume 1544–1590

Bibl. See Holmes–Lyons–Linker ed. of *The works* below.

The works, ed. U. T. Holmes, J. C. Lyons and R. W. Linker, 3 vols, Chapel Hill (NC) 1935–40 (incl. bibl. in vol 3).

La muse chrestiene, 1574; 1579.
La Judit, 1574 (in *La muse chrestiene* above); ed. A. Baîche, Toulouse 1971. Tr. J. Hudson, *The historie of Judith*, Edinburgh 1584 (ed. J. Craigie, 1941).
L'Uranie, 1574 (in *La muse chrestiene* above). Tr. James VI of Scotland, *Urania*, Edinburgh 1584; tr. R. Ashley, n.p. 1589.
La sepmaine, ou création du monde, 1578; 1585;
    La seconde semaine (unfinished), 1584;
  ed. K. Reichenberger, 2 vols, Tübingen 1963. Tr. J. Sylvester, *Divine weekes and workes*, London 1605–6.

PELLISSIER, G., *La vie et les oeuvres de Du Bartas*, 1882.

DU BELLAY, Joachim 1522–1560

CHAMARD, H., *Bibliographie des éditions*, 1949 (in *Bulletin du Bibliophile*). See also DICKENSON below.

Oeuvres françoises, ed. G. Aubert and J. de Morel, 1569; ed. H. Chamard, 7 vols, 1908–31; ed. E. Courbet, 2 vols, 1918 (with Latin poems).

Translated in many anthologies, incl. *Cassell's anthology of French poetry*, tr. A. Conder, London 1950, and *French lyrics in English verse*, tr. W. F. Giese, Madison (Wis) 1946.

La deffence et illustration de la langue françoyse, 1549; ed. H. Chamard, 1904 (revd 1961). Tr. G. M. Turquet, *The defence and illustration of the French language*, London 1939.
Recueil de poésie, 1549; 1561.
L'Olive, 1549 (with *L'Antérotique* and *Vers lyriques*); 1550 (enl.; with *Musagnoeomachie*).
Divers poèmes, 1552.
Divers jeux rustiques, et autres oeuvres poétiques, 1558; ed. V. L. Saulnier, Lille and Geneva 1947.
Les regrets et autres oeuvres poétiques, 1558; ed. E. Droz, 1945; ed. J. Joliffe and M. A. Screech, Geneva 1966.
Le premier livre des antiquitez de Rome, 1558; ed. E. Droz, 1945 (with *Les regrets* above); ed. J. Joliffe and M. A. Screech, Geneva 1966 (with *Les regrets* above). Tr. Edmund Spenser, *Ruins of Rome*, London 1591 (part tr., in his *Complaints*).

Lettres, ed. P. de Nolhac, 1883.

BOYER, F., *Joachim Du Bellay*, 1958.
CHAMARD, H., *Joachim Du Bellay*, Lille 1900.
 In his *Histoire de la Pléiade*, 4 vols, 1939–40.
DICKENSON, G., *Du Bellay in Rome*, Leiden 1960 (incl. bibl.).
GRIFFIN, R., *Coronation of the poet, Joachim du Bellay's debt to the Trivium*, Berkeley (Calif) 1969.
MERRILL, R. V., *The Platonism of Joachim Du Bellay*, Chicago (Ill) 1923.
SAULNIER, V. L., *Du Bellay, l'homme et l'oeuvre*, 1951; 1963.
VIANEY, J., *Les Regrets de Joachim Du Bellay*, 1930.

DU FAIL, Noël   c. 1520–1591

Bibl. See Lefèvre ed. of *Propos rustiques* below.

Propos rustiques, Lyon 1547; ed. J. M. Guichard, Paris 1842 (with *Baliverneries* below and *Les contes et discours* below); ed. J. Assézat, 2 vols, 1874 (with *Baliverneries* below and *Les contes et discours* below; as *Les oeuvres facétieuses*); ed. L. R. Lefèvre, 1928 (with *Baliverneries* below; incl. bibl.); ed. P. Jourda, 1964 (with *Baliverneries* below; in *Conteurs français du 16e siècle*).
 Baliverneries, ou contes nouveaux d'Eutrapel, 1548; Lyon 1549; ed. J. M. Guichard, Paris 1842 (with *Propos rustiques* above and *Les contes et discours* below); ed. J. Assézat, 2 vols, 1874 (with *Propos rustiques* above and *Les contes et discours* below; as *Les oeuvres facétieuses*); ed. L. R. Lefèvre, 1928 (with *Propos rustiques* above; incl. bibl.); ed. P. Jourda, 1964 (with *Propos rustiques* above; in *Conteurs français du 16e siècle*).
 Les contes et discours d'Eutrapel, Rennes 1585; ed. J. M. Guichard, Paris 1842 (with *Propos rustiques* above and *Baliverneries* above); ed. J. Assézat, 2 vols, 1874 (with *Propos rustiques* above and *Baliverneries* above; as *Les oeuvres facétieuses*).

PHILIPOT, E., *Essai sur le style et la langue de Noël Du Fail*, 1914.
 La vie et l'oeuvre littéraire de Noël Du Fail, 1914.
REYNIER, G., in his *Les origines du roman réaliste*, 1912.

DU GUILLET, Pernette   c. 1520–1545

Rymes de gentile et vertueuse dame, Pernette du Guillet, Lyonnoise, Lyon 1545; Paris 1546; Lyon 1552; ed. A. M. Schmidt, 1953 (in his *Poètes du 16e siècle*); ed. V. E. Graham, 1969.

DU VAIR, Guillaume 1556–1621

Les oeuvres, 1625; 1641.

There is some disagreement on first dates of publication.

De l'éloquence françoise. 1590; 1595; ed. R. Radouant 1908.
Manuel d'Epictète (tr. from *Epictetus*), 1591.
De la constance et consolation ès calamitez publiques, 1595; 1606 (in *Traictez philosophiques* below); ed. J. Flach and F. Funck-Brentano, 1915; ed. A. Reich, Toulouse 1941. Tr. Andrew Court, *A buckler against adversitie*, London 1622.
La philosophie morale des Stoïques, 1598. Tr. T. James, *The Moral Philosophie of the Stoicks*, London 1598 (ed. R. Kirk, New Brunswick (NJ) 1951).
La saincte philosophie; La philosophie des stoïques, Lyon 1600; ed. G. Michaut, Paris 1946.
Traictez philosophiques, 2 vols, 1606.
Recueil des harangues et traictez, 1606.
Actions et traictéz oratoires, 1641 (in *Les oeuvres* above); ed. R. Radouant, 1911 (with 10 *Discours*).

RADOUANT, R., *Guillaume du Vair, l'homme et l'orateur*, 1908.
ZANTA, L., In his *La renaissance du stoïcisme au 17e siècle*, 1914.

FAIL, Noël du
See DU FAIL, Noël.

GARNIER, Robert 1545–1590

Bibl. See MOUFLARD below.

Oeuvres complètes, ed. L. Pinvert, 2 vols, 1923; ed. R. Lebègue, 1949 onwards (4 vols pbd).
Les tragédies, 1585; ed. W. Förster, 4 vols, Heilbronn 1883.

Porcie, 1568.
Hippolyte, 1573.
Cornélie, 1574. Tr. Thomas Kyd, *Cornelia*, London 1594.
Marc-Antoine, 1578. Tr. Countess of Pembroke, *Antonius*, London 1592.
La Troade, 1579.
Antigone, 1580.
Bradamante, 1582; ed. M. Hervier, 1949.
Sédécie, ou les Juifves, 1583; ed. M. Hervier, 1945.

GRAS, M., *Robert Garnier, son art et sa méthode*, Geneva 1965.
JONDORF, G., *Robert Garnier and the themes of political tragedy in the 16th century*, Cambridge 1969.

LEBÈGUE, R., In his *La tragédie française de la Renaissance*, 1944.

MOUFLARD, M. M., *Robert Garnier*, 3 vols, La Roche sur Yon 1964 (incl. bibl. in vol 1).

WITHERSPOON, A. M., *The influence of Robert Garnier on Elizabethan drama*, New Haven (Conn) 1924.

GRÉVIN, Jacques   c. 1538–1570

Bibl. See PINVERT below.

Théâtre complet et poésies choisies, ed. L. Pinvert, 1922 (cntg 4 plays, with sonnets).

L'Olimpe, 1560 (pt 1).
   L'Olimpe, 1561 (pt 2).
La gélodacrye, 1560 (pt 1, with *L'Olimpe* above, pt 1);
   La gélodacrye, 1561 (pt 2, with *L'Olimpe* above, pt 2);
   ed. A. M. Schmidt, 1953 (selected poems, in *Poètes du 16e siècle*).
Le théâtre, 1561 (with *L'Olimpe* above, pt 2).
César, 1561 (in *Le théâtre* above); ed. G. A. O. Collischon, Marburg 1886;
   ed. E. S. Ginsberg, Geneva 1971.
La trésorière, 1561 (in *Le théâtre* above); ed. P. R. Auguis, 1824 (in *Les poètes françois*, vol 5).
Les esbahis, 1561 (in *Le théâtre* above); ed. Viollet-Le-Duc, 1855 (in *Ancien théâtre français*).

LEBÈGUE, R., in his *La tragédie française de la Renaissance*, 1944.

PINVERT, L., *Jacques Grévin, sa vie, ses écrits, ses amis*, 1898 (incl. bibl.).

GRINGORE, Pierre   1475–1538

Oeuvres complètes, ed. C. d'Héricault and A. de Montaiglon, 2 vols, 1858–77 (incomplete).

Tr. H. F. Cary, London 1846 (selected poems, in *The early French poets*).

Le présent livre appellé le chasteau de Labour, 1499. Tr. A. Barclay, *Here begynneth the castelle of Laboure*, London 1505? (ed. A. W. Pollard, London 1905).
La complainte de trop tard marié, 1505. Tr. R. Copland, *Here begynneth the complaynte of them that ben to late maryed*, n.p. 1505? (ed. J. P. Collier, London 1863 (in *Illustrations of early English popular literature*, vol 1)).
Le jeu du prince des sotz et mère sotte, 1511; ed. P. Tannin 1957.
Les fātasies de Mère Sote, 1516; 1538; ed. R. Frautschi, Chapel Hill (NC) 1962.

Le blazon des hérétiques, 1524; ed. C. Hérisson, 1832.

Rondeaulx en nombre trois cens cinquante (ascribed; incl. poems by other authors), 1527; 1530. Tr. J. R. Best, London 1838.

DITTMANN, W., *Pierre Gringore als Dramatiker*, Berlin 1923.

OULMONT, C., *La poésie morde, politique et dramatique à la veille de la Renaissance: Pierre Gringore*, 1911.

Etudes sur la langue de Pierre Gringore, 1911.

JODELLE, Étienne 1532–1573

Oeuvres, ed. C. de La Mothe, 1574; 1583; ed. C. Marty-Laveaux, 2 vols, 1868–70; ed. E. Balmas, 2 vols, 1968.

Tr. H. F. Cary, London 1846 (selected poems, in *The early French poets*).

Le recueil des inscriptions, 1558; ed. V. E. Graham and W. McA. Johnson, Toronto 1972.

L'Eugène, 1574 (in *Oeuvres* above); ed. E. Fournier, 1871 (in *Le théâtre français au 16e et au 17e siècle*); ed. E. Balmas, Milan 1955.

Cléopâtre captive, 1574 (in *Oeuvres* above); ed. L. Bryce Ellis, Philadelphia (Pa) 1946; ed. S. F. Baridon, Paris 1949.

Didon se sacrifiant, 1574 (in *Oeuvres* above); ed. D. Stone, Cambridge (Mass) 1966 (in *Four Renaissance tragedies*).

Les amours, 1574 (in *Oeuvres* above); ed. A. Van Bever, 1907; ed. A. M. Schmidt, 1953 (in *Poètes du 16e siècle*).

BALMAS, E., *Un poeta del Rinascimento francese*, Florence 1962.

HORVATH, K. A., *Etiénne Jodelle*, Budapest 1932 (largely in Hungarian).

LABÉ, Louise 1524–1566

Bibl. See Boy ed. of *Euvres* below.

Euvres, Lyon 1555; 1556; ed. C. Boy, 2 vols 1877 (incl. bibl.); ed. B. Jourdan, Paris 1953; ed. E. Giudici, Rome 1955; ed. G. Guillot, Paris 1962; ed. F. Zamaron, 1968 (elegies and sonnets); ed. A. M. Schmidt, 1953 (selection, in *Poètes du 16e siècle*).

Tr. F. Lobb, *The twenty-four love sonnets*, London 1950; tr. A. L. Cook, *Sonnets*, Toronto 1950; tr. B. L. Kemp, Paris 1964.

Un débat judiciel de Folie et d'Amour, Lyon 1555 (in *Euvres* above). Tr. E. M. Cox, *The debate between Folly and Cupid*, London 1925.

HARVEY, L. E., *The aesthetics of the Renaissance love sonnet*, Geneva 1962.

O'CONNOR, D., *Louise Labé, sa vie et son oeuvre*, 1926.

LA BOÉTIE, Étienne de   1530–1563

Oeuvres complètes, ed. L. Feugère, 1846; ed. P. Bonnefon, Bordeaux 1892.
Oeuvres politiques, ed. F. Hincker, 1963.

Vers françois, ed. M. de Montaigne, 1571; ed. A. M. Schmidt, 1953 (in *Poètes du 16e siècle*).
Discours de la servitude volontaire, ed. S. Goulart, Geneva 1574 (in *Mémoires de l'estat de France sous Charles neufiesme*, vol 3) ed. M. Coste and F. de Lamennais, Paris 1835; ed. P. Bonnefon, 1922; ed. E. Gilliard, Lausanne 1943; ed. M. Rat, Geneva 1963. Tr. H. Kurz, *Anti-Dictator*, New York 1942.
Vingt-neuf sonnetz, Bordeaux 1580 (in Montaigne's *Essais*); ed. A. M. Schmidt, 1953 (in *Poètes du 16e siècle*). Tr. L. How, *Twenty-nine sonnets*, Boston (Mass) 1915.
Mémoire sur l'édit de janvier, ed. P. Bonnefon, 1922 (with *Discours* above).

DESJARDINS, A., in his *Les moralistes français au 16e siècle*, 1870.
MESNARD, P., in his *L'essor de la philosophie politique au 16e siècle*, 1936.
MAZE-SENCIER, G., in his *Les vies closes*, 1902.

LARIVEY, Pierre de   c. 1540–1619

Bibl. See MORIN below.

Les six premières comédies facécieuses, 1579 (cntg *Les esprits* below, *Le laquais*, *Le morfondu*, *Les jalous* and *Les escholiers*); Lyon 1597; ed. Viollet-le-Duc, Paris 1855–6 (in *Ancien théâtre français*, vols 5–7).
Les esprits, 1579 (in *Les six premières comédies* above); ed. E. Fournier, 1871 (in *Le théâtre français au 16e et au 17e siècle*).
Trois comédies des six dernières, Troyes 1611 (cntg *La constance*, *Le fidelle* and *Les tromperies*).

JEFFREY, B., in his *French Renaissance comedy*, Oxford 1970.
MORIN, L., *Les trois Pierre de Larivey*, Troyes 1937 (incl. bibl.).

LA TAILLE, Jean de   c. 1540–after 1607

Oeuvres, ed. R. de Maulde, 4 vols, 1878–82 (incomplete; incl. *Les corrivaux* and *Le négromant*).
Dramatic works, ed. K. M. Hall and C. N. Smith, London 1972 (*Saül*, *La famine*, *Le négromant* and *Les corrivaux*).

Remonstrance pour le roy, 1562; 1571.
Saül le furieux [. . .] *et autres oeuvres poétiques*; 1572; ed. A. Werner, Leipzig 1908; ed. E. Forsyth, 1968.
De l'art de la tragédie, 1572 (with *Saül* above); ed. F. West, Manchester 1939.

47

La famine, ou les Gabéonites [. . .] *ensemble plusieurs autres oeuvres poëtiques*, 1573; ed. E. Forsyth, 1968.

DALEY, T. A., *Jean de La Taille*, 1934.
LEBÈGUE, R., in his *La tragédie religieuse en France*, 1929.

LEMAIRE DE BELGES, Jean   c. 1473–after 1514

MUNN, K. M., *A contribution to the study of Jean Lemaire de Belges; a critical study of bio-bibliographical data*, Scottdale (Pa) 1936.

Oeuvres, ed. J. Stecher, 4 vols, Louvain 1882–91; ed. E. Lommatzsch and M. L. Wagner, Berlin 1924 (poems).

La plainte du désiré, 1503; ed. D. Yabsley 1932.
Le temple d'honneur et de vertus, 1504; ed. H. Hornik, Geneva and Paris 1957. Tr. and adapt. A. Barclay, *The description of the toure of vertue and honour*, London 1521 (part tr.; in *The boke of Codrus and Menaclus*).
Les deux épistres de l'amant vert, Lyon 1509; 1512; ed. J. Frappier, Lille and Geneva 1948.
Les illustrations de Gaule et antiquitez de Troye, Lyon 1509 (bk 1, with *Les épistres* above); 1510–12 (bks 1–2); 1513 (bk 3).
La concorde des deux langages, 1513; ed. J. Frappier, 1947.

DOUTREPONT, G., *Jean Lemaire de Belges et la Renaissance*, Brussels 1934.
SPAAK, P., *Jean Lemaire de Belges, sa vie, son oeuvre et ses meilleures pages*, 1926.

MAGNY, Olivier de   c. 1529–c. 1561

Poésies complètes, ed. E. Courbet, 6 vols, 1871–80.
Poésies choisies, ed. M. de Beaurepaire, 1913.

Les amours, 1553; ed. P. Blanchemain, Turin 1870; ed. M. S. Whitney, Geneva 1970.
Les gayetez, 1554; ed. A. R. Mackay, Geneva 1968.
Les souspirs, 1557; ed. P. Blanchemain, Turin 1870.
Les odes, 1559; ed. M. S. Whitney, Geneva 1964.
Sonnets inédits, ed. T. de Larroque, 1880.

FAVRE, J., *Olivier de Magny*, 1885.

MALHERBE, François de   1555–1628

Bibl. See Lalanne ed. of *Oeuvres complètes* below.

Oeuvres complètes, ed. L. Lalanne, 5 vols, 1862–9 (incl. bibl. in vol 1); ed. A. Adam, 1971.

Poésies, 1626; 1722 (with *Vie de Malherbe* by RACAN below); ed. P. Martinon and M. Allem, 1926; ed. J. Lavaud, 2 vols, 1936–7; ed. R. Fromilhague and R. Lebègue, 2 vols, 1968.

Translated in anthologies.

Les larmes de S. Pierre, imitées du Tansille, 1587.
Ode [. . .] *à la reine*, Aix 1601.
Ode sur l'attentat commis en la personne de Sa Majesté le 19 décembre 1605; n.p. 1606.
Vers, 1611.
Pour le roy allant chastier la rébellion des Rochelois, Lyon 1628.

ALLAIS, G., *Malherbe et la poésie française à la fin de 16e siècle*, 1891.
BRUNOT, F., *La doctrine de Malherbe d'après son Commentaire sur Desportes*, 1891.
CELLES, J. de, *Malherbe: sa vie, son caractère, sa doctrine*, 1937.
FROMILHAGUE, R., *Malherbe, technique et création poétique*, 1954.
  La vie de Malherbe, apprentissages et luttes, 1555–1610, 1954.
PONGE, F., *Pour un Malherbe*, 1965.
RACAN, H. de, *La vie de Malherbe*, 1672 (in *Divers traitéz d'histoire, de morale et d'éloquence*); ed. P. Martinon, 1926 (in *Poésies* above).
WINEGARTEN, R., *French lyric poetry in the age of Malherbe*, Manchester 1954.

MAROT, Clément   1496–1544

VILLEY, P., *Tableau chronologique des publications de Marot*, 1921.
MAYER, C. A., *Bibliographie des oeuvres*, 2 vols, Geneva 1954.

Les oeuvres complètes, ed. P. R. Auguis, 5 vols, 1823; ed. G. Guiffrey and J. Plattard, 5 vols, 1875–1931; ed. A. Grenier, 2 vols, 1951; ed. C. A. Mayer, 5 vols, London 1958–70.

Translated in anthologies.

L'adolescence Clémentine, 1532 (incl. many poems first pbd in collections set to music 1528–30); Antwerp 1539;
  La suite de l'Adolescence Clémentine, 1534?;
  ed. V. L. Saulnier, 1958.
L'enfer, Antwerp 1539 (with *L'adolescence Clémentine* above); Lyon 1542.
Psalmes de David, Antwerp 1541; Paris 1541 (*Trente pseaulmes*). 1546 (*Cinquante-deux pseaumes*); ed. S. J. Lenselink, 1969.
Le balladin, 1545.

BECKER, P. A., *Clément Marot, sein Leben und seine Dichtung*, Munich 1926.
GUY, H., *Clément Marot et son école*, 1926.
JOURDA, P., *Marot, l'homme et l'oeuvre*, 1950; 1967.

MORLEY, H., *Clément Marot and other studies*, London 1871.
PLATTARD, J., *Marot, sa carrière poétique, son oeuvre*, 1938.
SAULNIER, V. L., *Les élégies de Clément Marot*, 1952.

MONLUC, Blaise de   1502–1577

Commentaires, ed. F. de Raemond, Bordeaux 1592; ed. P. Courteault, 3 vols, Paris 1911–25. Tr. C. Cotton, *The Commentaries*, London 1674.

COURTEAULT, P., *Blaise de Monluc, historien*, Toulouse 1908.

MONTAIGNE, Michel de   1533–1592

TANNENBAUM, S. A., *A concise bibliography*, New York 1942.

Oeuvres complètes, ed. A. Armaingaud, 12 vols, 1924–41; ed. A. Thibaudet and M. Rat, 1962; ed. R. Berral and P. Michel, 1967.

Tr. C. Cotton et al., ed. W. C. Hazlitt, *The complete works*, London 1842; tr. D. M. Frame, Stanford (Calif) 1948.

Tr. and ed. M. Lowenthal, *The autobiography*, Boston (Mass) and London 1935 (extracts from works).

Essais, Bordeaux 1580 (2 bks); Paris 1588 (enl. and with 3rd bk); ed. Marie de Gournay and P. de Brach, 1595; ed. F. Strowski, F. Gebelin et al., 5 vols, Bordeaux 1906–33 ('édition municipale'); ed. P. Villey, 3 vols, Paris 1922–3 (revd V. L. Saulnier, 1965); ed. A. Tilley and A. M. Boase, Manchester 1934 (selection); ed. P. Michel, 5 vols, Paris 1955–7; ed. M. Rat, 3 vols, 1958. Tr. J. Florio, London 1603; tr. C. Cotton, 3 vols, 1685–6 (ed. W. C. Hazlitt, 3 vols, 1877); tr. J. M. Cohen, Harmondsworth 1958.

Apologie de Raymond Sebond, 1589 (as preface to his tr. of Sebonde's *Theologia naturalis*); ed. E. P. Porteau, 1937. Tr. A. H. Beattie, *In defense of Raymond Sebond*, New York 1959.

Journal du voyage [. . .] en Italie, Rome and Paris 1774; ed. M. Rat, Paris 1942; ed. C. Dédéyan, 1946; ed. S. de Sacy, 1954. Tr. W. C. Hazlitt, *The journey into Germany and Italy*, London 1842; tr. and ed. E. J. Trechmann, *The diary of Michel de Montaigne's journey to Italy*, 1929.

BONNEFON, P., *Montaigne, l'homme et l'oeuvre*, Bordeaux 1893.

BOASE, A. M., *The fortunes of Montaigne, a history of the Essays in France, 1580–1669*, London 1935.

BRUNSCHVICG, L., *Descartes et Pascal, lecteurs de Montaigne*, Neufchâtel, 1945.

DÉDÉYAN, C., *Montaigne chez ses amis anglo-saxons*, 2 vols, 1946.

DRÉANO, M., *La pensée religieuse de Montaigne*, 1936; 1969.

EHRLICH, H., *Montaigne: la critique et le langage*, 1972.

FRAME, D. M., *Montaigne's discovery of Man*, New York 1955.
  Montaigne, a biography, New York 1965.
  Montaigne's Essays, a study, Englewood Cliffs (NJ) 1969.
FRIEDRICH, H., *Montaigne*, Berne 1949.
GIDE, A., *Essai sur Montaigne*, 1929. Tr. D. Bussy, *The living thoughts of Montaigne*, London and New York 1939.
JANSSEN, H., *Montaigne fidéiste*, Nijmegen and Utrecht 1930.
JOUKOVSKY, F., *Montaigne et le problème du temps*, 1972.
LANSON, G., *Les Essais de Montaigne, étude et analyse*, 1930.
MOREAU, P., *Montaigne, l'homme et l'oeuvre*, 1939.
NAUDEAU, O., *La pensée de Montaigne et la composition des Essais*, Geneva 1972.
PASCAL, Blaise, *Entretien avec M. de Saci*, c. 1655.
PLATTARD, J., *Montaigne et son temps*, 1933.
RIDER, F., *The dialectic of selfhood in Montaigne*, Stanford (Calif) 1973.
SAYCE, R. A., *The essays of Montaigne, a critical exploration*, London 1972.
STROWSKI, F., *Montaigne*, 1906.
VILLEY, P., *Les sources et l'évolution des Essais de Montaigne*, 2 vols, 1908; 1933.

NAVARRE, Marguerite de   1492–1549

JOURDA, P., *Tableau chronologique des publications*, 1925.
  Répertoire analytique et chronologique de la correspondance, 1930.

Les poésies, ed. F. Frank, 4 vols, 1880.
Théâtre profane, ed. V. L. Saulnier, 1946.
Chansons spirituelles, ed. G. Dottin, Geneva 1971.

Le miroir de l'âme pécheresse, Alençon 1531; ed. J. C. Allaire, Munich 1972. Tr. Elizabeth I of England, *A Godly medytacyon of the Christen soule*, London 1548; 1897.
Les Marguerites de la Marguerite des princesses, Lyon 1547; ed. F. Frank, 4 vols, 1873.
L'heptaméron, 1559; ed. F. Dillaye, 3 vols, Paris 1879; ed. F. Frank, 1879; ed. A. J. V. Le Roux de Lincy and A. de Montaiglon, 4 vols, 1880; ed. M. François, 1961; ed. P. Jourda, 1965 (in *Conteurs du 16e siècle*); ed. Y. Le Hir, 1967. Tr. 'A. B.', *The queene of Navarres tales, containing verie pleasant discourses of fortunate lovers*, London 1597; tr. J. S. Chartres, *The heptameron*, 5 vols, 1959.
Les dernières poésies, ed. A. Lefranc, 1895.
La Nativité, ed. P. Jourda, 1939.

Lettres, ed. F. Gernin, 2 vols, 1841–2.

FEBVRE, L., *Autour de l'Heptaméron: amour sacré, amour profane*, 1944.

JOURDA, P., *Marguerite d'Angoulême, duchesse d'Alençon, reine de Navarre; étude biographique et littéraire*, 2 vols, 1930.

PUTNAM, S., *Marguerite de Navarre: first modern woman*, New York 1935.

TELLE, E. V., *L'oeuvre de Marguerite d'Angoulême, reine de Navarre, et la querelle des femmes*, Toulouse 1937.

TETEL, M., *Marguerite de Navarre's Heptameron: themes, language and structure*, Durham (NC), 1973.

PASQUIER, Étienne   1529–1615

THICKETT, D., *Bibliographie des oeuvres*, Geneva 1956.

Oeuvres, 2 vols, Amsterdam 1723; ed. L. Feugère, 2 vols, 1849 (selection).
Ecrits politiques, ed. D. Thickett, Geneva 1966.

Le monophile, 1554. Tr. G. Fenton, *Monophylo*, London 1572.
Recueil des rymes et proses, 1555.
Des recherches de la France, 1560 (bk 1); 1565 (bk 2); 1596 (bks 1 to 6); 1607 (bks 1 to 7); 1621 (bks 1 to 10); ed. H. B. Ellis, Liverpool 1955–6 (bk 7).
Histoire prodigieuse d'un détestable parricide entrepris en la personne du roy, Melun 1594. Tr. anon., *A discourse of estate uppon the late hurte of the ffrenche king*, London 1595.
La jeunesse d'Estienne Pasquier (incl. *Le monophile* above), 1610.

Les lettres, 1586 (bks 1–10); 2 vols, 1619 (bks 1–22); ed. D. Thickett, Geneva 1956 (selection); ed. D. Thickett, 1966 (*Lettres historiques pour les années 1556–94*).

FEUGÈRE, L., *Essai sur la vie et les ouvrages d'Etienne Pasquier*, 1848.

MOORE, M. J., *Etienne Pasquier, historien de la poésie et de la langue françaises*, Poitiers 1934.

PELETIER DU MANS, Jacques   1517–1582

A few poems translated in anthologies, incl. *An anthology of French poetry*, tr. H. Carrington, London and New York 1900.

Oeuvres poétiques, 1547; ed. L. Séché, 1904.
Dialogue de l'ortografe e prononciacion françoese, Poitiers 1550; ed. L. C. Porter, 1966.
L'art poétique, Lyon 1555; ed. A. Boulanger, 1930.
L'amour des amours, Lyon 1555; ed. J. de Tournes and A Van Bever, 1926.
La Savoie, Annecy 1572; ed. C. Pagès, Moutiers 1898.

JUGÉ, C., *Jacques Peletier du Mans, essai sur sa vie, son oeuvre, son influence*, 1907.

SCHMIDT, A. M., in his *La poésie scientifique en France au 16e siècle*, 1939.

STAUB, H., *Le curieux désir: Scève et Peletier du Mans, poètes de la connaissance,* Geneva 1967.

WILSON, D. B., *The discovery of nature in the works of Jacques Peletier du Mans,* Manchester 1954.

PIBRAC, Guy de   1529–1584

PIBRAC, R. du Faur de, *Catalogue des ouvrages et éditions depuis 1542 jusqu'à nos jours,* Orléans 1901.
See also CABOS below.

Cinquante quatrains, 1574; Lyon 1575 (*Cent quatrains*); 1576 (*Quatrains;* enl.); ed. J. Claretie, 1874 (with other poems). Tr. J. Sylvester, *Tetrasticha, or the Quadrains,* London 1605 (with *Bartas his divine weekes and workes*); tr. E. Du Faur, *Quatrains,* 1907.

CABOS, A., *Guy du Faur de Pibrac, un magistrat poète au 16e siècle,* 1922 (incl. bibl.).

RABELAIS, François   1494?–1553

PLAN, P. P., *Bibliographie rabelaisienne, les éditions de Rabelais de 1532 à 1711,* 1904.
See also Boulenger–Scheler ed. of *Les oeuvres* below.

Les oeuvres, Lyon 1558; 9 vols, Paris 1823–6; ed. A. Lefranc et al., Paris, Geneva and Lille 1912 onwards (6 vols pbd); ed. J. Plattard, 5 vols, 1929; ed. J. Boulenger and J. Scheler, 1955 (incl. bibl.); ed. P. Jourda, 2 vols, 1962; ed. G. Demerson, 1973.

Gargantua et Pantagruel, 5 vols, Lyon and Paris 1532–64. Comprising:
  Pantagruel (later bk 2), Lyon 1532; ed. V. L. Saulnier, Paris 1946.
  [*Gargantua*], Lyon 1534 (title missing; later bk 1); 1542; ed. J. de Foucault, Paris 1949; ed. M. A. Screech, Geneva 1970.
  Tiers livre des faictz et dictz héroïques du noble Pantagruel, 1546; ed. H. Béraldi, 1933; ed. M. A. Screech, Geneva 1964.
  Le quart livre des faictz et dictz héroïques du noble Pantagruel. Lyon 1548 (incomplete); 1552; ed. J. Plattard, Paris 1909; ed. R. Marichal, Lille and Geneva 1947.
  L'isle sonante (authorship doubtful), n.p. 1562 (ed. A. Lefranc and J. Boulenger, 1905); Lyon 1564 (enl. as *Le cinquiesme et dernier livre des faicts et dicts héroïques du bon Pantagruel*).
  Tr. T. Urquart and P. A. Motteux (bks 3–5), *The works,* 2 vols, London 1653–94 (3 vols, Oxford 1934); tr. W. F. Smith, *The five books,* 2 vols, 1893; tr. Jacques Le Clerq, *The complete works,* 5 vols, New York 1936;

tr. J. Cowper Powys, *Selections from the Four books of Rabelais, to which is added the end of the Fifth book*, London 1948; tr. J. M. Cohen, *The histories of Gargantua and Pantagruel*, Harmondsworth 1955.

La sciomachie, Lyon 1549; ed. J. de Foucault, Paris 1949 (with *Gargantua* above).

ARONSON, N., *Les idées politiques de Rabelais*, 1973.

BEAUJOUR, M., *Le comique de Rabelais*, 1969.

BROWN, H., *Rabelais in English literature*, Cambridge (Mass) 1933.

CLEMENT, N. H., *The influence of the Arthurian romances on the five books of Rabelais*, Berkeley (Calif) 1926.

COLEMAN, D. G., *Rabelais: a critical study in prose fiction*, Cambridge 1971.

DIÉGUEZ, M. de, *Rabelais par lui-même*, 1960.

Etudes rabelaisiennes, Geneva 1956 onwards.

FEBVRE, L., *Le problème de l'incroyance au 16e siècle, la religion de Rabelais*, 1942.

FRANCE, A., *François Rabelais*, 1928.

GEBHART, E., *Rabelais, la Renaissance et la Réforme*, 1877.

GLAUSER, A. C., *Rabelais créateur*, 1966.

MACMINN, G. R., *English and American appreciation of Rabelais*, Berkeley (Calif) 1922 (in *The Charles Mills Gayley anniversary papers*)

METTRA, C., *Rabelais secret*, 1973.

PLATTARD, J., *L'invention et la composition dans l'oeuvre de Rabelais*, 1909.
  Vie de François Rabelais, Paris and Brussels 1928. Tr. L. P. Roche, *The life of François Rabelais*, New York 1931.

RIGOLOT, F., *Les langages de Rabelais*, Geneva 1972.

SAINÉAN, L., *La langue de Rabelais*, 2 vols, 1922–3.

VILLEY, P., *Marot et Rabelais*, 1923.

RONSARD, Pierre de   1524–1585

LAUMONIER, P., *Tableau chronologique des oeuvres*, 1911 (2nd ed.).

RAYMOND, M., *Bibliographie critique, 1550–1585*, 1927.

THIBAULT, G. and PERCEAU, L., *Bibliographie des poésies de Ronsard mises en musique au 16e siècle*, 1941.

Les oeuvres, 4 vols, Buon 1560; 1578; 1584; 1587; ed. P. Laumonier et al., 18 vols, 1914–67; ed. G. Cohen, 2 vols, 1938; ed. I. Silver, 8 vols, Abbeville and Chicago (Ill) 1966–71.

Poésies choisies, ed. P. de Nolhac, 1924.

Tr. C. H. Page, *Songs and sonnets*, Cambridge (Mass) and New York 1903 (selection).

Tr. C. Graves, *Selected poems*, Edinburgh 1924.

Tr. E. J. Dennis, *Salute to Ronsard. Salut ô Ronsard !*, Hull 1960 (selection).
Les quatres premiers livres des odes, 1550;
  Le cinquiesme des odes, 1552;
  ed. C. Guérin, 1952.
Le bocage, 1550 (with *Odes*, bks 1–4 above); 1554; ed. G. Cohen, 1937.
Les amours, 1552; (with *Odes*, bk 5 above); 1553;
  Continuation des Amours, 1555;
  Nouvelle continuation des Amours, 1556;
  ed. J. Porcher, 2 vols, 1942–4; ed. F. Simone, Milan 1947; ed. A. Micha,
  Geneva 1951 (bk 2); ed. H. W. and C. Weber, 1963.
Livret de folastries, 1553; Geneva? 1584; ed. F. Fleuret and L. Perceau,
  Paris 1920.
Les Hymnes, 1555.
  Le second livre des Hymnes, 1556.
Les meslanges, 1555.
  Le second livre des Meslanges, 1559.
Discours des misères de ce temps, 1562;
  Continuation du Discours, 1562;
  ed. J. Baillou, 1949.
Remonstrance au peuple de France, 1563; ed. J. Baillou, 1949.
Institution pour l'adolescence du Roi, 1562.
Abbregé de l'art poëtique françois, 1565.
  Art poëtique françois, 1585.
Elégies, Mascarades et Bergerie, 1565.
Sixiesme et septiesme livres des Poèmes, 1569 (bks 1 to 5 pbd in 1560 ed. of
  Oeuvres above).
Les quatre premiers livre [sic] *de la Franciade*, 1572; 1573.
Sonnets pour Hélène, 1578; ed. J. Lavaud, 1947; ed. M. Smith, Geneva and
  Paris 1970. Tr. W. van Wyck, *Sonnets for Helen*, So. Pasadena (Calif) 1932;
  tr. H. Wolfe, London 1934.

ALLIOT, M. and BAILLOU, J., *Ronsard et son quatrième centenaire*, 1926.
BINET, C., *La vie de Pierre de Ronsard*, 1586; ed. P. Laumonier, 1910.
BISHOP, M., *Ronsard, prince of poets*, New York and London 1940.
CAVE, T. (ed.), *Ronsard the poet*, London 1973.
CHAMPION, P., *Ronsard et son temps*, 1925.
COHEN, G., *Ronsard, sa vie et son oeuvre*, 1924.
DASSONVILLE, M., *Ronsard, étude historique et littéraire*, 2 vols, Geneva 1970.
GENDRE, A., *Ronsard, poète de la conquête amoureuse*, Neuchêtel 1970.
LAUMONIER, P., *Ronsard, poète lyrique*, 1909.
LEBÈGUE, R., *Ronsard, l'homme et l'oeuvre*, 1950.
LEWIS, D. B. Wyndham, *Ronsard*, New York 1944.
LUCAS, F. L., in his *Studies French and English*, London 1934.
NOLHAC, P de, *Ronsard et l'humanisme*, 1921.

RAYMOND, M., *L'influence de Ronsard sur la poésie française*, 2 vols, 1927; Geneva 1965.

SILVER, I., *The intellectual evolution of Ronsard*, 2 vols, 1973.

SONGUON, H., *Pierre de Ronsard: les ancêtres, la jeunesse*, 1912.

STONE, D., *Ronsard's sonnet cycles*, New Haven (Conn) 1966.

SAINT GELAIS, Mellin de   1491–1558

Oeuvres poétiques, Lyon 1574; Paris 1719.
Oeuvres complètes, ed. P. Blanchemain, 3 vols, 1873.

A few poems translated in anthologies.

Sophonisba (tr. of Trissino's *Sofonisba*), 1559.

BECKER, P. A., *Mellin de Saint Gelays, eine kritische Studie*, Vienna 1924.

MOLINIER, H. J., *Melin de Saint Gelays, étude sur sa vie et ses oeuvres*, Rodez 1910.

SAINT GELAIS, Octovien de   1468–1502

Le séjour d'honneur (in collab. with Andre La Vigne), c. 1503; 1519.
La chasse et le départ d'amours (incl. poems by Blaise d'Auriol and Charles d'ORLÉANS), 1509.

Also translated *The Aeneid* and Ovid's *Heroides*.

MOLINIER, H. J., *Essai biographique et littéraire sur Octovien de Saint Gelays*, Rodez 1910.

SATIRE MÉNIPPÉE, La   1594
(by Pierre Le Roy, with Jacques Gillot, Florent Chrestien, Nicolas Rapin, Pierre Pithou and Jean Passerat)

La vertu du catholicon d'Espagne, avec un abrégé de la tenue des Estats de Paris 1594 (some items first pbd separately from 1593); 1594 (enl., renamed *Satyre Ménippée de la vertu du catholicon d'Espagne et de la tenue des estatz de Paris*); ed. P. Dupuy, J. Le Duchat et al., 3 vols, Ratisbon 1711; ed. V. Verger, 2 vols, Paris 1824; ed. C. Read, 1876; ed. J. Frank, Oppeln 1884; ed. P. Demey, Dublin 1911. Tr. anon., *A pleasant satyre or poesie*, London 1595.

GIROUX, F., *La composition de la Satire Ménippée*, Laon 1904.

SCÈVE, Maurice   1501–c. 1560

Bibl. See Guégan ed. of *Oeuvres poétiques* below; also SAULNIER below.

Oeuvres poétiques complètes, ed. B. Guégan, 1927 (incl. bibl.).
Le opere minori, ed. E. Giudici, Parma 1958.

Tr. W. Fowlie, *Sixty poems,* New York 1949.
Also translated in anthologies.

Délie, object de plus haulte vertu, Lyon 1544; ed. E. Parturier, 1916; ed. A. M.
Schmidt, 1953 (in *Poètes du 16e siècle*); ed. I. D. McFarlane, 1966; ed.
D. B. Wilson, Menston (Yorks) 1972.
Saulsaye, Lyon 1547; ed. B. Guégan, Paris 1918.
Microcosme, Lyon 1562; ed. V. Larbaud and A. A. M. Stols, Maastricht
1929.

BAUR, A., *Maurice Scève et la renaissance lyonnaise,* 1906.
SAULNIER, V. L., *Maurice Scève,* 2 vols, 1948–9 (incl. bibl. in vol 2).

SPONDE, Jean de   1557–1595

Oeuvre poétique, ed. M. Arland, 1945 (selection); ed. A Boase and F. Ruchon,
Geneva 1949.

Tr. R. Nugent, *Sonnets on love and death,* Painesville (Ohio), 1962 (selection).
Tr. G. F. Cunningham et al., *Poems of love and death,* Edinburgh and
London 1964 (selection).
Also translated in anthologies.

Most poems originally published in miscellanies.

Méditations sur les pseaumes, n.p. 1588; ed. A. Boase, 1954.
La déclaration des principaux motifs, Melun 1594.
Stances et sonnets sur la mort, ed. A. Boase, 1947.

Also edited Homer, Hesiod and Aristotle's *Logic.*

RUCHON, F. and BOASE, A., *La vie et l'oeuvre de Jean de Sponde,* Geneva 1949.

TABOUROT DES ACCORDS, Étienne   1549–1590

Bibl. See CHOPTRAYANOVITCH below.

Les bigarrures et touches, [. . .] *avec les apophtegmes du Sieur Gaulard et les
escraignes dijonnoises,* 1603; 3 vols, Brussels 1866. Tr. 'J.B. of Charterhouse', *Bigarrures,* Glasgow 1884 (privately pbd). Containing the works
below, first pbd as follows:
   Les bigarrures, 1583 (bk 1); 1585 (bk 4).
   Les apophtegmes, 1585 (with *Les bigarrures,* bk 4 above); 1586.
   Les touches, 1585 (bks 1–3, not pbd in 1603 ed. above); 1588 (bk 4);
   1588 (bk 5).

Les escraignes dijonnoises, 1588.

CHOPTRAYANOVITCH, G., *Etienne Tabourot des Accords,* Dijon 1935 (incl. bibl.).

TURNÈBE, Odet de   1552–1581

Bibl. See Spector ed. below.

Les contens, 1584; ed. E. Fournier, 1871 (in *Le théâtre français au 16e et au 17e siècle*); ed. N. B. Spector, 1961 (incl. bibl.).

TYARD, Pontus de   1521–1605

Bibl. See JEANDET below.

Les oeuvres poétiques, 1573; ed. J. C. Lapp, 1966.
Oeuvres, ed. C. Marty-Laveaux, 1875.

Translated in anthologies.

Les Erreurs amoureuses, Lyon 1549.
    Continuation des Erreurs amoureuses, Lyon 1551.
    Erreurs amoureuses, augmentées d'une tierce partie, Lyon 1555.
L'Univers, Lyon 1557; ed. J. C. Lapp, Ithaca (NY) 1950.
Les discours philosophiques, 1587 (incl. *L'Univers* above).

BARIDON, S. F., *Pontus de Tyard,* Milan 1950.
HALL, K. M., *Pontus de Tyard and his Discours philosophiques,* London 1963.
JEANDET, J. P. A., *Pontus de Tyard, seigneur de Bissy, depuis évêque de Châlon* Aubry 1860 (incl. bibl.).
VIANEY, J., in his *Le pétrarquisme en France au 16e siècle,* Montpellier 1909.

3
The Seventeenth Century

BALZAC, Jean Louis Guez de   1597–1654

BEUGNOT, B., *Bibliographie générale*, Montreal 1967.
  Supplément, Montreal 1969.

Les oeuvres diverses, 1644; 1665; ed. L. Moreau and J. Lecoffre, 2 vols, 1854.
Oeuvres choisies, ed. A. Malitourne, 2 vols, 1822.

Le prince, 1631. Tr. 'H.G.', *The prince*, London 1648.
Le barbon, 1648.
Socrate chrestien, 1652.
Les entretiens, 1657; ed. B. Beugnot, 1972.
Aristippe, 1658. Tr. 'R.W.', *Aristippus*, London 1659; tr. B. Kennett, *Aristippus, or wise scholar*, 1709.

Lettres, 1624; 1627 (as *Les oeuvres*; enl.); ed. H. Bibas and K. T. Butler, 2 vols, 1933–4.
  Lettres, seconde partie, 2 vols, 1636; 1664 (enl.).
  Tr. various, [*Letters*], 5 vols, London and Oxford 1634–54:
  W. Tirwhyt, *The letters*, London 1634.
  R. Baker, *New epistles*, 2 vols, 1638.
  Anon., *A collection of some modern epistles*, Oxford 1639.
  R. B. Knight, *Letters*, London 1654.

GUILLAUMIE, G., *Jean-Louis Guez de Balzac et la prose française*, 1927.
SUTCLIFFE, F. E., *Guez de Balzac et son temps*, 1959.
YOUSSEF, Z., *Polémique et littérature chez Guez de Balzac*, 1972.

BAYLE, Pierre   1647–1706

Bibl. See LABROUSSE below; also REX below.
LABROUSSE, E., *Inventaire critique de la correspondance*, 1960.

Oeuvres diverses, 2 vols, The Hague 1725; 4 vols, 1727–31; ed. P. Des Maizeaux, 9 vols, 1730; ed. A. Calame, 3 vols, Hildesheim 1966.
Choix de textes, ed. M. Raymond, 1948; ed. E. Labrousse, 1965.
Oeuvres diverses, ed. A. Niderst, 1971 (selection).

Lettre, Rotterdam 1682; 2 vols, 1683 (renamed *Pensées diverses* [. . .] *a l'occasion de la planète qui parut au mois de décembre* 1680);
  Addition aux pensées diverses, Rotterdam 1694;
  Continuation des pensées diverses, Rotterdam 1705;
  ed. A. Adam, 2 vols, Paris 1911–12; ed. A. Prat, 2 vols, 1939. Tr. anon., *Miscellaneous reflections occasion'd by the comet which appear'd in December 1680,* 2 vols, London 1708.
Ce que c'est que la France toute Catholique, Saint Ouen 1686; ed. E. Labrousse, Paris 1973.
Avis important aux refugiéz sur leur prochain retour en France, The Hague 1690.
Dictionnaire historique et critique, 2 vols, Rotterdam 1695–7; 3 vols, 1702; 4 vols, 1740; ed. A. J. Beuchot, 16 vols, Paris 1820–4. Tr. P. Des Maizeaux, *An historical and critical dictionary,* 4 vols, London 1710 (revd, 5 vols, 1734–8; ed. E. A. Beller and M. du P. Lee Jr., *Selections,* Princeton (NJ) 1952); tr. and ed. R. H. Popkin and C. B. Brush, New York 1965 (selection).
Réponse aux questions d'un provincial, 5 vols, Rotterdam 1704–7.

BRUSH, C. B., *Montaigne and Bayle: variations on the theme of scepticism,* The Hague 1966.
CANTELLI, G., *Vico e Bayle: premesse per un confronto,* Naples 1971.
COURTINES, L. P., *Bayle's relations with England and the English,* New York 1938.
DIBON, P. et al., *Pierre Bayle, le philosophe de Rotterdam,* Amsterdam 1959.
LABROUSSE, E., *Pierre Bayle,* 2 vols, 1963–4 (incl. bibl. in vol 2).
RÉTAT, P., *Le Dictionnaire de Bayle et la lutte philosophique au 18e siècle,* 1971.
REX, W., *Essays on Pierre Bayle and religious controversy,* The Hague 1965 (incl. bibl.).
ROBINSON, H., *Bayle the sceptic,* New York 1931.

BOILEAU-DESPRÉAUX, Nicolas   1636–1711

MAGNE, E., *Bibliographie générale des oeuvres de Nicolas Boileau-Despréaux, et de Gilles et Jacques Boileau,* 2 vols, 1929.

Oeuvres, ed. J. de Valincour and E. Renaudot, 1713; ed. C. Brossette, 2 vols, Geneva 1716; ed. J. Berriat-Saint-Prix, 4 vols, Paris 1830; ed. C. Boudhors, 7 vols, 1934–43; ed. A. Adam and F. Escal, 1966.
Oeuvres poétiques, ed. F. Brunetière, 1893.

Tr. J. Dennis, in *Miscellanies of verse and prose,* n.p. 1693 (selection); *Miscellany poems,* n.p. 1697 (selection, incl. some *Satires*).
Tr. anon., *The works,* 3 vols, London 1712–13.
Tr. various, *Posthumous works,* London 1713.
Tr. E. Dilworth, *Selected criticism,* Indianapolis (Ind) 1965.

Le chapelain décoiffé (in collab. with brother Gilles and Antoine FURE-TIÈRE), 1665.

Satires, 1665–1711 (12 *satires*, pbd separately and in groups); ed. A. Cahen, 1932; ed. A. Adam, 1941 (*Satires* 1–11). Tr. H. Porter, *The satires*, Glasgow 1904 (with *Address to the King*).

Contre les femmes 1694 (as *Satire 10* in *Satires* above); ed. L. Perceau, 1927. Tr. anon., in *The fourth and tenth satires*, Dartford 1824.

Epistres, 1666–98 (12 *épîtres*, pbd separately and in groups); ed. A. Cahen, 1937. *L'art poétique*, 1674; ed. V. Delaporte, 3 vols, Lille 1888; ed. D. Nichol Smith, Cambridge 1898. Tr. W. Soames, London 1683; tr. Dilworth above, *Art of poetry*.

Oeuvres diverses, 1674 (incl. *Traité du sublime*, tr. from Longinus); 1701 (enl.; incl. *Satire 11* above).

Le lutrin, 1674 (last 2 cantos); 1683 (full text); ed. F. Brunetière, 1893. Tr. 'N.O.', London 1682; tr. J. Ozell, 1708.

Dialogues des morts, Emmerich 1688 (in *Le retour des pieces choisies*); ed. T. F. Crane, Boston (Mass) 1902 (as *Les héros de roman*).

Ode sur la prise de Namur, 1693. Tr. S. Cobb, *An ode on the taking of Namur*, London 1712.

Correspondance de Boileau-Despréaux et Brossette, ed. A. Laverdet, 1958.

BRAY, R., in his *La formation de la doctrine classique en France*, 1927.
    Boileau, l'homme et l'oeuvre, 1942.
CLARAC, P., *Boileau*, 1964.
FRANCE, P., in his *Rhetoric and truth in France*, Oxford 1972.
LANSON, G., *Boileau*, 1892.
MORNET, D., *Nicolas Boileau*, 1942.
ZDROJEWSKA, V., *Boileau*, Brescia 1948.

BOSSUET, Jacques-Bénigne   1627–1704

VERLAQUE, V., *Bibliographie raisonnée des oeuvres*, 1908.
CARRIÈRE, V., *Bossuet au 20e siècle: les travaux de Charles Urbain relatifs à Bossuet*, 1931 (in *Revue d'Histoire de l'Eglise en France*, vol. 17).
COULON, P., *Additions to the bibliography*, Geneva 1965 (in *Studies on Voltaire and the Eighteenth Century*, vol. 37).

Oeuvres, ed. C. Lequeux, Deforis and Coniac, 20 vols, 1772–88 ('Deforis ed.'; incomplete); ed. F. Lachat, 31 vols, 1862–6; ed. E. N. Guillaume, 11 vols, Bar-le-Duc 1877.

Oeuvres oratoires, ed. J. Lebarq et al., 7 vols, 1890–7; ed. C. Urbain and E. Levesque, 7 vols, 1922–7.

Extraits des oeuvres diverses, ed. G. Lanson, 1899.

Oraisons funèbres, ed. P. Jacquinet, 1885; ed. J. Truchet, 1961.

Réfutation du catéchisme du pasteur Ferry, Metz 1655.

Exposition de la doctrine catholique, 1671; ed. A. Vogt, 1911. Tr. anon., *An exposition of the doctrine of the Catholic Church*, London 1841.

L'histoire des variations des églises protestantes, 1688; ed. C. Lequeux and C. P. Le Roy, 5 vols, 1770. Tr. J. Brown, *The history of the variations of the Protestant Churches*, 2 vols, Antwerp 1742; Dublin 1836.

Discours sur l'histoire universelle, 1681; ed. J. B. Jeanin, 1884. Tr. anon., *A discourse on the history of the whole world*, London 1686; tr. Mrs Jenkins, *A survey of universal history*, 1819.

Traité de la communion sous les deux espèces, 1682. Tr. anon., *A treatise of communion under both species*, Paris 1685; tr. J. Davis, *A treatise of communion under both kinds*, London 1687.

Avertissements aux protestants, 7 vols, 1689–91; 2 vols, Liège 1710.

Recueil d'oraisons funèbres, 1689 (cntg 6 on royal individuals). Tr. anon., *A sermon preached at the funeral of Marie Terese of Austria*, London 1684; tr. E. Jerningham, London 1799 (in his *Biographical sketches of Henrietta, Duchess of Orleans and Louis of Bourbon Prince of Condé*).

Traité du libre arbitre et de la concupiscence, 1694; ed. C. Urbain and E. Levesque, 1930.

Maximes et réflexions sur la comédie, 1694; ed. C. Urbain and E. Levesque, 1930 (in *L'Eglise et le théâtre*). Tr. anon., *Maxims and reflections upon plays*, London 1699.

Politique tirée des propres paroles de l'Ecriture Sainte, 1709; ed. J. Le Brun, Geneva 1967.

Elévations sur les mystères, 1711; ed. M. Dréano, 1962.

Introduction à la philosophie, ou de la connoissance de soi-même, 1722; ed. M. L. Rossigneux, 1900.

Meditations sur l'Evangile, 4 vols, 1730–1; ed. M. Dréano, 1966.

Panégyriques des saints, 1821. Tr. anon., ed. D. O'Mahony et al., *Panegyrics of the Saints*, London 1924.

Correspondance, ed. C. Urbain and E. Levesque, 15 vols, 1909–25.

CALVET, J., *Bossuet, l'homme et l'oeuvre*, 1941; revd J. Truchet, 1968.
FRANCE, P., in his *Rhetoric and truth in France*, Oxford 1972.
HÜPPI, B., *Versuch über den Stil Bossuets*, Fribourg 1950.
LANSON, G., *Bossuet*, 1891.
LE BRUN, J., *La spiritualité de Bossuet*, 1972.
MARTIMORT, A. G., *Le gallicanisme de Bossuet*, 1953.
RÉBELLIAU, A., *Bossuet historien du protestantisme*, 1892; 1909.
TRUCHET, J., *La prédication de Bossuet*, 1960.

BOURDALOUE, Louis   1632–1704

GRISELLE, E., *Bibliographie critique*, 1900.
See also *Revue Bourdaloue* below.

Oeuvres complètes, 4 vols, Paris and Bar-le-Duc, 1876; ed. E. Griselle, 2 vols, 1919–22 (incomplete).

Sermons, ed. F. Bretonneau, 16 vols, 1707–34; ed. L. Dimier, 1936 (selection). Tr. A. Carroll, *Practical divinity*, 4 vols, London 1776 (selection); tr. anon., *Select sermons*, Harlow 1806.

CASTETS, F., *Bourdaloue: la vie et la prédication d'un religieux au 17e siècle*, 2 vols, 1901–4.
FEUGÈRE, A., *Bourdaloue, sa prédication et son temps*, 1874.
GRISELLE, E., *Bourdaloue, histoire critique de sa prédication*, 3 vols, 1901–6.
HITZ, M. F., *Die Redekunst in Bourdaloues Predigt*, Munich 1936.
PRINGY, Mme de, *La vie du Père Bourdaloue de la Compagnie de Jésus*, 1705.
Revue Bourdaloue, 3 vols, 1902–34 (incl. bibl.).

BUSSY-RABUTIN, Roger de   1618–1693

Oeuvres complètes, ed. L. Lalanne, 8 vols, 1857–9.

Histoire amoureuse des Gaules, Liège 1665 (circulated in ms from 1660); ed. P. Boiteau and C. L. Livet, Paris 1856–86; ed. G. Mongrédien, 2 vols, Paris 1930; ed. A. Adams, 1967. Tr. anon., *The amorous history of the Gauls*, London 1725.
Les mémoires, 2 vols, 1696.

Les lettres, 4 vols, 1697; 5 vols, 1711.

DINAR, A., *Bussy-Rabutin l'incorrigible*, 1948.
GÉRARD-GAILLY, E., *Un académicien grand seigneur et libertin au 17e siècle*, 1909.
ORIEUX, J., *Bussy-Rabutin; le libertin galant homme*, 1958; 1969.

CHAULIEU, (Abbé) Guillaume Amfrye de   1639–1720

Bibl. See Lachèvre ed. of *Poésies* below.

Oeuvres, ed. Saint-Marc, 2 vols, Amsterdam 1750; 2 vols, 1774.

A few poems tr. in anthologies, incl. *Flowers of France*, tr. J. Payne, London 1914.

Poésies, Lyon 1724 (with poems by de La Fare); ed. Camusat, 1731 (enl.); ed. Delaunay, 2 vols, Amsterdam 1733 (enl., as *Oeuvres diverses*); ed. F. Lachèvre, Paris 1924 (in *Le libertinage au 17e siècle*, vol 11, incl. bibl.).

BOURIQUET, G., *l'Abbé de Chaulieu et le libertinage au grand siècle*, 1972.
SCHWARTZKOPF, F., *Coulanges, Chaulieu und La Fare*, Leipzig 1908.

CORNEILLE, Pierre 1606–1684
PICOT, E., *Bibliographie cornélienne*, 1876.
 LE VERDIER, P. J. and PELAY, E., *Additions à la bibliographie cornélienne*, Rouen and Paris 1908.

Oeuvres, ed. C. Marty-Laveaux, 12 vols, 1862–8; ed. A. Stegman, 1963.
Théâtre complet, ed. P. Lièvre and R. Caillois, 2 vols, 1950; ed. M. Rat, 3 vols, 1960; ed. G. Couton, 1972 onwards (1 vol pbd).
Théâtre choisi, ed. M. Rat, 1963 (cntg *Cid, Horace, Cinna, Polyeucte, Mort de Pompée, Rodogune, Nicomède, Suréna, L'illusion comique, Le Menteur, Don Sanche* and *Poésies diverses*).
Corneille inconnu, ed. V. Klemperer, Munich 1933 (selection).
Writings on the theatre, ed. H. T. Barnwell, Oxford 1965.

Tr. and ed. L. Lockert, *The chief plays*, Princeton (NJ) 1952 (cntg *The Cid, Horace, Cinna, Polyeucte, Rodogune* and *Nicomede*); *Moot plays*, Nashville (Tenn) 1960 (cntg *La mort de Pompée, Héraclius, Don Sanche d'Aragon, Aertorius, Othon, Attila, Pulchérie* and *Suréna*).

Clitandre, 1632; ed. R. L. Wagner, Lille and Geneva 1949.
Mélite, ou les fausses lettres, 1633; ed. M. Roque and M. Lièvre, Lille and Geneva 1950. Tr. anon., *Melite*, London 1776.
La vefve, ou le traistre trahy, 1634; ed. M. Roque and M. Lièvre, Lille and Geneva 1954.
La galerie du palais, 1637; ed. T. B. Rudmose-Brown, Manchester 1920.
La suivante, 1637.
La Place Royalle, 1637; 1682; ed. J. C. Brunon, 1962.
Excuse à Ariste, 1637.
Le Cid, 1637; 1660; ed. M. Cauchie, 1946; ed. Y. Brunswick and P. Ginestier, 1970; ed. L. Lejealle and J. Dubois, 1970. Tr. J. Rutter ?, *The Cid*, London 1637; tr. D. Johnson, Bath 1873; tr. W. Fowlie, New York 1962 (in *Classical French Drama*).
Médée, 1639.
L'illusion comique, 1639; ed. J. Marks, Manchester 1944; ed. R. Garapon, Paris 1957.
Horace, 1641; ed. P. H. Nurse, London 1963; ed. P. Gaillard 1970. Tr. W. Lower, *Horatius*, London 1656; tr. C. Cotton, *Horace*, 1671; tr. A. Bermel, *Horatius*, San Francisco (Calif) 1962.
Cinna, Rouen and Paris 1643; ed. C. Dullin, 1948; ed. D. A. Watts, London 1964. Tr. Colley Cibber ?, *Cinna's conspiracy*, London 1713.
Polyeucte, 1643; 1682; ed. R. A. Sayce, Oxford 1949; ed. G. Delaisement, 1963. Tr. W. Lower, *Polyeuctes*, London 1655; tr. A. Meakin, Paris 1929.
La mort de Pompée, 1644; ed. H. T. Barnwell, Oxford 1971. Tr. K. Philips and J. Denham, *Pompey*, London 1667 (with *Horace* above).

Le menteur, 1644; ed. L. Petit de Julleville, 1898. Tr. anon., *The mistaken beauty, or the lyar*, London 1671.

La suite du menteur, 1645.

Théodore, vierge et martyre, Rouen and Paris 1646.

Rodogune, Rouen and Paris 1647; 1682; ed. J. Schérer, Lille and Paris 1946; ed. M. Cégretin, Paris 1694. Tr. S. Aspinall, London 1765.

Héraclius, empereur d'Orient, Rouen and Paris 1647. Tr. L. Carlell, *Heraclius, emperour of the East*, London 1664.

Don Sanche d'Arragon, Rouen and Paris 1650; ed. F. Hémon 1896. Tr. H. Brand, *The conflict*, n.p. 1798 (in *Plays and poems*).

Andromède, Rouen and Paris 1651.

Nicomède, Rouen and Paris 1651; ed. R. C. Knight, London 1960. Tr. J. Dancer, London 1671.

L'imitation de Jésus Christ (tr. from Thomas à Kempis), 1651.

Pertharite, roy des Lombards, Rouen and Paris 1653.

Oedipe, Rouen and Paris 1659.

La toison d'or, Rouen and Paris 1661.

Sertorius, 1662; ed. J. Streicher, Geneva and Paris 1959.

Sophonisbe, 1663.

Othon, 1665.

Agésilas, Rouen and Paris 1666.

Attila, roy des Huns, 1668.

Tite et Berenice, 1671.

Pulchérie, 1673.

Suréna, general des Parthes, 1675.

BELLESSORT, A., in his *Sur les grands chemins de la poésie classique*, 1914.

BÉNICHOU, P., in his *Morales du grand siècle*, 1948.

BRASILLACH, R., *Pierre Corneille*, 1938.

COUTON, G., *La vieillesse de Corneille, 1658–1684*, 1949.

CROCE, B., *Ariosto, Shakespeare e Corneille*, Bari 1920. Tr. D. Ainslie, *Ariosto, Shakespeare and Corneille*, New York 1920.

DORCHAIN, A., *Pierre Corneille*, 1918.

DORT, B., *Pierre Corneille, dramaturge*, 1957.

DOUBROVSKY, S., *Corneille et la dialectique du héros*, 1963.

KLEMPERER, V., *Pierre Corneille*, Munich 1933.

LANSON, G., *Corneille*, 1898.

LE BRUN, R., *Corneille devant trois siècles*, 1906.

MONGRÉDIEN, G., *Recueil des textes et des documents du 17e siècle relatifs à Corneille*, 1972.

NADAL, O., *Le sentiment de l'amour dans l'oeuvre de Pierre Corneille*, 1948.

NELSON, R., *Corneille, his heroes and their world*, Philadelphia 1963.

POCOCK, G., *Corneille and Racine: problems of tragic form*, Cambridge 1973.

RICHARD, A., *L'Illusion comique de Corneille et le baroque*, 1972.

ROUSSEAUX, A., in his *Le monde classique*, vol 1, 1941.
SCHLUMBERGER, J., *Plaisir à Corneille*, 1936.
STEGMANN, A., *L'héroïsme cornélien*, 2 vols, 1968.
YARROW, P. J., *Corneille*, London and New York, 1963.

CORNEILLE, Thomas   1625–1709

Oeuvres, ed. C. Louandre, 1853 (in *Oeuvres des deux Corneille*).
Théâtre complet, ed. E. Thierry, 1881 (incomplete).

Le feint astrologue, Rouen and Paris 1651. Tr. and adapt. anon., *The feign'd astrologer*, London 1668.
D. Bertran de Cigarral, Rouen and Paris 1652.
L'amour à la mode, Rouen and Paris 1653; ed. C. Cosnier, Paris 1973. Tr. J. Bulteel, *Amorous Orontus, or the love in fashion*, London 1665 (1675 as *The amorous gallant*).
Le berger extravagant, Rouen and Paris 1653; ed. F. Bar, Geneva and Paris 1960. Tr. T. Rawlins ?, *The extravagant sheepherd*, London 1654.
Timocrate, Rouen and Paris 1658; ed. Y. Giraud, Geneva 1970. Tr. C. L. Lockert, Nashville (Tenn) 1968 (in *More plays by rivals of Corneille and Racine*).
Camma, reine de Galatie, Rouen and Paris 1661.
Laodice, Paris and Rouen 1668. Tr. C. L. Lockert, Nashville (Tenn) 1956 (in *The chief rivals of Corneille and Racine*).
Ariane, 1673. Tr. and adapt., *The labyrinth*, Dublin 1795; tr. C. L. Lockert, *Ariane*, Nashville (Tenn) 1968 (in *More plays by rivals of Corneille and Racine*).
Circé, 1675.
Le comte d'Essex, Amsterdam 1678. Tr. C. L. Lockert, Nashville (Tenn) 1956 (in *The chief rivals of Corneille and Racine*).
La Devineresse, 1680; ed. P. J. Yarrow, Exeter 1971.
Les engagemens du hasard, 1689.
Le dictionnaire des arts et des sciences, 2 vols, 1694; ed. B. de Fontenelle, 2 vols, 1731.
Observations de l'Academie françoise sur les Remarques de M. de Vaugelas, 1704.
Dictionnaire historique et géographique, 3 vols, 1708.

COLLINS, D. A., *Thomas Corneille, protean dramatist*, The Hague 1966.
LANCASTER, H. C., in his *A history of French dramatic literature in the 17th century*, pt 3, vol 1, Baltimore (Md) 1936; 1952.
REYNIER, G., *Thomas Corneille, sa vie et son théâtre*, 1892.

CYRANO DE BERGERAC, Savinien   1619–1655

Bibl. See MONGRÉDIEN below.

Les oeuvres libertines, ed. F. Lachèvre, 2 vols, 1921 (in *Le libertinage au 17e siècle*).

Oeuvres diverses, lettres satiriques [etc.] ed. F. Lachèvre, 2 vols, 1933 (incl. *La mort d'Agrippine*).

Oeuvres, ed. G. Ribemont-Dessaignes, 1957 (selected works).

La mort d'Agrippine, 1653.

Le pédant joué, 1654; ed. T. Martel, 1888 (in *Comédies du 17e siècle*).

Les oeuvres diverses, 1654 (cntg *Les lettres, Les lettres satyriques, Les lettres amoureuses* and *Le pédant joué* above); ed. L. Erba, Milan 1965 (*Lettres*).
Tr. anon., *Satyrical characters*, London 1658 (from *Lettres satyriques*).

Histoire comique [. . .] *contenant les estats & empires de la lune*, 1657; ed. L. Jordan, Dresden 1910. Tr. T. St. Serf, *The government of the world in the moon*, London 1659;

> *Les nouvelles oeuvres* [. . .] *contenant l'histoire comique des estats & empires du soleil*, 1662;

ed. H. Weber, 1959. Tr. A. Lovell, *The comical history of the states and empires of the world of the moon and sun*, London 1687; tr. and ed. R. Aldington, *Voyages to the moon and the sun*, London and New York 1923; tr. G. Strachan, *Other worlds*, Oxford 1965.

ALCOVER, M., *La pensée philosophique et scientifique de Cyrano de Bergerac*, Geneva 1970.

BRUN, P. A., *Savinien Cyrano de Bergerac, sa vie et ses oeuvres*, 1893.

LANIUS, E. W., *Cyrano de Bergerac and the universe of the imagination*, Geneva 1967.

MONGRÉDIEN, G., *Cyrano de Bergerac*, 1964 (incl. bibl.).

DESCARTES, René 1596–1650

ALVERNY, T. d', *Notices bibliographiques et iconographiques*, 1937.

BOORSCH, J., *Etat présent des études sur Descartes*, 1937.

SEBBA, G., *Bibliographia cartesiana; a critical guide to the Descartes literature, 1800–1960*, The Hague, 1964.

GILSON, E., *Index scolastico-cartésien*, 1913 (glossary of philosophical terms).

Oeuvres, ed. C. Adam and P. Tannery, 13 vols, 1897–1913.

Oeuvres et lettres, ed. A. Bridoux, 1937; 1953 (enl.).

Oeuvres philosophiques, ed. F. Alquié, 3 vols, 1963–73.

Tr. E. S. Haldane and G. R. T. Ross, *The philosophical works*, 2 vols, Cambridge 1911 (revd 1931).

Tr. N. K. Smith, *Philosophical writings*, London 1953.

Tr. E. Anscombe and P. T. Geach, *Philosophical writings*, London 1954 (selection; revd 1971).

Tr. A. Wollaston, *Discourse on the method and other writings*, Harmondsworth 1960.

Tr. L. Bair, *Essential works,* New York 1961.

Tr. F. E. Sutcliffe, *Discourse on method and other writings,* Harmondsworth 1968.

Tr. and ed. J. M. Morris, *Descartes dictionary,* New York 1921.

Discours de la méthode, Leiden 1637; ed. E. Gilson, Paris 1925; ed. Alain, 1927; ed. G. Gadoffre, Manchester 1941; ed. J. Benda, Mulhouse, 1948. Tr. anon., *A discourse of a method,* London 1649.

Les méditations métaphysiques (French tr., by Duc de Luynes and C. Clerselier in collab. with Descartes, of *Meditationes de prima philosophia,* 1641), 1647; ed. G. Lewis, 1944. English tr. J. Veitch, *The meditations,* Edinburgh and London 1853 (introd. A. D. Lindsay, London and New York 1912).

Les principes de la philosophie (French tr., by Abbé Picot and C. Clerselier in collab. with Descartes, of *Principia philosophiae,* Amsterdam 1644), Paris 1647. English tr. J. Veitch, *Selections from the Principles of philosophy,* Edinburgh and London 1853 (with *The meditations* above).

Les passions de l'âme, 1649; ed. P. Mesnard, 1937; ed. G. Rodin-Lewis, 1955. Tr. anon., *The passions of the soule,* 3 vols, London 1650.

Lettres [. . .] où sont traittées les plus belles questions de la morale, physique, medecine & des mathématiques, 1657; ed. C. Clerselier, 3 vols, 1666–7.

Correspondance, ed. C. Adam and G. Milhaud, 8 vols, 1936–63; ed. M. Alexandre, 1955 (selection). Tr. A. Kenny, *Philosophical letters,* Oxford 1970 (selection).

Correspondence of Descartes and Constantijn Huygens, 1635–1647, ed. L. Roth, Oxford 1926.

ADAM, C., *Vie et oeuvres de Descartes; étude historique,* 1910.

ALAIN, *Etude sur Descartes,* 1928.

BRUNSCHVICG, L., *René Descartes,* 1937.

CHEVALIER, J., *Descartes,* 1921.

COLLINS, J., *Descartes' philosophy of nature,* Oxford 1971.

GOUHIER, H., *La pensée métaphysique de Descartes,* 1962.

KEELING, S. V., *Descartes,* London 1934; 1969.

LANSON, G., *L'influence de la philosophie cartésienne sur la littérature française,* 1929 (in his *Etudes d'histoire littéraire*).

LAPORTE, J., *Le rationalisme de Descartes,* 1945; 1950.

LE GUERN, M., *Pascal et Descartes,* 1971.

RODIN-LEWIS, G., *L'oeuvre de Descartes,* 2 vols, 1971.

SMITH, N. K., *New studies in the philosophy of Descartes,* London 1952.

DESMARETS DE SAINT-SORLIN, Jean   c. 1595–1676

Ariane, 2 vols, 1632. Tr. anon., *Ariana,* London 1636.

Les visionnaires, 1637; ed. T. Martel, 1888 (in *Comédies du 17e siècle*); ed. H. G. Hall, 1963.

Rosane, 1639.

Scipion, 1639.

Mirame (supposedly written in collab. with Richelieu), 1641.

Clovis, ou la France chrestienne, 1657; 1673; ed. F. Freudmann and H. G. Hall, 1971.

Marie-Madeleine, 1669.

Esther, 1670.

La deffense du poeme heroïque, 1674.

La défense de la poésie et de la langue françoise, 1675.

KERVILER, R., *Jean Desmaretz, sieur de Saint-Sorlin*, 1879.

LANCASTER, H. C., in his *A history of French dramatic literature in the 17th century*, pt 2, Baltimore (Md) 1932.

SAYCE, R. A., in his *The French biblical epic in the 17th century*, Oxford 1955.

DU RYER, Pierre   1605–1658

Bibl. See LANCASTER below.

Published some 20 tragicomedies; translated Cicero, Seneca and other Latin writers.

Alcionée, 1640; ed. H. C. Lancaster, Baltimore (Md) 1930.

Saül, 1642; ed. H. C. Lancaster, Baltimore (Md) 1931. Tr. C. L. Lockert, Nashville (Tenn) 1956 (in *The chief rivals of Corneille and Racine*).

Scévole, 1647; ed. G. Fasano, Bologna 1966.

LANCASTER, H. C., *Pierre du Ryer, dramatist*, Washington (DC) 1912 (incl. bibl.).

LOCKERT, C. L., in his *Studies in French classical tragedy*, Nashville (Tenn) 1958.

SCHÉRER, J., in his *La dramaturgie classique en France*, 1950.

FÉNELON, François de Salignac de la Mothe   1651–1715

CARCASSONNE, E., *Etat présent des travaux sur Fénelon*, 1939.

RASTOUL, A., *Bibliothèque nationale catalogue des ouvrages de Fénelon conservés au département des imprimés*, 1912.

Oeuvres spirituelles, 2 vols, 1718; ed. F. Varillon, 1954. Tr. anon., *The Archbishop of Cambray's Meditations, etc.*, Ipswich 1756 (extracts); tr. R. Houghton, *Part of the spiritual works*, Dublin 1771.

Oeuvres complètes, ed. J. E. A. Gosselin and A. Caron, 35 vols, 1820–30 ('Versailles ed.'); 10 vols, Paris 1848–52 ('Saint-Sulpice ed.').

Oeuvres choisies, ed. A. Chérel, 1930.

Fénelon, ce méconnu, ed. M. P. Chaintreuil and Daniel-Rops, 1961 (selection).

Suite du quatrième livre d l'Odysée d'Homère, ou les avantures de Télémaque, 1699 (incomplete); Brussels 1699; The Hague 1701; ed. Bosquillon, 2 vols, Paris 1799; ed. A. Cahen, 2 vols, 1920–7; ed. J. L. Goré, 1968. Tr. J. Ozell, *The adventures of Telemachus,* 2 vols, London 1720; tr. T. Smollett, 2 vols, London 1776; tr. J. L. Ross, 1860.

Education des filles, 1687; ed. C. Defodon, 1881; ed. A. Gasté, 1882. Tr. G. Hicks, *Instructions for the education of a daughter,* London 1707; tr. T. F. Dibdin, *Fénelon's treatise on the education of daughters,* Cheltenham 1805.

Explication des maximes des saints sur la vie intérieure, 1697; Brussels 1698; ed. A. Chérel, 1911. Tr. W. W. Williams, *Maxims of the mystics,* n.p. 1904.

Reflexions sur la grammaire, la rhétorique, la poétique et l'histoire, 1716; ed. E. Caldarini, Geneva 1970 (as *Lettre à l'Academie*).

Correspondance, ed. A. Caron, 11 vols, 1827–30 (in *Oeuvres complètes* above). Tr. H. L. Sidney Lear, *Letters to men and women,* London 1957 (selection); tr. J. McEwen, *Letters,* 1964 (selection).

BREMOND, H., *Apologie pour Fénelon,* 1910.

CARCASSONNE, E., *Fénelon, l'homme et l'oeuvre,* 1946.

CHÉREL, A., *Fénelon, ou la religion du pur amour,* 1934.

GORÉ, J. L., *L'itinéraire de Fénelon: humanisme et spiritualité,* 1957.

LITTLE, K. D., *François de Fénelon, a study of a personality,* New York 1951.

VARILLON, F., *Fénelon et le pur amour,* 1957.

FLÉCHIER, Esprit   1632–1710

Oeuvres complètes, ed. G. M. Du Creux, 10 vols, Nîmes 1782; ed. J. P. Migne, 2 vols, Paris 1856.

Oeuvres choisies, ed. H. Bremond, 1911.

Histoire de Théodose le Grand, 1679. Tr. M. Manning, *The life of the Emperour Theodosius the Great,* London 1693.

Mémoires [. . .] sur les grands jours tenus à Clermont, ed. B. Gonod, 1844; ed. P. A. Chéruel and C. A. de Sainte-Beuve, 1862. Tr. W. W. Comfort, *The Clermont assizes,* Philadelphia (Pa) 1937.

FABRE, A., *Fléchier orateur 1672–1690; étude critique,* 1885.

GRENTE, G., *Cardinal Fléchier,* 1934.

FONTENELLE, Bernard le Bovier de   1657–1757

Oeuvres, 11 vols, 1766; ed. G. B. Depping, 3 vols, 1818.

Fontenelle, ed. H. Potez, 1909 (selection).

Textes choisis, ed. E. Faguet, 1912; ed. M. Roelens, 1967.

Lettres diverses de Mr le Chevalier d'Her ***, 1683; 1699 (enl., renamed *Lettres galantes* [etc.]); ed. D. Delafarges, 1961. Tr. anon., London 1683; tr. G. Russel, in *The works of the late Rev. G. Russel*, 2 vols, Cork 1769.

Nouveaux dialogues des morts, 2 vols, 1683–4; ed. J. Dagan, 1971. Tr. J. Dryden, *New dialogues of the dead*, 3 vols, London 1683–5; tr. J. Hughes, 1708; tr. E. Pound, *Dialogues*, 1917.

Entretiens sur la pluralité des mondes, 1686; n.p. 1719 (with 6th *Entretien*); ed. R. Shackleton, Oxford 1955; ed. A. Calame. Paris 1966; ed. J. Gué-henno 1971; ed. J. Bergier, 1973. Tr. J. Glanvill, *A plurality of worlds*, London 1688 (ed. D. Garnett, 1929); tr. Mrs Aphra Behn, *A discovery of new worlds*, 1688; tr. W. Gardiner, *Conversations on the plurality of worlds*, 1715.

Histoire des oracles (adapt. from A. van Dale's *De oraculum ethnicorum dissertationes duae*, Amsterdam 1683), 1686; ed. L. Maigron, Paris 1908. Tr. Mrs Aphra Behn, *The history of oracles*, n.p. 1688; tr. S. Whatley, London 1750.

Poésies pastorales [. . .] *avec un traité sur la nature de l'eglogue, & une digression sur les anciens et les modernes*, 1688, ed. R. Shackleton, Oxford 1955 (*Digression*, with *Entretiens* above); tr. Mr Hughes, *A discourse concerning antients and moderns*, London 1688 (with Glanvill's tr. of *Entretiens* above).

De l'origine des fables (derived from *Sur l'histoire*, pbd 1758), 1724; ed. J. R. Carré, 1932.

Eloges des académiciens de l'Académie royale des sciences, morts depuis l'an 1699, 2 vols, 1766 (certain *Eloges* first pbd 1708–33).

CARRÉ, J. R., *La philosophie de Fontenelle*, 1932.

MAIGRON, L., *Fontenelle: l'homme, l'oeuvre, l'influence*, 1906.

NIDERST, A., *Fontenelle à la recherche de lui-même, 1657–1702*, 1972.

FURETIÈRE, Antoine   1619–1688

Bibl. See FISCHER below; also Mongrédien ed. of *Roman bourgeois* below.

Aenéide travestie, 1649.

Nouvelle allégorique, ou histoire des derniers troubles arrivez au royaume d'éloquence, 1658; ed. E. van Ginneken, Geneva and Paris 1967. Tr. anon., *The rebellion*, n.p. 1704.

Roman bourgeois, 1666; ed. G. Mongrédien, 1955 (with *Nouvelle allégorique* above; incl. bibl.). ed. A. Adam, 1958 (in *Romanciers du 17e siècle*). Tr. anon., *City romance*, London 1671.

Fables morales et nouvelles, 1671.

Essai d'un Dictionnaire universel, n.p. 1684; 3 vols, The Hague and Rotterdam 1690 (enl., as *Dictionnaire universel*).

Factum, Amsterdam 1685;
>   *Second factum*, Amsterdam 1686;

Troisième factum, Amsterdam 1688;
Nouveau recueil des factums, Amsterdam 1694;
ed. C. Asselineau, 2 vols, Paris 1859.

FISCHER, H., *Antoine Furetière; ein französischer Literat des 17. Jahrhunderts*, Berlin 1937 (incl. bibl.).

REYNIER, G., in his *Le roman réaliste au 17e siècle*, 1914.

GOMBAULD, Jean Oger de   c. 1590–1666

Bibl. See MOREL below.

L'Endimion, 1624. Tr. R. Hurst, *Endimion, an excellent fancy*, London 1639.
L'Amaranthe, 1631.
Les poésies, 1646.
Sonnets, 1649.
Les épigrammes, 1657; ed. J. V. F. Liber, Lille 1861.
Les Danaïdes, 1658.

MOREL, L., *Jean Ogier de Gombauld: sa vie, son oeuvre*, Neuchâtel 1910 (incl. bibl.).

HARDY, Alexandre   c. 1570–1632

Le théâtre, 5 vols, 1624–8; ed. E. Stengel, 5 vols, Marburg 1883–4.

Mariamne, 1625 (in *Le théâtre*, vol 2 above). Tr. C. L. Lockert, Nashville (Tenn) 1968 (in *More plays by rivals of Corneille and Racine*).
Les ramoneurs (ascribed to Hardy), ed. A. Gill, 1957.

BRERETON, G., in his *French tragic drama in the 16th and 17th centuries*, London 1972.

LANCASTER, H. C., in his *A history of French dramatic literature in the 17th century*, pt 1, vol 1, Baltimore (Md) 1929; 1952.

RIGAL, E., *Alexandre Hardy et le théâtre français*, 1889.

LA BRUYÈRE, Jean de   1645–1696

Bibl. See Servois ed. of *Oeuvres* below; also RICHARD below.

Oeuvres, ed. G. Servois, 3 vols, 1865–82 (revd 1922; incl. bibl.); ed. J. Benda, 1935 (revd 1951).
Tr. M. Coste, *The works*, 2 vols, London 1713.

Les caractères de Théophraste traduits du grec, avec les caractères ou les moeurs de ce siècle, 1688 (cntg 420 *caractères*); 1689 (764); 1690 (923); 1691 (997); 1692 (1072); 1694 (1120 *caractères*); ed. R. Garapon, 1962. Tr. various, *The characters, or the manners of the age*, London 1699; tr. H. van Laun, 1885.

LANGE, M., *La Bruyère, critique des conditions et des institutions sociales*, 1909.

MICHAUT, G., *La Bruyère*, 1936.

RICHARD, P., *La Bruyère et ses Caractères*, Amiens 1946 (incl. bibl.).

ROSSO, C., in his *Virtù e critica della virtù nei moralisti francesi*, Turin 1964; Pisa 1971.

STEGMANN, A., *Les Caractères de La Bruyère: bible de l'honnête homme*, 1972.

LA FAYETTE, Madame de 1634–1693
(Marie-Madeleine de la Vergue, Comtesse de La Fayette)

SCOTT, J. W., *Selective critical bibliography*, London 1974.
See also Lejeune ed. of *Oeuvres* below; also Magne ed. of *Romans et nouvelles* below.

Oeuvres, ed. R. Lejeune, 3 vols, 1925–30 (incl. bibl.).

Romans et nouvelles, ed. E. Magne, 1939 (cntg *Princesse de Montpensier*, *Zaïde*, *Princesse de Clèves*, *Comtesse de Tende*; incl. bibl.).

La princesse de Monpensier, 1662; 1674; ed. A. Beaunier, 1926. Tr. anon., *The Princess of Montpensier*, n.p. 1666.

Zayde, 2 vols, 1670–1. Tr. P. Porter, London 1678.

La princesse de Clèves (probably in collab. with Segrais and La Rochefoucauld), 4 vols, 1678; ed. E. Magne, 1946; ed. B. Pingaud, 1957; ed. A. Adam, 1958 (in *Romanciers du 17e siècle*); ed. N. Scarlyn Wilson, London 1958. Tr. anon., *The Princess of Cleves*, London 1679; tr. H. Ashton, London 1925; tr. Nancy Mitford, 1950; tr. W. J. Cobb, New York 1961.

Histoire de Madame Henriette d'Angleterre, Amsterdam 1720; ed. E. Henriot, Paris 1925; ed. G. Sigaux, 1965; ed. M. T. Hipp, Geneva and Paris 1967. Tr. anon., *Fatal gallantry*, London 1722; tr. J. M. Shelmerdine, *The secret history of Henrietta, Princess of England*, 1929.

Mémoires de la cour de France pour les années 1688 et 1689, Amsterdam 1731; ed. G. Sigaux, Paris 1965 (with *Histoire de Madame Henriette* above).

La comtesse de Tende, 1804 (in *Oeuvres complètes de Mesdames de La Fayette et de Tencin;* first pbd in *Nouveau Mercure*, May 1724).

Correspondance, ed. A. Beaunier and G. Roth, 2 vols, 1942.

ASHTON, H., *Madame de La Fayette, sa vie et ses oeuvres*, Cambridge 1922.

BEAUNIER, A., *L'amie de La Rochfoucauld*, 1927.

DÉDÉYAN, C., *Madame de La Fayette*, 1955.

DURRY, M. J., *Madame de La Fayette*, 1962.

LAUGAA, M., *Lectures de Madame de La Fayette*, 1971.

MAGNE, E., *Madame de La Fayette en ménage*, 1926.

PINGAUD, B., *Madame de La Fayette par elle-même*, 1959.

LA FONTAINE, Jean de   1621–1695

ROCHAMBEAU, R. de, *Bibliographie des oeuvres*, 1911.
See also Régnier ed. of *Oeuvres* below; also CLARAC below.

Oeuvres, 3 vols, Antwerp 1726; ed. C. A. Walckenaer, 6 vols, Paris 1822–3; ed. C. Marty-Laveaux, 5 vols, 1857–77; ed. H. Régnier, 11 vols, 1883–92 (incl. bibl. in vol 9); ed. E. Pilon and F. Dauphin, 7 vols, 1922–7; ed. E. Pilon, R. Groos, J. Schiffrin and P. Clarac, 2 vols, 1932–42 (as *Fables, contes et nouvelles* and *Oeuvres diverses*).
Oeuvres diverses, 3 vols, 1729.

Tr. anon., *Fables and tales*, London 1734 (selection); tr. M. Moore, New York 1952.

L'eunuque, 1654.
Nouvelles en vers tirée [sic] *de Boccace et de l'Arioste*, 1665 (incl. 2 tales); 1665 (10 tales, as *Contes et nouvelles en vers*);
>   *Deuxiesme partie des contes et nouvelles en vers*, 1666 (13 tales); 1669 (16 tales, incl. 3 first pbd Rheims? 1667; with pt 1 above);
>   *Contes et nouvelles en vers* [. . .] *troisiesme partie*, 1671 (13 tales);
>   *Nouveaux contes* [. . .] *quatriesme partie*, Mons 1674 (16 tales);
>   ed. P. Clarac, 2 vols, 1934 (incl. 2 tales first pbd 1682, with *Le poëme du quinquina* below, 5 tales first pbd 1685, in *Ouvrages de prose et de poésie*, vol 1, and 1 tale first pbd 1696, in *Les oeuvres posthumes* below); ed. E. Pilon and F. Dauphin, 1951; ed. G. Couton, 1961. Tr. W. Congreve et al., *Tales and novels in verse*, Edinburgh 1762 (incomplete); tr. anon., *Tales*, 2 vols, London 1814; tr. anon., New York 1933.
Fables choisies, mises en vers, 1668 (cntg bks 1–6);
>   *Le soleil et les grenouilles*, 1672;
>   *Fables choisies*, 2 vols, 1678–9 (cntg bks 7–11, incl. 8 fables first pbd 1671, in *Fables nouvelles et autres poésies*);
>   *Fables choisies*, 1694 (cntg bk 12, incl. 10 fables first pbd 1685, in *Ouvrages de prose et de poésie*, vol 1);
>   ed. L. Clément, 1894; ed. F. Gohin, 2 vols, 1934; ed. G. Couton, 1962. Tr. R. Thomson, *Fables*, 1806; tr. E. Marsh, London 1931; tr. M. Ponsot, 1959.
Discours à Madame de la Sablière, 1668 (in *Fables choisies*, bk 9 above); ed. H. Busson and F. Gohin, 1938.
Les amours de Psiché et de Cupidon, 1669. Tr. J. Lockman, *The loves of Cupid and Psyche*, London 1744.
Adonis, 1669 (with *Les amours de Psiché et de Cupidon* above). Tr. D. M. Glixon, London 1957.
Recueil de poésies chrestiennes et diverses, 1671.
Poëme de la captivité de Saint Malc, 1673.
Poëme du quinquina et autres ouvrages en vers, 1682.

Les oeuvres posthumes, ed. Mme Ulrich, 1696.

Le songe de Vaux, 1729 (in *Oeuvres diverses*, vol 1 above; 9 fragments, incl. 1 first pbd 1665, in *Contes et nouvelles en vers* above, and 3 first pbd 1671, in *Fables nouvelles et autres poésies*); ed. E. Titcomb, Geneva 1967.

CLARAC, P., *La Fontaine, l'homme et l'oeuvre*, 1947; 1959 (incl. bibl.).

COLLINET, J. P., *Le monde littéraire de La Fontaine*, 1970.

COUTON, G., *La poétique de La Fontaine*, 1957.

GOHIN, F., *L'art de La Fontaine dans ses fables*, 1929.

LUGLI, V., *Il prodigio di La Fontaine*, Messina and Milan 1939.

MICHAUT, G., *La Fontaine*, 2 vols, 1913–4.

MONGRÉDIEN, G., *Recueil des textes et des documents du 17e siècle relatifs à La Fontaine*, 1974.

ROCHE, L., *La vie de Jean de La Fontaine*, 1913.

SUTHERLAND, M., *La Fontaine*, London 1953.

WADSWORTH, P., *Young La Fontaine*, Evanston (Ill) 1952.

LA ROCHEFOUCAULD, François, Duc de   1613–1680

BRIX, E., *Die Entwicklungsphasen der Maximen*, Erlangen 1913.

MARCHAND, J., *Bibliographie générale raisonnée*, 1948.

Oeuvres, ed. D. L. Gilbert and J. Gourdault, 4 vols, 1868–83; ed. L. Martin-Chauffier, 1935 (revd J. Marchand and R. Kanters, 1964).

Mémoires, Cologne 1662; 1663. Tr. anon., *The memoirs*, London 1684.

Sentences et maximes de morale, The Hague 1664 (pirate ed. cntg 189 maxims); Paris 1665 (*Réflexions, ou sentences et maximes morales*, cntg 314 maxims); 1678 (504 maxims); 1693 (532 maxims); ed. J. Marchand, 1931; ed. J. Truchet, 1967; ed. D. Secretan, Geneva and Paris 1967 (with English tr.). Tr. J. Davies, *Epictetus Junior, or maxims of modern morality*, London 1670; tr. W. Scott, *The maxims*, 1901; tr. C. Fitzgibbon, 1957; tr. L. W. Tancock, Harmondsworth 1959.

BISHOP, M., *The life and adventures of La Rochefoucauld*, Ithaca (NY) 1951.

BOURDEAU, J., *La Rochefoucauld*, 1895.

GOSSE, E., in his *Three French moralists*, London 1918.

GRUBBS, H. A., *The originality of La Rochefoucauld's Maxims*, Oxford 1929.

MAGNE, E., *Le vrai visage de La Rochefoucauld*, 1923.

MOORE, W. G., *La Rochefoucauld, his mind and art*, Oxford 1969.

MORA, E., *La Rochefoucauld*, 1965.

STROWSKI, F., *La Rochefoucauld et la mondanité*, 1925.

VINET, A., in his *Moralistes des 16e et 17e siècles*, 1904.

ZELLER, M. F., *New aspects of style in the Maxims*, Washington (DC) 1954.

LETTRES PORTUGAISES, Les 1669
(published under the name of Marianna Alcoforado, but now generally ascribed to Gabriel-Joseph de Guilleragues, 1628–1685).

DOS SANTOS, J., *Descriçao bibliográfica das ediçoes das cartas de amor de soror Mariana Alcoforado*, Lisbon 1918.

Lettres portugaises, traduites en françois, 1669; The Hague 1682 (entitled *Lettres d'amour d'une religieuse portugaise*); ed. E. Asse, Paris 1873; ed. F. Deloffre and J. Rougeot, 1962. Tr. R. L'Estrange, *Five love-letters from a nun to a cavalier*, n.p. 1678; tr. E. A. Ashwin, *The letters of a Portuguese nun*, Dyffryn (Wales) 1929.

CORDEIRO, L., *Sóror Marianna a freira portugueza*, Lisbon 1888; 1891 (enl.).
LEBOIS, A., in his *Le 17e siècle*, 1966.

MAIRET, Jean 1604–1686

Bibl. See Marsan ed. of *La Sylvie* below; also Vollmöller ed. of *La Sophonisbe* below.

La Sylvie, 1628; ed. J. Marsan, 1905 (incl. bibl.).
Chryseide et Arimand (adapt. from d'URFÉ's *L'Astrée*), Rouen 1630 (pirate ed.); Paris 1630; ed. H. C. Lancaster et al., Baltimore (Md) and Paris 1925.
La Silvanire (adapt. from d'URFÉ's *Silvanire*; with *Dissertation* advocating the unities), 1632; ed. R. Otto, Bamberg 1890.
La Virginie, 1635.
La Sophonisbe, 1635; ed. K. Vollmöller, Heilbronn 1888 (incl. bibl.); ed. C. Dédéyan, Paris 1945. Tr. C. L. Lockert, Nashville (Tenn) 1956 (in *The chief rivals of Corneille and Racine*).
Les galanteries du duc d'Ossonne, 1637; ed. E. Fournier, 1871 (in *Le théâtre français du 16e et du 17e siècle*); ed. G. Dotoli, 1972.
Le Marcantoine, ou la Cléopatre, 1637.
Le grand et dernier Solyman, 1639.
L'illustre corsaire, 1640.
Le Roland furieux, 1640.
Athénais, 1642.
La Sidonie, 1643.

BIZOS, G., *Étude sur la vie et les oeuvres de Jean de Mairet*, 1877.
BRERETON, G., in his *French tragic drama in the 16th and 17th centuries*, London 1972.

DANNHEISSER, E., *Studien zu Jean de Mairets Leben und Werke*, Ludwigshafen 1888.

LANCASTER, H. C., in his *A history of French dramatic literature in the 17th century*, vol 1, Baltimore (Md) 1929.

MALEBRANCHE, Nicolas de 1638–1715

SEBBA, G., *A preliminary bibliography*, Athens (Ga) 1959.
See also NOCE below; also Robinet ed. of *Oeuvres complètes* below.

Oeuvres complètes, ed. D. Roustan and P. Schrecker, 1938 (only 1 vol pbd); ed. A. Robinet et al., 20 vols, 1958–68 (incl. bibl. in vol 20).

De la recherche de la vérité, 3 vols, 1674–8; 3 vols, 1701 (enl.); ed. G. Lewis, 3 vols, 1946. Tr. T. Taylor, *Father Malebranche's Search after truth*, 2 vols, Oxford 1694.

Entretiens sur la métaphysique et la religion, Rotterdam 1688; 2 vols, Paris 1696 (with *Entretiens sur la mort*); ed. P. Fontana, 2 vols, 1922. Tr. M. Ginsberg, *Dialogues on metaphysics and on religion*, London 1923.

Traité de l'amour de Dieu, Lyon 1707; ed. D. Roustan, Paris 1922.

ALQUIÉ, F., *Le cartésianisme de Malebranche*, 1974.

GOUHIER, H., *La philosophie de Malebranche et son expérience religieuse*, 1926; 1948.

GUÉROULT, M., *Malebranche*, 3 vols, 1955.

NOCE, A. del, *Malebranche nel terzo centenario della nacità*, Milan 1938 (incl. bibl.).

ROBINET, A., *Système et existence dans l'oeuvre de Malebranche*, 1965.
Malebranche, l'homme et l'oeuvre, 1967.
Malebranche de l'Académie des Sciences: l'oeuvre scientifique, 1674–1715, 1970.

WALTON, C., *De la recherche du bien: a study of Malebranche's science of ethics*, The Hague 1972.

MOLIÈRE 1622–1673
(stage name of Jean-Baptiste Poquelin)

LACROIX, P., *Bibliographie moliéresque*, Nice 1872; Paris 1875.

CURRIER, T. F. and GAY, E. L., *Catalogue of the Molière collection in Harvard College library*, Cambridge (Mass) 1906.

Catalogue des ouvrages de Molière conservés au Département des Imprimés, et dans les bibliothèques Mazarine, Sainte-Geneviève, de l'Arsenal et de l'Université de Paris, 1933.

SAINTONGE, P. and CHRIST, R. W., *Fifty years of Molière studies, 1892–1941*, Baltimore (Md) 1942 (supplemented in *Modern Language Notes*, vol 59, New York 1944).

GUIBERT, A. J., *Bibliographie des oeuvres de Molière publiées au 17e siècle*, 2 vols, 1961 (supplements pbd 1965 and 1973).
See also Despois-Mesnard ed. of *Oeuvres* below.

Oeuvres, 7 vols, 1673 (1st complete ed.); 7 vols, 1674–5; 8 vols, 1682 (enl.); ed. E. Despois, P. Mesnard et al., 13 vols, 1873–93 (incl. bibl.); ed. J. Copeau, 10 vols, 1926–9; ed. M. Rat, 2 vols, 1933; ed. R. Bray, 8 vols, 1935–52; ed. R. Bray and J. Schérer, 3 vols, 1954–6; ed. R. Jouanny, 2 vols, 1956; ed. G. Couton, 2 vols, 1971.

Tr. J. Ozell, *The works*, 6 vols, London 1714.
Tr. H. Baker, J. M. Clare et al., *Select comedies*, 8 vols, London 1732.'
Tr. H. Baker and J. Miller, *Works*, 10 vols, London 1739; ed. F. C. Green, 1929 (comedies).
Tr. anon., *The works*, 10 vols, London 1755.
Tr. A. R. Waller, *The plays*, London 1902.
Tr. M. Bishop, *Eight plays*, New York 1957 (cntg *The precious damsels*, *The school for wives*, *The critique of the school for wives*, *The Versailles impromptu*, *The would-be gentleman*, *Tartuffe*, *The misanthrope*, *The physician in spite of himself*).

Les précieuses ridicules, 1660. Tr. anon., *The precious ridiculous*, New York 1888; tr. R. Waldinger, *The pretentious young ladies*, Great Neck (NY) 1959; tr. W. Fowlie, *The intellectual ladies*, New York 1962 (in *Classical French drama*).
Sganarelle, ou le cocu imaginaire, 1660. Tr. C. Molloy, *The perplex'd couple*, London 1715.
L'escole des maris, 1661.
Les facheux, 1662. Tr. anon., *The impertinents*, London 1732.
L'estourdy, 1663; ed. P. Melèse, Geneva 1951. Tr. anon., *The blunderer*, London 1732; tr. S. Foote, London 1762 (in *The comic theatre*, vol 4).
L'escole des femmes, 1663. Tr. Earl of Longford, *The school for wives*, Dublin 1948.
Le dépit amoureux, 1663. Tr. F. Spencer, *The love-tiff*, Oxford 1930.
La critique de l'escole des femmes, 1663. Tr. D. M. Frame, *The critique of the school for wives*, New York 1967 (in *Tartuffe and other plays*).
L'amour medecin, 1666. Tr. B. H. Clark, *Doctor Love*, New York, 1915.
Le medecin malgré luy, 1667; ed. J. Guicharnaud, New York 1962; ed. J. Boullé, Paris 1970. Tr. and adapt. H. Fielding, *The mock doctor*, London 1732; tr. anon., *The faggot-binder*, 1762 (in *The comic theatre*, vol 5); tr. L. Beer, *The unwilling doctor*, Boston (Mass) 1962.
Le misantrope, 1667; ed. G. Rudler, Oxford 1947; ed. E. Lop and A. Sauvage, Paris 1963; ed. S. Rossat-Mignaud, 1970. Tr. R. Wilbur, London and New York 1955.
Amphitryon, 1668; ed. P. Melèse, Geneva 1950.

L'avare, 1669; ed. C. Dullin, 1946; ed. L. Lejealle, 1971. Tr. W. Fowlie, *The miser*, Great Neck (NY) 1964.

Le Tartuffe, 1669; ed. J. Guicharnaud, New York 1962 (with *Le medecin malgré lui* above). Tr. J. M. Clare, London 1732; tr. R. W. Hartle, Indianapolis (Ind) 1965; tr. J. Neugroschel, New York 1967.

George Dandin, 1669. Tr. anon., London 1732.

Le bourgeois gentilhomme, 1671; ed. H. G. Hall, London 1966; ed. Y. Hucher, Paris 1970. Tr. M. Baker, *The merchant gentleman*, New York and London 1915; tr. J. S. Dugdale, *The would-be gentleman*, Bath 1964.

Les fourberies de Scapin, 1671; ed. L. Jouvet, 1951. Tr. Lady Gregory, *The rogueries of Scapin*, Dublin 1910 (in *The Kiltartan Molière*).

Les femmes sçavantes, 1672; ed. J. Cazalbou and D. Sevely, 1972. Tr. R. Waldinger, *The learned ladies*, Great Neck (NY) 1957.

Le malade imaginaire, 1674; ed. P. H. Nurse, London and New York 1965; ed. Y. Brunswick and P. Ginestier, Paris 1971. Tr. I. Bickerstaffe, *Dr Last in his chariot*, London 1769; tr. R. Morgan, *The imaginary invalid*, 1879.

Dom Juan, ou le festin de pierre, 1682 (in *Oeuvres*, vol 7 above); Amsterdam 1683; ed. W. D. Howarth, Oxford 1968. Tr. W. Fowlie, *Don Juan*, New York 1964.

ADAM, A., in his *Histoire de la littérature française au 17e siècle*, vol 3, 1952.

BRAY, R., *Molière, homme de théâtre*, 1954.

DESCOTES, M., *Les grands rôles du théâtre de Molière*, 1960.

GUICHARNAUD, J., *Molière, une aventure théâtrale*, 1963.

(ed.), *Molière, 20th century views*, Englewood Cliffs (NJ) 1964.

GUTWIRTH, M., *Molière, ou l'invention comique*, 1966.

HUBERT, J. D., *Molière and the comedy of intellect*, Berkeley (Calif) 1962.

JASINSKI, R., *Molière*, 1943.

LANCASTER, H. C., in his *History of French dramatic literature in the 17th century*, pt 3, 2 vols, Baltimore (Md) 1936; 1952.

MATTHEWS, B., *Molière, his life and works*, New York 1910.

MICHAUT, G., *Le jeunesse de Molière*, 1922.

Les débuts de Molière à Paris, 1925.

Les lettres de Molière, 1925.

MONGRÉDIEN, G., *Recueil des documents et des textes du 17e siècle relatifs à Molière*, 2 vols, 1965.

MOORE, W. G., *Molière, a new criticism*, Oxford 1949.

MORNET, D., *Molière*, 1943.

PELLISSON, M., *Les comédies-ballets de Molière*, 1914.

PICO, F., *Molière*, Florence 1930.

RIGAL, E., *Molière*, 1908.

ROMANO, D., *Essai sur le comique de Molière*, Berne 1950.

SARCEY, F., in his *Quarante ans de théâtre*, 1900.

TILLEY, A., *Molière*, Cambridge, 1921.

TURNELL, M., in his *The classical moment*, 1947.

MONTCHRESTIEN, Antoine de   c. 1575–1621

Bibl. See Seiver ed. of *Aman* below.

Les tragédies, Rouen 1601; 1604 (enl.); ed. L. Petit de Julleville, Paris 1891.

Sophonisbe, Caen 1596; Rouen 1601 (renamed *Les Carthaginois*, in *Les tragédies* above); ed. L. Fries, Marburg 1889.

L'Ecossaise, ou le désastre, Rouen 1601 (in *Les tragédies* above); ed. G. Michaut et al., Paris 1905; ed. C. N. Smith, London 1972.

Lacènes, ou la constance, Rouen 1601 (in *Les tragédies* above); ed. G. E. Calkins, Philadelphia (Pa) 1943.

David, ou l'adultère, Rouen 1601 (in *Les tragédies* above); ed. L. E. Dabney, Austin (Tex) 1958.

Aman, ou la vanité, Rouen 1601 (in *Les tragédies* above); ed. G. O. Seiver, Philadelphia (Pa) 1939 (incl. bibl.).

Hector, Rouen 1604 (in *Les tragédies* above); ed. C. N. Smith, London 1972 (with *L'Ecossaise* above).

Traicté de l'oeconomie politique, Rouen 1615; ed. T. Funck-Brentano, Paris 1889.

GRIFFITHS, R., *The dramatic technique of Antoine de Montchrestien*, Oxford 1970.

PASCAL, Blaise   1623–1662

MAIRE, A. and WEBER–SILVAIN, L., *Bibliographie générale des oeuvres*, 5 vols, 1925–7.

See also MESNARD below.

Oeuvres complètes, ed. L. Brunschvicg, P. Boutroux and F. Gazier, 14 vols, 1904–14; ed. F. Strowski, 3 vols, 1923–31; ed. J. Mesnard, 2 vols, 1964–70.

Tr. G. Pearce, *The miscellaneous writings*, London 1849.

Tr. D. W. Wight, *Minor works*, New York 1910.

Tr. E. Cailliet and J. C. Blankenagel, *Great shorter works*, Philadelphia (Pa) 1948 (without *Pensées* and *Provinciales*).

Tr. R. Scofield, *Scientific treatises*, Chicago (Ill) 1952.

Les lettres provinciales, 1656–7 (18 letters pbd separately, as *Lettre* [*Seconde lettre*, etc] *escrite à un provincial par un de ses amis*); Leiden ? 1657 (renamed *Les Provinciales*); ed. M. V. Maynard, 2 vols, Paris 1851; ed. A. Molinier, 2 vols, 1891; ed. H. F. Stewart, Manchester 1920; ed. Z. Tourneur, 2 vols, Paris 1944; ed. J. Steinmann, 2 vols, 1962; ed. L. Cognet, 1965. Tr. anon., *Les Provinciales, or the mysterie of Jesuitisme discover'd*, London

1657; tr. T. McCrie, *The provincial letters*, Edinburgh 1751 (new ed. Chicago (Ill) 1952).

Pensées [. . .] *sur la religion*, 1669; ed. C. Bossut, 5 vols, 1779; ed. Frantin, Dijon 1835; ed. P. Faugère, 2 vols, Paris 1844; ed. A. Molinier, 2 vols, 1877–9; ed. G. Michaut, Fribourg 1896; ed. L. Brunschvicg, Paris 1897; ed. J. Dedieu, 1937; ed. Z. Tourneur, 2 vols, 1938; ed. H. F. Stewart, London and New York 1950 (with English tr.); ed. L. Lafuma, 3 vols, Paris 1951; ed. M. Guersant, 1954 (with selected letters). Tr. J. Walker, *Monsieur Pascall's thoughts, meditations and prayers*, London 1688; tr. W. F. Trotter, *The thoughts*, London 1904 (introd. T. S. Eliot, London and New York 1931); tr. J. Warrington, *Pensées, Notes on religion and other subjects*, London and New York 1961; tr. J. M. Cohen, *The Pensées*, Harmondsworth 1961; tr. M. Turnell, London 1962; tr. A. Krailsheimer, Harmondsworth 1966.

ADAM, A., in his *Histoire de la littérature française au 17e siècle*, vol 2, 1951.

BÉGUIN, A., *Pascal par lui-même*, 1952.

Blaise Pascal, l'homme et l'oeuvre, 1956 (Cahiers de Royaumont).

BISHOP, M., *Pascal, the life of genius*, New York 1936.

BROOME, G. H., *Pascal*, London 1965.

BRUNSCHVICG, L., *Pascal*, 1932.

CHEVALIER, J., *Pascal*, 1922.

DEMOREST, J. J., *Dans Pascal, essai en partant de son style*, 1953.

DU BOS, C. in his *Approximations*, 2nd series, 1932.

FLETCHER, F. T. H., *Pascal and the mystical tradition*, Oxford 1954.

GOLDMANN, L., *Le dieu caché*, 1955. Tr. P. Thody, *The hidden god*, London 1963.

Pascal présent: 1662–1962, Clermont-Ferrand 1963.

LANSON, G., in his *L'art de la prose*, 1909.

LE GUERN, M., *Pascal et Descartes*, 1971.

MESNARD, J., *Pascal, l'homme et l'oeuvre*, 1951.

Pascal et les Roannez, 2 vols, Bruges 1965 (incl. bibl. in vol 2).

RUSSIER, J., *La foi selon Pascal*, 2 vols, 1949.

SAINTE-BEUVE, C. A. de, *Port-Royal*, vols 2–3, 1842–8.

SPOERRI, T., *Der verborgene Pascal*, Hamburg 1955.

STEWART, H. F., *The secret of Pascal*, Cambridge 1941.

STROWSKI, F., *Histoire du sentiment religieux en France au 17e siècle, Pascal et son temps*, 3 vols, 1907–8.

TOPLISS, P., *The rhetoric of Pascal*, Leicester 1966.

PERRAULT, Charles   1628–1703

DELARUE, P. and TENEZE, M. L., in their *Le conte populaire français, catalogue raisonné*, 2 vols, 1957–65.

See also NOURRY below.

Oeuvres complètes, ed. J. J. Pauvert and M. Soriano, 3 vols, 1968–9.

Saint Paulin, évesque de Nole, 1686.

Le siècle de Louis le Grand, 1687. Tr. M. Bladen, *The age of Lewis the Great,* London 1705 (in *Fénelon's Characters and criticisms upon the ancient and modern orators*).

Paralèlle des anciens et des modernes, 4 vols, 1688–92; ed. M. Imdahl, W. Iser and H. R. Jauss, Munich 1964.

L'apologie des femmes, 1694. Tr. R. Gant, *The vindication of wives,* London 1954.

Grisélidis nouvelle, avec le conte de Peau d'Asne, et celui des Souhaits ridicules (tales in verse), 1694 (*Grisélidis* first pbd 1691, as *La marquise de Salusses, ou la patience de Grisélidis*); 1695 (with *Préface*);
> *Histoires ou contes du temps passé* (tales in prose), 1697;
>> ed. A. Lang, Oxford 1888 (as *Popular tales*); ed. E. Nourry, Paris 1923 (in his *Les contes de Perrault* below); ed. E. Henriot, 1928; ed. J. Barchilon, 2 vols, New York 1956 (as *Tales of Mother Goose*); ed. G. Rouger, Paris 1967. Tr. G. Miège and R. Samber, *Histories or tales of past times,* London 1729; tr. G. Brereton, *Fairy tales,* Harmondsworth 1957; tr. A. E. Johnson et al., *Complete fairy tales,* London 1962; tr. R. Howard, introd. Simone de BEAUVOIR, *Bluebeard and other fairy tales,* London and New York 1964 (introd. tr. P. Green).

Les hommes illustres qui ont paru en France pendant ce siècle, 2 vols, 1696–1700. Tr. J. Ozell, *Characters historical and panegyrical of the greatest men that have appear'd in France during the last century,* 2 vols, London 1704–5.

Mémoires, Avignon 1759; ed. P. Bonnefon, Paris 1909.

HALLAYS, A., *Les Perrault,* 1926.

NOURRY, E., *Les contes de Perrault et les récits parallèles, leurs origines,* 1923 (incl. text. of *Contes* above, and bibl.).

SORIANO, M., *Les contes de Perrault,* 1968.

QUINAULT, Philippe   1635–1688

Théâtre choisi, ed. V. Fournel, 1882.

La mort de Cyrus, 1659.
Astrate, roy de Tyr, 1665.
La mère coquette, 1666; ed. E. Gros, 1926.
Amalasonte, 1666.
Cadmus et Hermione, 1673.
Armide, 1686. Tr. C. Aveling et al., *Armida,* London 1906; tr. M. and E. Radford et. al., n.p. 1936.

BUIJTENDORP, J. B. A., *Philippe Quinault, sa vie, ses tragédies et ses tragi-comédies,* Amsterdam 1928.

GROS, E., *Philippe Quinault, sa vie et son oeuvre*, Paris and Aix-en-Provence 1926.

LANCASTER, H. C., in his *A history of French dramatic literature in the 17th century*, pt 3, vol 1, Baltimore (Md) 1936; 1952.

RACAN, Honorat de Bueil de   1589–1670

Bibl. See ARNOULD below.

Oeuvres, 2 vols, 1724; ed. T. de La Tour, 2 vols, 1857; ed. L. Arnould, 2 vols, 1930–7 (cntg poetry and *Les bergeries*).

Translated in anthologies, incl. *Flowers of France*, tr. J. Payne, London 1907.

Les bergeries, 1625; 1635; ed. P. Camo, 1929 (with other poems).
Les sept pseaumes, 1631; 1660 (in *Dernières oeuvres* below).
Odes sacrées, 1651; 1660 (in *Dernières oeuvres* below).
Dernières oeuvres et poésies chrestiennes, 1660.
La vie de Malherbe, 1672 (in *Divers traitez d'histoire, de morale, et d'éloquence*); ed. P. Martinon, 1926 (in *Les poésies de Malherbe*).

ADAM, A., in his *Histoire de la littérature française au 17e siècle*, vol 1, 1949.

ARNOULD, L., *Un gentilhomme de lettres au 17e siècle, Honorat de Bueil, seigneur de Racan*, 1901 (incl. bibl. of works).

RACINE, Jean   1639–1699

PONS, A. J., *Les éditions illustrées*, 1878.

WILLIAMS, E. E., *Racine depuis 1885; bibliographie raisonnée des livres, articles, comptes-rendus critiques*, Baltimore (Md) and London 1940.

GUIBERT, A. J., *Bibliographie des oeuvres de Racine publiées au 17e siècle et oeuvres posthumes*, 1968.

GOLDMANN, L., *Situation de la critique racinienne*, 1971.

See also Mesnard ed. of *Oeuvres* below.

Oeuvres, 2 vols, 1697 (cntg 12 plays); ed. P. Mesnard, 10 vols, 1865–73 (revd 1885, incl. bibl. in vol 7); ed. R. Picard et al., 2 vols, 1951–2.
Théâtre, ed. G. Truc, 4 vols, 1929–30; ed. P. Mélèse, 5 vols, 1951–3.

Tr. R. B. Boswell, *The dramatic works of Jean Racine*, n.p. 1889.
Tr. C. L. Lockert, *The best plays of Racine*, Princeton (NJ) 1936.
  Racine's mid-career tragedies, Princeton (NJ) 1958.
Tr. K. Muir, *Five plays*, London 1960 (*Andromache, Britannicus, Berenice, Phaedra, Athaliah*).
Tr. G. Dillon, *Three plays*, Chicago (Ill) and London 1961 (*Phaedra, Andromache, Britannicus*).

Tr. J. Cairncross, *Iphigenia, Phaedra, Athalia*, Harmondsworth 1963.
Tr. S. Solomon, *The complete plays*, New York 1967.

La nymphe de la Seine, 1660.
Ode sur la convalescence du roy, 1663.
La renommée aux muses, n.p. 1663.
La thebaÿde, 1664; 1697 (in *Oeuvres* above).
Alexandre le Grand, 1665; 1697 (in *Oeuvres* above). Tr. J. Ozell, *Alexander the Great*, London 1714.
Lettre à l'auteur des hérésies imaginaires, et des deux Visionnaires, 1666; ed. G. Truc, 1933 (in *Port-Royal*).
Andromaque, 1668; 1697 (in *Oeuvres* above); ed. P. Grosclaude, 1954. Tr. J. Crowne et al., *Andromache*, London 1675; tr. J. Hobday, Bath 1965; tr. J. Neugroschel, New York 1967.
Les plaideurs, 1669; 1697 (in *Oeuvres* above); ed. V. L. Saulnier, 1950. Tr. J. Ozell, *The litigants*, London 1715; tr. I. Brown, New York 1871.
Britannicus, 1670; 1697 (in *Oeuvres* above); ed. R. Moriset, 1933; ed. V. L. Saulnier, 1950 (with *Les plaideurs* above). Tr. J. Ozell, London 1714; tr. E. Vaughn, San Francisco (Calif) 1962.
Bérénice, 1671; 1697 (in *Oeuvres* above); ed. V. L. Saulnier, 1950 (with *Les plaideurs* and *Britannicus* above). Tr. John Masefield, London 1922.
Bajazet, 1672; 1697 (in *Oeuvres* above); ed. X. de Courville, 1947. Tr. Y. M. Martin, London 1964.
Mithridate, 1673; 1697 (in *Oeuvres* above); ed. G. Rudler, Oxford 1943. Tr. H. D. Spoerl, *Mithridates*, Tufts College (Mass) 1926.
Iphigénie, 1675; 1697 (in *Oeuvres* above). Tr. A. Wallace, *Iphiginia*, Worthing 1861; tr. J. Gibson, London 1892.
Phèdre & Hippolyte, 1677; 1697 (in *Oeuvres* above); ed. R. C. Knight, Manchester 1943; ed. J. L. Barrault, Paris 1946. Tr. anon., *Phedra*, London 1776; tr. M. Rawlings, *Phèdre*, 1961.
Idylle sur la paix, n.p. 1685.
Esther, 1689; 1697 (in *Oeuvres* above); ed. C. M. Des Granges, 1929. Tr. T. Brereton, London 1715; tr. and adapt. John Masefield, London 1922.
Athalie, 1691; 1697 (in *Oeuvres* above); ed. G. Le Roy, 1952. Tr. W. Duncombe, *Athaliah*, London 1722; tr. T. Constable, 1898 (in *The great French triumvirate*).
Cantiques spirituels, 1694.
Abrégé de l'histoire de Port-Royal, 2 vols, Cologne 1742 (first pt); Vienne and Paris 1767 (full text); ed. G. Truc, 1933 (in *Port-Royal*).
Principes de la tragédie, ed. E. Vinaver, Manchester 1944.

Lettres d'Uzès, ed. J. J. Brousson, Uzès 1929; ed. J. Dubu, 1963.

AUERBACH, E., in his *Mimesis*, Berne 1946. Tr. W. R. Trask, Princeton (NJ) 1953.
BARTHES, R., *Sur Racine*, 1963. Tr. R. Howard, *On Racine*, New York 1964.

BRERETON, G., *Jean Racine, a critical biography*, London 1951.

CLARK, A. F. B., *Jean Racine*, Cambridge (Mass) and London 1939.

ECCLES, F. Y., *Racine in England*, Oxford 1922.

EDWARDS, M., *La tragédie racinienne*, 1972.

FRANCE, P., *Racine's rhetoric*, Oxford 1965.

GIRAUDOUX, J., *Racine*, 1930. Tr. P. M. Jones, Cambridge 1938.

GOLDMANN, L., *Jean Racine, dramaturge*, 1956. Tr. A. Hamilton, Cambridge 1972.

HUBERT, J. D., *Essai d'exégèse racinienne*, 1956.

JASINSKI, R., *Vers le vrai Racine*, 2 vols, 1958.

KNIGHT, R. C., *Racine et la Grèce*, 1950.

LAPP, J. C., *Aspects of Racinian tragedy*, Toronto 1955.

MAULNIER, T., *Racine*, 1935; 1954.

MAURIAC, F., *La vie de Jean Racine*, 1928.

ORCIBAL, J., *La genèse d'Esther et d'Athalie*, 1950.

PICARD, R., *La carrière de Jean Racine*, 1956.

> *Corpus racinianum: recueil-inventaire des textes et documents du 17e siècle concernant Jean Racine*, 1956 (supplement pbd 1961).

POMMIER, J., *Aspects de Racine*, 1954.

ROUBINE, J. J., *Lectures de Racine*, 1971.

STRACHEY, G. L., in his *Landmarks in French literature*, New York and London 1912.

> In his *Books and characters*, New York 1922.

TURNELL, M., *Jean Racine, dramatist*, London 1972.

VINAVER, E., *Racine et la poésie tragique*, 1951. Tr. P. M. Jones, *Racine and poetic tragedy*, Manchester 1955.

VOSSLER, K., *Jean Racine*, Munich 1926. Tr. I. and F. McHugh, New York, 1972.

WEINBERG, B., *The art of Jean Racine*, Chicago (Ill) 1963.

REGNARD, Jean-François   1655–1709

COMPAIGNON DE MARCHÉVILLE, M., *Bibliographie et iconographie*, 1877.

Oeuvres, 5 vols, Rouen and Paris 1731; ed. M. Beuchot et al., 2 vols, Paris 1854; ed. E. Fournier, 1875.

Attendez-moy sous l'orme, 1694.

Satyre contre les maris, 1694; ed. E. Pilon, 1920. Tr. R. Grant, *Satire against husbands*, London 1954.

Le joueur, 1697; ed. R. Gautheron, 1921. Tr. S. Carroll, *The Gamester*, London 1705.

Le distrait, 1698.

Le retour impréveu, 1700. Tr. Henry Fielding, *The intriguing chambermaid,* London 1734.

Les folies amoureuses, 1704; ed. A. Rion, 1878.

Le légataire universel, 1708; ed. O. Grosjean, Brussels 1942. Tr. R. Aldington, *The residuary legatee,* London 1923.

La Provençale, 1731 (in *Oeuvres* above); ed. E. Pilon, 1920 (with *Satyre contre les maris* above).

CALAME, A., *Regnard, sa vie et son oeuvre,* Algiers 1960 (incl. bibl.).

HALLAYS, A., *La vie aventureuse de Regnard,* 1929.

LANCASTER, H. C., in his *A history of French dramatic literature in the seventeenth century,* vol 4, Baltimore (Md) 1940; 1952.

in his *Sunset,* 1945; 1954.

RÉGNIER, Mathurin   1573–1613

Cherrier, H., *Bibliographie,* 1884.

Oeuvres complètes, ed. E. Courbet, 1875; ed. J. Plattard, 1930; ed. G. Raibaud, 1958.

Les premières oeuvres, 1608 (incl. 10 satires and *Discours au Roy*); 1609 (as *Les satyres,* incl. *Satires 1–12*); 1612 (with *Satire 13* below); 1613 (with *Satires 14–17,* 3 elegies and 6 other poems); Leiden 1652 (as *Satyres et autres oeuvres,* with *Satires 18–19* and other poems); ed. F. Fleuret and L. Perceau, 1923 (in *Satires françaises des 16e et 17e siècles*).

Macette (Satire 13), 1612 (in *Les satyres* above); ed. F. Brunot et al., 1900.

ADAM, A., in his *Histoire de la littérature française au 17e siècle,* vol 1, 1948.

VIANEY, J., *Mathurin Régnier,* 1896.

RETZ, Paul de Gondi, Cardinal de   1613–1679

Oeuvres, ed. A. Feillet, J. Gourdault, R. Chantelauze and C. Cochin, 11 vols, 1870–1920.

Mémoires, Pamphlets, Conjuration de Fiesque, Correspondance, ed. C. Verrier, 1909.

La conjuration du comte Jean-Louis de Fiesque (adapt. from Mascardi), 1665 (circulated from 1632 in ms); ed. D. A. Watts, Oxford 1967.

Mémoires, 3 vols, Amsterdam and Nancy 1717; 7 vols, Amsterdam 1731–8; ed. G. Mongrédien, 4 vols, 1935. Tr. D. Ogg, *Memoirs,* 2 vols, London 1917.

BATTIFOL, L., *Le cardinal de Retz,* 1929.

LORRIS, P. G., *Le cardinal de Retz, un agitateur au 17e siècle,* 1956.

ROTROU, Jean de   1609–1650

Bibl. See Leiner ed. of *Venceslas* below.

Oeuvres, ed. Viollet-le-Duc, 5 vols, 1820.
Théâtre choisi, ed. L. de Ronchaud, 2 vols, 1883 (cntg *Hercule mourant, Antigone* and *Dom Bernard de Cabrère*).

L'hypocondriaque, 1631; ed. F. Gohin, 1924.
Hercule mourant, 1636; ed. D. A. Watts, Exeter 1971.
Agésilan de Colchos, 1637.
Le filandre, 1637.
Clorinde, 1637.
Antigone, 1639.
La belle Alphrède, 1639.
Le Bélissaire, 1644.
La soeur, 1647; ed. A. Tissier, 1970.
Le véritable St Genest, 1647; ed. T. F. Crane, New York 1907; ed. R. W. Ladborough, Cambridge 1954; ed. E. T. Dubois, Geneva 1972. Tr. C. L. Lockert, Nashville (Tenn) 1968 (in *More plays by rivals of Corneille and Racine*).
Dom Bernard de Cabrère, 1647.
Venceslas, 1648; ed. T. F. Crane, New York 1907 (with *Saint Genest* above); ed. W. Leiner, Saarbrücken 1956 (incl. bibl.). Tr. C. L. Lockert, Nashville (Tenn) 1956 (in *The chief rivals of Corneille and Racine*).
Cosroës, 1649; ed. J. Schérer, 1950. Tr. C. L. Lockert, Nashville (Tenn) 1956 (in *The chief rivals of Corneille and Racine*).

CHARDON, H., *La vie de Rotrou mieux connue*, 1884.
KNUTSON, H. C., *The ironic game, a study of Rotrou's comic theatre*, Berkeley (Calif) 1966.
MOREL, J., *Rotrou, dramaturge de l'ambiguité*, 1968.
NELSON, R. J., *Immanence and transcendence: the theatre of Jean Rotrou*, Columbus (Ohio) 1969.
SCHÉRER, J., in his *La dramaturgie classique en France*, 1950.
VAN BAELEN, J., *Rotrou*, 1965.

SAINT-AMANT, Antoine Girard de   1594–1661

LAGNY, J., *Bibliographie des éditions anciennes des oeuvres*, 1961.
See also GOURIER below.

Oeuvres complètes, ed. C. L. Livet, 2 vols, 1855 (incomplete); ed. J. Lagny and J. Bailbé, 1968 onwards (4 vols pbd).
Oeuvres poétiques, ed. L. Vérane, 1930 (selection).

Translated in anthologies, incl. *Penguin book of French verse*, vol 2.

La Solitude, 1627 (in *Les dernières oeuvres de Theophile*). Tr. anon., London 1678 (in *Poems by the most deservedly admired Mrs Katherine Philips*).
Les oeuvres, 1629 (incl. *La Solitude* above).
    La suitte des oeuvres, 1631.
    Seconde partie, 1643 (incl. *Caprice*).
    Troisiesme partie, 1649.
    Dernier recueil de diverses poësies, 1658.
La Rome ridicule n.p. c. 1640.
Le passage de Gibraltar, 1640.
Moyse sauvé, 1650.

ADAM, A., in his *Histoire de la littérature française au 17e siècle*, vols 1–3, 1948–56.
AUDIBERT, R. and BOUVIER, R., *Saint-Amant, capitaine du Parmasse*, 1946.
BORTON, S. L., *Six modes of sensibility in Saint-Amant*, The Hague 1966.
BUFFUM, I., in his *Studies in the baroque*, New Haven (Conn) 1957.
GOURIER, F., *Etude des oeuvres poétiques de Saint-Amant*, Geneva and Paris 1961 (incl. bibl.).
LAGNY, J., *Le poète Saint-Amant*, 1964.

SAINT-ÉVREMOND, Charles de   c. 1613–1703

Bibl. See BARNWELL below.

Oeuvres, ed. R. de Planhol, 3 vols, 1927 (selection); ed. R. Ternois, 4 vols, 1962–9 (prose works).
Critique littéraire, ed. M. Wilmotte, 1921 (selection).
Textes choisis, ed. A. Niderst, 1970.

Tr. anon., *The works*, 2 vols, London 1700; 3 vols, 1928 (enl.).

La comédie des Académistes (in collab.), n.p. 1650 (circulated from c. 1640 in ms); 1680 (renamed *Les Académiciens*, in *Oeuvres meslées*, vol 8 below); ed. G. L. Van Roosbroeck, New York 1931; ed. P. Carile, Milan 1969.
Conversation du maréchal d'Hocquincourt avec le P. Canaye, Emmerich 1687 (in collective work *Le retour des pièces choisies*).
Oeuvres meslées, 11 vols, 1668–84; 2 vols, 1689–92 (enl.); ed. P. Des Maizeaux, 2 vols, London 1705 (enl. and revd, 5 vols, Amsterdam 1726); ed. L. de Nordis, Rome 1966. Tr. J. Dryden et al., *Miscellaneous essays*, London 1692–4.

Lettres, ed. R. Ternois, 2 vols, 1967–8.
Tr. anon., ed. J. Hayward, *The letters*, London 1930 (mainly based on trs in *The works* above).

BARNWELL, H. T., *Les idées morales et critiques de Saint-Evremond*, 1957 (incl. bibl.).

COHEN, G., *Le séjour de Saint-Evremond en Hollande*, 1926.

DANIELS, W. M., *Saint-Evremond en Angleterre*, Versailles 1907.

HOPE, Q. M., *Saint-Evremond: the Honnête Homme as critic*, Bloomington (Ind) 1962.

SCHMIDT, A. M., *Saint-Evremond, ou l'humaniste impur*, 1932.

SALES, (Saint) François de   1567–1622

BRASIER, V. and MORGANTI, E., *Bibliografia salesiana; opere e scritti riguardenti s. Francesco di Sales, 1623–55*, Turin and Milan 1956.

Les oeuvres, Toulouse 1637; 2 vols, 1641; ed. H. B. Mackey and J. J. Navatel, 26 vols, Annecy 1892–1932; ed. A. Ravier and R. Devos, Paris 1969 (main works).

Tr. H. B. Mackey, *Library of Saint François de Sales. Works of this doctor of the Church*, 5 vols, London 1886–1910 (incl. *Life* by Jean-Pierre Camus in vol 5).

Défense de l'estendart de la saincte croix, Lyon 1600.

Introduction à la vie dévote, Lyon 1609; 1619; ed. C. Florisoone, 2 vols, Paris 1930. Tr. A. Ross, *Introduction to the devout life*, London 1924; tr. and ed. J. K. Ryan, New York 1950.

Traité de l'amour de Dieu, Lyon 1616; ed. B. Laurès, 2 vols, Paris 1953. Tr. M. Car, *A treatise of the love of God*, Douai 1630; tr. H. B. Mackey, *The love of God*, London and Edinburgh 1931 (abr.).

Sermons, 1641 (in *Oeuvres* above).

Lettres, Lyon 1626; 6 vols, Paris 1758; 11 vols, Annecy 1900–23 (in *Oeuvres*, vols 11–21 above). Tr. E. Stopp, *Selected letters*, London 1960.

HAMON, A. J., *Vie de saint François de Sales, évêque et prince de Genève*, 2 vols, 1854; ed. J. G. Gouthier and G. Letourneau, 2 vols, 1920.

LAJEUNIE, E. J., *Saint François de Sales, l'homme, la pensée, l'action*, 2 vols, 1966.

VINCENT, F., *Le travail du style chez saint François de Sales*, 1923.

SCARRON, Paul   1610–1660

MAGNE, E., *Bibliographie générale des oeuvres*, 1924.

Oeuvres, 2 vols, 1659; 2 vols, 1663 (enl.); ed. A. A. de La Martinière, 10 vols, Amsterdam 1737 (incomplete); 7 vols, Paris 1786.

Poésies diverses, ed. M. Cauchie, 2 vols, 1947–8.

Tr. J. Davies of Kidwelly, *Scarron's novels*, London 1694.

Tr. T. Brown, J. Savage et al., *The whole comical works of Monsieur Scarron*, London 1700 (ed. B. Boyce, 2 vols, New York 1968, entitled *The comical romance* and *The innocent adultery and other short novels*).

Recueil de quelques vers burlesques, 1643; 1648 (enl.; renamed *Recueil des oeuvres burlesques*).

    Suitte des oeuvres burlesques, 1644.

    Les oeuvres burlesques [. . .] *IIIe partie,* 1651.

Typhon, ou la gigantomachie, 1644. Tr. J. Phillips, *Typhon, or the gyants war with the gods,* London 1665; tr. B. Mandeville, 1704.

Le Jodelet, ou le Me valet, 1645.

Le Virgile travesty en vers burlesques, 7 vols, 1648–53; 8 vols, 1659 (with bk 8); ed. V. Fournel, 1858. Tr. C. Cotton, *Scarrönides,* London 1715 (in *The genuine works*); tr. anon., 1804.

Le romant comique, 2 vols, 1651–7; ed. E. Magne, 1938; ed. H. Bénac, 2 vols, 1951; ed. A. Adam, 1958 (in *Romanciers du 17e siècle*). Tr. anon., 2 vols, London 1651–7; tr. 'J.B.', *The comical romance,* London 1665; tr. O. Goldsmith, 2 vols, 1775.

Epistres chagrines, 1652–60 (addressed to Rousteau, d'Albret, d'Elbène and Madeleine de Scudéry). Tr. J. Davies of Kidwelly, *Monsieur Scarron's letters, to persons of the greatest eminence and quality,* London 1677.

Don Japhet d'Arménie, 1653; ed. R. Garapon, 1967.

Le testament, 1660; 1660 (in *Le burlesque malade*).

Les nouvelles tragi-comiques, 1661 (cntg 4 stories first pbd separately 1655–7: *La précaution; Les hypocrites; L'adultère innocent,* tr. anon., *The innocent adultery,* n.p. 1722; and *Plus d'effets que de parolles*); ed. J. Cassou, 1948.

La fausse apparence, 1663.

ARMAS, F. A. de, *Paul Scarron,* New York 1972.

BAR, F., *Le genre burlesque en France au 17e siècle,* 1960.

CHARDON, H., *Scarron inconnu, et les types des personnages du Roman comique,* 2 vols, 1903–4.

MAGNE, E., *Scarron et son milieu,* 1905; 1924.

MOORE, F. W., *The drama of Paul Scarron,* New Haven (Conn) 1956.

MORILLOT, P., *Scarron et le genre burlesque,* 1888.

PHELPS, N. F., *The queen's invalid,* Baltimore (Md) 1951.

SCUDÉRY, Georges de   1601–1667

MONGRÉDIEN, G., *Bibliographie des oeuvres de Georges et de Madeleine de Scudéry,* 1933–5 (in *Revue d'histoire littéraire de France,* vols 40 and 42).

Published 16 plays in all; also collaborated with his sister Madeleine on *Le grand Cyrus,* 1649–53.

Oeuvres poétiques, 1631.

La mort de Caesar, 1636; ed. H. L. Cook, New York 1930.

Le prince déguisé, 1636; ed. B. Matulka, New York 1929.

Observations sur Le Cid, 1637; ed. A. Gastí, 1898 (in *La querelle du Cid*).
L'amour tirannique, 1639; ed. V. C. Fairholt, Chicago (Ill) 1938.
Poésies diverses, 1649.
Alaric, ou Rome vaincue, 1654.

CLERC, C., *Un Matamore des lettres*, 1929.
MONGRÉDIEN, G., in his *La vie littéraire au 17e siècle*, 1947.

SCUDÉRY Madeleine de   1607–1701

MONGRÉDIEN G., *Bibliographie des oeuvres de Georges et de Madeleine de Scudéry*, 1933–5 (in *Revue d'histoire littéraire de France*, vols 40 and 42). See also MacDOUGALL below.

Mademoiselle de Scudéry, sa vie et sa correspondance, avec un choix de ses poesies, ed. Rathéry and Boutron, 1873.

Published 8 novels in all, 1641–71, under brother Georges' name.

Ibraham, ou l'illustre Bassa, 4 vols, 1641; ed. E. Seillière, Monaco 1923 (as *Isabelle Grimaldi*). Tr. H. Cogan, *Ibrahim, or the illustrious Bassa*, London 1652; tr. E. Settle, 1677.
Artamène, ou le grand Cyrus (in collab. with brother Georges), 10 vols, 1649–53. Tr. 'F.G.', *Artamenes, or the Grand Cyrus*, 5 vols, London 1653–5.
Clélie, histoire romaine, 10 vols, 1654–61. Tr. J. Davies and G. Havers, *Clelia*, 5 vols, London 1656–61.
Mathilde, 1667.
Conversations sur divers sujets, 1680. Tr. F. Spense, *Conversations upon several subjects*, 2 vols, London 1683 (part tr.).

ARAGONNÈS, C., *Madeleine de Scudéry, reine du tendre*, 1934.
MacDOUGALL, D., *Madeleine de Scudéry, her romantic life and death*, London 1938 (incl. bibl.).
MAGENDIE, M., in his *Le roman français au 17e siècle*, 1932.
MONGRÉDIEN, G., *Madeleine de Scudéry et son salon*, 1946.

SÉVIGNÉ, Madame de   1626–1696
(Marie de Rabutin-Chantal, Marquise de Sévigné)

[*Lettres*], 1696 (6 in Bussy-Rabutin's *Mémoires*); Amsterdam and Paris 1775 (109, as *Lettres* [. . .] *au comte de Bussy-Rabutin*);
    Lettres choisies [. . .] *à Madame de Grignan*, ed. Voltaire?, Troyes 1725 (31 letters);

Lettres, 2 vols, ed. Thiriot, Rouen 1726 (78 letters); 2 vols, The Hague 1726 (117 letters); ed. Chevalier de Perrin, 6 vols, Paris 1734–7 (614 letters, as *Recueil des lettres*); ed. Chevalier de Perrin, 8 vols, 1754 (747 letters); *Lettres* [. . .] *à Monsieur de Pomponne*, Amsterdam 1756; Paris 1773 (enl.); *Lettres inédites*, ed. C. Capmas, 2 vols, 1876; ed. L. J. N. Monmerqué, A. Régnier and P. Mesnard, 14 vols, 1862–5 (without *Lettres inédites* above); ed. E. Gérard-Gailly, 3 vols, 1953–7; ed. N. Scarlyn Williams, London 1955 (selection); ed. M. Jouhandeau, Paris 1959 (selection); ed. R. Duchêne, 1972 onwards (1 vol pbd). Tr. anon., *Letters to the Countess de Grignan*, London 1727; tr. anon., *Letters from the Marchioness of Sévigné to her daughter*, 10 vols, 1764; tr. R. Aldington, *Letters*, 2 vols, 1927; tr. anon., 1928; tr. H. T. Barnwell, *Selected letters*, London and New York 1960.

BAILLY, A., *Madame de Sévigné*, 1955.

BRUNET, G., in his *Evocations littéraires*, 1931.

CELARIÉ, H., *Madame de Sévigné, sa famille et ses amis*, 1926.

CORDELIER, J., *Madame de Sévigné par elle-même*, 1967.

DUCHÊNE, R., *Madame de Sévigné*, 1968.

Madame de Sévigné et la lettre d'amour, 1970.

GÉRARD-GAILLY, E., *Madame de Sévigné*, 1971.

KAUFFMANN, L., *Die Briefe der Madame de Sévigné*, Cologne 1954.

TILLEY, A. A., *Madame de Sévigné*, Cambridge 1936.

WALCKENAER, C. A., *Mémoires touchant la vie et les écrits de Marie de Rabutin-Chantal, dame de Bourbilly, marquise de Sévigné*, 5 vols, 1842–52.

SOREL DE SOUVIGNY, Charles   c. 1600–1674

Bibl. See ROY below.

Les nouvelles françoises, 1623; 1645 (enl.).

Histoire comique de Francion, 1623; 1633 (enl.); ed. E. Colombey, 1858; ed. A. Thérive, 1922 (bk 1 only); ed. E. Roy, 4 vols, 1924–31; ed. A. Adam, 1958 (in *Romanciers du 17e siècle*).

Le berger extravagant, 1627; 3 vols, 1627–8. Tr. anon., *The extravagant shepherd*, n.p. 1653.

Polyandre, 1648.

GODENNE, R., in his *Histoire de la nouvelle française aux 17e et 18e siècles*, Geneva 1970.

ROY, E., *La vie et les oeuvres de Charles Sorel*, 1891 (incl. bibl.).

SUTCLIFFE, F. E., *Le réalisme de Charles Sorel*, 1965.

TALLEMANT DES RÉAUX, Gédéon 1619?-1690?

Bibl. See MAGNE below.

Les historiettes, ed. L. J. N. de Monmerqué et al., 6 vols, 1834-5; (revd P. Paris, L. J. N. de Monmerqué et al., 9 vols, 1854-60); ed. G. Mongrédien, 8 vols, 1932-4; ed. A. Adam and G. Delessault, 2 vols, 1960-1. Tr. H. Miles, *Miniature portraits,* London 1925 (selection); tr. anon., *Love-tales from Tallemant,* 1925.

BRUN, P., in his *Autour du 17e siècle,* Grenoble 1901.
GOSSE, E. W., *Tallemant des Réaux,* Oxford 1925.
MAGNE, E., *Tallemant des Réaux,* 2 vols, 1921-2 (incl. bibl.).
WORTLEY, W. V., *Tallemant des Réaux, the man through his style,* The Hague and Paris 1969.

THÉOPHILE DE VIAU

See VIAU, Théophile de.

TRISTAN L'HERMITE   c. 1601-1655
(pseudonym of François l'Hermite)

CARRIAT, A., *Bibliographie des oeuvres,* Limoges 1955.
See also Van Bever collected ed. below.

Théâtre complet, ed. E. Girard, 8 vols, 1900-4.
Les amours [etc], ed. A. van Bever, 1909 (main works; incl. bibl.).
Les plaintes d'Acante et autres oeuvres, ed. J. Madeleine, 1909 (with *Les amours*).
Poésies chrestiennes, ed. F. Lachèvre, 1941.
Poésies choisies, ed. P. A. Wadsworth, 1962.

A few poems translated in anthologies.

Les plaintes d'Achante, 1633.
La Mariane, 1635; 1637; ed. J. Madeleine, 1917; ed. P. A. Jannini, Varese and Milan 1953 (revd Paris 1970). Tr. C. L. Lockert, Nashville (Tenn) 1956 (in *The chief rivals of Corneille and Racine*).
Les amours, 1638 (incl. poems first pbd in *Les plaintes d'Achante* above); ed. P. Camo, 1925.
Panthée, 1639.
La lyre, 1641.
Le page disgracié, 2 vols, 1643; ed. A. Dietrich, 1898; ed. J. Savarin, 1924.
La mort de Chrispe, 1645; ed. E. Girard, 1904.
La mort de Senèque, 1645; ed. J. Madeleine, 1919. Tr. C. L. Lockert, Nashville (Tenn) 1968 (in *More plays by rivals of Corneille and Racine*).

La folie du sage, 1645; ed. J. Madeleine, 1936.
Les vers héroiques, 1648; ed. C. M. Grisé, Geneva 1967.
Le parasite, ed. P. Quinault, 1654; ed. J. Madeleine, 1934.
Osman, 1656. Tr. C. L. Lockert, Nashville (Tenn) 1968 (in *More plays by rivals of Corneille and Racine*).

BERNARDIN, N. M., *Un précurseur de Racine*, 1895.
CARRIAT, A., *Tristan, ou l'éloge d'un poète*, Limoges 1955.
SCHÉRER, J., in his *La dramaturgie classique en France*, 1950.
VALLE, D. della, *Il teatro di Tristan l'Hermite*, Turin 1965.

URFÉ, Honoré d'   c. 1567–1625

See Vaganay ed. of *L'Astrée* below; also Charlier ed. of *Les amours d'Alcidon* below.

L'Astrée (completed by d'Urfé's secretary, Balthazar Bars), 5 vols, 1607–28; ed. H. Vaganay, 5 vols, Lyon 1925–8 (incl. bibl. of eds 1607–47); ed. M. Magendie, Paris 1927 (extracts). Tr. anon., *The history of Astrea, The first part*, London 1620; tr. J. Davies, *Astraea*, 3 vols, 1657–8.
Les amours d'Alcidon, 1619 (as episode in *L'Astrée*, vol 3, above); ed. G. Charlier, 1920 (incl. bibl.).
La Sylvanire, 1627.

EHRMANN, J., *Un paradis désespéré: l'amour et l'illusion dans l'Astrée*, New Haven (Conn) and Paris 1963.
MAGENDIE, M., *L'Astrée d'Honoré d'Urfé*, 1929.
REURE, C. O., *La vie et les oeuvres de Honoré d'Urfé*, 1910.

VAUGELAS, Claude Favre de   c. 1585–1650

Remarques sur la langue françoise, 1647; ed. T. Corneille, 2 vols, 1687; ed. J. Streicher, 1934;
    Nouvelles remarques sur la langue françoise, 1690;
ed. A. Chassang, 2 vols, Versailles, 1880.

ADAM, A., *Pour le troisième centenaire des Remarques*, June 1947 (in *Mercure de France*).
STREICHER, J. (ed.), *Commentaires sur les Remarques de Vaugelas*, 2 vols, 1936.

VIAU, Théophile de   c. 1590–1626

Bibl. See Lefèvre ed. of *Oeuvres poétiques* below; also LACHÈVRE below.

Les oeuvres, 1626; ed. C. Alleaume, 2 vols, 1855–6.

Oeuvres poétiques, ed. L. R. Lefèvre, 1926 (selection; incl. bibl.); ed. J. Streicher, 2 vols, Geneva and Paris 1951–8.
Prose, ed. G. Saba, Turin 1965.

Translated in anthologies, incl. *Penguin book of French verse,* vol 2, Harmondsworth 1959.

Les oeuvres, 1621 (cntg *Traicté de l'immortalité de l'âme* and poems).
  Seconde partie, 1623.
  Recueil de toutes les pièces, 1625 (pt 3).
[Poèmes], 1622 (in *Le Parnasse des poëtes satiriques*).
Les amours tragiques de Pyrame et Thisbé, 1626 (in *Les oeuvres* above); ed. J. Hankiss, Strasbourg 1933; ed. G. Saba, Naples 1967.

ADAM, A., *Théophile de Viau et la libre pensée française en 1620,* Geneva 1935.
LACHÈVRE, F., *Le libertinage devant le Parlement de Paris; le procès du poète Théophile de Viau,* 2 vols, 1909 (incl. bibl.).

VOITURE, Vincent   1597–1648

Bibl. See MAGNE below.

Oeuvres, ed. M. de Pichesne, 1650;
  Nouvelles oeuvres, 1658;
  ed. A. Ubicine, 2 vols, 1855; ed. H. Lafay, 2 vols, 1972.

Tr. J. Ozell, J. Dryden et al., *The works* (incl. *Familiar letters to gentlemen and ladies*), 2 vols, London 1705; Dublin 1735.
Tr. J. Webster, *Select poems,* London 1735.

Lettres, ed. O. Uzanne, 2 vols, 1880.

MAGNE, E., *Voiture et l'Hôtel de Rambouillet,* 2 vols, 1929–30 (incl. bibl.).
RAHSTEDE, H. G., in his *Wanderungen durch die französische Literatur,* vol 1, Oppeln 1891.

4

The Eighteenth Century

ALEMBERT, Jean (d') 1717–1783

See also *L'ENCYCLOPÉDIE*.

Bibl. See GRIMSLEY below.

Oeuvres philosophiques, historiques et littéraires, ed. J. F. Bastien, 18 vols, 1805; ed. A. Bossange, 5 vols, 1821–2.

Traité de dynamique, 1743; 2 vols, 1921.
Discours préliminaire, 1751 (as introduction to vol 1 of the *ENCYCLO-PÉDIE*); ed. F. Picavet, 1894; ed. G. Klaus, Berlin 1958. Tr. R. N. Schwab and W. E. Rex, *Preliminary discourse to the Encyclopaedia*, Indianapolis (Ind) 1963.
Geneva, 1757 (entry in the *ENCYCLOPÉDIE*, vol 7; in collab. with VOL-TAIRE).
Elémens de musique, théorique et pratique, 1752; Lyon 1762.
Mélanges de littérature, d'histoire et de philosophie, 2 vols, Berlin 1753; 5 vols, Paris 1759. Tr. anon., *Miscellaneous pieces in literature, history and philosophy*, London 1764.
Sur la destruction des Jésuites en France, Edinburgh 1765. Tr. anon., *An account of the destruction of the Jesuits in France*, London 1766.
Oeuvres posthumes, ed. M. C. Pugens, 2 vols, 1799.
Oeuvres et correspondances inédites, ed. C. Henry, 1887.

BERTRAND, J., *D'Alembert*, 1889.
BOUISSOUNOUSE, J., in her *Julie de Lespinasse: ses amitiés, sa passion*, 1958. Tr. P. de Fontnouvelle, *Julie, the life of Mlle de Lespinasse: her salon, her friends, her loves*, New York 1962.
CONDORCET, A. N., *Eloge de M. d'Alembert*, 1784; 1804 (in his *Oeuvres complètes*, vol 3).
GRIMSLEY, R., *Jean d'Alembert*, Oxford 1963 (incl. bibl.).
HANKINS, T. L., *Jean d'Alembert: science and the Enlightenment*, Oxford 1970.
MULLER, M., *Essai sur la philosophie de Jean d'Alembert*, 1926.
PAPPAS, J. N., *Voltaire & d'Alembert*, Bloomington (Ind) 1962.

BARTHÉLEMY, (Abbé) Jean-Jacques   1716–1795

Oeuvres diverses, ed. G. E. J. de Sainte-Croix, 2 vols, 1798.
Oeuvres complètes, ed. M. G. B. Villenave, 5 vols, 1821–2.
Voyage du jeune Anacharsis en Grèce, 4 vols, 1788; ed. anon., 7 vols, 1815.
Tr. W. Beaumont, *Travels of Anacharsis the Younger in Greece*, 7 vols,
London 1794.
Voyage en Italie, ed. A. Sérieys, 1801. Tr. anon., *Travels in Italy*, London
1802.

BADOLLE, M., *L'abbé Jean-Jacques Barthélémy et l'hellénisme en France dans
la seconde moitié du 18e siècle*, 1923.

BEAUMARCHAIS, Pierre-Augustin de   1732–1799

CORDIER, H., *Bibliographie des oeuvres*, 1883.

Oeuvres complètes, 3 vols, Amsterdam 1775; 5 vols, Paris 1780–5; ed. P. P.
Gudin de la Brenellerie, 7 vols, 1809; ed. E. Fournier, 1876.
Théâtre, Lettres relatives à son théâtre, ed. M. Allem, 1934 (revd M. Allem
and Paul-Courant, 1957).
Théâtre complet, ed. G. d'Heylli and F. de Marescot, 4 vols, 1869–71; ed.
R. d'Hermies, 1952; ed. P. Pia, 1956.

Eugénie, Besançon 1762. Tr. E. Griffith, *The School for Rakes*, London 1795.
Les deux amis, ou le négociant de Lyon, 1770. Tr. 'C.H.', *The Two Friends, or
the Liverpool Merchant*, London 1800.
Le Barbier de Séville, 1775; ed. C. M. Des Granges, 1947; ed. E. J. Arnould,
Oxford 1963. Tr. E. Griffith, *The barber of Seville*, London 1776; tr. J.
Wood, Harmondsworth 1964.
La folle journée, ou le mariage de Figaro, 1785; ed. E. J. Arnould, Oxford
1952; ed. A. Ubersfeld, Paris 1957. Tr. and adapt. T. Holcroft, *The
follies of a day, or the marriage of Figaro*, London 1785; tr. J. Wood, *The
marriage of Figaro*, Harmondsworth 1964.
Tarare, 1787.
L'autre Tartuffe, ou la mère coupable, 1794. Tr. J. Wild, *Frailty and hypocrisy*,
London 1804.
Mémoires, [. . .] dans l'affaire Goezmann, 1878.

Correspondance, ed. B. N. Morton, 1969 onwards (3 vols pbd).

BRUNETIÈRE, F., in his *Les époques du théâtre français*, 1896.
GAIFFE, F., *Le mariage de Figaro*, 1928.
LEMAÎTRE, G., *Beaumarchais*, New York 1949.
LINTILHAC, E. F., *Beaumarchais et ses oeuvres*, 1887.
LOMÉNIE, L. L. de, *Beaumarchais et son temps*, 2 vols, 1856; 1880. Tr. H. S.
Edwards, *Beaumarchais and his times*, 4 vols, London 1856.

POMEAU, R., *Beaumarchais, l'homme et l'oeuvre*, 1956; 1967.
PUGH, A. R., *Beaumarchais, le mariage de Figaro*, 1968.
SCHÉRER, J., *La dramaturgie de Beaumarchais*, 1954.
TIEGHEM, P. van, *Beaumarchais par lui-même*, 1960.

BERNARDIN DE SAINT-PIERRE, Jacques-Henri

See SAINT-PIERRE, Jacques-Henri Bernardin de.

BUFFON, Georges-Louis Leclerc de   1707–1788

Bibl. See *Oeuvres philosophiques* below; also BERTIN below.

Oeuvres complètes, 25 vols, 1774–88; ed. J. L. de Lanessan and M. Nadault de Buffon, 14 vols, 1884–5.
Oeuvres philosophiques, ed. J. Piveteau et al., 1954 (incl. bibl.).

Histoire naturelle (in collab. with Daubenton, Guéneau de Montbeillard and Bexon, and incl. 8-vol continuation by Lacépède after Buffon's death), 44 vols, 1749–1804. Tr. Barr?, *Barr's Buffon*, 10 vols, London 1792 (revd 1810); tr. anon., *Buffon's natural history*. London 1869. Pbd as follows:

> *Histoire naturelle générale et particulière*, 15 vols, 1749–67 (cntg *Discours généraux*, *Théorie de la Terre*, *L'homme* below, and *Les quadrupèdes*). Tr. W. Kenrick and J. Murdoch, *The natural history of animals, vegetables and minerals, with the theory of the Earth in general*, 6 vols, London 1775–6.
> *Histoire naturelle des oiseaux*, 9 vols, 1770–83. Tr. W. Smellie, *The natural history of birds*, 9 vols, London 1793.
> *Suppléments*, 7 vols, 1774–9.
> *Histoire naturelle des minéraux*, 5 vols, 1783–8.
> *Ovipares et serpens*, 2 vols, 1788–9.
> *Poissons*, 5 vols, 1798–1803.
> *Cétacées*, 1804.

L'homme, 3 vols, 1749 (as vols 2–4 of *Histoire naturelle* above); ed. M. Duchet, 1971.
Traité des époques de la nature, 1778 (as vol 5 of *Suppléments* above); ed. J. Roger, 1962.
Discours prononcé dans l'Académie françoise, 1753; ed. H. Guyot, 1923 (as *Discours* [. . .] *sur le style*).

Correspondance, ed. H. Nadault de Buffon, 1885 (as vols 14–15 of *Oeuvres complètes* above).

BERTIN, L., BOURDIER, F. et al., *Buffon*, 1952 (incl. bibl.).
DUCLAUX, M., in his *The French ideal*, London 1911.

FELLOWS, O. E. and MILLIKEN, S. F., *Buffon*, New York 1973.
MORNET, D., in his *Le sentiment de la nature en France, de J. J. Rousseau à Bernardin de Saint-Pierre*, 1907.

CARMONTELLE 1717–1806
(pseudonym of Louis Carrogis)

Bibl. See DONNARD below.

Proverbes dramatiques, 8 vols, 1768–81; ed. C. de Méry, 4 vols, 1822;. ed. G. Maçon, 2 vols, 1947. Tr. T. Holcroft, London 1805 (four proverbs: *The opera dancer*, *The pullet*, *The portrait*, *False indifference*, in *The Theatrical Recorder*, vols 1 and 2).

BRENNER, C. D., in his *Le développement du proverbe dramatique en France*, Berkeley (Calif) 1937.
DONNARD, J. H., *Le théâtre de Carmontelle*, 1967 (incl. bibl.).
HERRMANN, M., *Das Gesellschaftstheater des Louis Carrogis de Carmontelle*, Meisenheim 1968.

CHAMFORT, Sébastien-Roch Nicolas de 1740–1794

Bibl. See TEPPE below; also Grosclaude ed. of *Maximes* below.

Oeuvres, ed. P. L. Ginguené, 4 vols, 1795; ed. P. R. Auguis, 5 vols, 1824–5; ed. C. Roy, 1960 (selection).
In *Collection complète de tableaux historiques de la Révolution française*, n.p. 1804 (texts from Chamfort and others). Tr. anon., *Historical pictures representing the most remarkable events which occurred during the early period of the French Revolution*, n.p. 1803.

La jeune indienne, 1764; ed. G. Chinard, Princeton (NJ) 1945.
Eloge de Molière, 1769.
Eloge de La Fontaine, Marseille 1774.
Des académies, 1791.
Maximes, pensées, caractères et anecdotes, ed. P. L. Ginguené, London and Paris 1796; ed. anon., Paris 1860 (with letters to Mirabeau); ed. A. Van Bever, 2 vols, 1922–4 (with *Dialogues philosophiques*); ed. A. Camus, Monaco 1944; ed. P. Grosclaude, 2 vols, Paris 1953 (as *Produits de la civilisation perfectionnée*; incl. bibl.). Tr. W. G. Hutchinson, *The cynic's breviary*, London 1902; tr. E. Powys Mathers, *Maxims and considerations*, 2 vols, Waltham Saint Lawrence 1926; tr. W. S. Mervin, *Products of the perfected civilization*, New York 1969 (selection); tr. C. G. Pearson, *Maxims, anecdotes, personalities, letters, historical writings, etc.*, Glastonbury 1973 (selection).

RICHARD, P. J., *Aspects de Chamfort*, 1959.
ROSSO, C., in his *Virtú e critica della virtú nei moralisti francesi*, Pisa 1971.
TEPPE, J., *Chamfort, sa vie, son oeuvre, sa pensée*, 1950 (incl. bibl.).
TREICH, L., *L'esprit de Chamfort*, 1927.

CHASLES (or CHALLES), Robert   1659–after 1721

Bibl. See Deloffre ed. of *Les illustres Françoises* below.

Les illustres Françoises, 1713; ed. F. Deloffre, 2 vols, 1959 (cntg bibl.).
    Tr. Mrs Aubin, *The illustrious French Lovers*, London 1727.
Journal d'un voyage fait aux Indes, 3 vols, Rouen 1721. Tr. anon., *A new
    voyage to the East Indies*, London 1696.
Mémoires, ed. A. Augustin Thierry, 1831.

DELOFFRE, F., in his *La nouvelle en France à l'âge classique*, 1967.
FORNO, L. J., *Robert Challe: intimations of the Enlightenment*, Cranbery (NJ)
    1972.

CHÉNIER, André-Marie   1762–1794

Bibl. See DIMOFF below; SCARFE below.

Oeuvres complètes, ed. H. Latouche, 1819 (incomplete); ed. P. Dimoff, 3
    vols, 1908–19 (poetical works); ed. H. Clouard, 3 vols, 1927; ed. G. Walter,
    1940 (incl. Malherbe commentary).
Oeuvres en prose, ed. Le Becq de Fouquières, 1872.
Poems, ed. F. Scarfe, Oxford 1961.
Tr. A. Symons, New York 1913 (3 elegies, in *Knave of Hearts*).
Also translated in anthologies.

Le serment du Jeu de Paume, 1791.
Hymne aux Suisses de Châteauvieux, 1792.
La jeune captive, 1795 (in magazine *Décade philosophique*). Tr. anon., *The
    young captive*, New York c. 1897 (in *The Warner library of the world's best
    literature*).
La jeune Tarentine, 1801 (in magazine *Mercure*).
Poésies diverses, 1818; ed. C. Labitte, 1842.
Les bucoliques, 1819 (in *Oeuvres complètes* above); ed. J.-M. de Hérédia, 1905.
L'invention, 1819 (in *Oeuvres complètes* above); ed. P. Dimoff 1966.

AUBARÈDE, G. d', *André Chénier*, 1970.
BECQ de FOUQUIÈRES, L., *Documents nouveaux sur André Chénier*, 1875.
DIMOFF, P., *La vie et l'oeuvre d'André Chénier jusqu'à la Révolution française*,
    2 vols, 1936 (incl. bibl. in vol 2).
FABRE, J., *André Chénier, l'homme et l'oeuvre*, 1955.
LOGGINS, V., *André Chénier, his life, death and glory*, Athens (Ohio) 1965.

SCARFE, F., *André Chénier, his life and work, 1762–1794*, Oxford 1965 (incl. bibl.).
WALTER, G., *André Chénier, son milieu et son temps*, 1947.

CHÉNIER, Marie-Joseph   1764–1811

Oeuvres, ed. D. C. Robert et al., 5 vols, 1823.
Théâtre, 3 vols, 1821.

Charles IX, 1790.
Henri VIII, 1793.
Caïus Gracchus, 1793.
Fénelon, ou les religieuses de Cambrai, 1793. Tr. R. Merry, *Fenelon, or the nuns of Cambray*, n.p. 1795.
Timoléon, 1795.
Tableau de la littérature française de 1789 à 1808, 1816.
Tibère, ed. N. Lemercier, 1819.

BINGHAM, A. J., *Marie-Joseph Chénier, early political life and ideas*, New York 1939.
LIEBY, A., *Etude sur le théâtre de Marie-Joseph Chénier*, 1901.

CONDILLAC, Étienne Bonnot de   1715–1780

See also *L'ENCYCLOPÉDIE*

Bibl. See MEYER below.

Oeuvres philosophiques, 4 vols, 1792; ed. G. Le Roy, 3 vols, 1947–51.
Oeuvres, ed. G. Arnoux and Mousnier, 23 vols, 1798; ed. A. F. Théry, 21 vols, 1821–2.
Condillac, ou la joie de vivre, ed. R. Lefèvre, 1966 (selection).

Essai sur l'origine des connoissances humaines, 2 vols, Amsterdam 1746; ed. R. Lenoir, Paris 1924; ed. C. Porset, Auvers-sur-Oise 1973. Tr. T. Nugent, *An essay on the origin of human knowledge*, London 1756.
Traité des sistèmes, 2 vols, The Hague, 1749.
Traité des sensations, 2 vols, London and Paris 1754; ed. F. Picavet, 1885. Tr. G. Carr, *Treatise on the sensations*, London 1930.
Traité des animaux, 2 vols, 1754.
La logique, 1780. Tr. J. Neef, *The logic of Condillac*, Philadelphia (Pa) 1809.

BAGUENAULT DE PUCHESSE, G., *Condillac: sa vie, sa philosophie, son influence*, 1910.
KNIGHT, I. F., *The geometric spirit: the Abbé de Condillac and the French Enlightenment*, New Haven (Conn) 1968.

LEBEAU, A., *Condillac économiste*, 1903.

LEFÈVRE, R., *Hommage à Condillac*, Clermont-Ferrand 1956 (in *Cahiers d'Histoire*).

MEYER, P., *Etienne Bonnot de Condillac*, Zurich 1944 (incl. bibl.).

SCHAUPP, Z., *The naturalism of Condillac*, Lincoln (Nebr) 1925.

CRÉBILLON (Père), Prosper Jolyot de   1674–1762

Les oeuvres, 1716 (cntg 4 plays); 1750 (cntg all 9 plays and speeches).
Théâtre complet, ed. A. Vitu, 1885; 1938.
Tragédies choisies, ed. P. Ciureanu, Genoa 1963.

Rhadamiste et Zénobie, 1711. Tr. A. Murphy, *Zenobia*, London 1768; tr. C. L. Lockert, Nashville (Tenn) 1956 (in *The chief rivals of Corneille and Racine*).
Atrée et Thyeste, 1716.

CIUREANU, P., *Crébillon*, Genoa 1965.

DUTRAIT, M., *Etude sur la vie et le théâtre de Crébillon*, Bordeaux 1895.

LANCASTER, H. C., in his *French tragedy in the time of Louis XV*, Baltimore (Md) and Oxford 1950.

VOLTAIRE, *Eloge de M. de Crébillon*, Geneva 1762.

DELILLE, (Abbé) Jacques   1738–1813

Oeuvres complètes, 17 vols, 1818–20; ed. P. F. Tissot, 10 vols, 1832–3.
Oeuvres choisies, ed. Mme Woilliez, 1850.

Translated in anthologies.

Les jardins, 1782; 1810. Tr. M. H. Montolieu, *The gardens*, London 1798.
L'homme des champs, Strasbourg 1800; Paris 1808; ed. F. Estienne, 1873. Tr. J. Maunde, *The rural philosopher*, London 1801.
La pitié, 1803; Brunswick 1804 (renamed *Le malheur et la pitié*).
L'imagination, ed. Esmenard, 2 vols, 1806.
Les trois règnes de la nature, ed. Cuvier, 2 vols, 1808; ed. Cuvier and Lefèvre-Gineau, 2 vols, Strasbourg 1809.
La conversation, 1812.

Also translated Virgil, Pope and Milton.

FABRE, J. et al., *Delille est-il mort?*, Clermont-Ferrand 1967.

SOUZA, R. de, *Un préparateur de la poésie romantique: Delille*, 1938 (in *Mercure de France*).

DIDEROT, Denis 1713–1784

See also *L'ENCYCLOPÉDIE*

DIECKMANN, H., *Bibliographical data*, St Louis (Mo) 1942 (in *Studies in honor of Frederick W. Shipley*).
See also PROUST below.

Oeuvres de théâtre, Amsterdam 1772.
Oeuvres philosophiques, 6 vols, Amsterdam 1772; ed. P. Vernière, 1961.
Oeuvres, ed. J. A. Naigeon, 15 vols, 1798; ed. J. Assézat and M. Tourneux, 20 vols, 1875–7; ed. R. Lewinter, 15 vols, 1970–3.
Writings on the theatre, ed. F. C. Green, London 1936.
Oeuvres esthétiques, ed. P. Vernière, 1959.
Textes politiques, ed. Y. Benot, 1960.
Oeuvres romanesques, ed. H. Bénac, 1962.
Oeuvres politiques, ed. P. Vernière, 1963.
Contes, ed. H. Dieckmann, London 1963.
Quatre contes, ed. J. Proust, Geneva 1964 (cntg *Les deux amis de Bourbonne*, *Ceci n'est pas un conte*, tr. A. Bonner, New York 1960, in *Great French short stories*, *Madame de la Carlière*, and *Mystification*).

Tr. B. L. Tollemache, *Diderot's thoughts on art and style, with some of his shorter essays*, London 1893.
Tr. and ed. M. Jourdain, *Early philosophical works*, Chicago (Ill) and London 1916.
Tr. F. Birrell, *Dialogues*, London 1927.
Tr. J. Stewart and J. Kemp, *Diderot, interpreter of nature, selected writings*, London 1927.
Tr. D. Coltman, *Selected writings*, New York 1966.
Also tr. in short story anthologies, incl. *Great French short novels*, New York 1952, and in *Les Philosophes*, New York 1960.

Principes de la philosophie morale (adapt. of Shaftesbury's *Inquiry concerning merit and virtue*), Amsterdam 1745.
Pensées philosophiques, The Hague 1746; ed. R. Niklaus, Geneva 1950. Tr. anon., London 1819 (selection, with *Thoughts on religion* below).
  Addition aux pensées philosophiques, ed. J. A. Naigeon, Amsterdam 1770 in *Recueil philosophique*, as *Pensées sur la religion*); ed. J. A. Naigeon, Paris 1770 (in his *Philosophie ancienne et moderne*); 1798 (in *Oeuvres* above). Tr. anon., *Thoughts on religion*, London 1819.
Les bijoux indiscrets, 2 vols, 1748; ed. J. Hervez, 1920; ed. J. Proust, 1973. Tr. anon., *The indiscreet toys*, 2 vols, London 1749; tr. Stewart and Kemp above (part).
Lettre sur les aveugles, London 1749; ed. R. Niklaus, Geneva and Lille 1951 (revd 1963). Tr. anon., *An essay on blindness*, London c. 1750; tr. S. C.

Howe, *A letter upon the blind*, Boston (Mass) 1857; tr. Tollemache above (part).

Lettre sur les sourds et muets, n.p. 1751; ed. P. H. Meyer, Geneva 1965. Tr. Tollemache above (part).

Pensées sur l'interprétation de la nature, n.p. 1753; London 1754; ed. J. Varloot, Paris 1953 (in *Textes choisis II*). Tr. Stewart and Kemp above (part).

L'histoire et le secret de la peinture en cire, n.p. 1755.

Le fils naturel, 1757 (with *Entretiens avec Dorval*); ed. J. P. Caput, 1970. Tr. anon., *Dorval, or the test of virtue*, London 1767.

Le père de famille, Amsterdam 1758. Tr. anon., London 1770; tr. anon., *The family picture*, 1871.

Un discours sur la poésie dramatique, Amsterdam 1758 (with *Le père de famille* above).

Eloge de Richardson, 1762 (with Prévost's tr., *Supplément aux lettres anglaises de Miss Clarisse Harlow*). Tr. Tollemache above.

De la suffisance de la religion naturelle, ed. J. A. Naigeon, Amsterdam 1770 (in *Recueil philosophique*, vol 2).

Contes moraux, Zurich 1773 (cntg *Entretiens d'un père avec ses enfants*, tr. Tollemache above, and *Les deux amis de Bourbonne*); Paris 1822.

Entretiens d'un philosophe avec la maréchale de ***, n.p. 1776. Tr. 'E.N.', *A philosophical conversation*, London 1875; tr. Stewart and Kemp above.

Supplément au voyage de Bougainville, ed. Bourlet de Vauxcelles, 1796 (in *Opuscules philosophiques et littéraires*); ed. G. Chinard, 1935; ed. H. Dieckmann, Geneva 1955. Tr. Stewart and Kemp above.

Essai sur la peinture, n.p. 1796; ed. R. Desné and J. Pierre, Paris 1955.

Jacques le fataliste et son maître, 2 vols, 1796; ed. Y. Belaval, 1953. Tr. anon., *James the fatalist and his master*, 3 vols, London 1797; tr. and ed. J. R. Loy, *Jacques the fatalist and his master*, New York 1959.

La religieuse, 1797; ed. G. Deleuze, 1947; ed. R. Mauzi, 1961; ed. J. Parrish, Geneva 1963. Tr. anon., *The nun*, 2 vols, London and Dublin 1797; tr. F. Birrell, *Memoirs of a nun*, London 1959; tr. M. Sinclair, *The nun*, 1966.

Les Eleuthéromanes, 1798 (in *Oeuvres*, vol 15 above).

Le neveu de Rameau, 1823 (first pbd in Goethe's German tr., *Rameaus Neffe*, Leipzig 1805); ed. E. Thoinan, Paris 1891; ed. J. Fabre, Lille and Geneva 1950; ed. H. Dieckmann, Paris 1957. Tr. S. M. Hill, *Rameau's nephew*, London 1897; tr. Stewart and Kemp above; tr. L. W. Tancock, Harmondsworth 1966.

Paradoxe sur le comédien, 1830; ed. E. Dupuy, 1902; ed. J. Copeau, 1929. Tr. W. H. Pollock, *The paradox of acting*, London 1883.

Mémoires, correspondance et ouvrages inédits, 4 vols, 1830–1.

Entretien entre d'Alembert et Diderot, Rêve d'Alembert, Suite de l'entretien, 1831 (in *Mémoires* [etc], vol 4 above); ed. G. Maire, 1921; ed. P. Vernière, 1951; ed. J. Roger, 1965.

Est-il bon? Est-il méchant?, 1875 (in *Oeuvres*, vol 8 above; first pbd in *Revue rétrospective*, vol 3, 1834); ed. J. Undank, Geneva 1961.

Les salons, 1759–1781, ed. R. Desné, 1955 (collected art criticism); ed. J. Seznec and J. Adhémar, 4 vols, Oxford 1957–67.

Lettres à Mademoiselle Voland [sic], 1830–1 (in *Mémoires* [etc], vols 1–3, above). Tr. P. France, *Letters to Sophie Volland*, Oxford 1972 (selection).

Correspondance inédite, ed. A. Babelon, 2 vols, 1931.

Correspondance, ed. G. Roth and J. Varloot, 16 vols, 1955–70.

BILLY, A., *Vie de Diderot*, 1932.

CROCKER, L., *Two Diderot studies: ethics and esthetics*, Baltimore (Md) 1952.
  The embattled philosopher; a biography of Denis Diderot, East Lansing (Mich) 1954.

Diderot Studies, Syracuse (NY) and Geneva 1949 onwards.

DIECKMANN, H., *Cinq leçons sur Diderot*, Geneva 1959.

DUCROS, L., *Diderot, l'homme et l'écrivain*, 1894.

GILMAN, M., in her *The idea of poetry in France*, Cambridge (Mass) 1958.

NAIGEON, J. A., *Mémoires historiques et philosophiques sur la vie et les ouvrages de Diderot*, 1821.

POMEAU, R., *Diderot, sa vie et son oeuvre*, 1967.

PROUST, J., *Diderot et l'Encyclopédie*, 1962 (incl. bibl.).

ROSENKRANZ, K., *Diderots Leben und Werke*, 2 vols, Leipzig 1866.

VENTURI, F., *Jeunesse de Diderot, 1713 à 1753*, 1939 (tr. from Italian by J. Bertrand).

VERNIÈRE, P., in his *Spinoza et la pensée française avant la Révolution*, 1954.

WILSON, A. M., *Diderot: the testing years, 1713–1759*, New York 1957; 1972.

DU BOS, (Abbé) Jean-Baptiste   1670–1742

Bibl. See LOMBARD below.

Histoire de la ligue faite à Cambray, 2 vols, 1709; 2 vols, 1729. Tr. 'R.F.', *The history of the league made at Cambray*, London 1712.

Reflexions critiques sur la poésie et la peinture, 2 vols, 1719; 3 vols, 1733; 3 vols, 1770. Tr. T. Nugent, *Critical reflections on poetry, painting and music*, 3 vols, London 1748.

Histoire critique de l'établissement de la monarchie françoise dans les Gaules, 3 vols, 1734; 2 vols, 1742.

LOMBARD, A., *L'abbé Du Bos, un initiateur de la pensée moderne*, 1913 (incl. bibl.).

DUCLOS, Charles Pinot   1704–1772

Oeuvres diverses, 5 vols, 1802.

Oeuvres complètes, ed. L. S. Auger, 10 vols, 1806; ed. L. Clément de Ris, 1855.

Histoire de Mme de Luz, The Hague 1741; ed. J. Brengues, Saint-Brieuc 1971.

Les confessions du Comte de ***, 2 vols, Amsterdam 1741; ed. H. Frichet, Paris 1929; ed. R. Etiemble, 1965 (in *Romanciers du 18e siècle*); ed. L. Versini, 1969. Tr. anon., *A course of gallantries, or the inferiority of the tumultuous joys of the passions to the serene pleasures of reason, attested by the confession of a nobleman who had tried both*, 2 vols, London 1775.

Acajou et Zirphile, n.p. 1744.

Histoire de Louis XI, 4 vols, The Hague 1745–6. Tr. anon., *The history of Louis XI, King of France*, 2 vols, London 1746.

Les considerations sur les moeurs de ce siècle, 1751; ed. F. C. Green, Cambridge 1939.

> *Mémoire pour servir à l'histoire des moeurs du 18e siècle*, 2 vols, 1751. Tr. anon., *Memoirs illustrating the manners of the present age*, 2 vols, London c. 1775 (incl. tr. of chs 1–14 of *Les considérations* above).

Mémoires secrets sur les règnes de Louis XIV et de Louis XV, 2 vols, 1791; ed. C. B. Petitot, 2 vols, 1819–29 (in *Collection des mémoires relatifs à l'histoire de France*, vols 76–7); 2 vols, 1864. Tr. E. J. Meras, *Secret memories of the Regency*, London 1912.

Correspondance, ed. J. Brengues, Saint-Brieuc 1969.

BRENGUES, J., *Charles Duclos, ou l'obsession de la vertu*, Saint-Brieuc 1971.
MEISTER, P., *Charles Duclos, 1704–1772*, Geneva 1956.
SAINTE-BEUVE, C. A. de, in his *Causeries du lundi*, vol 9, 1854.
SILVERBLATT, B. G., *The maxims in the novels of Duclos*, The Hague 1973.

ENCYCLOPÉDIE, L' 1751–1780

Compiled by DIDEROT, as general editor, assisted by Louis de Jaucourt (mainly technical and scientific entries), with the collaboration of d'ALEMBERT (*Discours préliminaire*, entries on mathematics, and '*Geneva*' with VOLTAIRE), and with some 200 contributors, including CONDILLAC and Helvétius (philosophy), Daubenton (natural history), Dumarsais (grammar), d'Holbach (chemistry and mineralogy), MARMONTEL (literary criticism), MONTESQUIEU ('*goût*'), morellet and Yvon (theology), ROUSSEAU (music), Turgot (political economy) and VOLTAIRE ('*élégance*', '*éloquence*', '*esprit*', '*force*', etc.).

Bibl. See PROUST below.

Prospectus (by Diderot), 1750.

Encyclopédie, ou dictionnaire raisonné des sciences, des arts et des métiers, 35 vols, 1751–80. Tr. S. J. Gendzier, *The Encyclopedia, selections*, New York 1967. Pbd as follows:

Entries A–Z, 17 vols, 1751–65.
    vol. 1 (incl. d'ALEMBERT's *Discours préliminaire*), 1751;
    vols 2–7, 1752–7;
    vols 8–17 (after d'Alembert's withdrawal and government ban), 1765.
Plates, 11 vols, 1765–72.
Supplement (not ed. Diderot), 5 vols, 1777.
Index, 2 vols, 1780.

DUCROS, L., *Les encyclopédistes*, 1900.
LE GRAS, J., *Diderot et l'Encyclopédie*, Amiens 1928.
PROUST, J., *Diderot et l'Encyclopédie*, 1962 (incl. bibl.).
    L'Encyclopédie, 1965 (incl. bibl.).
WEIS, E., *Geschichtsschreibung und Staatsauffassung in der französischen Enzyclopädie*, Wiesbaden 1956.
WILSON, A. M., *Diderot, the testing years, 1713–1759*, New York 1957.

FLORIAN, Jean-Pierre Claris de   1755–1794

Oeuvres complètes, 16 vols, 1820.
Oeuvres inédites, ed. R. C. G. de Pixérécourt, 4 vols, 1824.
Théâtre, 3 vols, 1792.

Tr. Mr Robinson, *The works*, 2 vols, London 1786 (cntg *Galatea* and other romances).

Les deux billets, 1780.
    Le bon ménage, ou la suite des Deux billets, 1783.
Galatée, 1783. Tr. anon., *Galatea*, Dublin 1791; tr. W. M. Craig, London 1813.
Numa Pompilius, 1786; ed. L. T. Ventouillac, 2 vols, London 1823. Tr. anon., *The adventures of Numa Pompilius*, 2 vols, London 1787; tr. E. Morgan, *The history of Numa Pompilius*, 3 vols, 1787; tr. A. Murphy, London 1811; tr. J. A. Ferris, *Numa Pompilius*, Boston (Mass) 1850.
La bonne mère, London 1786; ed. J. Truffier, 1910. Tr. H. Robson, *Look before you leap*, London 1788.
Estelle, 1788; ed. A. Hiard, 1831 (as *Estelle et Némorin*, with *Galatée* above). Tr. E. Morgan, *Stella*, 2 vols, London 1791; tr. Mr Maxey, *Estelle*, London 1803.
Gonzalve de Cordoue, 2 vols, 1791. Tr. anon., *Gonzala of Cordova*, Dublin 1793; tr. anon., *Gonsalvo, or the Spanish knight*, 2 vols, New York 1801.
Fables, 1792; ed. L. Humbert, 1908. Tr. J. W. Phelps, New York 1888; tr. P. Perring, London 1896.
Nouvelles, 1792.
    Nouvelles nouvelles, 1792. Tr. anon., *New tales*, London 1792.
La jeunesse de Florian, ou mémoires d'un jeune Espagnol, 1807; ed. A. Louis, 1923.

CLARETIE, L., *Florian*, 1888.
SAILLARD, G., *Florian, sa vie, son oeuvre*, Toulouse 1912.

GRESSET, Louis   1709–1777

Oeuvres complètes, ed. F. J. M. Fayolle, 3 vols, 1804; ed. A. A. Renouard, 2 vols, 1811; 4 vols, 1824.
Poésies choisies, ed. L. Derome, 1883.
Vair-vert, ou les voyages du perroquet de la Visitation de Neverts, The Hague 1734; ed. G. d'Heylli, Paris 1872. Tr. anon., *Green-green, or the nunnery parrot*, Dublin 1762.
La Chartreuse, n.p. 1735; Rotterdam 1736.
Edouard III, 1740.
Sidney, The Hague, 1745.
Le méchant, 1747; ed. H. Labaste, 1922.
Poésies inédites, ed. V. de Beauvillé, 1863.

FINCH, R., in his *The sixth sense; individualism in French poetry, 1686–1760*, Toronto 1966.
WOGUE, J., *J. B. L. Gresset; sa vie, ses oeuvres*, 1894.

JOUBERT, Joseph   1754–1824

Recueil des pensées, ed. A. Joubert and R. de Chateaubriand, 1838 (selection); ed. P. de Raynal, 2 vols, 1842 (complete, as *Pensées, essais et maximes*, with *Lettres à ses amis*); ed. R. Dumay and M. Andrieux, 1954 (extracts, as *Pensées et lettres*). Tr. G. H. Calvert, *Some of the Thoughts*, Boston (Mass) 1867; tr. H. Attwell, *Pensées*, London 1896 (selection); tr. K. Lyttleton, *A selection from his Thoughts*, 1898; tr. H. P. Collins, *Pensées and Letters*, London and New York 1928.

Carnets, ed. A. Beaunier et al., 1955.
Correspondance de Louis de Fontanes et de Joubert, ed. R. Tessonneau, 1943.

BILLY, A., *Joubert énigmatique et délicieux*, 1969.
EVANS, J., *The unselfish egoist: a life of Joseph Joubert*, London and New York 1947.
GIRAUD, V., in his *Moralistes français*, 1923.
MONGLOND, A., in his *Le préromantisme français*, Grenoble 1930.

LA CHAUSSÉE, Pierre-Claude Nivelle de   1692–1754

Oeuvres de théâtre, 2 vols, 1741–7.
Oeuvres, ed. Sablier, 5 vols, 1762.

La fausse antipathie, 1734.

Le préjugé à la mode, 1735.
L'école des amis, 1737.
Maximinien, 1738.
Mélanide, 1741.
Amour pour amour, 1742.
L'école des mères, 1745.
L'amour castillan, 1747.
La gouvernante, 1747.

LANSON, G., *Nivelle de La Chaussée et la comédie larmoyante,* 1887; 1903.

LACLOS, Pierre Choderlos de   1741–1803

Bibl. See Maynial ed. of *Les liaisons dangereuses* below; also THELANDER below.

Oeuvres complètes, ed. M. Allem, 1944.
Poésies, ed. A. Symons and L. Thomas, 1908.

Les liaisons dangereuses, 4 vols, 1782; ed. M. Allem, 1932; ed. E. Maynial, 1943 (incl. bibl.); ed. R. Vailland, 1957. Tr. anon., *Dangerous connections,* 4 vols, London 1784; tr. R. Aldington, *Dangerous acquaintances,* 1924; tr. P. W. K. Stone, *Les liaisons dangereuses,* Harmondsworth 1961; tr. L. Bair, *Dangerous Liaisons,* New York 1962.
Lettre à Messieurs de l'Académie françoise sur l'éloge de M. le Maréchal de Vauban, Amsterdam and Paris 1786.
De l'éducation des femmes, ed. E. Champion, 1903 (with notes by Baudelaire).

Lettres inédites, ed. L. de Chauvigny, 1904.

DARD, E., *Un acteur caché du drame révolutionnaire: le général Choderlos de Laclos,* 1905; 1936.
DELMAS, A. and Y., *A la recherche des Liaisons dangereuses,* 1964.
FAURIE, J., *Essai sur la séduction,* 1948.
NATOLI, G., in his *Figure e problemi della cultura francese,* Messina 1956.
SEYLAZ, J. L., *Les liaisons dangereuses et la création romanesque chez Laclos,* Geneva 1958.
THELANDER, D. R., *Laclos and the epistolary novel,* Geneva 1963 (incl. bibl.).
VAILLAND, R., *Laclos par lui-même,* 1953; 1962.
VERSINI, L., *Laclos et la tradition,* 1968.

LESAGE, Alain-René   1668–1747

CORDIER, H., *Essai bibliographique sur les oeuvres,* 1910.

Oeuvres complètes, 12 vols, 1828 (not incl. *Théâtre de la foire*).

Théâtre, ed. M. Bardon, 1948 (incl. *Turcaret* and *Crispin*).

Tr. anon., *Gil Blas, The devil on two sticks* and *Vanillo Gonzales*, London 1822 (in *Novelist's Library*, vol 4).

Crispin, rival de son maître, 1707; ed. C. Simond, 1890; ed. T. E. Lawrenson, London 1961. Tr. D. Garrick, *Neck or nothing*, London 1766; tr. B. H. Clark, *Crispin, rival of his master*, New York 1915; tr. W. S. Merwin, *The rival of his master*, New Orleans (La) 1962 (in *The Tulane Drama Review*, vol 6).

Le diable boiteux, 1707 (chs 1–16); 1720 (chs 1–17); 2 vols, 1726 (chs 1–21); 2 vols 1737; ed. R. Etiemble, 1960 (in *Romanciers du 18e siècle*, vol 1); ed. R. Laufer, Paris and The Hague, 1970. Tr. anon., *The devil upon two sticks*, London 1708; tr. J. Thomas, *Asmodeus*, 1841; tr. anon., New York 1932.

Turcaret, 1709; ed. F. Duval, 1938; ed. M. Spaziani, Milan 1965. Tr. R. Aldington, London 1923 (in *French comedies of the 18th century*).

Histoire de Gil Blas de Santillane, 4 vols, 1715–35; 1747; ed. A. Dupouy, 1935; ed. M. Bardon, 2 vols, 1947; ed. R. Etiemble, 1960 (in *Romanciers du 18e siècle*, vol 1). Tr. anon., *The history of Gil Blas of Santillane*, 4 vols, London 1735; tr. T. Smollett, 4 vols, *Gil Blas*, 1749 (ed. and abr. B. B. Evans, Greenwich (Conn) 1962); tr. H. van Laun, 4 vols, London 1897.

Théâtre de la foire (ed. Lesage and Dorneval and incl. farces by Lesage), 10 vols, 1721–37.

Les avantures de M. Robert Chevalier, dit de Beauchesne, 2 vols, 1732; ed. H. Kurz, New York 1926; ed. E. Henriot, 1933. Tr. anon., *The adventures of Robert Chevalier*, 2 vols, London 1745.

Histoire de Guzman d'Alfarache, 2 vols, 1732. Tr. A. O'Connor, *Pleasant adventures of Gusman of Alfarache*, 3 vols, London 1812.

Histoire d'Estevanille Gonzalez, 1734. Tr. anon., *The comical history of Estevanille Gonzalez*, n.p. 1735.

Une journée des Parques, 1735. Tr. A. L. Gowans, *A day of the Fates*, London and Boston (Mass) 1922.

Le bachelier de Salamanque, 1736; 2 vols, 1736. Tr. J. Lockman, *The bachelar of Salamanca*, 2 vols, London 1737–39; tr. J. Townsend *The bachelor of Salamanca*, 1822 (and New York 1892 as *The merry bachelor*).

Recueil des pièces mises au théâtre françois, 2 vols, 1739; 2 vols, 1774; ed. M. Bardon, 1948.

La valise trouvée, 1740; Maastricht 1779.

ALTER, R., in his *The rogue's progress: studies in the picaresque novel*, Cambridge 1964.

BRUNETIÈRE, F., in his *Histoire et littérature*, 3 vols, 1884.

DÉDÉYAN, C., *Lesage et Gil Blas*, 2 vols, 1965.

LAUFER, R., *Lesage, ou le métier de romancier*, 1971.

LINTILHAC, E., *Lesage*, 1893.

MAISTRE, Joseph de   c. 1754–1821

Bibl. See HOLDSWORTH below.

Oeuvres complètes, 15 vols, Lyon 1884–7.
Textes choisis, ed. E. M. Cioran, Monaco 1957 (incl. *Du pape* and *Les soirées de Saint-Petersbourg*).

Tr. J. Lively, *The works*, London 1965 (selection, incl. *Saint-Petersburg dialogues, Pope, Considerations on France*).

Considérations sur la France, Basle 1797; Paris 1821; ed. R. Johannet and F. Vermale, 1936; ed. H. Guillemin, Geneva 1943.
Du pape, 2 vols, Lyon 1819; 2 vols, 1821; 1845; ed. J. Lovie and J. Chetail, Geneva 1966. Tr. A. E. McD. Dawson, *The Pope*, London 1850.
Les soirées de Saint Petersbourg, 1821; ed. A. de La Valette, 2 vols, 1924.
Lettres à un gentilhomme russe, 1822. Tr. A. E. McD. Dawson, *Letters to a Russian gentleman*, London 1851.

GIGNOUX, C. J., *Joseph de Maistre, prophète du passé, historien de l'avenir*, 1963.
HOLDSWORTH, F., *Joseph de Maistre et l'Angleterre*, 1935 (incl. bibl.).
LAMARTINE, A. de, *Vie et oeuvres du comte de Maistre*, 1859 (in his *Cours familier de littérature*).

MAISTRE, Xavier de   1763–1852

Bibl. See MAYSTRE and PERRIN below.

Oeuvres complètes, ed. C. A. de Sainte-Beuve, 1862; ed. E. Réaume, 1876.
Oeuvres inédites, ed. E. Réaume, 2 vols, 1877.

Voyage autour de ma chambre, Lausanne 1795. Tr. H. Attwell, *A journey round my room*, London 1871.
Le lépreux de la cité d'Aoste, Saint Petersburg 1811. Tr. H. Attwell, *The leper of the city of Aosta*, London 1873.
Les prisonniers du Caucase, 1815.
La jeune Sibérienne, 1815 (with *Les prisonniers du Caucase* above). Tr. anon., *Prasca Loupouloff, a Russian narrative*, London 1838.

BERTHIER, A., *Xavier de Maistre*, 1921.
LA FUYE, M. de, *Xavier de Maistre, gentilhomme européen*, Tours 1934.
MAYSTRE, H. and PERRIN, A., *Un chapitre inédit d'histoire littéraire et bibliographique: Xavier de Maistre*, Geneva 1895.

MARIVAUX, Pierre de Chamblain de   1688–1763

POULET-MALASSIS, A., *Théâtre de Marivaux; bibliographie des éditions originales et des éditions collectives données par l'auteur*, 1876.

See also DELOFFRE below.

Oeuvres complètes, 12 vols, 1781; ed. M. Duviquet, 10 vols, 1825–30.
Théâtre complet, romans, ed. M. Arland, 2 vols, 1949.
Théâtre complet, ed. B. Dort, 1964.
Oeuvres de jeunesse, ed. F. Deloffre and C. Rigault, 1972.

Le Spectateur François, 2 vols, 1722–3 (cntg issues of periodical); 1727 (enl.);
2 vols, 1761 (with issues of *L'Indigent Philosophe* and *Le Cabinet du Philosophe*).
Arlequin poli par l'amour, 1723; ed. R. and T. Niklaus, London 1959.
La surprise de l'amour, 1723; ed. G. d'Heylli, 1890. Tr. J. Rule? *The agreeable surprise*, London 1766.
La double inconstance, 1724; ed. G. Marcel, 1947.
L'île des esclaves, 1725.
Annibal, 1727.
Le dénouement imprévu, 1727.
Le prince travesti, 1727.
L'isle de la raison, 1727.
La seconde surprise de l'amour, 1728.
La fausse suivante, 1729.
L'héritier, 1729.
Le jeu de l'amour et du hasard, 1730; ed. M. Shackleton, London 1955; ed. R. Labreaux 1972. Tr. H. Ford and M. L. Le Verrir, *Love in livery*, New York 1907; tr. R. Aldington, *The game of love and chance*, London 1923; tr. W. Fowlie, New York 1962.
La vie de Marianne, Paris/The Hague 1731–41 (11 pts pbd separately, pts 1–7 and 10 in Paris, pts 8, 9? and 11 in The Hague); 4 vols, Amsterdam 1745 (pts 1–12; unfinished); ed. F. Deloffre, Paris 1957. Tr. anon., *The life of Marianne*, 3 vols, London 1736–42; tr. G. Campbell, *The hand of destiny, or the life of Marianne*, 1889.
L'école des mères, 1732; ed. G. Michaud, 1937.
Les serments indiscrets, 1732.
Le triomphe de l'amour, 1732.
L'heureux stratagème, 1733. Tr. anon., *The agreeable surprise*, n.p. 1766.
Le petit maître corrigé, 1734; ed. F. Deloffre, Geneva 1955.
La mère confidente, 1735.
Le paysan parvenu (unfinished), 4 vols 1735; ed. F. Deloffre, 1959. Tr. anon., *The fortunate peasant*, London 1735; tr. and adapt. anon., *The fortunate villager*, 2 vols, Dublin 1765.
Le Télémaque travesti, Amsterdam 1736; ed. F. Deloffre, Lille and Geneva 1956.
Le legs, 1736. Tr. B. H. Clark, *The legacy*, New York 1915.
Pharsamon, ou les nouvelles folies romanesques, 2 vols, The Hague, 1737; Paris 1781 (as *Le Don Quichotte françois*, vol 11 of *Oeuvres complètes* above). Tr. J. Lockman, *Pharsamond, or the new knight-errant*, 2 vols, London 1750.

Les fausses confidences, 1738; ed. C. M. Des Granges, 1947; ed. H. T. Mason, Oxford 1964; ed. R. Morisse, Paris 1973.

La joie imprévue, 1738.

Le triomphe de Plutus, 1739.

La méprise, 1739.

Les sincères, 1739.

L'épreuve, 1740; 1760 (with *Discours prononcé à l'Académie françoise*); ed. G. Marcel, 1947 (with *La double inconstance* above). Tr. W. K. Jones, *The test,* Boston (Mass) 1924.

La dispute, 1747.

Le préjugé, 1747.

Journaux et oeuvres diverses, ed. F. Deloffre and M. Gilot, 1969.

ARLAND, M., *Marivaux,* 1950.

DELOFFRE, F., *Une préciosité nouvelle: Marivaux et le marivaudage,* 1955; 1967 (incl. bibl.).

DESCHAMPS, G., *Marivaux,* 1897.

DESCOTES, M., *Les grands rôles du théâtre de Marivaux,* 1972.

DURRY, M. J., *A propos de Marivaux,* 1960.

GREENE, E. J. H., *Marivaux,* Toronto 1965.

JAMIESON, R. K., *Marivaux,* New York 1941.

LAGRAVE, H., *Marivaux et sa fortune littéraire,* Bordeaux 1971.

LAMBERT, P., *Réalité et ironie: les jeux de l'illusion dans le théâtre de Marivaux,* Fribourg 1973.

RATERMANIS, J. B., *Etude sur le comique dans le théâtre de Marivaux,* Geneva 1961.

ROUSSET, J., in his *Forme et signification,* 1962.

RUGGIERO, O., *Marivaux e il suo teatro, saggio critico,* Milan 1953.

MARMONTEL, Jean-François 1723–1799

See also *L'ENCYCLOPÉDIE*

RENWICK, J., *La destinée posthume de Jean-François Marmontel; bibliographie critique,* Clermont-Ferrand 1972.

Oeuvres posthumes, 11 vols, 1804–6.

Oeuvres complètes, 19 vols, 1818–20.

Denis le tyran, 1749.

Cléopâtre, 1750.

24 other plays published 1750–1804.

Contes moraux, 2 vols, The Hague 1761 (first pbd in *Mercure de France* from 1756); 4 vols, 1771 (enl.); 7 vols, Paris 1829. Tr. C. Dennis and R. Lloyd, *Moral Tales,* 3 vols, London 1764–6.

Nouveaux contes moraux, 1765; 4 vols, 1801 (enl.).

Tr. G. Saintsbury, *Moral Tales*, London 1895 (selection).

La bergère des Alpes, 1766. Tr. 'J.F.M.', *The shepherdess of the Alps*, n.p. 1810?

Bélisaire, 1767; 1770 (with *Pièces relatives à Bélisaire*, first pbd 1767). Tr. anon., *Belisarius*, London 1767; tr. A. Murphy, 1811.

Les Incas, 2 vols, 1777. Tr. anon., *The Incas*, 2 vols, Dublin 1777.

Mémoires d'un père, 4 vols, 1804 (in *Oeuvres posthumes*, vols 1–4 above); ed. M. Tourneux, 3 vols, 1891; ed. J. Renwick, 2 vols, Clermont-Ferrand 1972. Tr. anon., *Memoirs*, 4 vols, London 1805; tr. B. Patmore 1930.

EHRARD, J. (ed.), *De l'Encyclopédie à la Contre-Révolution: Jean-François Marmontel*, Clermont-Ferrand 1970.

LENEL, S., *Une homme de lettres au 18e siècle*, 1902.

MERCIER, Louis-Sébastien   1740–1814

Théâtre complet, 4 vols, Amsterdam and Leiden 1778–84 (cntg 23 plays; 10 others pbd separately 1784–1809).

Le déserteur, 1770.

L'an deux mille quatre cent quarante, rêve s'il n'en fut jamais, London 1771; 2 vols, 1785 (enl.); ed. R. Trousson, Bordeaux 1971. Tr. H. A. Freeman, *Astraea's return, or the halycon days of France in the year 2440*, London? 1797.

L'indigent, 1772. Tr. anon., *The distressed family*, London 1787.

La brouette du vinaigrier, London and Paris 1775; ed. R. Aggéri, 1972.

Tableau de Paris, 2 vols, Hamburg and Neuchâtel, 1781; 12 vols, Amsterdam 1782–8 (enl.); ed. L. Chaumeil, Paris 1947 (extracts). Tr. H. Simpson, *The waiting city: Paris 1782–88*, London 1933 (abr.).

    Le nouveau Paris, 6 vols, 1798; ed. L. Lacour, 2 vols, 1862. Tr. anon. *New picture of Paris*, 2 vols, Dublin 1800.

L'habitant de Guadeloupe, 1782. Tr. J. Wallace, *The merchant of Guadeloupe*, London 1802.

BÉCLARD, L., *Sébastien Mercier, sa vie, son oeuvre, son temps*, 1903.

MAJEWSKI, H., *Preromantic imagination of Louis-Sébastien Mercier*, New York 1971.

MONTESQUIEU, Charles de Secondat, Baron de   1689–1755

See also *L'ENCYCLOPÉDIE*.

DANGEAU, L., *Bibliographie de ses oeuvres*, 1874.

CABEEN, D. C., *A bibliography*, New York 1947.

    A supplementary Montesquieu bibliography, 1955 (in *Revue Internationale de Philosophie*, vol 9).

Montesquieu, Bibliothèque Municipale de Bordeaux, 1955 (exhibition catalogue).
See also SHACKLETON below.

Oeuvres, ed. F. Richer, 3 vols, Amsterdam and Leipzig 1758; ed. E. Laboulaye, 7 vols, Paris 1875–9; ed. R. Caillois, 2 vols, 1949–51; ed. A. Masson, 3 vols, 1949–55.
Extraits, ed. R. Guichemerre, 1957.
Textes choisis, ed. F. Strowski, c. 1912.

Tr. anon., *The complete works*, 4 vols, London 1777.

Les lettres persanes, 2 vols, Cologne 1721; 2 vols Amsterdam 1730; ed. E. Carcassonne, 2 vols, Paris 1929; ed. A. Adam, Geneva and Lille 1954; ed. P. Vernière, Paris 1960; ed. J. F. Revel, 1971; ed. J. Starobinski, 1973. Tr. J. Ozell, *Persian letters*, 2 vols, London 1722; tr. J. R. Loy, New York 1961; tr. G. A. Healy, Indianapolis (Ind) 1964.
Considérations sur les causes de la grandeur des Romains et de leur décadence, Amsterdam 1734; Paris 1748; ed. H. Barckhausen, 1900; ed. C. Jullian, 1923; ed. G. Truc, 1945. Tr. anon., *Reflections on the cause of the greatness of the Romans and their decline*, London 1734; tr. anon., *Considerations on the cause of the grandeur and declension of the Roman empire*, Glasgow 1883 (revd); tr. D. Lowenthal, *Consideration on the cause of the greatness of the Romans and their decline*, New York 1965.
Le temple de Gnide, 1742 (first pbd in *Bibliothèque françoise*, Amsterdam 1724); London 1760; ed. O. Uzanne, Rouen 1881. Tr. anon., *The temple of Gnidus*, London 1797.
Voyage à l'isle de Paphos, Florence 1747 (first pbd in *Mercure*, Paris 1727).
De l'esprit des loix, 2 vols, Geneva 1748; ed. C. Jullian, Paris 1896 (revd 1920; extracts); ed. J. Brethe de La Gressaye, 4 vols, 1950–61; ed. R. Derathé, 2 vols, 1973. Tr. T. Nugent, *The spirit of laws*, 2 vols, London 1750.
  Defense de l'Esprit, à laquelle on a joint quelques éclaircissements, Geneva 1750.
Dialogue de Sylla et d'Eucrate, 1748 (with *Considérations* above); ed. M. P. Cruice et al., 1848.
Goût, 1757 (entry in *L'Encyclopédie*, vol 7); London 1760 (renamed *Essai sur le goût*, with *Le temple de Gnide* above); Paris 1945. Tr. A. Gerard, Edinburgh 1764 (as appendix to his *An Essay on Taste*).
Mélanges inédits, ed. G. de Montesquieu, Bordeaux 1892.
Histoire véritable, n.p. 1892.
Voyages, ed. A. de Montesquieu et al., 2 vols, Bordeaux 1894–6.

Correspondance, ed. F. Gebelin and A. Morize, 2 vols, 1914.
Cahiers, 1716–1755, ed. B. Grasset and A. Masson, 1941.

BERLIN, I., *Montesquieu*, London 1956.

CARCASSONNE, E., *Montesquieu et le problème de la constitution française au 18e siècle*, 1927.

COTTA, S., *Montesquieu e la scienza della società*, Turin 1953.

DEDIEU, J., *Montesquieu et la tradition politique anglaise en France*, 1909; 1966.

DESTUTT DE TRACY, A. L. C., *Commentaire sur l'Esprit des lois*, 1819.

DODDS, M., *Les récits de voyages, sources de l'Esprit des lois*, 1929.

FERNANDEZ, R., in his *Itinéraire français*, 1943.

LEVIN, L. M., *The political doctrine of Montesquieu's Esprit des lois: its classical background*, New York 1936.

LOY, J. R., *Montesquieu*, New York 1968.

MOLIÈRE, J. J. G., *La théorie de la constitution anglaise chez Montesquieu*, Leiden 1972.

SAINTE-BEUVE, C. A. de, in his *Causeries du lundi*, vol 7, 1853.

SHACKLETON, R., *Montesquieu, a critical biography*, Oxford 1961 (incl. bibl.).

SOREL, A., *Montesquieu*, 1887.

STAROBINSKI, J., *Montesquieu par lui-même*, 1953.

VIAN, L., *Historique de Montesquieu, sa vie et ses oeuvres*, 1878.

WADDICOR, M. H., *Montesquieu and the philosophy of natural law*, The Hague, 1970.

PARNY, Évariste-Désiré de Forges de   1753–1814

Oeuvres, Ile de Bourbon 1780; 4 vols, Paris 1831; ed. J. A. Pons and C. A. de Sainte-Beuve, 1862.

Translated in anthologies, incl. *Anthology of French poetry*.

Poésies érotiques, Ile de Bourbon 1778; ed. L. de Forges de Parny, Paris 1949 (in his *Le Chevalier de Parny et ses poésies érotiques*).
Opuscules poétiques, Amsterdam 1779.
Poésies de Sapho, London 1781.
Chansons madécasses traduites en françois, London and Paris 1787.
La guerre des dieux, 1799; Paris 1808.
Goddam !, 1804.
Le portefeuille volé, 1805.
Le voyage de Céline, 1806.
Poésies inédites, ed. P. F. Tissot, 1827.

BARQUISSAU, R., in his *Les poètes créoles du 18e siècle*, 1949.

PIRON, Alexis   1689–1773

Bibl. See CHAPONNIÈRE below.

Oeuvres complettes, ed. Rigoley de Juvigny, 7 vols, 1776; ed. P. Dufay, 10 vols, 1928–31.

Oeuvres inédites, ed. H. Bonhomme, 2 vols, 1859.

Translated in anthologies, incl. *French lyrics in English verse* and *Anthology of French poetry*.

Gustave, 1733; 1788 (as *Gustave Wasa*).

La métromanie, 1738; 1765; ed. A. Rion, 1878.

Fernand Cortès, 1757.

Poésies diverses, London 1787.

La Priapée [. . .] *et l'Antipriapée*, n.p. 1795?; n.p., n.d. (as *Ode à Priape*).

CHAPONNIÈRE, P., *Alexis Piron, sa vie et ses oeuvres*, Geneva and Paris 1910 (incl. bibl. of works).

PRÉVOST D'EXILES, (Abbé) Antoine-François   1697–1763

Bibl. See HAZARD below.

Published some 50 novels, and travel and philosophy books, as well as translating Richardson's *Pamela* and *Clarissa*.

Oeuvres choisies, 39 vols, Amsterdam and Paris, 1783–4 (reissued Paris 1810–16).

Memoires et avantures d'un homme de qualité, 4 vols, Amsterdam 1730; 7 vols, 1731; ed. H. Frichet, Paris 1924 (vol 3); ed. M. E. I. Robertson, 1927 (vol 5: *Séjour en Angleterre*). Tr. anon., *Memoirs of a man of quality*, 3 vols, London 1738; tr. M. E. I. Robertson, *Adventures of a man of quality* (*in England*), London 1930 (tr. of vol 5).
    Suite des memoires, Amsterdam 1733.

Les avantures du chevalier des Grieux et de Manon Lescaut, Amsterdam 1731 (in *Memoires et avantures*, vol 7, above); 2 vols, 1753; ed. M. de Lescure, Paris, 1879; ed. L. Landré, New York 1930; ed. M. E. I. Robertson, 2 vols, Oxford 1943; ed. G. Matoré, Geneva 1953; ed. P. Vernière, Paris 1957; ed. F. Deloffre and R. Picard, 1965; ed. J. L. Borny and S. S. de Sacy, Paris 1972. Tr. C. Smith, *Manon Lescaut, or the fatal attachment*, London 1786; tr. H. Waddell, *The history of the Chevalier des Grieux and of Manon Lescaut*, 1931 (tr. of 1731 ed.); tr. L. W. Tancock, *Manon Lescaut*, Harmondsworth 1949; tr. D. M. Frame, New York 1961.

Le Pour et le Contre, 20 vols, 1733–40 (cntg 296 issues of periodical edited by Prévost).

Le doyen de Killerine, 6 vols, 1735–40. Tr. C. Davis, *The Dean of Coleraine*, 3 vols, London 1752.

Histoire d'une Grecque moderne, 2 vols, Amsterdam 1740; ed. R. Mauzi, Paris 1965. Tr. anon., *The history of a fair Greek*, London 1755.

Mémoires d'un honnête homme, 1745.

AUERBACH, E., in his *Mimesis,* Berne 1946. Tr. W. R. Trask, Princeton (NJ) 1953.

BILLY, A., *Un singuliar bénédictin: l'abbé Prévost,* 1969.

ENGEL, C. E., *Le véritable abbé Prévost,* Monaco 1958.

HARRISSE, H., *L'abbé Prévost: histoire de sa vie et de ses oeuvres,* 1896.

HAVENS, G. R., *The abbé Prévost and English literature,* Paris and Princeton (NJ) 1921.

HAZARD, P. et al., *Etudes critiques sur Manon Lescaut,* Chicago (Ill) 1929 (incl. critical bibl.).

KORY, O. A., *Subjectivity and sensibility in the novels of the Abbé Prévost,* 1972.

LAUFER, R., in his *Style rococo, style des lumières,* 1963.

LE BRETON, A., in his *Le roman au 18e siècle,* 1898.

MONTY, J. R., *Les romans de l'Abbé Prévost,* 1970.

RODDIER, H., *L'abbé Prévost, l'homme et l'oeuvre,* 1955.

SCHROEDER, V., *Un romancier français au 18e siècle: l'abbé Prévost,* 1898.

SGARD, J., *Prévost romancier,* 1968.

TRAHARD, P., in his *Les maîtres de la sensibilité française au 18e siècle,* vol 1, 1931.

RAYNAL, (Abbé) Guillaume   1713–1796

FEUGÈRE, A., *Bibliographie critique,* Angoulême 1922.

Oeuvres, 4 vols, Geneva 1784.

L'histoire du stathouderat, The Hague 1747; ed. M. Rousset, Amsterdam 1749. Tr. anon., *The history of the Stadtholdership,* n.p. 1749.

Histoire du parlement d'Angleterre, London 1748; Paris 1821.

Histoire philosophique et politique des établissemens et du commerce des Européens dans les deux Indes, 6 vols, Amsterdam 1770 (pbd clandestinely); 5 vols, Geneva 1780; 12 vols, Paris 1820–1. Tr. J. O. Justamond, *A philosophical and political history of the settlements and trade of the Europeans in the East and West Indies,* 4 vols, London 1776; Dublin 1779.

    Révolution de l'Amerique, London 1781. Tr. anon., *The revolution of America,* London 1781.

Tr. anon., *A philosophical and political history of the settlements and trade of the Europeans in the West Indies [. . .] to which is added the Revolution of America,* 6 vols, Edinburgh 1782.

Lettre [. . .] a l'Assemblée Nationale, n.p. 1790. Tr. anon., *A letter [. . .] to the National Assembly of France,* London 1791.

FEUGÈRE, A., *Un précurseur de la Révolution: l'abbé Raynal,* Angoulême 1922.

RESTIF (or RÉTIF) DE LA BRETONNE, Nicolas 1734–1806

LACROIX, P., *Bibliographie et iconographie de tous les ouvrages*, 1875.

BÉGUÉ, A., *Etat présent des études sur Restif da la Bretonne*, 1948.

CHILDS, J. R., *Témoignages et jugements; bibliographie*, 1949.

Published some 250 volumes in all.

Oeuvres, ed. H. Bachelin, 9 vols, 1930–2 (selection).

Le paysan perverti, 4 vols, The Hague and Paris 1776;
  La paysane pervertie, 4 vols, The Hague and Paris 1784;
  4 vols, The Hague 1787; ed. M. Talmeyr, Paris 1888 (abr.). Tr. and ed.
  A. H. Walton, *The corrupted ones*, London 1967.

La vie de mon père, 2 vols, Neuchâtel 1779; ed. M. Boisson, Paris 1924; ed.
  G. Rouger, 1970.

Les contemporaines, 42 vols, Leipzig 1780–5; ed. J. Assézat, 3 vols, Paris
  1875–6 (extracts).

Les nuits de Paris, ou le spectateur nocturne, 16 vols, London and Paris 1788–
  94; ed. H. Bachelin, Paris 1960. Tr. L. Asher and E. Fertig, *Les nuits de
  Paris, or the nocturnal spectator*, New York 1964 (selection).

Monsieur-Nicolas, ou le coeur-humain devoilé, 16 vols, 1794–7; ed. M. Renard,
  1924 (extracts). Tr. R. C. Mathers, *Monsieur Nicolas, or the human heart
  unveiled*, 6 vols, London 1930–1 (tr. of vols 1–12); tr. and ed. R. Baldick,
  Monsieur Nicolas, or the human heart laid bare, London 1966.

Histoire de Sara, 1797 (as episode in *Monsieur Nicolas*, vol 12 above); ed.
  P. O. Walzer, Lausanne 1947; ed. M. Blanchot, Paris 1949. Tr. R. C.
  Mathers, *Sara*, London 1927.

L'anti-Justine, 2 vols, 1798; ed. L. Perceau, n.d. Tr. P. Casavini, *Pleasures
  and follies of a good-natured libertine*, 1955.

Les posthumes, 4 vols, 1802.

Mes inscriptions, journal intime, 1780–1787, ed. P. Cottin, 1889.

CHADOURNE, M., *Restif de La Bretonne, ou le siècle prophétique*, 1958.

PORTER, C. A., *Restif's novels*, New Haven (Conn) and London 1967.

POSTER, M., *The utopian thought of Restif de la Bretonne*, New York 1971.

TABARANT, A., *Le vrai visage de Réstif de La Bretonne*, 1936.

RIVAROL, Antoine de 1753–1801

Bibl. See *La fiche bibliographique française*, La Rochelle, Sept. 1923; also
  LE BRETON below.

Oeuvres complètes, ed. C. J. Chênedollé and F. Fayolle, 5 vols, 1808 (cntg
  about two-thirds of works).

Oeuvres choisies, ed. M. de Lescure, 2 vols, 1880 (incl. collected articles from
  Journal Politique National in vol 2).

Ecrits politiques et littéraires choisis, ed. V. H. Debidour, 1957.

Rivarol: collection des plus belles pages, 1923.

Rivarol, ed. J. Dutourd, 1963 (extracts).

Le chou et le navet, n.p. 1782.

> *Lettre critique sur le poème des Jardins, suivi du Chou et du navet,* Amsterdam and Paris 1782.

De l'universalité de la langue françoise, Berlin 1784; Hamburg 1897; ed. M. Hervier, Paris 1929; ed. T. Suran, 1930; ed. H. Juin, 1966.

Le petit almanach de nos grands hommes, n.p. 1788; 1788.

> *Le petit almanach de nos grands hommes pour l'année 1790* (in collab. with Champcenetz), n.p. 1790.

Petit dictionnaire des grands hommes de la Révolution (in collab. with Champcenetz), 1790.

Une lettre à la noblesse françoise, Brussels 1792.

GOURMONT, R. de, in his *Promenades littéraires,* 1909.

GROOS, R., *La vraie figure de Rivarol,* 1927.

HARRIS, G. W., *Antoine Rivarol, journalist of the French Revolution,* Oxford 1940.

LE BRETON, A., *Rivarol, sa vie, ses idées, son talent,* 1895 (incl. bibl. of works).

LOISEAU, Y., *Rivarol,* 1961.

ROUSSEAU, Jean-Jacques   1712–1778

See also *L'ENCYCLOPÉDIE.*

LEDOS, E. G., *Catalogue des ouvrages de J. J. Rousseau conservés dans les grandes bibliothèques de Paris,* 1912.

COURTOIS, L. J., *Chronologie critique de la vie et des oeuvres,* Geneva 1924.

DUFOUR, T. A., *Recherches bibliographiques sur les oeuvres imprimées,* 2 vols, 1925.

SÉNELIER, J., *Bibliographie générale des oeuvres,* 1949.

SCHINZ, A., *Etat présent des travaux sur J. J. Rousseau,* Paris and New York 1941.

Annales de la Société Jean-Jacques Rousseau, tables des tomes 1–35, 1905–1962, Geneva 1965.

Oeuvres complètes, ed. P. Moultou and P. A. Du Peyrou, 33 vols, Geneva 1780–9; ed. J. A. Naigeon et al., 25 vols, Paris 1801; ed. B. Gagnebin, M. Raymond et al., 4 vols, 1959; ed. M. Launay, 3 vols, 1967–71.

Political writings, ed. C. E. Vaughan, 2 vols, Cambridge 1915.

Morceaux choisis, ed. D. Mornet, Toulouse 1910.

Vie et oeuvres, ed. A. Schinz, Boston (Mass) and New York 1921.

Tr. anon., *The works,* 10 vols, Edinburgh 1763–73.

Tr. anon., *The miscellaneous works*, 5 vols, London 1767.
Tr. G. D. H. Cole, *The social contract and the discourses*, London 1906 (revd
J. H. Brumfitt and J. C. Hall, 1973).
Tr. and ed. F. Watkins, *Political writings*, Edinburgh 1953.

Discours qui a remporté le prix à l'Académie de Dijon, Geneva 1750; 1763;
ed. G. R. Haven, New York 1946 (as *Discours sur les sciences et les arts*).
Tr. anon., *The discourse which carried the praemium at the Academy of
Dijon*, London 1751; tr. R. Wynne, *A discourse, to which the prize was
adjudged by the Academy of Dijon*, London 1752.
Le devin du village, 1753; ed. G. Duret, Geneva 1924. Tr. C. Burney, *The
cunning-man*, London 1766.
Discours sur l'origine et les fondements de l'inégalité, Amsterdam 1755; ed.
J. L. Lecercle, Paris 1954; ed. A. Kremer-Marietti, 1973. Tr. anon.,
A discourse upon the origin and foundation of the inequality among mankind,
London 1761; tr. anon., ed. C. W. Eliot, *On the inequality of mankind*,
Harvard 1910.
Economie ou Oeconomie, (morale et politique), 1755 (as entry in the *Encyclo-
pédie*, vol 5); Geneva 1758 (renamed *Discours sur l'œconomie politique*).
Tr. anon., *A dissertation on political economy*, New York 1797.
[Lettre] à Mr. d'Alembert [. . .], sur son article Genève, Amsterdam 1758; ed.
L. Brunel, Paris 1896; ed. M. Fuchs, Lille and Geneva 1948 (as *Lettre
à d'Alembert sur les spectacles*). Tr. anon., *A letter [. . .] to M. d'Alembert
concerning the effects of theatrical entertainments*, London 1759.
Lettre [. . .] à Monsieur de Voltaire, Berlin 1759 (pirate ed.); Paris 1764.
Lettres de deux amans, habitans d'une petite ville au pied des Alpes, 6 vols,
Amsterdam 1761 (with half-title *Julie, ou la nouvelle Héloïse*); ed. D.
Mornet, 4 vols, Paris 1925; ed. R. Pomeau, 1960. Tr. W. Kenrick, *Eloisa,
or a series of original letters*, 4 vols, London and Dublin 1761; tr. J. H.
McDowell, *Julie, or the new Eloise*, University Park (Pa) 1968 (abr.).
Du contract social, Amsterdam 1762; ed. E. Dreyfus-Brisac, Paris 1896; ed.
C. E. Vaughan, Manchester 1918; ed. M. Halbwachs, Paris 1942; ed.
J. M. Fataud and M. C. Bartholy, Paris 1972. Tr. anon., *A treatise on the
social contract*, London 1764; tr. G. Hopkins, in *Social contract; essays by
Locke, Hume and Rousseau*, New York and Oxford 1948; tr. W. Kendall,
Chicago (Ill) 1954; tr. M. Cranston, Harmondsworth 1969.
Emile, ou de l'éducation, 4 vols, The Hague 1762; ed. F. and P. Richard,
Paris 1939; ed. E. P. Duharcourt, 2 vols, 1958 (extracts); ed. H. Wallon
and J.-L. Lecercle, 1973 (selection). Tr. W. Kenrick, *Emilius and Sophia*,
4 vols, London 1762–3; tr. M. Nugent, *Emilius*, 2 vols, 1763; tr. B. Foxley,
Emile, London and New York 1911; tr. W. Boyd, *Emile for today*, London
1956 (extracts).
Emile et Sophie, ou les solitaires, Geneva 1782 (in *Oeuvres complètes*, vol 10
above).

121

Rousseau juge de Jean-Jacques, London and Lichfield 1780 (1st dialogue); Geneva 1782 (in *Oeuvres complètes*, vols 21–2 above).

Le vicaire savoyard, tiré du livre intitulé Emile, n.p., n.d.; Paris 1822 (as *La profession de foi du vicaire savoyard*); ed. P. M. Masson, Fribourg and Paris 1914. Tr. O. Schreiner, *The profession of a Savoyard vicar*, New York 1889; tr. anon., ed. C. W. Eliot, *Profession of faith of a Savoyard vicar*, Cambridge (Mass) 1910; tr. A. H. Beattie, *The creed of a priest of Savoy*, New York 1956.

Lettre [. . .] *à Christophe de Beaumont*, Amsterdam 1763. Tr. anon., *An expostulatory letter* [. . .] *to Christophe de Beaumont, Archbishop of Paris*, London 1763.

Lettres écrites de la montagne, Amsterdam 1764; ed. J. S. Spink, 1931.

Dictionnaire de musique, 1767; London 1776. Tr. W. Waring, *A complete dictionary of music*, London 1779.

Discours sur la vertu, Lausanne 1769.

Considérations sur le gouvernement de la Pologne, London 1772; The Hague and Lausanne 1783 (with *Lettres sur la législation de la Corse*, etc.). Tr. Watkins above, *Considerations on the government of Poland*.

Les confessions, 2 vols, Geneva 1782;
    Seconde partie des Confessions, 2 vols, Geneva 1789;
ed. A. van Bever, 2 vols, 1912; ed. E. Seillier, 3 vols, 1929; ed. J. Fournier, 2 vols, 1949; ed. J. Voisine, 1964. Tr. anon., *The confessions*, 5 vols, London 1783–90 (revd A. S. B. Glover, 2 vols, London 1938); tr. J. M. Cohen, Harmondsworth 1953.

Les rêveries du promeneur solitaire, Geneva 1782 (with *Les confessions* above); ed. A. van Bever, Paris 1912 (with *Les confessions* above); ed. M. Jobin, 1944 (extracts); ed. M. Raymond, Lille and Geneva 1948; ed. J. S. Spink, Paris 1948; ed. H. Roddier, 1960. Tr. anon., *The reveries of the solitary walker*, London 1783 (with *The confessions* above); tr. J. G. Fletcher, *The reveries of a solitary*, London and New York 1927.

Le nouveau Dédale, c. 1801; ed. collectively, Pasadena (Calif) 1950.

Recueil de lettres, 5 vols, Neuchâtel 1790.

Lettres originales [. . .] *à Madame de* . . ., *à Madame la maréchale de Luxembourg, à Monsieur de Malesherbes, à d'Alembert*, etc., ed. C. Pougens, 1798; ed. G. Rudler, London 1928 (*Lettres à M. de Malesherbes*). Tr. anon., *Letters* [. . .] *to M. de Malesherbes, d'Alembert, Madame la M. de Luxembourg*, etc., London 1799.

Correspondance générale, ed. T. Dufour and P. P. Plan, 20 vols, Paris and Geneva 1924–34; ed. R. A. Leigh, Geneva and Banbury 1965 onwards (21 vols pbd). Tr. anon., *Letters*, London 1790 (in *The Confessions*, above, vol 5); tr. C. W. Hendel, *Citizen of Geneva, selections from the letters of Jean-Jacques Rousseau*, New York and Oxford 1937.

Annales de la Société Jean-Jacques Rousseau, Geneva 1905 onwards.

BAUD-BOVY, S. et al., *Jean-Jacques Rousseau*, Neuchâtel 1962.

BURGELIN P., *La philosophie de l'existence de Rousseau*, 1952.

CASSIRER, E., *Das Problem Jean-Jacques Rousseau*, Berlin 1932 (in *Archiv für die Geschichte der Philosophie*, vol 41). Tr. and ed. P. Gay, *The question of Jean-Jacques Rousseau*, New York 1954.

CROCKER, L. G., *Jean-Jacques Rousseau*, 2 vols, New York 1968–73.

DERATHÉ, R., *Jean-Jacques Rousseau et la science politique de son temps*, 1950.

DOBINSON, E. H., *Rousseau; his thought and its relevance today*, London 1969.

DUCROS, L., *Jean-Jacques Rousseau*, 3 vols, Paris and Geneva 1908–18.

ELLIS, M. B., *Julie ou la nouvelle Héloïse: a synthesis of Rousseau's thought, 1749–1759*, Toronto 1949.

GREEN, F. C., *Jean-Jacques Rousseau: a study in his life and writings*, Cambridge 1955.

GRIMSLEY, R., *Jean-Jacques Rousseau; a critical study of self-awareness*, Cardiff 1961.

The philosophy of Rousseau, Oxford 1973.

GROETHUYSEN, B., *Jean-Jacques Rousseau*, 1949.

GUÉHENNO, J., *Jean-Jacques*, 3 vols, 1948–52. Tr. J. G. and D. Weightman, 2 vols, London and New York 1966.

HALL, J. C., *Rousseau: an introduction to his political thought*, London 1973.

HENDEL, C. W., *Jean-Jacques Rousseau, moralist*, 2 vols, London and New York 1934.

Jean-Jacques Rousseau et son oeuvre; problèmes et recherches, 1964 (conference organized by *Comité national pour la commémoration de Rousseau*).

Journées d'étude sur le Contrat social, Dijon 1962; Paris 1964.

JOST, F., *Jean-Jacques Rousseau, Suisse*, Fribourg 1961.

LECERCLE, J. L., *Rousseau et l'art du roman*, 1969.

LEMAÎTRE, J., *Jean-Jacques Rousseau*, 1907. Tr. J. Mairet and C. Bigot, New York 1907.

LICHET, R., *Rousseau, l'homme et l'oeuvre*, 1971.

MASSON, P. M., *La religion de Jean-Jacques Rousseau*, 3 vols, 1916.

MASTERS, R. D., *The political philosophy of Rousseau*, Princeton (NJ) 1968.

MORNET, D., *La nouvelle Héloïse de Jean-Jacques Rousseau; étude et analyse*, 1929.

Rousseau, l'homme et l'oeuvre, 1950.

RAYMOND, M., *Jean-Jacques Rousseau: la quête de soi et la rêverie*, 1962.

ROCHE, K. F., *Rousseau, stoic and romantic*, London 1974.

ROUSSEL, J., *Jean-Jacques Rousseau en France après la Révolution, 1795–1830*, 1972.

STAROBINSKI, J., *Jean-Jacques Rousseau: la transparence et l'obstacle*, 1957; 1971.

TEMMER, M. J., *Art and influence of Jean-Jacques Rousseau*, Chapel Hill (NC) 1973.

TROUSSON, R., *Rousseau et sa fortune litteraire*, Bordeaux 1971.

WRIGHT, E. H., *The meaning of Rousseau*, London 1929.

SADE, Donatien Alphonse François, Marquis de   1740–1814

CHANOVER, E. P., *A bibliography*, Metuchen (NJ) 1973.

See also Paulhan ed. of *Les infortunes de la vertu* below; also LÉLY below.

Oeuvres complètes, 27 vols, 1958; 13 vols, 1960–3 (incomplete); 15 vols, 1962–4; 16 vols, 1966–7.
L'oeuvre (selections), ed. G. Apollinaire, 1909; ed. M. Nadeau, 1947; ed. G. Lély, 1948.
Système de l'agression: textes politiques et philosophiques, ed. N. Chatelet, 1972.

Tr. L. de Saint-Yves, *Selected writings*, London 1953; tr. M. Crosland, 1953 (revd 1964).
Tr. R. Seaver and A. Wainhouse, *The complete Justine, Philosophy in the bedroom and other writings*, New York 1965; *The 120 days of Sodom and other writings*, 1966.
Tr. P. J. Gillette, *The complete Marquis de Sade*, 2 vols, Los Angeles (Calif) 1966.

Justine, ou les malheurs de la vertu, 2 vols, 1791; 1797. Tr. and ed. A. H. Watson, *Justine, or the misfortunes of virtue*, London 1964; tr. Gillette above, vol 1, *Justine*.
  La nouvelle Justine, ou les malheurs de la vertu, 4 vols, 1797; 10 vols, 1797 (with *L'histoire de Juliette, sa soeur, ou les prospérités du vice*), Netherlands 1797; 1963.
Aline et Valcour, 4 vols, 1793–5; ed. G. Lély 1962 (episode *Histoire de Sainville et de Léonore*); ed. P. Klossowski, c. 1963.
La philosophie dans le boudoir, 2 vols, 1795; 1924. Tr. P. Casavini, *The bedroom philosophers*, 1957.
Juliette, 4 vols, n.p. 1796; 1797 (with *La nouvelle Justine* above). Tr. Gillette above, vol 2, *Juliette, or vice amply rewarded*.
Pauline et Belval (ascribed), 3 vols, 1798.
Zoloé et ses deux acolytes (ascribed), 1800; ed. F. Mitton, 1928.
Les crimes de l'amour, 4 vols, 1800 (incl. *Idée sur les romans*, ed. O. Uzanne, 1878); ed. G. Lély, 3 vols, 1961. Tr. L. Bair et al., *The crimes of love*, New York 1964 (cntg *Eugénie de Franval, Miss Henrietta Stralson, Florille and Courval*); tr. W. Baskin, *Crimes of passion*, 1965 (cntg *Florille and Courval, Juliette and Raunai, Miss Henrietta Stralson*).
Les 120 journées de Sodome, ed. E. Dühren, 1904; ed. M. Heine, 3 vols, 1931–5. Tr. P. Casavini et al., *The 120 days of Sodom*, 1954.
Historiettes, contes et fabliaux, ed. M. Heine, 2 vols, 1926.
Dialogue entre un prêtre et un moribond, ed. M. Heine, 1926. Tr. Gillette above, vol 2, *Dialogue between a priest and a dying man*.
Les infortunes de la vertu, ed. M. Heine, 1930; ed. J. Paulhan, 1946 (incl. bibl. by R. Valençay); ed. B. Didier, 1970.

Histoire secrète d'Isabelle de Bavière, ed. G. Lély, 1953.
Cahiers personnels, 1803–4, ed. G. Lély, 1953.
Journal inédit, 1970.
Correspondance, ed. P. Bourdin, 1929.
Lettres, 3 vols, Avignon and Paris 1949–53. Comprising:
  L'Aigle Mlle, ed. G. Lély, Avignon 1949.
  Le carillon de Vincennes, ed. G. Lély, 1953.
  Monsieur le 6, ed. G. Daumas, 1954.
Lettres choisies, ed. G. Lély, 1963.
  Tr. W. J. Strachan, ed. M. Crosland, *Selected letters*, London 1965.

BARTHES, R., *Sade, Fourier, Loyola*, 1970.
BEAUVOIR, S. de, *Faut-il brûler Sade?*, 1955 (in *Privilèges*). Tr. A. Michelson, *Must we burn Sade?*, London and New York 1953.
BLANCHOT, M., *Lautréamont et Sade*, 1949.
BLIN, G., *Le sadisme de Baudelaire*, 1948.
DAWES, C. R., *The Marquis de Sade, his life and works*, London 1927.
DESBORDES, J., *Le vrai visage du marquis de Sade*, 1939.
GORER, G., *The revolutionary ideas of the Marquis de Sade*, London 1934; New York 1963 (enl., renamed *The life and ideas of the Marquis de Sade*).
HEINE, M., *Le marquis de Sade*, 1950.
KLOSSOWSKI, P., *Sade mon prochain*, 1947.
LAUGAA-TRAUT, F., *Lectures de Sade*, 1973.
LÉLY, G., *Vie du marquis de Sade*, 2 vols, 1952–7 (incl. bibl. of works in vol 2).
  Tr. A. Brown, *The Marquis de Sade, a biography*, London 1961.
  Le Marquis de Sade: étude sur sa vie et son oeuvre, 1967.
PRAZ, M., in his *La carna, la morte e il diavolo nella letteratura romantica*, Milan and Rome 1930. Tr. A. Davidson, *The romantic agony*, Oxford 1933.

SAINT-PIERRE, Jacques-Henri Bernardin de   1737–1814

TOINET, P., *Paul et Virginie: répertoire bibliographique et iconographique*, 1963.

Oeuvres complètes, ed. L. Aimé-Martin, 12 vols, 1826.

Tr. E. Clarke, *The works of Saint-Pierre, comprising his Studies of nature, Paul and Virginia, and Indian cottage*, 2 vols, London 1846.

La vie et les ouvrages de Jean-Jacques Rousseau, 1772; ed. A. M. Souriau, 1907.
L'Arcadie, Angers 1781. Tr. J. B. de la Roche, *Voyages of Amasis*, Boston (Mass) 1795 (part tr.).
Voyage à l'isle de France, 2 vols, Amsterdam and Paris 1783. Tr. J. Paris, *A voyage to the Island of Mauritius*, London 1775; tr. anon., *A voyage to the Isle of France*, London 1800.
Etudes de la nature, 3 vols, 1784; 4 vols, 1787 (with *Paul et Virginie* below). Tr. H. Hunter, *Studies of nature*, 5 vols, London 1796; tr. F. Shoberl, 4 vols, 1807.

Voeux d'un solitaire, 2 vols, 1789–92.

Harmonies de la nature, ed. L. Aimé-Martin, 3 vols, 1815; ed. A. M. Souriau, Caen, 1904 (in *Mémoires de l'Académie Nationale de Caen*); ed. S. F. Baridon, 2 vols, Milan and Varese 1958–9. Tr. W. Meeston, *Harmonies of nature*, 3 vols, London 1815.

Paul et Virginie, 1787 (in *Études de la nature*, vol 4 above); ed. V. P. Underwood, Manchester 1942; ed. P. Trahard, Paris 1959; ed. R. Etiemble and M. Du Cheyrdu, 1965 (in *Romanciers du 18e siècle*, vol 2); ed. R. Mauzi, 1966. Tr. D. Malthus, *Paul and Mary*, London 1789; tr. H. M. Williams, *Paul and Virginia*, Paris 1795; tr. anon., London and Philadelphia (Pa) 1923.

La chaumière indienne, 1791; ed. L. T. Ventouillac, London 1824. Tr. R. A. Kendall, *The Indian cottage*, 1791; tr. A. de Kosakoff, Nice 1862.

Le café de Surate, 1792 (in *Voeux d'un solitaire*, vol 2 above); ed. L. T. Ventouillac, London 1824.

Oeuvres posthumes, ed. L. Aimé-Martin, 1833.

Correspondance, ed. L. Aimé-Martin, 4 vols, 1826.

MAURY, F., *Etude sur la vie et les oeuvres de Bernardin de Saint-Pierre*, 1892.

ROULE, L., *L'histoire de la nature vivante d'après l'oeuvre des grands naturalistes français*, vol 5, 1930.

SOURIAU, M., *Bernardin de Saint-Pierre d'après ses manuscrits*, 1905.
      Bernardin de Saint-Pierre, son caractère, 1905.

TRAHARD, P., in his *Les maîtres de la sensibilité française au 18e siècle*, vol 4, 1933.

SAINT-SIMON, Louis de Rouvroy, Duc de   1675–1755

Bibl. See Truc ed. of *Mémoires* below.

Oeuvres complètes, ed. R. Dupuis, H. Comte and F. Bouvet, 1965 onwards (1 vol pbd).

Mémoires, 7 vols, London 1788–9 (incomplete; extract first pbd Brussels 1781, in *Pièces intéressantes et peu connues*); 13 vols, Paris and Strasbourg 1791 (incomplete); ed. H. J. V. de Saint-Simon, 21 vols, Paris 1829–30; ed. A. Chéruel, 20 vols, 1956–8; ed. A. de Boislisle et al., 45 vols, 1879–1928 (incl. 4 vols of indexes); ed. A. Tilley, Cambridge 1920 (selection); ed. L. Bertrand, Paris 1946 (extracts); ed. G. Truc, 7 vols, 1947–58 (incl. bibl.). Tr. B. St. John, *The memoirs*, 4 vols, London 1857 (abr.); tr. F. Arkwright, 6 vols, 1915–18 (abr.); tr. D. Flower, *Louis XIV at Versailles, a selection*, London 1953; tr. S. de Gramont, *The age of magnificence*, New York 1963 (selection); tr. L. Norton et al., *Historical memoirs*, 3 vols, London 1967–72.

BOISSIER, G., *Saint-Simon*, 1892.
CRUYSSE, D. van der, *Le portrait dans les Mémoires*, 1971.
LE BRETON, A., *La comédie humaine de Saint-Simon*, 1914.
SAINTE-BEUVE, C. A. de, in his *Causeries du lundi*, vols 2, 3, 11 and 15, 1851–62.
In his *Nouveaux lundis*, vol 10, 1870.
POISSON, G., *Monsieur de Saint-Simon*, 1973.

SEDAINE, Michel   1719–1797

Published over 30 plays and libretti in all.

Théâtre, ed. G. d'Heylli, 1877.

Poésies fugitives, n.p. 1752; 2 vols, London and Paris 1760.
Rose et Colas, 1764.
Le philosophe sans le savoir, 1766; ed. T. E. Oliver, Urbana (Ill) 1913; ed. E. Feuillerat, Paris 1936. Tr. W. H. Kent, Reading 1888.
La gageure imprévue, 1768; ed. C. Simond, 1890. Tr. anon., *A key to the lock*, London 1788.
Le déserteur, 1769. Tr. and adapt. C. Dibdin the Elder, *The deserter*, n.p. 1773.
Richard Coeur de Lion, 1786. Tr. J. Burgoyne, Dublin 1786.

LANSON, G., in his *Hommes et livres*, 1895.
REY, A., *Notes sur mon village; la vieillesse de Sedaine*, 1906.

VAUVENARGUES, Luc de Clapiers de   1715–1747

Bibl. See Gaillard de Champris ed. of *Oeuvres choisies* below; also CAVALUCCI below.

Oeuvres complètes, ed. A. de Fortia d'Urban, 2 vols, 1797; ed. J. B. Suard, A. Morellet and Voltaire, 2 vols, 1806; ed. D. L. Gilbert, 2 vols, 1857; ed. P. Varillon, 3 vols, 1929; ed. H. Bonnier, 2 vols, 1968.
Oeuvres choisies, ed. H. Gaillard de Champris, 1942 (incl. bibl.).

Introduction à la connoissance de l'esprit humain, suivie de réflexions et de maximes, 1746; 1747; ed. J. Roger-Charbonnel, 1934 (*Réflexions et maximes*). Tr. E. Lee, *Selections from the Characters, reflexions and maxims*, London 1903; tr. F. G. Stevens, *The reflections and maxims*, London 1940.

CAVALUCCI, G., *Vauvenargues dégagé de la légende*, Naples and Paris 1939 (incl. bibl.).
LANSON, G., *Le marquis de Vauvenargues*, 1930.
MORNET, D., in his *La pensée française au 18e siècle*, 1926; 1929.
PRÉVOST-PARADOL, L. A., in his *Etudes sur les moralistes français*, 1865.
SAITSCHICK, R., in his *Denker und Dichter*, Zurich 1948.
WALLAS, M., *Luc de Clapiers, Marquis de Vauvenargues*, Cambridge 1928.

VOLTAIRE 1694–1778
(pseudonym of François-Marie Arouet)

See also *L'ENCYCLOPÉDIE*

BENGESCO, G., *Bibliographie de ses oeuvres*, 4 vols, 1882–90.
> CROWLEY, F. J., *Corrections and additions*, Baltimore (Md) 1935 (in *Modern Language Notes*, vol 50).
> MALCOLM, J., *Table de la bibliographie*, Geneva 1953.

BARR, M. M., *A century of Voltaire study; a bibliography of writings on Voltaire, 1825–1925*, New York 1929.
> *Quarante anées d'études voltairiennes, bibliographie analytique de livres et articles sur Voltaire, 1926–1965*, 1968.

EVANS, H. B., *A provisional bibliography of English editions and translations*, Geneva 1959 (in *Studies on Voltaire and the Eighteenth Century*, vol 8).

Studies on Voltaire and the Eighteenth Century, general index to volumes 1–30, Geneva 1967 (as vol 31).

Oeuvres, 3 vols, The Hague 1728; 10 vols, Dresden 1748–54; 11 vols, Paris 1751; 45 vols, Geneva and Paris 1768–96; ed. P. A. de Beaumarchais et al., 70 vols (92 vols 12mo), Kehl 1784–93; ed. A. Beuchot, 72 vols, Paris 1828–40 (incl. 2 vols of tables by Miger); ed. L. Moland, 52 vols, 1877–85 (incl. tables by C. Pierrot, vols 51–2); ed. T. Besterman et al., Geneva 1969 onwards (8 vols pbd).

Romans et contes philosophiques, 2 vols, London 1775; ed. P. Van Tieghem, 4 vols, Paris 1930; ed. J. Fournier, 1948.

Selections, ed. G. R. Havens, New York 1925.

Dialogues et anecdotes philosophiques, ed. R. Naves, 1939.

Oeuvres historiques, ed. R. Pomeau, 1957.

Mélanges, ed. J. v.d. Heuvel, 1961.

Tr. Dr Smollett et al., *The works*, 25 vols, London 1761–5; 38 vols, 1761–81.

Tr. anon., *Select pieces (prose)*, London 1754.

Tr. anon., *A collection of the tales and smaller pieces*, 2 vols, Edinburgh 1792.

Tr. anon., *The philosophical tales, romances and satires*, London 1871.

Tr. W. Walton, *The whole prose romances*, 3 vols, London 1900.

Tr. anon., *The best known works of Voltaire, the complete romances, dialogues, and philosophic criticisms*, London 1932.

Oedipe, 1719; 1730.

La Ligue, ou Henri le Grand, Geneva 1723; London 1728 (renamed *La Henriade*); ed. J. Ravenel, Paris 1835; ed. O. R. Taylor, 3 vols, Geneva 1965. Tr. J. Lockman, *Henriade*, London 1732; tr. D. French, 1807.

Hérode et Mariamne, 1725; n.p. 1730 (renamed *Mariamne*).

Essay upon the civil wars of France, London 1727 (written in English); *Essai sur les guerres civiles de France*, The Hague 1729.

Histoire de Charles XII, roi de Suède, 2 vols, Rouen 1731; ed. M. Tourneux,

Paris 1882. Tr. anon., *The history of Charles XII*, London 1732; tr. W. Todhunter, 1908.

Le Brutus, 1731; Amsterdam 1731.

Le temple de goust, Rouen 1733; Amsterdam 1733; ed. E. Carcassonne, Paris 1938. Tr. anon., *The temple of taste*, London 1734.

Zaïre, Rouen and Paris 1733; Paris 1736; ed. M. Fontaine et al., 1889. Tr. and adapt., A. Hill, *The tragedy of Zara*, London 1736; tr. A. Wallace, Worthington 1854; tr. C. L. Lockert, Nashville (Tenn) 1956 (in *The chief rivals of Corneille and Racine*).

Lettres écrites de Londres sur les Anglois, London 1734 (first pbd in J. Lockman's tr., *Letters concerning the English nation*, London 1733); 1734 (renamed *Lettres philosophiques*); ed. G. Lanson, 2 vols, 1915–17; ed. R. Naves, 1939. Tr. E. Dilworth, *Philosophical letters*, Indianapolis (Ind) 1961.

La mort de César, Amsterdam 1735 (pbd clandestinely); Amsterdam 1736.

Alzire, ou les Américains, 1736; ed. E. Géruzez, 1849. Tr. and adapt. A. Hill, *Alzira*, London 1736.

Le mondain, n.p. 1736; ed. A. Morize, Paris 1909.

Elémens de la philosophie de Neuton, Amsterdam 1738; 1741 (enl.). Tr. J. Hanna, *The elements of Sir Isaac Newton's philosophy*, London 1738.

Lettres, The Hague 1738 (incl. *Epître à Uranie*).

Vie de Molière, 1739; Amsterdam 1739.

Mahomet, Brussels 1742 (pbd clandestinely); Amsterdam 1743; ed. A. M. Gossez, Lille 1932. Tr. J. Miller and J. Hoadly, *Mahomet the impostor*, London 1744; tr. R. L. Myers, *Mohomet the prophet*, New York 1964.

Le Mérope françoise, 1744; 1758; ed. T. E. Oliver, New York, 1925. Tr. J. Theobald, *Mérope*, London 1744; tr. and adapt. A. Hill, 1749.

La bataille de Fontenoy, 1745; 1745.

Princesse de Navarre, 1745.

Memnon, Amsterdam 1747 (pbd clandestinely); Nancy 1748 (renamed *Zadig, ou la destinée*); ed. G. Ascoli, 2 vols, Paris 1929; ed. V. L. Saulnier, 1946; ed. H. T. Mason, Oxford 1971. Tr. anon., *Zadig, or the book of fate*, London 1749; tr. R. B. Boswell, New York 1929; tr. R. Aldington, 1959; tr. J. Butt, Harmondsworth 1964.

Le monde comme il va, Dresden 1748 (in *Oeuvres*, vol 8 above); 1749 (renamed *Babouc, ou le monde comme il va*, in *Recueil de pièces en vers et en prose*). Tr. anon., *Babouc, or the world as it goes*, London 1754.

Nanine, 1749.

La tragédie de Sémiramis, 1749; ed. J. J. Olivier, 1946. Tr. anon., *Semiramis, a tragedy*, London 1760.

Oreste, 1750.

Le siècle de Louis XIV, 2 vols, Berlin 1751; 4 vols, Geneva 1768; ed. E. Bourgeois, Paris 1906. Tr. anon., *The age of Lewis XIV*, 2 vols, London 1752; tr. M. P. Pollack, *The age of Louis XIV*, London and Toronto 1926.

Discours en vers sur l'homme, Dresden 1752 (in *Oeuvres,* vol 3 above; cntg 7 poems first pbd separately or in groups, Amsterdam and Paris 1738–52). Tr. anon., *Three epistles in the ethic way,* London n.d.; tr. W. Gordon, *Epistles on happiness, liberty and envy,* 1738 (tr. of *Epîtres* 1–3: *Epîtres sur le bonheur, la liberté et l'envie*).

Le Micromégas, London 1752; ed. I. O. Wade, Princeton (NJ) and Oxford 1950. Tr. anon., *Micromegas,* London 1753.

Rome sauvée, Berlin 1752; Dresden and Geneva 1753 (renamed *Catalina, ou Rome sauvée*). Tr. anon., *Rome preserv'd,* London 1760.

Abrégé de l'histoire universelle, 2 vols, The Hague 1753.

Essai sur l'histoire universelle, Dresden and Leipzig 1754.

Annales de l'Empire depuis Charlemagne, 2 vols, The Hague and Berlin 1754. Tr. D. Williams et al., *Annals of the Empire from the reign of Charlemagne,* London 1781.

Histoire de la guerre de mil sept cent quarante et un, 2 vols, 1755; ed. J. Maurens, 1971. Tr. anon., *The history of the war of 1741,* London 1756 (revd Dublin 1756).

La pucelle d'Orléans, Frankfurt 1755; Geneva 1762; ed. J. Ravenel, Paris 1833; ed. J. Vercruysse, Geneva 1970 (in *Oeuvres* above). Tr. anon., *La Pucelle, or the Maid of Orleans,* London 1785–6; tr. E. Dowson, 1899; tr. H. Nelson, *The virgin of Orleans,* Denver (Colo) 1965.

Poèmes sur le désastre de Lisbonne et sur la loi naturelle, Geneva 1756 (following pirate eds the same year); ed. F. J. Crowley, Berkeley (Calif) 1938 (*Poème sur la loi naturelle*).

Essai sur l'histoire générale et sur les moeurs et l'esprit des nations, 7 vols, Geneva 1756; 8 vols, 1761–3; ed. R. Pomeau, Paris 1963. Tr. T. Nugent, *The general history and state of Europe,* 3 vols, London 1754 (revd and enl., 4 vols, Dublin 1759).

Candide, ou l'optimisme, Geneva 1759; ed. A. Morize, Paris 1913; ed. G. R. Havens, New York 1934; ed. R. Pomeau, Paris 1959; ed. C. Thacker, Geneva 1968; ed. C. Blum, Paris 1972. Tr. anon., *Candid, or all for the best,* London 1759; tr. R. Aldington, in *Candide and other romances,* 1927; tr. J. Butt, *Candide, or optimism,* West Drayton 1947; tr. L. Bair, New York 1959; tr. R. M. Adams, New York 1966.

Histoire de l'Empire de Russie sous Pierre le Grand, 2 vols, Geneva 1759–63; 2 vols, 1765. Tr. anon., *The history of the Russian Empire under Peter the Great,* London 1763.

Tancrède, 1761; Geneva 1761.

Pièces originales concernant la mort des sieurs Calas, Geneva 1762. Tr. anon., *Original pieces relating to the trial and execution of Mr John Calas,* London 1762.

Traité sur la tolérance, Geneva 1763; 1765 (enl.). Tr. anon., *A treatise on religious toleration,* London 1764; tr. J. McCabe, in *Toleration and other essays,* New York and London 1912.

Olimpie, Frankfurt and Leipzig 1763; Paris 1764.

Contes de Guillaume Vadé, Geneva 1764.

Dictionnaire philosophique portatif, Geneva 1764; London 1767; ed. J. Benda and R. Naves, 2 vols, Paris 1935–6. Tr. anon., *A philosophical dictionary for the pocket*, London 1765; tr. H. I. Woolf, *Philosophical dictionary*, 1945; tr. and ed. W. Baskin, 1962; tr. and ed. T. Besterman, Harmondsworth 1971.

La philosophie de l'histoire, Geneva 1765. Tr. anon., *The philosophy of history*, London 1766.

L'ingénu, Geneva 1767; Paris 1767 (renamed *Le Huron, ou l'ingénu*); ed. W. R. Jones, 1936; ed. J. H. Brumfitt and M. I. G. Davies, Oxford 1960 (with *Histoire de Jenni*, first pbd 1775). Tr. anon., *The pupil of nature*, London 1771; tr. J. Butt, Harmondsworth 1964 (with *Zadig* above).

Défense de mon oncle, Geneva 1767. Tr. anon., *A defence of my uncle*, London 1768.

Relation de la mort du chevalier de La Barre, n.p. 1768.

Droits des hommes, Geneva 1768.

Les singularités de la nature, Geneva 1768.

La princesse de Babilone, Geneva 1768; ed. P. Grimal, Paris 1942 (with other tales). Tr. T. E. Graham, *The Princess of Babylon*, Calcutta 1944.

L'homme aux quarante écus, Geneva and Paris 1768. Tr. anon., *The man of forty crowns*, Glasgow 1768.

Histoire du Parlement de Paris, 2 vols, Amsterdam 1769; Geneva 1773.

Fragments sur l'Inde, sur le général Lalli et sur le comte de Morangiès, Geneva 1773. Tr. F. Bedi, *Fragments on India*, Lahore 1937.

Les loix de Minos, Geneva and Paris 1773; 1773.

Le taureau blanc, Geneva 1774; ed. R. Pomeau, Lyon 1956. Tr. anon., *The white bull*, London 1774; tr. C. E. Vulliamy, London 1929 (with *Saul* and various short pieces).

Irène, 1779.

Prix de la justice et de l'humanité, Geneva 1778.

Traité de métaphysique, Kehl 1784 (in *Oeuvres*, vol 32 above); ed. H. T. Patterson, Manchester 1937.

Mémoires pour servir à la vie de M. de Voltaire écrits par lui-même, Geneva 1784; ed. J. Brenner, Paris 1965. Tr. anon., *Memoirs of the life of Voltaire*, London 1784.

Voltaire's notebooks, ed. T. Besterman, 2 vols, Geneva 1952.

Correspondance, ed. T. Besterman, Geneva and Banbury 1953 onwards (114 vols pbd). Tr. and ed. T. Besterman, *Select letters*, London 1963.

Lettres d'amour de Voltaire à sa nièce, ed. T. Besterman, Paris and Lausanne 1957. Tr. T. Besterman, *The love letters of Voltaire to his niece*, London 1958.

Lettres choisies, ed. R. Naves, 1963.

Tr. R. Aldington, *Letters of Voltaire and Frederick the Great*, London 1927 (selection).

BESTERMAN, T., *Voltaire*, London and Harlow 1969.

BRAILSFORD, H. N., *Voltaire and reform in the light of the French Revolution*, New York and London 1935; 1969.

BRUMFITT, J. H., *Voltaire, historian*, Oxford 1958.

CHAMPION, E., *Voltaire, études critiques*, 1893; 1921.

DESNOIRESTERRES, G., *Voltaire et la société au 18e siècle*, 8 vols, 1867–76.

GAY, P., *Voltaire's politics*, Princeton (NJ) 1959.

LANSON, G., *Voltaire*, 1906; 1910; ed. R. Pomeau, 1960. Tr. R. A. Wagoner, New York 1966 (enl.).

LION, H., *Les tragédies et les théories dramatiques de Voltaire*, 1895.

MAUROIS, A., *Voltaire*, London 1932. Tr. H. Miles, 1932.

MORLEY, J., *Voltaire*, London 1872.

NAVES, R., *Voltaire et l'Encyclopédie*, 1938.

  Le goût de Voltaire, 1938.

  Voltaire, l'homme et l'oeuvre, 1942.

POMEAU, R., *La religion de Voltaire*, 1956; 1969.

  Voltaire par lui-même, 1955.

RIDGWAY, D. S., *Voltaire and sensibility*, Montreal and London 1973.

SAKMANN, P., *Voltaires Geistesart und Gedankenwelt*, Stuttgart 1910.

SAREIL, J., *Voltaire et la critique*, Englewood Cliffs (NJ) 1966.

Studies on Voltaire and the 18th Century, ed. T. Besterman, Geneva and Banbury 1955 onwards.

TORREY, N. L., *The spirit of Voltaire*, New York 1938.

WADE, I. O., *Voltaire and Mme du Châtelet, an essay on the intellectual activity at Cirey*, Princeton (NJ) 1941.

5

The Nineteenth Century

AMIEL, Henri-Frédéric   1821–1881

Bibl. See MATTHEW below.

Fragments d'un journal intime, ed. E. Scherer, 2 vols, Paris and Geneva 1884;
   2 vols 1887 (enl.); ed. B. Bouvier, 3 vols, 1923 (enl.); ed. B. Bouvier, 2
   vols, Paris 1927 (enl.). Tr. and ed. Mrs H. Ward, *Amiel's journal*, 2 vols,
   London and New York 1885; tr. Van Wyck Brooks and C. Wyck Brooks,
   The private journal of Henri-Frédéric Amiel, New York 1935.
   Philine, fragments inédits du Journal intime, ed. B. Bouvier and E. Jaloux,
      1927. Tr. Van Wyck Brooks, *Philine*, London 1931.
   Journal intime 1839–50, ed. L. Bopp, 3 vols, Geneva 1948–58.
   Journal intime de l'année 1866, ed. L. Bopp, 1959.
   Journal intime de l'année 1857, ed. G. Poulet, 1965.
Essais critiques, ed. B. Bouvier, 1931.

La jeunesse d'Henri-Frédéric Amiel, lettres à sa famille, ses amis, ed. B. Bouvier,
   1935.

BOPP, L., *H. F. Amiel*, 1926; 1931.
HALDA, B., *Amiel et les femmes*, 1964.
MATTHEW, J., *Amiel et la solitude*, Annemasse (Hte. Savoie) 1932 (incl. bibl.).
PFISTER, S., *Expansion et concentration dans la pensée d'Amiel*, Berne and
   Frankfurt 1971.

BALZAC, Honoré de   1799–1850

SPOELBERCH DE LOVENJOUL, C. de, *Histoire des oeuvres*, 1879; 1886.
ROYCE, W. H., *A Balzac bibliography*, 2 vols, Chicago (Ill) 1929–30.
GEORGE, A. J., *Books by Balzac*, Syracuse (NY) 1960.
LONGAUD, F., *Dictionnaire de Balzac*, 1969.

Oeuvres complètes de Horace de Saint Aubin, 16 vols, 1836–40 (cntg 8 early
   novels written under pseudonym).
Oeuvres complètes, 17 vols, 1842–8 ('Furne ed.', cntg collected works under
   general title *La comédie humaine* for first time); 26 vols, 1869–76 ('Edition

définitive'); ed. M. Bouteron and H. Longnon, 40 vols, 1912–40; ed. M. Bouteron, R. Pierrot and F. Lotte, 11 vols, 1935–59; ed. M. Bardèche et al., 28 vols, 1957–63; ed. J. A. Ducourneau et al., 1965 onwards (27 vols pbd).

La comédie humaine, 17 vols, 1842–8 (as *Oeuvres complètes* above); 17 vols, 1869–70 (in *Oeuvres complètes*, édition définitive above); ed. P. G. Castex and P. Citron, 7 vols, 1965. Tr. K. P. Wormeley, *The comedy of human life*, 40 vols, Boston 1896; tr. C. Bell, E. Marriage, J. Waring and R. S. Scott, ed. G. Saintsbury, *Comédie humaine*, 40 vols, London 1895–8; tr. G. B. Ives et al., *The human comedy*, 53 vols, 1911 (vols 1–11 first pbd 1895–6). Many vols also tr. separately, below.

Tr. E. de Valcourt-Vermont, *The dramatic works*, 2 vols, Chicago 1901.

Many of the following works were first published in serial form in various periodicals. '*Ed. déf.*' refers to the 1869–76 edition of the *Oeuvres complètes* above; for works in the *Comédie humaine*, the division to which they belong in this edition is also given, unless it has remained unchanged since first publication.

Le centenaire, 4 vols, 1822; 2 vols, 1837 (renamed *Le Sorcier*, in *Oeuvres complètes de Horace de Saint Aubin* above).

Le vicaire des Ardennes, 4 vols, 1822; 2 vols, 1836 (in *Oeuvres complètes de Horace de Saint Aubin* above).

Annette et le criminel, ou suite du Vicaire des Ardennes, 4 vols, 1824; 2 vols, 1837 (renamed *Argow le pirate*, in *Oeuvres complètes de Horace de Saint Aubin* above).

Physiologie du mariage, 2 vols, 1829; 1870 (in *Ed. déf., Etudes analytiques*). Tr. F. Macnamara, *The physiology of marriage*, London 1925.

Le dernier Chouan, 4 vols, 1829; 2 vols, 1834 (renamed *Les Chouans*); 1870 (in *Ed. déf., Etudes de moeurs: scènes de la vie militaire*); ed. M. Allem, 1952. Tr. G. Saintsbury, *The Chouans*, London 1890; tr. M. A. Crawford, Harmondsworth 1972.

Scènes de la vie privée, 2 vols, 1830; 4 vols, 1832 (enl.).

La maison du chat qui pelote, 1830 (as *Gloire et malheur*, in *Scènes de la vie privée* above); 1869 (in *Ed. déf.*).

Gobseck, 1830 (as *Les dangers de l'inconduite*, in *Scènes de la vie privée* above); 1869 (in *Ed. déf.*).

La paix du ménage, 1830 (in *Scènes de la vie privée* above); 1869 (in *Ed. déf.*). Tr. M. A. Crawford, *Domestic peace*, Harmondsworth 1958.

La peau de chagrin, 2 vols, 1831; 2 vols, 1831 (as vols 1 and 2 of *Romans et contes philosophiques* below); 1870 (in *Ed. déf., Etudes philosophiques*). Tr. C. Paul, *The fatal skin*, London 1946.

Romans et contes philosophiques, 3 vols, 1831.

[*La femme de trente ans*], 1832–5; 1869 (in *Ed. déf., Etudes de moeurs: scènes de la vie privée*); ed. M. Allem, 1944. Comprising:

1 *Premières fautes*, 1832 (as *Le rendez-vous*, in *Scènes de la vie privée* above).

2 *Souffrances inconnues*, 1834 (in *Etudes de moeurs: scènes de la vie privée* below).

3 *A trente ans*, 1832 (as *La femme de trente ans*, in *Scènes de la vie privée* above).

4 *Le doigt de Dieu*, 1832 (in *Scènes de la vie privée* above); 1834–5 (combined with *La vallée du torrent*).

5 *Les deux rencontres*, 1832 (in *Scènes de la vie privée* above).

6 *La vieillesse d'une mère coupable*, 1832 (as *L'expiation*, in *Scènes de la vie privée* above).

[*Les célibataires*], 1832–43; 1869 (in *Ed. déf.*, *Etudes de moeurs: scènes de la vie de province*). Comprising:

1 *Pierrette*, 2 vols, 1840.

2 *Le curé de Tours*, 1832 (as *Les célibataires*, in *Scènes de la vie privée* above). Tr. M. Lawrence, *The curé of Tours*, Boston (Mass) 1964.

3 *La rabouilleuse*, 2 vols, 1843 (as *Les deux frères*). Tr. E. Wilkins, *A bachelor's establishment*, London 1951; tr. D. Adamson, *The black sheep*, Harmondsworth 1972.

Nouveaux contes philosophiques, 1832.

Louis Lambert, 1832 (as *Notice biographique sur Louis Lambert*, in *Nouveaux contes philosophiques* above); 1833 (enl. and renamed *Histoire intellectuelle de Louis Lambert*); 1870 (in *Ed. déf.*, *Etudes philosophiques*); ed. M. Bouteron and J. Pommier, 1961.

Adieu, 1832 (as *Le devoir d'une femme*); 1870 (in *Ed. déf.*, *Etudes philosophiques*).

Les cent contes drolatiques, *1er dixain*, 1832.

 Deuxième dixain, 1833.

 Troisième dixain, 1837.

 Quatriesme dixain, 1925 (in *Cahiers balzaciens*).

 Quint dixain, ed. M. Bouteron and H. Longnon, 1938 (in *Oeuvres complètes*, vol 37 above).

 Dixiesme dixain, ed. M. Bouteron and H. Longnon, 1938 (in *Oeuvres complètes*, vol 37 above).

 Tr. G. R. Sims, *Contes drôlatiques*, London 1874; tr. A. Brown, 2 vols, 1958.

Le medecin de campagne, 2 vols, 1833; 1870 (in *Ed. déf.*, *Etudes de moeurs: scènes de la vie de campagne*); ed. M. Allem, 1931. Tr. anon., *The country doctor*, London 1911.

Etudes de moeurs au XIXe siècle, 12 vols, 1834–7 (consisting of *Scènes de la vie privée*, 4 vols; *Scènes de la vie de province*, 4 vols; *Scènes de la vie parisienne*, 4 vols).

[*Histoire des Treize*], 1834–5; 1869 (in *Ed. déf.*, *Etudes de moeurs: scènes de la vie parisienne*). Tr. H. J. Hunt, *History of the Thirteen*, Harmondsworth 1974. Comprising:

1 *Ferragus, chef des dévorants*, 1834 (in *Etudes de moeurs: scènes de la vie parisienne* above). Tr. Lady Knutsford, *The mystery of the rue Solymane*, London, 1894.

2 *Duchesse de Langeais*, 1834 (as *Ne touchez pas la hache*, in *Etudes de moeurs: scènes de la vie parisienne* above); ed. G. Mayer, 1948. Tr. D. Mitford, *The Duchesse de Langeais*, London 1949.

3 *La fille aux yeux d'or*, 1834–5 (in *Etudes de moeurs: scènes de la vie parisienne* above). Tr. E. Dowson, *The girl with the golden eyes*, London 1896.

Eugénie Grandet, 1834 (in *Etudes de moeurs: scènes de la vie de province* above); 1869 (in *Ed. déf.*); ed. M. Allem, 1929. Tr. anon., London and New York 1859; tr. M. A. Crawford, Harmondsworth 1955; tr. H. Reed, New York 1964; tr. M. Lawrence, Boston (Mass) 1964 (with *The Curé of Tours* above).

La recherche de l'absolu, 1834 (in *Etudes de moeurs: scènes de la vie privée* above); 1870 (in *Ed. déf.*, *Etudes philosophiques*). Tr. W. Robson, *Balthazar, or science and love*, London and New York 1859; tr. H. Blanchamp, *The tragedy of a genius*, London 1911.

L'illustre Gaudissart, 1834 (in *Etudes de moeurs: scènes de la vie de province* above); 1869 (in *Ed. déf.*).

Le père Goriot, 2 vols, 1835; 1869 (in *Ed. déf.*, *Etudes de moeurs: scènes de la vie privée*). Tr. anon. *Daddy Goriot*, London 1860; tr. M. A. Crawford, *Old Goriot*, Harmondsworth 1951; tr. H. Reed, New York 1962.

Le contrat de mariage, 1835 (as *La fleur des pois*, in *Etudes de moeurs: scènes de la vie privée* above); 1869 (in *Ed. déf.*).

Séraphita, 1835 (in *Le livre mystique*); 1870 (in *Ed. déf.*, *Etudes philosophiques*).

Etudes philosophiques, 20 vols, 1835–40.

Le lys dans la vallée, 2 vols, 1836; 1869 (in *Ed. déf.*, *Etudes de moeurs: scènes de la vie de province*); ed. M. Allem, 1931. Tr. L. Hill, *The lily in the valley*, London 1957.

[*Illusions perdues*], 1837–43; 1869 (in *Ed. déf.*, *Etudes de moeurs: scènes de la vie de province*); ed. G. Mayer, 1946. Tr. K. Raine, *Lost illusions*, London 1951. Comprising:

1 *Les deux poètes*, 1837 (as *Illusions perdues*, in *Etudes de moeurs: scènes de la vie de province* above).

2 *Un grand homme de province à Paris*, 2 vols, 1839.

3 *Les souffrances de l'inventeur*, 1843 (as *Eve et David*, in *La comédie humaine* above, *Scènes de la vie de province*).

La messe de l'athée, 1837 (in *Etudes philosophiques* above); 1869 (in *Ed. déf.*, *Etudes de moeurs: scènes de la vie privée*).

Histoire de la grandeur et de la décadence de César Birotteau, 2 vols, 1837; 1869 (in *Ed. déf.*, *Etudes de moeurs: scènes de la vie parisienne*); ed. M. Allem, 1930. Tr. J. H. Simpson, *History of the grandeur and downfall of*

César Birotteau, London 1860; tr. F. Frenaye, London 1956.

[*Splendeurs et misères des courtisanes*], 1838–48; 1869 (in *Ed. déf.*, *Etudes de moeurs: scènes de la vie parisienne*). Comprising:

1   *Comment aiment les filles*, 1838 (incomplete, as *La Torpille*, in *La femme supérieure*); 1845 (complete, with *A combien l'amour revient aux vieillards*, as *Splendeurs et misères des courtisanes: Esther*).

2   *A combien l'amour revient aux vieillards*, 1844 (with *Comment aiment les filles* above, as *Splendeurs et misères des courtisanes: Esther*).

3   *Où mènent les mauvais chemins*, 1846 (in *La comédie humaine* above, *Scènes de la vie parisienne*).

4   *La dernière incarnation de Vautrin*, 3 vols, 1848 (with *Les martyrs ignorés* and *Une rue de Paris et son habitant*).

Les employés, 2 vols, 1838 (as *La femme supérieure*, with *La Torpille* above); 1869 (in *Ed. déf.*, *Etudes de moeurs: scènes de la vie parisienne*).

La Maison Nucingen, 1838 (with *La femme supérieure* above); 1869 (in *Ed. déf.*, *Etudes de moeurs: scènes de la vie parisienne*).

Une fille d'Eve, 2 vols, 1839 (with *Massimilla Boni*); 1869 (in *Ed. déf.*, *Etudes de moeurs: scènes de la vie privée*).

Béatrix, 2 vols, 1839 (pts 1–2); 2 vols, 1845 (pt 3, as *La lune de miel*); 1869 (in *Ed. déf.*, *Etudes de moeurs: scènes de la vie privée*). Tr. R. and S. Harcourt-Smith, *Love in duress*, London and New York 1957.

Vautrin, 1840.

Le curé de village, 2 vols, 1841; 1870 (in *Ed. déf.*, *Etudes de moeurs: scènes de la vie de campagne*). Tr. anon., *The country parson*, London 1914.

Ursule Mirouet, 2 vols, 1842; 1869 (in *Ed. déf.*, *Etudes de moeurs: scènes de la vie de province*).

Une ténébreuse affaire, 3 vols, 1842; 1870 (in *Ed. déf.*, *Etudes de moeurs: scènes de la vie politique*). Tr. G. Hopkins, *The Gondreville mystery*, London and New York 1958.

Mémoires de deux jeunes mariés, 2 vols, 1843; 1869 (in *Ed. déf.*, *Etudes de moeurs: scènes de la vie privée*). Tr. anon., introd. H. James, *The two young brides*, London 1902.

Un début dans la vie, 2 vols 1844 (with *La fausse maîtresse*); 1869 (in *Ed. déf.*, *Etudes de moeurs: scènes de la vie privée*); ed. G. Robert and G. Matoré, Geneva and Lille 1950.

Modeste Mignon, 2 vols, 1844 (as *Les trois amoureux*); 1869 (in *Ed. déf.*, *Etudes de moeurs: scènes de la vie privée*).

Petites misères de la vie conjugale, 1845 (pbd in 50 pts); 1870 (in *Ed. déf.*, *Etudes analytiques*). Tr. G. Tickell, *Pinpricks of married life*, London 1957.

[*L'envers de l'histoire contemporaine*], 1846–8; 1870 (in *Ed. déf.*, *Etudes de moeurs: scènes de la vie politique*). Comprising:

1   *Madame de la Chanterie*, 1846 (as *L'envers de l'histoire contemporaine*, in *Comédie humaine* above, *Scènes de la vie politique*).

2   *L'initié*, 2 vols, 1848 (with *El Verdugo*).

Les parents pauvres, 1847 (as *Histoire des parens pauvres*, with *Les grands danseurs du roi*, by C. Rabou); 1869 (in *Ed. déf.*, *Etudes de moeurs: scènes de la vie parisienne*); ed. M. Allem, 1937. Comprising:

1 *La cousine Bette*, 1847 (in *Histoire des parens pauvres*). Tr. K. Raine, *Cousin Bette*, London 1948; tr. M. A. Crawford, Harmondsworth 1965.

2 *Le cousin Pons*, 1847 (as *Les deux musiciens*, in *Histoire des parens pauvres*). Tr. N. Cameron, *Cousin Pons*, London 1950; tr. H. J. Hunt, Harmondsworth 1968.

La marâtre, 1848. Tr. E. Saunders, *The stepmother*, London 1958.

Les paysans, 5 vols, 1855 (pbd by Balzac's wife from serial version of Dec. 1844 and proofs of 1847, and possibly completed by her, with *Traité des excitants* and *Voyage de Paris à Java*); 1870 (in *Ed. déf.*, *Etudes de moeurs: scènes de la vie de campagne*).

Correspondance 1819–1850, 2 vols, 1876. Tr. C. L. Kenny, *The correspondence*, 2 vols, London 1878.

Lettres à l'étrangère, 1833–44, 4 vols, 1899–1950. Tr. K. P. Wormeley, *Letters to Madame Hanska*, Boston 1900 (tr. of vol 1); tr. anon., *The love letters*, 2 vols, London 1901 (tr. of vol 1).

Lettres à sa famille, 1809–1850, ed. W. S. Hastings, Princeton (NJ) 1934.

Correspondance inédite avec Zulma Carraud, ed. M. Bouteron, 1951. Tr. J. L. May, *The unpublished correspondence of Honoré de Balzac and Madame Zulma Carraud*, London 1937.

Correspondance, ed. R. Pierrot, 1960 onwards (4 vols pbd).

ALAIN, *Avec Balzac*, 1937.

BARBÉRIS, P., *Le monde de Balzac*, 1973.

BARDÈCHE, M., *Balzac romancier*, 1940.

BÉGUIN, A., *Balzac lu et relu*, 1965.

BÉRARD, S. J., *Le genèse d'un roman de Balzac: Illusions perdues*, 2 vols, 1961.

BERTAULT, P., *Balzac, l'homme et l'oeuvre*, 1947; 1968.

BILLY, A., *Vie de Balzac*, 1944.

BOREL, J., *Le lys dans la vallée, et les sources profondes de la création balzacienne*, 1961.

BOUTERON, M., *Etudes balzaciennes*, 1954.

FOREST, J., *L'aristocratic balzacienne*, 1973.

HEMMINGS, F., *Balzac, an interpretation of La comédie humaine*, New York 1967.

HUNT, H. J., *Honoré de Balzac*, London 1957.

LAUBRIET, P., *L'intelligence de l'art chez Balzac*, 1961.

MCCORMICK, D. F., *Les nouvelles de Balzac*, 1973.

MARCEAU, F., *Balzac et son monde*, 1955. Tr. D. Coltman, *Balzac and his world*, London 1967.

MAUROIS, A., *Prométhée, ou la vie de Balzac*, 1963. Tr. N. Denny, *Prometheus*, London and New York 1965.

NYKROG, P., *La pensée de Balzac*, Copenhagen 1965.
OLIVER, E. J., *Honoré de Balzac*, London 1965.
PICON, G., *Balzac par lui-même*, 1956.
PRITCHETT, V. S., *Balzac*, London 1973.
THOORENS, L., *La vie passionnée de Honoré de Balzac*, 1959.
WURMSER, A., *La comédie inhumaine*, 1964; 1970.

BANVILLE, Théodore de   1823–1891

Oeuvres, 3 vols, 1925.
Poésies complètes, 3 vols, 1878–9; 3 vols, 1891–1907.
Tr. in anthologies.

Les cariatides, 1842.
Les stalactites, 1846; ed. E. M. Souffrin, 1942.
Odes funambulesques, 1857.
Scènes de la vie, 7 vols, 1859–1888 (collections of articles, entitled *Esquisses parisiennes*, *Contes pour les femmes*, *Contes féeriques*, *Contes héroiques*, *Contes bourgeois*, *Dames et demoiselles* and *Les belles poupées*).
Gringoire, 1866. Tr. and adapt. A. Shirley, *Pity*, n.p. 1882; tr. A. B. Myrick, *Gringoire*, Boston 1916.
Petit traité de poésie française, 1872.
Trente-six ballades joyeuses, 1873. Tr. A. T. Strong, *The Ballades*, London 1913.
Mes souvenirs, 1882.

CHARPENTIER, J., *Théodore de Banville, l'homme et son oeuvre*, 1925.
DENOMMÉ, R. T., in his *The French Parnassian poets*, Carbondale (Ill) and London 1972.
FUCHS, M., *Théodore de Banville*, 1912.
SICILIANO, I., *Dal romanticismo al simbolismo, Théodore de Banville*, Turin 1927.

BARBEY D'AUREVILLEY, Jules   1808–1889

SEGUIN, J. P., *Etudes de bibliographie critique*, Avranches 1949.
See also PETIT and YARROW below.

Oeuvres complètes, 17 vols, 1926–7.
Oeuvres romanesques complètes, ed. J. Petit, 2 vols, 1964–6.

Du dandysme et de G. Brummell, Caen 1845; Paris 1879 (with *Un dandy d'avant les dandys*). Tr. D. Ainslie, *Of dandyism and of George Brummell*, London 1897; tr. D. B. Wyndham Lewis, *The anatomy of dandyism*, 1928.
Une vieille maîtresse, 1851.

L'ensorcelée, 2 vols, 1855. Tr. L. C. Willcox, *Bewitched*, New York and London 1928.

XIXe siècle, les oeuvres et les hommes, 26 vols, 1860–1909; ed. J. Petit, 2 vols, 1964–6.

Les chevalier des Touches, 1864.

Un prêtre marié, 1865.

Les diaboliques, 1874 (incl. *Le rideau cramoisi*); ed. J. H. Bornecque, 1963. Tr. E. Boyd, *The diaboliques*, London and New York 1926; tr. J. Kimber, introd. E. Starkie, *The she-devils*, London 1964.

Une histoire sans nom, 1883.

Ce qui ne meurt pas, 1884. Tr. S. Melmoth, *What never dies*, Paris 1902.

Le théâtre contemporain, 5 vols, 1887–96.

Omnia (carnet de notes), ed. A. Hirschi and J. Petit, Besançon 1970.

Lettres à Trébutien, 4 vols, 1927.

BÉSUS, R., *Barbey d'Aurevilly*, 1958.

BORDEAUX, H., *Le Walter Scott normand*, 1925.

CANU, J., *Barbey d'Aurevilly*, 1945.

Barbey d'Aurevilly, 1966 onwards.

CORBIÈRE-GILLE, G., *Barbey d'Aurevilly, critique littéraire*, Geneva 1962.

PETIT, J. and YARROW, S. J., *Barbey d'Aurevilly, journaliste et critique*, 1959 (incl. bibl.).

ROGERS, B. G., *The novels and stories of Barbey d'Aurevilly*, 1967.

YARROW, P. J., *La pensée politique et religieuse de Barbey d'Aurevilly*, Geneva and Paris 1961.

BARRÈS, Maurice   1862–1923

ZARACH, A., *Bibliographie barrésienne, 1881–1948*, 1951.

Oeuvres complètes, ed. P. Barrès, 1965 onwards (18 vols pbd).

Le culte du moi, 1887–91. Comprising:
    Sous l'oeil des barbares, 1887.
    Un homme libre, 1889.
    Le jardin de Bérénice, 1891.

Du sang, de la volupté et de la mort, 1894; 1903 (enl., with *Trois stations de psychothérapie*, first pbd 1891).

Le roman de l'énergie nationale, 1897–1902. Comprising:
    Les déracinés, 1897.
    L'appel au soldat, 1900.
    Leurs figures, 1902.

Scènes et doctrines du nationalisme, 1902.

Amori et dolori sacrum. La mort de Venise, 1903.

Les amitiés françaises, 1903.

Les bastions de l'est, 1905–9. Comprising:
   Au service de l'Allemagne, 1905.
   Colette Baudoche, 1909. Tr. F. V. Huard, New York 1918.
Le Greco, 1911; 1912 (renamed *Greco, ou le secret de Tolède*).
La colline inspirée, 1913; ed. J. Barbier, 1962. Tr. M. Cowley, *The sacred hill*, New York 1929.
La grande pitié des églises de France, 1914.
L'âme française et la guerre, 11 vols, 1915–20; 14 vols, 1920–4 (renamed *Chronique de la Grande Guerre*); 1968 (selection). Tr. anon., *The soul of France*, London 1916 (selection from vols 1–5).
Un jardin sur l'Oronte, 1922.
Une enquête aux pays de Levant, 2 vols, 1923.
Le mystère en pleine lumière, 1927.

Mes cahiers, 14 vols, 1929–57; 1963 (extracts).

BOISDEFFRE, P. de, *Barrès parmi nous*, 1952; 1969 (enl.).
DOMENACH, J. M., *Barrès par lui-même*, 1954; 1960.
FRANDON, I. M., *L'Orient de Maurice Barrès*, Geneva 1952.
GODFRIN, J., *Barrès mystique*, Neuchâtel 1962.
LALOU, R., *Maurice Barrès*, 1950.
MAURIAC, F., *La rencontre avec Barrès*, 1945.
MOREAU, P., *Maurice Barrès*, 1946.
VIER, J., *Barrès et la culte du Moi*, 1958.

BAUDELAIRE, Charles   1821–1867

BANDY, W. T. and PICHOIS, C., *Baudelaire devant ses contemporains*, Monaco 1957 (covering 1845–67); Paris 1967.
Charles Baudelaire, exposition, 1957 (Bibliothèque nationale catalogue).
CARTER, A. E., *Baudelaire et la critique française, 1868–1917*, Columbia (SC) 1963.
CARGO, R. T., *Baudelaire criticism, 1950–1967*, University of Alabama 1968.
See also Gautier-Le Dantec ed. of *Oeuvres complètes* below.

Oeuvres complètes, ed. C. Asselineau and T. de Banville, 7 vols, 1868–70; ed. F. F. Gautier and Y. Le Dantec, 15 vols, 1918–34 (incomplete; incl. bibl. for 1843–1932 in vol 15); ed. J. Crépet and C. Pichois, 19 vols, 1922–53; ed. Y. Le Dantec, 1961 (revd C. Pichois, 1966).

Tr. and ed. J. Mayne, *The mirror of art, critical studies*. London 1955; *The painter of modern life and other essays*, Greenwich (Conn) 1964.
Tr. 'H.C.', *Some translations*, London 1894.
Tr. F. P. Sturms, *The poems*, 1906 (selection).
Tr. J. Huncker, *The poems and prose*, New York 1919.
Tr. A. H. Walton, *Selections*, 1943.
Tr. G. Wagner, introd. E. Starkie, *Selected poems*, 1946.

Tr. and ed. F. Scarfe, *Baudelaire*, Harmondsworth 1961 (selection).

Salon de 1845, 1845.
   Salon de 1846, 1846.
   Tr. J. Mayne, in *Art in Paris 1845–1862*, London 1965.
Translations from Edgar Allan Poe, 1856–65. Comprising:
   Histoires extraordinaires, 1856.
   Nouvelles histoires extraordinaires, 1857.
   Aventures d'Arthur Gordon Pym, 1858.
   Eurêka, 1864.
   Histoires grotesques et sérieuses, 1865.
Les fleurs du mal, 1857; 1861 (incl. 23 new poems, but without 6 banned poems from 1857 ed.); ed. G. Apollinaire, 1917; ed. A. Adam, 1959. Tr. C. Scott, *The flowers of evil*, London 1909 (selection); tr. G. Dillon and E. St. Vincent Millay, New York and London 1936; tr. R. Campbell, *Poems*, London 1952; tr. F. L. Friedman, *Flowers of evil*, 1962; tr. and ed. W. Fowlie, New York 1964 (with other works).
   Les épaves, Amsterdam 1866 (incl. 6 banned poems from *Fleurs du mal* above).
Les paradis artificiels, 1860; ed. C. Pichois, 1961.
Curiosités esthétiques, 1868 (in *Oeuvres complètes* above); ed. J. Adhémar, 1956.
   L'art romantique, 1868 (in *Oeuvres complètes* above); ed. D. Parmée, Cambridge 1949 (selection, with two studies on Poe);
ed. H. Lemaître, 1962 (with other critical works).
Petits poèmes en prose, 1869 (in *Oeuvres complètes* above); ed. A. Van Bever, 1917 (as *Le spleen de Paris*); ed. R. Kopp, 1969. Tr. A. Symons, *Poems in prose*, London 1905; tr. A. Crowley, *Little poems in prose*, Paris 1928; tr. and ed. M. Hamburger, *Twenty prose poems*, London 1946.
Oeuvres posthumes et correspondance inédite, ed. E. Crépet, 1887.
La fanfarlo, 1919 (first pbd in *Bulletin de la Société des Gens de Lettres*, Jan. 1847); ed. C. Pichois, Monaco 1957.
Vers retrouvés, 1929.

Journaux intimes, ed. G. Kahn, 1909 (cntg *Mon coeur mis à nu*, first pbd in *Oeuvres posthumes* above, and *Fusées*). Tr. C. Isherwood, introd. T. S. Eliot, *Intimate journals*, London and New York 1930 (introd. W. H. Auden, London 1949); tr. N. Cameron, ed. P. Quennell, *My heart laid bare*, London 1950 (with other prose writings).
   Années de Bruxelles, ed. G. Garonne, 1926.
Carnet, ed. F. F. Gautier, 1911; 1920.
Correspondance générale, ed. J. Crépet and C. Pichois, 6 vols, 1947–53 (in *Oeuvres complètes*, vols 14–19 above); ed. C. Pichois and J. Zeigler, 2 vols, 1973.
Lettres inédites à sa mère, ed. J. Crépet, 2 vols, 1918–26. Tr. A. Symons, *The letters* [. . .] *to his mother*, London 1927.

Lettres inédites aux siens, ed. P. Auserve, 1966.

Tr. and ed. L. B. and F. E. Hyslop, *Baudelaire: a portrait, selected letters,* London and New York 1957.

AUSTIN, L. J., *L'univers poétique de Baudelaire,* 1956.
BLIN, G., *Baudelaire,* 1940.
BOPP, L., *Psychologie des Fleurs du mal,* 5 vols, Geneva 1964–9.
BORGAL, C., *Baudelaire,* 1961.
CRÉPET, J., ed., *Propos sur Baudelaire,* 1957.
EMMANUEL, P., *Baudelaire devant Dieu,* 1967.
Etudes baudelairiennes, Neuchâtel 1969 onwards.
FAIRLIE, A., *Les fleurs du mal,* London 1960.
FERRAN, A., *L'esthétique de Baudelaire,* 1933.
GILMAN, M., *Baudelaire the critic,* New York 1943.
HUBERT, J., *L'esthétique des Fleurs du mal,* Geneva 1953.
JONES, P. M., *Baudelaire,* Yale and Cambridge 1952.
MANOLL, M., *La vie passionnée de Baudelaire,* 1957.
MELANÇON, J. A., *Le spiritualisme de Baudelaire,* 1963.
MOSSOP, D. J., *Baudelaire's tragic hero,* London 1961.
PICHOIS, C., *Baudelaire, études et témoignages,* 1973.
PRÉVOST, J., *Baudelaire, essai sur l'inspiration et la création poétique,* 1953.
RUFF, M. A., *Baudelaire, l'homme et l'oeuvre,* 1958.
    L'esprit du mal et l'esthétique baudelairienne, 1955.
SARTRE, J. P., *Baudelaire,* 1947; 1963. Tr. M. Turnell, Norfolk (Conn) 1950.
STARKIE, E., *Baudelaire,* London 1957; 1971.
TURNELL, M., *Baudelaire,* London 1953.

BECQUE, Henry   1837–1899

Bibl. See ARNAOUTOVITCH below.

Théâtre complet, 2 vols, 1890 (ed. E. Fasquelle, 2 vols 1910–16); 3 vols, 1898 ('La Plume' ed.).
Oeuvres complètes, 7 vols, 1924–6.

Tr. F. Tilden, *Three plays,* New York 1913.

Sardanaple, 1867.
L'enfant prodigue, 1868.
Michel Pauper, 1871.
La navette, 1878. Tr. Tilden, *The merry-go-round* in *Three plays* above.
Les honnêtes femmes, 1880.
Les corbeaux, 1882; 1897. Tr. Tilden, *The vultures* in *Three plays* above.
La Parisienne, 1885. Tr. Tilden, *The woman of Paris* in *Three plays* above; tr. A. Dukes, *Parisienne,* London 1943; tr. C. Shattuck, *The woman of Paris,* New York 1957.

Querelles littéraires, 1890.
Souvenirs d'un auteur dramatique, 1895.
Les polichinelles (unfinished), 1910.

ANTOINE, A., in his *Mes souvenirs sur le Théâtre Libre*, 1922.
ARNAOUTOVITCH, A., *Henry Becque*, 3 vols, 1927 (incl. bibl. of works and critical bibl. in vol 3).
DESCOTES, M., *Henry Becque et son théâtre*, 1962.
DUMESNIL, R., in his *Le réalisme et le naturalisme*, 1955.
HYSLOP, L. B., *Henry Becque*, New York 1972.

BÉRANGER, Pierre-Jean de   1780–1857

BRIVOIS, J., *Bibliographie de l'oeuvre*, 1876.

Oeuvres complètes, 5 vols, 1834; 9 vols, 1875–6.

Tr. W. Anderson, *Lyrical poems*, Edinburgh 1847 (selection).
Tr. W. Young, *Two hundred songs*, New York 1850.
Tr. various, *Poems*, London 1888.
Tr. W. Toynbee, *Songs*, London 1892.

Chansons morales et autres, 1816.
Chansons nouvelles, 1825.
Chansons inédites, 1828.
Dernières chansons, 1834–1851, 1857.
Ma biographie, 1857.
Oeuvres inédites, ed. L. H. Lecomte, 1909 (cntg 3 plays).

Correspondance, ed. P. Boiteau, 4 vols, 1860.

FOUR, L., *La vie en chansons de Béranger*, 1930.
LUCAS-DUBRETON, J., *Béranger, la chanson, la politique, la société*, 1934.
TOUCHARD, J., *La gloire de Béranger*, 2 vols, 1968.

BERTRAND, Aloysius   1807–1841

Oeuvres poétiques, ed. C. Sprietsma, 1926.

Gaspard de la nuit, fantaisies à la manière de Rembrandt et de Callot, ed. C. A. de Sainte-Beuve, 1842; ed. R. Prévost, 1953; ed. J. Palou, 1962. Tr. anon., New York 1960 (in *Nineteenth century French tales*); tr. P. Zweig, *A selection*, Paris 1964.

SPRIETSMA, C., *Louis Bertrand, dit Aloysius Bertrand, une vie romantique*, 1926.

BLOY, Léon 1846–1917

LAQUERRIÈRE, A. L. and BOLLERY, J., *Biblio-iconographie*, 1935.
See also SAINT-LOUIS DE GONZAGUE below.

Oeuvres complètes, ed. J. Bollery, 20 vols, 1947–9; ed. J. Bollery and J. Petit, 1964 onwards (10 vols pbd).
Choix de textes, ed. A. Béguin, Fribourg 1943.

Tr. J. Coleman and H. L. Binsse, *Pilgrim of the absolute: a selection of his writings*, New York and London 1947.

Propos d'un entrepreneur de démolitions, 1885.
Le désespéré, 1886; 1913; ed. J. Bollery, 1955.
Le salut par les Juifs, 1892; 1906.
Le femme pauvre, 1897. Tr. I. J. Collins, *The woman who was poor*, London and New York 1939.
Le sang du pauvre, 1909.

Journal, Brussels and Paris 1897–1920. Comprising:
  Le mendiant ingrat, Brussels 1897; ed. J. Bollery, Paris 1956.
  Mon journal, 1904; ed. J. Bollery, 1956.
  Quatre ans de captivité à Cochons-sur-Marne, 1905; ed. J. Bollery, 1958.
  L'invendable, 1909; ed. J. Bollery, 1958.
  Le vieux de la montagne, 1911.
  Le pèlerin de l'absolu, 1914.
  Au seuil de l'apocalypse, 1916.
  La porte des humbles, 1920.
Lettres, 7 vols, Paris and Bruges, 1920–33.
Lettres à sa fiancée, 1922. Tr. B. Wall, *Letters to his fiancée*, London and New York 1937.

BÉGUIN, A., *Léon Bloy l'impatient*, Fribourg 1944. Tr. E. M. Riley, *A study in impatience*, London 1947.
  Léon Bloy mystique de la douleur, 1948.
BOLLERY, J., *Léon Bloy*, 3 vols, 1947–54.
HEPPENSTALL, R., *Léon Bloy*, Cambridge 1953.
JUIN, H., *Léon Bloy*, 1957.
SAINT-LOUIS DE GONZAGUE, Sister M., *Léon Bloy face à la critique*, Montreal 1959 (incl. critical bibl.).
TISON-BRAUN, M., in his *La crise de l'humanisme*, 1958.

BOURGET, Paul 1852–1935

Bibl. See MANSUY below.

Oeuvres complètes, 9 vols, 1899–1911 (incomplete).

Essais de psychologie contemporaine, 1883.
    Nouveaux essais, 1886.
Cruelle énigme, 1885. Tr. J. Cray, *A cruel enigma*, London 1887 (and New York 1891 as *Love's cruel enigma*).
Poésies, 2 vols, 1885–7.
Un crime d'amour, 1886. Tr. anon., *A love crime*, London 1888.
Mensonges, 1887; 1901. Tr. G. F. Monkshood and E. Tristan, *Our lady of lies*, London 1910.
André Cornélis, 1887; 1903. Tr. Mrs C. Hoey, London 1889 (and New York 1893 as *The son*); tr. anon., *Sins of desire*, London 1929.
Le disciple, 1889; 1901. Tr. anon., *The disciple*, New York 1898.
Etudes et portraits, 2 vols, 1889; 3 vols, 1906.
Un coeur de femme, 1890. Tr. E. Tristan, *A woman's heart*, London 1909.
Le terre promise, 1892. Tr. anon., *The land of promise*, Chicago and New York 1895.
Cosmopolis, 1893; 1903. Tr. H. E. Miller, Chicago (Ill) 1893.
La duchesse bleue, 1898. Tr. E. Tristan, *The blue duchess*, London 1908.
Drames de famille, 1900. Tr. W. Marchant, *Domestic dramas*, London and New York 1901.
Un divorce, 1904. Tr. E. L. Charlwood, *Divorce*, London and New York 1904.
L'émigré, 1902. Tr. G. B. Ives, *The weight of the name*, London and Boston 1909.
Le démon de midi, 2 vols, 1914.
Le sens de la mort, 1915. Tr. G. F. Lees, *The night cometh*, London and New York 1916.
La géôle, 1923. Tr. F. M. Robinson, *The gaol*, London 1924.
Nos actes nous suivent, 2 vols, 1927.
Au service de l'ordre, 2 vols, 1929–32.

AUSTIN, L. J., *Paul Bourget, sa vie et son oeuvre jusqu'en 1889*, 1940.

FEUILLERAT, A., *Paul Bourget, histoire d'un esprit sous la 3e République*, 1937.

LARDEUR, J. B., *La vérité psychologique et morale dans l'oeuvre de Paul Bourget*, 1912.

MANSUY, M., *Un moderne, Paul Bourget, de l'enfance au Disciple*, 1961 (incl. bibl.).

CHATEAUBRIAND, René de   1768–1848

KERVILER, R., *Essai d'une bio-bibliographie de Chateaubriand et de sa famille*, Vannes 1895.
See also DUCHEMIN below.

Oeuvres complètes, 28 vols, 1826–31; 36 vols, 1836–9 (enl.).
Oeuvres romanesques et voyages, ed. M. Regard, 2 vols, 1969.
Oeuvres choisies, ed. C. Florisoone, 1912 (revd V. L. Tapié, 1949).

Essai historique, politique et moral sur les révolutions, London 1797; Paris 1815 (abr.); 1826 (in *Oeuvres complètes,* vols 1–2 above). Tr. anon., *An historical, political, moral essay on revolutions,* London 1815 (tr. of 1815 ed.).

Atala, 1801; 1802 (in *Génie du christianisme* below); 1826 (in *Oeuvres complètes,* vol 16 above); ed. G. Chinard, 1930; ed. A. Weil, 1950; ed. P. Crump, Manchester 1951; ed. J. M. Gautier, Geneva 1973. Tr. C. Bingham, Boston 1802 (ed. W. L. Schwartz, Stanford (Calif) 1930); tr. I. Putter, Berkeley (Calif) 1952; tr. R. Heppenstall, London 1963.

Le génie du christianisme, 5 vols, 1802; 5 vols, 1826–7 (in *Oeuvres complètes,* vols 11–15 above). Tr. C. I. White, *The genius of Christianity,* Boston 1802; tr. E. O'Donnell, Paris 1854.

René, 1802 (in *Génie du christianisme* above); ed. G. Chinard, 1930 (with *Atala* above); ed. A. Weil, Paris 1935; ed. P. Crump, Manchester 1951 (with *Atala* above); ed. J. M. Gautier, Geneva 1970; ed. P. Barbéris, Paris 1973. Tr. anon., London 1813; tr. I. Putter, Berkeley (Calif) 1952 (with *Atala* above); tr. R. Heppenstall, London 1963 (with *Atala* above).

Les martyrs, 2 vols, 1809; 3 vols, 1826–7 (in *Oeuvres complètes,* vols 17–18 above); ed. B. d'Andlau, 1951. Tr. anon., *The martyrs,* 3 vols, New York 1812; tr. W. J. Walter, *The two martyrs,* London 1819.

Itinéraire de Paris à Jérusalem, 3 vols, 1811; 3 vols, 1826 (in *Oeuvres complètes,* vols 8–10 above); ed. E. Malakis, Baltimore (Md) 1946. Tr. F. Shoberl, *Travels in Greece, Egypt and Barbarry,* London 1811 (part tr.).

De Buonaparte, des Bourbons, 1814; 1814. Tr. anon., *On Buonaparte and the Bourbons,* London 1814.

De la monarchie, selon la charte, 1816. Tr. anon., *The monarchy according to the charter,* London 1816.

Le dernier des Abencerrages, 1826 (in *Oeuvres complètes,* vol 16 above); ed. P. Hazard and M. J. Durry, 1926. Tr. anon., *Aben-Hamet, the last of the Abencerages,* London 1826; tr. I. Hill, *The last of the Abencerages,* 1835; tr. E. M. Nuttall, *The last Abencerage,* 1922.

Les Natchez, 2 vols, 1826 (in *Oeuvres complètes,* vols 19–20 above); 2 vols, 1829; ed. G. Chinard, Baltimore (Md) 1932. Tr. anon., *The Natchez,* 3 vols, London 1827.

Souvenirs d'Italie, d'Angleterre et d'Amérique, 2 vols, London 1815. Tr. anon., *Recollections of Italy, England and America,* 2 vols, London 1815.

Voyage en Amérique, 2 vols, 1827 (in *Oeuvres complètes* above, vols 6 and 7); ed. R. Switzer, 2 vols, 1964. Tr. R. Switzer, *Travels in America,* Lexington (Ky) 1969.

Voyage en Italie, 1827 (in *Oeuvres complètes* above, vol 7, with *Voyage en Amérique* above); ed. J. M. Gautier, Geneva 1951 (*Lettre à M. de Fontanes sur la campagne romaine*).

Essai sur la littérature anglaise et considérations sur le génie, 2 vols, 1836 (extracts first pbd in *Mercure,* 1802–30). Tr. anon., *Sketches on English literature,* 2 vols, London 1836.

Vie de Rancé, 1844; ed. F. Letessier, 2 vols, 1955.

Mémoires d'outre-tombe, 12 vols, 1849–50; ed. E. Biré, 6 vols, 1899–1900 (revd P. Moreau, 6 vols, 1947); ed. M. Levaillant and G. Moulinier, 2 vols, 1946–8; ed. M. Levaillant, 4 vols, 1948. Tr. anon., *Memoirs,* London 1848 (part tr.); tr. A. Teixeira de Mattos, 6 vols, London 1902; tr. R. Baldick, London 1961 (selection).

Correspondance générale, ed. L. Thomas, 1912 onwards (13 vols pbd).

BASSAN F., *Chateaubriand et la Terre sainte,* 1959.

CHINARD, G., *L'exotisme américain dans l'oeuvre de Chateaubriand,* 1918.

DECHAMPS, J. A., *Chateaubriand en Angleterre,* 1934.

DUCHEMIN, M., *Chateaubriand,* 1938 (incl. bibl.).

DURRY, M. J., *La vieillesse de Chateaubriand,* 2 vols, 1933.

EVANS, J., *Chateaubriand, a biography,* London 1939.

FLOORISOONE, C. and TAPIE, V. L., *Chateaubriand,* 1948.

GAUTIER, J. M., *Le style des Mémoires d'outre-tombe,* 1959.

LE SAVOUREUX, H., *Chateaubriand,* 1930.

LEVAILLANT, M., *Splendeurs et misères de M. de Chateaubriand,* 1922.
   Chateaubriand, prince des songes, 1960.

MARTIN-CHAUFFIER, L., *Chateaubriand,* 1969.

MAUROIS, A., *Chateaubriand,* 1938. Tr. V. Fraser, London and New York 1938.

MOREAU, P., *Chateaubriand, l'homme et l'oeuvre,* 1956.

MOUROT, J., *Le génie d'un style: Chateaubriand et les Mémoires d'outre-tombe,* 1960.
   Etudes sur les premières oeuvres, 1962.

SAINTE-BEUVE, C. A. de, *Chateaubriand et son groupe littéraire sous l'Empire,* 2 vols, 1860; 1873 (enl.); ed. M. Allem, 2 vols, 1948.

SWITZER, R., *Chateaubriand,* New York 1971.

VIAL, A., *Chateaubriand et le temps perdu,* 1963.

CONSTANT, Benjamin   1767–1830

RUDLER, G., *Bibliographie critique des oeuvres,* 1909 (to 1794 only).

LÉON, P. L., *Benjamin Constant,* 1930.

See also CORDIÉ below.

Oeuvres politiques, ed. C. Louandre, 1874.

Oeuvres, ed. A. Roulin, 1957.

Ecrits et discours politiques, ed. O. Pozzo di Borgo, 1954.

L'apothéose de Benjamin Constant, ed. G. Chinard, 1955 (selection).

De la force du gouvernement actuel, 1796; 1814.

De l'esprit de conquête et de l'usurpation, Hanover 1813; Paris 1814; ed. M. T. Génin, 1947. Tr. H. B. Lippmann, *Prophecy from the past: Benjamin Constant on conquest and usurpation,* New York 1941.

Adolphe, Paris and London 1816; Paris 1824; ed. G. Rudler, Manchester 1919; ed. J. Bompard, Paris 1946; ed. J. H. Bornecque, 1955; ed. J. Mistler and V. Bernard, 1957; ed. C. Cordie, Naples 1963. Tr. A. Walker, London 1816; tr. C. Wildman, introd. H. Nicolson, London 1948; tr. J. M. Murry, London and New York 1951 (in *The conquest of death*); tr. L. W. Tancock, Harmondsworth 1964.

Mémoires sur les Cent Jours, 2 vols, 1820–2; ed. O. Pozzo de Borgo, 1961.

De la réligion, 5 vols, 1824–31.

Mélanges de littérature et de politique, 1829.

Cécile, ed. A. Roulin, 1931. Tr. N. Cameron, London 1952.

Le Cahier rouge, 1907; ed. J. Mistler and V. Bernard, 1957 (with *Adolphe* above). Tr. N. Cameron, introd. H. Nicolson, *The red notebook*, London 1948 (with *Adolphe*, tr. Wildman above).

Journal intime [. . .] *et Lettres à sa famille et à ses amis*, 1895.

Journaux intimes, ed. A. Roulin and C. Roth, 1952 (complete text).

Lettres à Mme Récamier, ed. L. Colet, 1864; ed. Mme Lenormant, 1882 (enl.).

Lettres [. . .] *à sa famille 1775–1830*, ed. J. H. Menos, 1888.

L'inconnue d'Adolphe; correspondance de Benjamin Constant et d'Anna Lindsay, 1933.

Benjamin Constant et Mme de Staël—lettres à un ami (letters to Claude Hochet), ed. J. Mistler, Neuchâtel, 1949.

Benjamin Constant et Rosalie de Constant, correspondance 1786–1830, ed. A. and S. Roulin, 1955.

BASTID, P., *Benjamin Constant et sa doctrine*, 1966.

CORDIE, C., *Benjamin Constant*, Milan 1946 (incl. bibl.).

DELBOUILLE, P., *Genèse, structure et destin d'Adolphe*, 1972.

GOUHIER, H., *Benjamin Constant*, 1967.

GUILLEMIN, H., *Mme de Staël, Benjamin Constant et Napoléon*, 1958.

    Benjamin Constant muscadin (1795–1799), 1958.

HOLDEIM, W. M., *Benjamin Constant*, London 1961.

JASINSKI, R., *L'engagement de Benjamin Constant*, 1971.

NICOLSON, H. G., *Benjamin Constant*, London 1961.

OLIVER, A. R., *Benjamin Constant: écriture et conquête du moi*, 1970.

POULET, G., *Benjamin Constant par lui-même*, 1968.

CORBIÈRE, Tristan   1845–1875

GIOVINE, E., in her *Bibliographie de Corbière, Lautréamont et Laforgue*, 1962; Florence 1969.

See also Walzer ed. of *Oeuvres complètes* below.

Oeuvres complètes, ed. Y. G. Le Dantec, 1942 (revd 1953); ed. P. O. Walzer and F. F. Burch, 1970 (incl. bibl.); ed. J. L. Lalanne, 1973.

Ça, Les amours jaunes, Raccrocs, Sérénade des sérénades, Armor, Les gens de mer, Rondels pour après, 1873; 1912. Tr. W. McElroy, *Poems*, New York 1947; tr. C. F. MacIntyre, *Selections*, Berkeley (Calif) 1954.

ARNOUX, A., *Une âme et pas de violon, Tristan Corbière*, 1929.
GRIN, M., *Tristan Corbière, poète maudit*, 1972.
MARTINEAU, R., *Tristan Corbière*, 1925.
THOMAS, H., *Tristan le dépossédé*, 1972.

COURTELINE, Georges   1858–1929

Oeuvres, 24 vols, 1905; 13 vols, 1925–7.
Théâtre complet, 10 vols, 1929–31; 1961.

Tr. and adapt. A. Bermel and J. Barzun, *The plays*, London 1961 (selection).

Les gaîtés de l'escadron (stories), 1886; 1926 (in *Oeuvres* above); ed. F. Pruner, 1971.
    Les gaîtés de l'escadron, revue, 1905.
La vie de caserne, Le train de 8h. 47, 1888; 1928 (in *Oeuvres* above).
Lidoire et La Biscotte, 1892 (stories).
Messieurs les ronds-de-cuir, tableaux-romans, 1893; 1929 (in *Oeuvres* above); ed. F. Pruner, 1966.
    Messieurs les ronds-de-cuir, comédie, 1911 (in *L'Illustration*). Tr. Eric Sutton, *The Bureaucrats*, London 1928.
Boubouroche, pièce, 1893.
    Boubouroche (stories), 1893 (first version of *Boubouroche* pbd in *Lidoire et La Biscotte* above).
Un client sérieux, contes, 1897; 1929 (in *Oeuvres* above).
    Un client sérieux, comédie, 1898.
Le gendarme est sans pitié, comédie (in collab with Edouard Norès), 1899.
    Tr. H. I. Williams, *The pitiless policeman*, Boston (Mass) 1917.
Le commissaire est bon enfant, comédie (in collab with Jules Lévy), 1900. Tr. A. Bermel, *The Commissioner*, New York 1960 (in *Four modern French comedies*).
L'article 330, comédie, 1901.
Le miroir concave, 1901.
Le paix chez soi, comédie, 1903. Tr. V. and F. Vernon, *Peace at Home*, New York 1933.
La cruche, ou J'en ai plein le dos de Margot, comédie, 1910.
Les linottes, roman, 1912; 1929 (*in Oeuvres* above).
La philosophie de Georges Courteline, 1917; 1929 (in *Oeuvres* above).

BORNECQUE, P., *Le théâtre de Georges Courteline*, 1969.
PORTAIL, J., *Courteline, l'humoriste française*, 1928.

DAUDET, Alphonse   1840–1897

BRIVOIS, J., *Essai de bibliographie des oeuvres*, 1895.
See also SACHS below.

Oeuvres complètes, 18 vols, 1899–1901; ed. H. Bérand and A. Ebner, 20 vols, 1929–31; ed. J. L. Curtis, Lausanne and Paris 1966.
Oeuvres maîtresses, 2 vols, 1969.

Tr. G. B. Ives et al., *The works*, 24 vols, Boston 1898–1900.

Les amoureuses, poésies, 1858; 1873 (enl.).
Le petit chose, 1868; ed. J. H. Bornecque, 1947. Tr. E. Harris, *The little weakling*, Edinburgh 1917.
Lettres de mon moulin, 1869 (first pbd in *Le Figaro*, 1866); 1887; ed. J. H. Bornecque, 1947. Tr. M. Carey, *Letters from my mill*, London 1880; tr. E. Harris, Edinburgh 1915; tr. J. MacGregor, London 1962.
L'Arlésienne, 1872.
Aventures prodigieuses de Tartarin de Tarascon, 1872; ed. J. H. Bornecque, 1965. Tr. C. Roland, *The new Don Quixote*, Boston 1875; tr. anon., *Tartarin of Tarascon*, London and New York 1910; tr. J. Leclercq, 2 vols, New York 1930; tr. J. M. Cohen, London 1968.
> *Tartarin sur les Alpes*, 1885. Tr. H. Frith, *Tartarin on the Alps*, London and New York 1884; tr. anon., *Tartarin in the Alps*, London and New York 1910.
> *La défense de Tarascon*, 1873 (in *Contes du lundi* below); 1886.
> *Port Tarascon*, 1890. Tr. H. James, *Port Tarascon*, London 1891.
Contes du lundi, 1873; 1876 (enl.); ed. J. H. Bornecque, 2 vols, 1947. Tr. P. Forbes, London 1950.
Contes et récits, 1873 (incl. stories already pbd).
Fromont jeune et Risler aîné, 1874. Tr. anon., *Fromont the Younger and Risler the Elder*, London 1880; tr. C. Haldane, *Sidonie*, London 1958.
Robert Helmont, 1874. Tr. L. Ensor, *Robert Helmont*, London 1888.
Les femmes d'artistes, 1874. Tr. L. Ensor, *Artists' wives*, London 1890.
Jack, 2 vols, 1876. Tr. L. Ensor, *Jack*, London 1890.
Le nabab, 1877. Tr. E. Clavequin, *The nabob*, 3 vols, London 1878; tr. W. Blaydes, New York 1902.
Les rois en exil, 1879. Tr. E. Clavequin, *Kings in exile*, 3 vols, London 1880; tr. L. Ensor, London 1890; tr. H. Blanchamp, *The popinjay*, London 1909.
Numa Roumestan, 1881. Tr. V. Champlin, Boston and New York 1882; tr. Mrs J. G. Layard, London 1884; tr. H. Blanchamp, *A passion of the south*, London 1910.
L'évangéliste, 1883. Tr. C. H. Meltzer, *Port Salvation*, 2 vols, London 1883.

La Belle-Nivernaise, 1886 (incl. stories already pbd). Tr. R. Routledge, London 1887.

Sapho, 1884; ed. R. Kemp, Monaco 1957. Tr. anon., *Sappho*, London 1886: tr. E. Wilkins, London and New York 1951; tr. A. Brown, London 1959.
  Sapho (dramatized version in collab with Adolphe Belot), 1893. Tr. E. B. Ginty, New York 1895.

L'Immortel, 1888. Tr. and adapt. A. W. and M. de G. Verrall, *One of the Forty*, London 1888.

Souvenirs d'un homme de lettres, 1888. Tr. L. Ensor, *Recollections of a literary man*, London 1889.

  Trente ans de Paris, 1888. Tr. L. Ensor, *Thirty years of Paris and of my literary life*, London 1888.

  Notes sur la vie, 1899.

  Premier voyage, premier mensonge, 1900. Tr. R. W. Sherard, *My first voyage, my first lie*, London 1901.

Rose et Ninette, 1892. Tr. M. J. Serrano, *Rose and Ninette*, London 1892.

La petite paroisse, 1895. Tr. G. B. Ives, *The little parish church*, Boston (Mass) 1900.

Soutien de famille, 1899. Tr. and adapt. L. Carnac, *The hope of a family*, London 1898.

La doulou (extracts from unpbd notebooks), 1931 (in *Oeuvres complètes*, vol 17 above); 1931 (enl.).

BENOÎT-GUYOD, G., *Alphonse Daudet, son temps, son oeuvre*, 1947.

BORNECQUE, J. H., *Les années d'apprentissage d'Alphonse Daudet*, 1951.

DOBIE, V., *Alphonse Daudet*, London and New York 1949.

SACHS, M., *The career of Alphonse Daudet, a critical study*, Cambridge (Mass) 1965.

DESBORDES-VALMORE, Marceline   1786–1859

CAVALUCCI, G., *Bibliographie critique*, 2 vols, Naples 1935–41.

Poésies complètes, ed. B. Guégan, 4 vols, 1932; ed. M. Bertrand, 1972.
Poésies choisies, ed. M. Allem, 1935; ed. Y. Le Dantec, 1950.

Tr. H. W. Preston, in her tr. of Sainte-Beuve's *Madame Desbordes-Valmore* below (selected poems).
Also translated in anthologies.

Elégies, Marie et Romances, 1819; 1822.
Elégies et poésies nouvelles, 1825; Brussels 1825.
Les pleurs, 1833.
Pauvres fleurs, 1839.
Bouquets et prières, 1843.
Poésies inédites, ed. G. Revilliod, Geneva 1860.

JASÉNAS, E., *Marceline Desbordes-Valmore devant la critique*, 1962.
MOULIN, J., *Marceline Desbordes-Valmore*, 1955.
SAINTE-BEUVE, C. A. de, *Madame Desbordes-Valmore, sa vie et sa correspondance*, 1870 (in his *Nouveaux lundis*, vol 12). Tr. H. W. Preston, *Memoirs of Madame Desbordes-Valmore*, Boston 1873 (with selected trs).
SESMA, M. G., *Le secret de Marceline Desbordes-Valmore*, 1945.

DUMAS (Père), Alexandre   1802–1870

Catalogue des ouvrages des Dumas père et fils, conservés à la Bibliothèque nationale, 1911.
REED, F. W., *A bibliography of Alexandre Dumas Père*, London 1933 (*Supplement* pbd, 1952).

Oeuvres complètes, 301 vols, 1846–77.
Théâtre complet, 15 vols, 1863–74.

Tr. anon., *The romances*, 60 vols, London and Boston 1893–7.
Tr. anon., *The romances*, 10 vols, New York 1896.
Tr. A. Allinson, *The novels*, 56 vols, London 1903–11.

Published over 200 works, many written in collaboration.

La chasse et l'amour (first play; in collab.), 1825.
Henri III et sa cour, 1829.
Napoléon Bonaparte, 1831.
Antony, 1831.
Charles VII chez ses grands vassaux, 1831.
Térésa, 1832.
La tour de Nesle (in collab. with Gaillardet), 1832.
Richard Darlington (in collab.), 1832.
Madame et la Vendée (first novel), 1833; 1834.
Angèle, 1834.
Catherine Howard, 1834.
Don Juan de Marana, 1836.
Kean, 1836. Tr. anon., *Edmund Kean*, London 1847.
Caligula, 1837.
Mademoiselle de Belle-Isle, 1839.
Les crimes célèbres, 8 vols, 1839–41. Tr. anon., *Celebrated crimes*, London 1843; tr. I. G. Burnham, 8 vols, Philadelphia and London 1895–6.
Impressions de voyage, 5 vols, 1833–7. Tr. R. W. Plummer and A. C. Bell, *Travels in Switzerland*, London 1958.
   Quinze jours à Sinai, 2 vols, 1839.
   Midi de la France, 3 vols, 1841.
   Excursions sur les bords du Rhin., 3 vols, 1841.
   Une année à Florence, 2 vols, 1841.

De Paris à Cadix, 5 vols, 1848. Tr. and ed. A. E. Murch, *From Paris to Cadiz*, London 1958.

Le véloce, ou Tanger, Alger et Tunis, 4 vols, 1848–51. Tr. and ed. A. E. Murch, *Tangier to Tunis*, London 1959.

L'Arabie heureuse, 3 vols, 1855.

Le Caucase, 1859. Tr. and ed. A. E. Murch, *Adventures in the Caucasus*, London 1962.

La route de Varennes, 1860. Tr. and ed. A. C. Bell, *The flight to Varennes*, London 1962.

De Paris à Astrakhan, 1860.

Impressions de voyage en Russie, 4 vols, 1865; ed. A. Maurois and J. Suffel, 1960. Tr. and ed. A. E. Murch, *Adventures in Czarist Russia*, London 1960.

Un mariage sous Louis XV, 1841. Tr. S. Grundy, *A marriage of convenience*, London 1899.

Les demoiselles de Saint Cyr (in collab.), 1843.

Les trois mousquétaires, 8 vols, 1844; ed. C. Samaran, 1968. Tr. W. Barrow, *The three musketeers*, London 1846; tr. W. Robson, 1853.

    Vingt ans après (in collab. with Auguste Maquet) 10 vols, 1845; ed. J. Suffel, 2 vols, 1968; ed. G. Sigaux, 1962.

    Le vicomte de Bragelonne, 26 vols, 1848–50 (in collab. with A. Maquet). ed. A. Maurois, 1965.

Le comte de Monte-Cristo, 18 vols, 1845–6; ed. J. H. Bornecque, 2 vols, 1956. Tr. anon., *The Count of Monte Cristo*, 2 vols, London 1846; tr. L. Bair, New York 1956 (abr.).

La Reine Margot (in collab. with A. Maquet), 6 vols, 1845. Tr. S. F. Wright, *Marguerite de Valois*, London 1947.

    La dame de Monsoreau (in collab. with A. Maquet), 8 vols, 1846.

    Les quarante-cinq (in collab. with A. Maquet), 10 vols, 1847–8.

Le chevalier de Maison Rouge (in collab. with A. Maquet), 6 vols, 1846.

Le collier de la reine, 11 vols, 1849–50.

La Tulipe noire (in collab. with A. Maquet), 3 vols, 1850. Tr. A. J. O'Connor, *The black tulip*, London 1902.

Mes mémoires, 22 vols, 1852–4, 26 vols, Brussels 1852–6.

Mes mémoires, 22 vols, 1852–4; 26 vols, Brussels 1852–6; ed. P. Josserand, 5 vols, 1954–68. Tr. E. M. Waller, *My Memoirs*, 6 vols, London 1907–9; tr. J. E. Goodman, *The road to Monte Cristo*, New York 1956 (abr.); tr. and ed. A. C. Bell, *Memoirs*, London 1961 (abr.). First published as:

    Souvenirs de 1830 à 1842, 8 vols, 1854–5 (part first pbd in Brussels ed. of *Mes mémoires*.

Les Mohicans de Paris, 10 vols, Brussels and Leipzig 1854–5.

    Salvator, 13 vols, Brussels and Leipzig 1855–8; 14 vols, 1856–9.

L'Orestie, 1856.

    Les compagnons de Jehu, 5 vols, Brussels 1857.

BELL, A. C., *Alexandre Dumas*, London 1950.
BOUVIER-AJAM, M., *Alexandre Dumas, ou cent ans après*, 1973.
CLOUARD, H., *Alexandre Dumas*, 1955.
GAILLARD, R., *Alexandre Dumas*, 1953.
GRIBBLE, F. H., *Dumas, father and son*, London and New York 1930.
JAN, I., *Alexandre Dumas, romancier*, 1973.
MAUROIS, A., *Les trois Dumas*, 1957. Tr. G. Hopkins, *Three musketeers*, London 1957 (and New York, as *The Titans*).
THOORENS, L., *La vie passionnée d'Alexandre Dumas*, 1957.

DUMAS (Fils), Alexandre   1824–1895

Catalogue des ouvrages des Dumas, père et fils, conservés à la Bibliothèque nationale, 1911.
See also TAYLOR below.

Théâtre complet, 10 vols, 1923.

Diane de Lys, 3 vols, 1851 (with *Grangette*).
　Diane de Lys, comédie, 1853.
Le demi-monde, comédie, 1855. Tr. E. G. Squier, *The demi-monde*, Philadelphia (Pa) 1858.
La question d'argent, comédie, 1857. Tr. B. W. Gragin et al., *The money question*, Boston (Mass) 1915.
Le fils naturel, comédie, 1858. Tr. T. L. Oxley, London 1859.
La dame aux camélias, 2 vols, 1848; 1872. Tr. anon., *The lady of the camelias*, London 1856; tr. H. Metcalfe, New York 1931; tr. and ed. E. Gosse, *Camille*, London 1934.
　La dame aux camélias, pièce, 1852. Tr. F. A. Schwab, New York 1880; tr. E. Reynolds and N. Playfair, *The lady of the camellias*, London 1930.
L'ami des femmes, comédie, 1864.
Les idées de Madame Aubray, comédie, 1867. Tr. anon., Englewood Cliffs (NJ) 1965.
La femme de Claude, pièce, 1873.
L'étrangère, comédie, 1877. Tr. F. A. Schwab, New York 1888.

HARTOY, M. d', *Dumas fils inconnu*, 1964.
LAMY, P., *Le théâtre d'Alexandre Dumas fils*, 1928.
MAUROIS, A., *Les trois Dumas*, 1957. Tr. G. Hopkins, *Three musketeers*, London 1957 (and New York, as *The Titans*).
SCHWARZ, H. S., *Alexandre Dumas fils, dramatist*, New York 1927.
TAYLOR, F. A., *The theatre of Alexandre Dumas fils*, Oxford 1937 (incl. bibl.).

FEYDEAU, Georges   1862–1921

Théâtre complet, 9 vols, 1948–56.

Wrote 33 plays in all between 1884 and 1911.

Monsieur chasse !, 1896.
Un fil à la patte, 1899.
La puce à l'oreille, 1909. Tr. J. Mortimer, *A flea in her ear*, London 1968.
On purge bébé !, 1914.
Occupe-toi d'Amélie !, 1914. Tr. B. Duffield, *Keep an eye on Amélie*, New York 1958; tr. and adapt. Noel Coward, *Look after Lulu*, London 1959.
Mais n'te promène donc pas toute nue, 1914.
La dame de chez Maxim's, 1914.
Feu la mère de Madame, 1924.
L'hôtel de libre-échange (in collab. with Maurice Desvallières), 1928. Tr. P. Glenville, *Hotel Paradiso*, London 1957.

Cahiers Renaud-Barrault, no. 32, Dec. 1960.
LORCEY, J., *Georges Feydeau*, 1972.
SHENKAN, A., *Georges Feydeau*, 1973.

FLAUBERT, Gustave   1821–1880

DUMESNIL, R. and DEMOREST, D. L., *Bibliographie*, 1937.
MILLER, L. G., *Index de la correspondance*, Strasbourg 1934.
CARLUT, C., *La correspondance de Flaubert, étude et répertoire critique*, Columbus (Ohio) 1968.

Oeuvres complètes, 8 vols, 1885 (incomplete); 22 vols, 1910–33 ('Conard ed'); ed. R. Dumesnil, 10 vols, 1945–8; ed. A. Thibaudet and R. Dumesnil, 2 vols, 1946–8; ed. B. Masson, 2 vols, 1964; ed. M. Nadeau, 18 vols, Lausanne 1964–5.

Tr. anon., *The complete works*, 10 vols, New York 1904.

Madame Bovary, 2 vols, 1857; 1873 (with speeches and verdict at trial); ed. E. Maynial, 1957; ed. C. Gothot-Mersch, 1971. Tr. E. Marx-Aveling, London 1886; tr. anon., introd. H. James, London 1902; tr. G. Hopkins, 1948; tr. A. Russel, Harmondsworth 1950; tr. J. L. May, New York 1950; tr. F. Steegmuller, 1957; tr. L. Bair, 1959; tr. M. Marmur, introd. M. McCarthy, 1964 (with *The trial of Madame Bovary*, tr. E. Gendel); tr. P. de Man, 1965 (in *Madame Bovary, background and sources*).
Salammbô, 1863; 1879; ed. E. Maynial, 1963. Tr. M. F. Sheldon, London 1886; tr. J. C. Chartres, 1886 (ed. F. C. Green, London and New York 1963); tr. E. Powys Mathers, Waltham Saint Lawrence 1931; tr. R. Goodyear and P. J. R. Wright, London 1962.
L'éducation sentimentale, 2 vols, 1870; 1880; ed. E. Maynial, 1958. Tr. D. F.

Hannigan, *Sentimental education*, 2 vols, London 1898; tr. A. Goldsmith, London and New York 1941; tr. R. Baldick, Harmondsworth 1964.

La tentation de Saint Antoine, 1874; ed. E. Faguet, London 1913. Tr. D. F. Hannigan, *The temptation of Saint Antony*, 1895; tr. A. K. Chignell, 1928 (in *Tales from Flaubert*).

Le candidat, 1874; 1885.

Trois contes: Un coeur simple, La légende de Saint Julien l'Hospitalier, Hérodias, 1877; ed. E. Pilon, 1931; ed. C. Duckworth, London 1959. Tr. G. B. Ives, *Three tales*, New York 1903; tr. J. Gilmer, 1928; tr. M. Savill, 1950; tr. R. Baldick, Harmondsworth 1961; tr. W. F. Cobb, New York and Toronto 1964.

Bouvard et Pécuchet, 1881; ed. C. Haroche, 1957; ed. A. Cento, Naples 1964; ed. E. Maynial, Paris 1965. Tr. D. F. Hannigan, London 1896; tr. T. W. Earp and G. W. Stonier, *Bouvard and Pecuchet*, 1936.

Le château des coeurs, 1885 (with *Le candidat* above).

Par les champs et par les grèves (in collab. with Maxime Du Camp), 1886.

Dictionnaire des idées reçues, 1910 (in *Oeuvres complètes*, above); ed. E. L. Ferrière, 1913; ed. C. Haroche, 1957 (with *Bouvard et Pécuchet* above). Tr. J. Barzun, *Dictionary of accepted ideas*, London 1954; tr. E. J. Fluck, *A dictionary of platitudes*, 1954.

Premières oeuvres, 4 vols, 1914–20 (incl. *Novembre*, tr. F. Jellinek, ed. F. Steegmuller, *November*, London 1966, *Mémoires d'un fou, Smarh*, and early versions of *L'éducation sentimentale* and *La tentation de Saint Antoine* above).

Souvenirs, notes, et pensées intimes, ed. L. Chevalley-Sabatier, 1965. Tr. and ed. F. Steegmuller, *Intimate notebook 1840–41*, London and New York 1967.

Correspondance 1830–1880, ed. C. Commanville, 4 vols, 1887–93; 13 vols, 1926–54 (enl.); ed. J. Bruneau, 2 vols, 1973. Tr. J. M. Cohen, *Letters*, London 1950 (selection); tr. and ed. F. Steegmuller, *The selected letters of Gustave Flaubert*, 1954.

BART, B. F., *Flaubert*, New York 1967.

BROMBERT, V., *The novels of Flaubert, a study of themes and technique*, Princeton (NJ) 1966.

BRUNEAU, J., *Les débuts littéraires de Gustave Flaubert, 1831–1845*, 1962.

CULLER, J., *Flaubert, the uses of uncertainty*, London 1974.

DANGER, P., *Sensations et objets dans le roman de Flaubert*, 1973.

DESCHARMES, R., *Flaubert, sa vie, son caractère et ses idées avant 1857*, 1909.

DUMESNIL, R., *Flaubert*, 1903.

  Gustave Flaubert, l'homme et l'oeuvre, 1932.

  Gustave Flaubert, 1947.

  La vocation de Gustave Flaubert, 1961.

DURRY, M. J., *Flaubert et ses projets inédits*, 1950.

GOTHOT-MERSCH, C., *La genèse de Madame Bovary*, 1966.

NADEAU, M., *Gustave Flaubert, écrivain*, 1961. Tr. B. Bray, *The greatness of Flaubert*, London 1972.

SARTRE, J. P., *L'idiot de la famille*, 4 vols, 1971–3.

SHERRINGTON, R. J., *Three novels by Flaubert*, Oxford 1970.

STARKIE, E., *Flaubert the master*, 2 vols, 1967–71.

STEEGMULLER, F., *Flaubert and Madame Bovary*, London 1939; New York 1968.

THIBAUDET, A., *Gustave Flaubert, sa vie, ses romans, son style*, 1922.

THORLBY, A. K., *Gustave Flaubert and the art of realism*, London 1956.

FRANCE, Anatole   1844–1924
(pseudonym of Anatole-François Thibault)

LION, J., *Bibliographie des ouvrages consacrés à Anatole France*, 1935.
See also BANCQUART below.

Oeuvres complètes, ed. L. Carias, 25 vols, 1925–35; ed. J. Suffel, 27 vols, 1969–71.

Tr. various, *The complete works*, 21 vols, New York and London 1908–28.

Tr. A. Dukes, *The plays*, 2 vols, London 1925.

Alfred de Vigny, étude, 1868; 1923. Tr. J. L. May and A. Allinson, in *Marguerite and Count Morin, Deputy, together with Alfred de Vigny and The path of glory*, London 1927.

Les poèmes dorés, 1873. Tr. anon., *The golden poems*, New York 1926.

Les noces corinthiennes, 1876; 1923. Tr. W. and E. Jackson, *The bride of Corinth and other poems and plays*, New York and London 1920.

Le crime de Sylvestre Bonnard, 1881; 1902. Tr. L. Hearn, *The crime of Sylvestre Bonnard*, New York 1890; tr. anon., New York 1932.

Le livre de mon ami, 1885. Tr. J. L. May, *My friend's book*, New York 1913; tr. R. Feltenstein, New York 1951.

La vie littéraire, 4 vols, 1888–92 (collected articles pbd in *Le Temps*). Tr. A. W. Evans, D. B. Stewart and B. Miall, *On life and letters*, 4 vols, New York 1910–24.

> *La vie littéraire, 5e série*, 1950.

Thaïs, 1891; 1921. Tr. E. de L. Pierson, New York 1892; tr. E. Tristan, London 1902; tr. R. B. Douglas, 1909.

La rôtisserie de la Reine Pédauque, 1893; 1921. Tr. J. A. V. Stritzko, *The Queen Pédauque*, London 1910; tr. W. Jackson, *At the sign of the Reine Pédauque*, New York 1912.

Les opinions de M. Jérome Coignard, 1893; 1922. Tr. W. Jackson, *The opinions of Jérome Coignard*, New York 1913.

Le lys rouge, 1894; 1921. Tr. anon., *The red lily*, London 1898; tr. W. Stephens, New York 1908.

Le jardin d'Epicure, 1895; 1924. Tr. A. Allinson, *The garden of Epicurus*, New York 1908.

Histoire contemporaine, 4 vols, 1897–1901. Comprising:
Le mannequin d'osier, 1897; 1923. Tr. M. P. Willcocks, *The wicker-work woman*, New York 1910.
L'orme du mail, 1897; 1923. Tr. M. P. Willcocks, *The elm-tree on the Mall*, New York, 1910.
L'anneau d'améthyste, 1899; 1924. Tr. B. Drillien, *The amethyst ring*, New York 1919.
Monsieur Bergeret à Paris, 1901; 1925. Tr. B. Drillien, *Monsieur Bergeret in Paris*, New York 1921.

Pierre Nozière, 1899; 1927. Tr. J. L. May, New York 1916.

Sur la pierre blanche, 1905. Tr. C. E. Roche, *The white stone*, New York 1910.

Vers les temps meilleurs, 3 vols, 1906 (collected speeches, etc, 1899–1906); ed. C. Aveline, 4 vols, 1949.

Contes de Jacques Tournebroche, 1908. Tr. A. Allinson, *The merrie tales of Jacques Tournebroche*, London and New York 1910.

L'île des pingouins, 1908. Tr. A. W. Evans, *Penguin island*, New York 1909; tr. anon., New York 1933.

Les dieux ont soif, 1912. Tr. A. Allinson, *The gods are athirst*, New York 1913; tr. A. Brown, London 1951.

Génie latin (collected prefaces), 1913. Tr. W. S. Jackson, *The Latin genius*, New York and London 1924.

La révolte des anges, 1914. Tr. W. Jackson, *The revolt of the angels*, New York 1914.

Le petit Pierre, 1918; 1928. Tr. J. L. May, *Little Pierre*, New York 1920.

Les autels de la peur, 1926; ed. J. de Gardony Gilman, 1971.

Trente ans de vie sociale, 3 vols, 1949–63.

AXELRAD, J., *Anatole France: a life without illusion*, New York 1944.

BANCQUART, M. C., *Anatole France, polémiste*, 1962 (incl. bibl.).

CHEVALIER, H., *Anatole France, the ironic temper*, New York 1932.

DARGAN, E. P., *Anatole France, 1844–1896*, London and New York 1937.

LE GOFF, M., *Anatole France à la Béchellerie, 1914–1924*, 1924; 1947.

LEVAILLANT, J., *Les aventures du scepticisme: essai sur l'évolution intellectuelle d'Anatole France*, 1965.

MARNAUD, J., *Anatole France, écrivain français*, 1962.

SAREIL, J., *Anatole France et Voltaire*, Geneva 1961.

SUFFEL, J., *Anatole France par lui-même*, 1946; 1954.

TYLDEN-WRIGHT, D., *Anatole France*, London 1967.

VANDEGANS, A., *Anatole France, les années de formation*, 1954

GAUTIER, Théophile   1811–1872

TOURNEUX, M., *Théophile Gautier, sa bibliographie*, 1876.

SPOELBERCH DĘ LOVENJOUL, C. de, *Histoire des oeuvres*, 2 vols, 1887.

Poésies complètes, 1845; 2 vols, 1875–6 (enl.); ed. R. Jasinski, 3 vols, 1932 (enl. 1970).
Théâtre, 1877.
Nouvelles, 1923.
Romans et contes, n.d.
Contes fantastiques, 1962 (shorter stories).

Tr. and ed. F. C. de Sumichrast (vols 1–23) and A. Lee (poetry, vol 24). *The works*, 24 vols, New York and London 1900–3.

Tr. L. Hearn, *One of Cleopatra's nights, and other fantastic romances*, New York 1882 (cntg six tales).

Tr. B. Hill, *Gentle enchanter*, London 1960 (selected poems).

Poésies, 1830; 1845 (in *Poésies complètes* above); ed. H. Cockerham, London 1973.
Albertus, 1833 (incorporating *Poésies* above).
Les Jeunes France, romans goguenards, 1833; 1851 (with *Une larme du diable* below); 1873 (enl.); ed. R. Jasinski, 1974.
Mademoiselle de Maupin, 2 vols, 1835–6; ed. A. Boschot, 1930. Tr. I. G. Burnham, 2 vols, New York 1897; tr. R. and E. Powys Mathers, London 1938; tr. P. Selver, 1948.
La Préface de Mlle de Maupin, 1835 (in *Mlle de Maupin*, vol 1 above); ed. G. Matoré, Geneva 1946.
L'Eldorado, 1837; 1838 (renamed *Fortunio*); ed. A. Boschot, 1930 (in *Fortunio et autres nouvelles*). Tr. anon. *Fortunio*, London 1915.
La comédie de la mort, 1838.
Une larme du diable, 1839 (with *La morte amoureuse*).
Giselle, ou les Wilis, ballet (in collab. with Saint-Georges and Coraly), 1841.
Tra los montes, 2 vols, 1843; 1845 (renamed *Voyage en Espagne*). Tr. anon., *Wanderings in Spain*, London 1853; tr. C. A. Phillips, *A romantic in Spain*, 1926.
La Péri (in collab. with Coralli), 1843.
Les grotesques, 2 vols, 1844.
España, 1845 (in *Poésies complètes* above); ed. R. Jasinski, 1929.
Nouvelles, 1845 (incl. *Le roi Candaule*).
Zigzags, 1845; 1852 (enl., renamed *Caprices et zigzags*).
Italia, 1852; 1875 (enl., renamed *Voyage en Italie*). Tr. D. B. Vermilye, *Journeys in Italy*, New York 1902.
Emaux et camées, 1852; 1872 (enl.); ed. J. Madeleine, 1927; ed. G. Matoré, Lille and Geneva 1947; ed. A. Boschot, Paris 1954 (with other selected poems).
La peau de tigre, 3 vols, 1852 (incl. *Le pavillon sur l'eau*); 1866 (without *Le pavillon sur l'eau*).
Constantinople, 1853. Tr. R. H. Gould, *Constantinople of today*, London 1854.

Les beaux-arts en Europe, 2 vols, 1855 (mostly collected articles from *Moniteur Universel*), 2 vols, 1855.

Le roman de la momie, 1858; ed. A. Boschot, 1955. Tr. M. Young, *The romance of a mummy*, London 1886; tr. G. F. Monkshood, *The mummy's romance*, 1908.

Histoire de l'art dramatique en France depuis vingt-cinq ans (collected articles from *La Presse*), 6 vols, 1858–9. Tr. C. W. Beaumont, *The romantic ballet*, London 1932 (extracts).

Le capitaine Fracasse, 2 vols, 1863; ed. F. Gobin and R. Tisserand, 2 vols, 1929. Tr. E. M. Beam, *Captain Fracasse*, New York 1880.

Voyage en Russie, 2 vols, 1867. Tr. M. N. Ripley, *A winter in Russia*, New York 1874; tr. anon., *Russia*, 2 vols, Philadelphia (Pa) 1905.

Histoire du romantisme (unfinished), 1874; ed. L. Vincent, 1930. Tr. Sumichrast above, *A history of Romanticism*.

BOSCHOT, A., *Théophile Gautier*, 1933.

DU CAMP, M., *Théophile Gautier*, 1890. Tr. J. E. Gordon, London 1893.

FAUCHEREAU, S., *Théophile Gautier*, 1972.

JASINSKI, R., *Les années romantiques de Théophile Gautier*, 1929.

RICHARDSON, J., *Théophile Gautier, his life and times*, London 1958.

SPENCER, M. C., *The art criticism of Théophile Gautier*, Geneva 1969.

TILD, J., *Théophile Gautier et ses amis*, 1951.

TUIN, H. van der, *l'Evolution psychologique esthétique et littéraire de Théophile Gautier*, Amsterdam 1933.

GOBINEAU, Arthur de   1816–1882

Bibl. See ROWBOTHAM below.

Nouvelles, ed. J. J. Pauvert, 2 vols, 1956.

Le prisonnier chanceux, 3 vols, 1847. Tr. F. M. Atkinson, *The lucky prisoner*, London 1926.

Essai sur l'inégalité des races humaines, 4 vols, Paris and Hanover 1853–5; 2 vols, Paris 1884; ed. J. J. Pauvert, 1967. Tr. H. Hotz, *The moral and intellectual diversity of races*, Philadelphia (Pa) 1856 (sel.); tr. A. Collins, *The inequality of human races*, London and New York 1915; tr. M. D. Biddiss, *Selected political writings*, London 1970 (extracts).

Trois ans en Asie, 1859.

L'abbaye de Typhaines, 1867.

L'Aphroessa, 1869.

Souvenirs de voyage, 1872; ed. J. Gaulmier, 1968. Tr. H. L. Stuart, *The crimson handkerchief and other stories*, New York and London 1927.

Les Pléiades, Stockholm and Paris 1874; ed. J. Mistler, Paris 1946. Tr. J. F. Scanlan, *The Pleiads*, New York and London 1928; tr. D. Parmée, *Sons of Kings*, 1966.

Amadis, 1876.

Nouvelles asiatiques, 1876; ed. J. Gaulmier, 1965. Tr. H. M. Fox, *The dancing girl of Shamakha and other Asiatic tales*, London and New York 1926; tr. J. L. May, *Tales of Asia*, London 1947.

La Renaissance, 1877; ed. J. Mistler, 1947. Tr. P. V. Cohn, *The Renaissance*, New York 1913.

Histoire d'Ottar Jarl, 1879.

Études critiques, 1844–1848 (selected reviews), 1927.

Correspondance d'Alexis de Tocqueville et d'Arthur de Gobineau, ed. L. Schemann, 1908; ed. M. Degros, 1959 (as vol 9 of TOCQUEVILLE's *Oeuvres complètes*). Tr. and ed. G. Lukacs, *Correspondence with Gobineau*, New York 1959 (with *The European revolution*).

Lettres persanes, ed. A. B. Duff, 1957.

Comte de Gobineau et Mère Bénédicte de Gobineau, ed. A. B. Duff, 2 vols, 1958.

BIDDISS, M. D., *Father of racist ideology; the social and political thought of Count Gobineau*, New York 1970.

BUENZOD, J., *La formation de la pensée de Gobineau*, 1967.

COMBRIS, A., *La philosophie des races du comte de Gobineau et sa portée actuelle*, 1937.

Etudes gobiniennes, 1966 onwards.

GAULMIER, J., *Spectre de Gobineau*, 1965.

LANGE, M., *Le comte Arthur de Gobineau, étude biographique et critique*, Strasbourg 1924.

RIFFATERRE, M., *La style des Pléiades de Gobineau*, Geneva 1957.

ROWBOTHAM, A. H., *The literary works of Count of Gobineau*, 1929 (incl. bibl.).

GONCOURT, Edmond de   1822–1896
GONCOURT, Jules de   1830–1870

Bibl. See BILLY below.

[*Oeuvres*], 41 vols, 1922–37 (Académie Goncourt standard ed., by various editors, and incl. part pbn of *Journal* below).
Tr. M. A. Belloc and M. Shedlock, in *Edmond and Jules de Goncourt, with letters, and leaves from their Journals*, 2 vols, London 1895 (selection).

En 18, 1851; 1884.

Histoire de la société française pendant la Révolution, 1854.

Histoire de la société française pendant le Directoire, 1855.

Sophie Arnould, 1857; 1885.

Portraits intimes du XVIIIe siècle, 2 vols, 1857–8; 1878.

Histoire de Marie Antoinette, 1858; 1859.

L'art du dix-huitième siècle, 1859–75 (as 12 booklets on individual artists); 3 vols, 1881–2. Tr. R. Ironside, *French eighteenth century painters*, London and New York 1948 (selection).

Les hommes de lettres, 1860; 1868 (renamed *Charles Demailly*).

Les maîtresses de Louis XV, 2 vols, 1860 (3 pts); 3 vols, 1878–91 (enl.):

1 *La Du Barry*, 1878.

2 *Madame de Pompadour*, 1878.

3 *La duchesse de Châteauroux et ses soeurs*, 1879.

Tr. E. Dowson, *The confidantes of a king*, 2 vols, London and Edinburgh 1907.

Soeur Philomène, 1861. Tr. L. Ensor, *Sister Philomène*, London 1890.

La femme au dix-huitième siècle, 1862; 1877. Tr. J. Leclercq and R. Roeder, *The woman of the eighteenth century*, New York 1927.

Renée Mauperin, 1864. Tr. anon., London 1888; tr. anon., New York 1919.

Germinie Lacerteux, 1864. Tr. anon., London 1887; tr. anon., *Germinie*, London and New York 1955.

Henriette Maréchal, drame, Paris and Brussels 1866.

Manette Salomon, 2 vols, Paris and Brussels 1867.

Madame Gervaisais, Paris and Brussels 1869.

Gavarni, l'homme et l'oeuvre, 1873.

Works by Edmond de Goncourt alone.

La fille Elisa, 1877. Tr. M. Crosland, *Elisa*, London 1959; tr. C. Harrald, in *Woman of Paris*, 1959.

Les frères Zemganno, 1879. Tr. anon., *The Zemganno brothers*, London 1886; tr. L. Clark and I. Allam, 1957.

La Faustin, 1882. Tr. J. Stirling, Philadelphia (Pa) 1882; tr. G. F. Monkshood and E. Tristan, London 1906.

La Saint-Huberty, 1882.

Mademoiselle Clairon, 1890.

Outamaro, 1891.

La Guimard, 1893.

Hokousaï, l'art japonais du XVIIIe siècle, 1896.

Journal, 9 vols, 1887–96 (incomplete); ed. R. Ricatte, 22 vols, Monaco, 1956. Tr. Belloc and Shedlock above (selection); tr. and ed. L. Galantiere, *The Goncourt journals, 1851–1870*, New York 1937 (selection); tr. and ed. R. Baldick, *Pages from the Goncourt journal*, Oxford 1962; tr. and ed. G. T. Becker and E. Philips, *Paris and the arts, 1851–1896, from the Goncourt journal*, Ithaca (NY) 1971.

BALDICK, R., *The Goncourts*, London 1960.

BILLY, A., *Vie des frères Goncourt*, 3 vols, Monaco 1956 (incl. bibl.). Tr. M. Shaw, *The Goncourt brothers*, London and New York 1960.

GRANT, R. B., *The Goncourt brothers*, 1973.

RICATTE, R., *La création romanesque chez les Goncourt, 1851–1870*, 1953.
SABATIER, P., *L'esthétique des Goncourt*, 1920.

GUÉRIN, Maurice de   1810–1839

Bibl. See DECAHORS below.

Oeuvres, ed. H. Clouard, 2 vols, 1930; ed. B. d'Harcourt, 2 vols, 1947.

Reliquiae, ed. G. S. Trebutien, 2 vols, 1861; 1862 (enl., as *Journal, lettres et poèmes*).
Le centaure, 1861 (in *Reliquiae* above; first pbd in *Revue des Deux Mondes*, May 1840); ed. E. Decahors, Toulouse 1932. Tr. S. Merrill, *The centaur*, New York 1890; tr. T. S. Moore, London 1899; tr. H. Bedford Jones, New York 1929 (with unpbd correspondence).
La bacchante, 1862 (in *Journal, lettres et poèmes* above); ed. E. Decahors, Toulouse 1932 (with *Le centaure* above). Tr. T. S. Moore, *The bacchante*, London 1899 (with *The centaur* above).

Journal, 1861 (in *Reliquiae* above); ed. A. Van Bever, 1921 (as *Le cahier vert, journal intime, 1832–1835*). Tr. E. T. Fisher, *The journal*, New York 1867; tr. J. P. Frothingham, London 1891.
Lettres à Barbey d'Aurevilly, 1908.
Lettres d'adolescence, ed. G. Chinard, 1929.

DECAHORS, E., *Maurice de Guérin, essai de biographie psychologique*, 1932 (incl. bibl.).
GUÉRIN, E. de, *Journal intime*, 1862. Tr. W. M. Lightbody, *The journal*, London 1908.
HARCOURT, B. d', *Maurice de Guérin et le poème en prose*, 1932.
LEFRANC, A., *Maurice de Guérin*, 1910.

HÉRÉDIA, José-Maria de   1842–1905

IBROVAC, M., *Bibliographie*, 1923 (in *J. M. de Hérédia* below); 1927.

Les trophées, 1893; 1924 (enl.). Tr. E. R. Taylor, *Sonnets from the Trophies*, San Francisco (Calif) 1898; tr. J. M. O'Hara and J. Hervey, *The trophies, with other sonnets*, New York 1929; tr. B. Hill, *Fifty sonnets*, London 1962.

CHATELAIN, U. V., *José-Maria de Hérédia, sa vie et son milieu*, 1930.
IBROVAC, M., *José-Maria de Hérédia, sa vie et son oeuvre*, 1923 (incl. bibl.).
    Les sources des Trophées, 1923.
LANGEVIN, E., *José-Maria de Hérédia, études et sources*, 1907.
MOUSSAT, E., *Expliquez-moi les sonnets de José-Maria de Hérédia*, 1949.

HUGO, Victor   1802–1865

RUDWIN, M., *Bibliographie*, 1926.
GRANT, E. M., *A select and critical bibliography*, Chapel Hill (NC) 1967.

Oeuvres complètes, 57 vols, 1880–92 ('*édition Hetzel-Quantin*'); ed. P. Meurice,
G. Simon and C. Daubray, 45 vols, 1904–52 ('*édition de l'Imprimerie nation-*
ale'); ed. J. Massin, 36 vols, 1967–72 ('*édition chronologique*', incl. 4 vols
of drawings, etc.).
La légende des siècles, La fin de Satan, Dieu, ed. J. Truchet, 1950.
Théâtre, ed. J. J. Thierry and J. Mélèse, 2 vols, 1963–4.
Oeuvres poétiques, ed. P. Albouy, 1964 onwards (2 vols pbd); ed. B. Leuilliot,
3 vols, 1972.
Choix de poèmes, ed. J. Gaudon, Manchester 1957.

Tr. various, ed. H. L. Willies, *The literary life and poetical works of Victor*
Hugo, New York 1883.
Tr. anon., *Works*, New York 1887; tr. A. Baillot et al., 30 vols, Boston 1892.
Tr. M. W. Artois, J. C. Beckwith et al., *The novels*, 28 vols, London 1895.
Tr. I. G. Burnham, *The dramas*, 4 vols, Philadelphia (Pa) 1895–6.

Odes et poésies diverses, 1822; 1823 (enl.).
    Nouvelles odes, 1824;
    Odes et ballades, 1826;
    1826 (collected ed., enl., as *Odes et ballades*).
Han d'Islande, 4 vols, 1823. Tr. anon., *Hans of Iceland*, London 1845; tr.
G. Campbell, *The outlaw of Iceland*, 1885; tr. H. Smith, *Hans of Iceland*,
New York and Boston (Mass) 1896.
Bug-Jargal, 1826. Tr. anon., *The noble rival*, London 1845; tr. C. E. Wilbour,
Jargal, New York 1866.
Cromwell, 1827 (with *Préface*, ed. M. Souriau, 1897).
Les Orientales, 1829; ed. E. Barineau, 2 vols, 1952–54. Tr. J. N. Fazakerley,
Eastern lyrics, London 1879.
Le dernier jour d'un condamné, 1829; 1832 (with preface). Tr. G. W. M.
Reynolds, *The last day of a condemned* London 1840; tr. M. Wood,
The last day of a condemned man, 1931.
Hernani, 1830; ed. M. Levaillant, 1933; ed. C. Beuchat, Lausanne 1945.
Tr. F. L. Gower, London 1830; tr. R. F. Sharp, 1898.
Notre Dame de Paris, 2 vols, 1831; 3 vols, 1832; ed. M. F. Guyard, 1959.
Tr. F. Shoberl, *The hunchback of Notre Dame*, London 1833; tr. anon.,
Notre Dame de Paris, 1910; tr. J. Haynes, 2 vols, Paris 1930; tr. L. Bair,
The hunchback of Notre Dame, New York 1956; tr. W. J. Cobb, 1965.
Marion de Lorme, 1831.
Les feuilles d'automne, 1831; ed. L. Bisson, Oxford 1944.
Le roi s'amuse, 1832. Tr. H. T. Haby, *The king's fool*, London? 1842; tr.
F. L. Slow, *Le roi s'amuse!*, London 1843.

Lucrèce Borgia, drame, 1833. Tr. H. T. Haby, *Lucretia Borgia*, London? 1841.

Marie Tudor, 1833.

Angelo, tyran de Padoue, 1835. Tr. E. O. Coe, *Angelo*, London 1880.

Les chants du crépuscule, 1835. Tr. G. W. M. Reynolds, *Songs of twilight*, 1836.

Les voix intérieures, 1837.

Ruy Blas, Leipzig and Paris 1838 (with *Préface*, ed. E. Wahl, Oxford 1932). Tr. W. D. S. Alexander, London 1890; tr. B. Hooker, New York 1931.

Les rayons et les ombres, 1840.

Le Rhin, lettres à un ami, 2 vols, 1842; 4 vols, 1845 (enl.). Tr. D. M. Aird, *The Rhine*, London 1843; tr. E. and A. Birrell, *The story of the bold Pécopin*, 1902.

Les Burgraves, trilogie, 1843.

Napoléon-le-petit, London and Brussels 1852.

Châtiments, Saint Hélier (Jersey) 1853; Paris 1870 (enl.); ed. P. Berret, 2 vols, 1932.

Les contemplations, 1856; ed. J. Vianey, 1922; ed. P. Albouy, 1967 (revd 1973); ed. L. Cellier, 1970.

Les contemporains, 3 vols, Brussels 1856; ed. J. Vianey, 3 vols, Paris 1922.

La légende des siècles, 5 vols, 1859–83; ed. P. Benet, 6 vols, 1921–7. Tr. anon., *The legend of the centuries*, New York 1894. Comprising:
>   *La légende des siècles, première série*, 2 vols, Leipzig and Brussels 1859.
>   *Nouvelle série*, 2 vols, 1877.
>   *Tome cinquième et dernier*, 1883.

Les misérables, 10 vols, Brussels and Paris 1862; ed. M. Allem Paris, 1951; ed. M. F. Guyard, 2 vols, 1957. Tr. F. C. L. Wraxall, London 1862 (abr. 1931); ed. C. E. Wilbour, 1887; tr. I. F. Hapgood, New York and Boston (Mass) 1887; tr. M. Schaeffer, New York 1925.

William Shakespeare, 1864; ed. J. Seebacher, 1966. Tr. A. Baillot, London 1864.

Les chansons des rues et des bois, Paris and Brussels 1865.

Les travailleurs de la mer, 3 vols, Brussels 1866. Tr. W. M. Thomas, *Toilers of the sea*, 3 vols, London 1866; tr. M. Artois, 2 vols, Philadelphia (Pa) 1892.

L'homme qui rit, 4 vols, Paris and Brussels 1869. Tr. W. Young, *The man who laughs*, New York 1869; tr. A. C. Steele, *By order of the King*, 3 vols, London 1870; tr. I. Hapwood, *The man who laughs*, 2 vols, New York, 1888.

L'année terrible, 1872 (incomplete); 1879; ed. H. Guillemin, 1971.

Quatre-vingt treize, 3 vols, 1874. Tr. F. L. Benedicte and J. H. Friswell, *Ninety-three*, 3 vols, London 1874; tr. L. Bair, New York 1962.

Histoire d'un crime, 2 vols, 1877–8 (vol 1 first pbd Brussels 1852, as *Enquête sur le deux décembre*). Tr. T. H. Joyce and A. Locker, *The history of a crime*, 4 vols, London 1877–8; tr. G. Campbell, 1888.

L'art d'être grand-père, 1877.

Les quatre vents de l'esprit, 2 vols, 1881.

La fin de Satan, 1886 (in *Oeuvres complètes*, vol 50 above).

Dieu, 1891 (in *Oeuvres complètes*, vol 55 above); ed. R. Journet and G. Robert, 5 vols, 1960–9 (ed. of 3 parts only).

Choses vues, 1887–1900; ed. P. Souchon, Paris and Geneva 1962. Tr. and ed. D. Kimber, *Things seen*, London 1964 (selection). Comprising:
Choses vues, 1887 (in *Oeuvres complètes* above). Tr. anon., *Things seen*, 2 vols, London 1887.
Nouvelle série, 1900.

Toute la lyre, 2 vols, 1888; 2 vols, 1935 (in *Oeuvres complètes*, vols 12–13 above).

Les années funestes, 1852–1870, 1898 (incl. poems first pbd in *Toute la lyre* above).

Dernière gerbe, 1902.

Journal, 1830–1848, ed. H. Guillemin, 1954.

Correspondance, 4 vols, 1947–52 (in *Oeuvres complètes*, vols 41–5 above). Tr. N. H. Dole, *Victor Hugo's letters to his wife and others*, Boston (Mass) 1895; tr. F. Clarke, *The letters of Victor Hugo*. London 1896 (selection); tr. E. W. Latimer, *The love letters of Victor Hugo, 1820–1822*, London and New York 1901.

ALBOUY, P., *La création mythologique chez Victor Hugo*, 1963.

BARRÈRE, J. B., *La fantaisie de Victor Hugo*, 3 vols, 1949–60; 1972.
Victor Hugo à l'oeuvre: le poète en exil et en voyage, 1966.

GAUDON, J., *Le temps de la contemplation*, 1969.

GLACHANT, P. and V., *Essai critique sur le théâtre de Hugo*, 2 vols, 1902–3.

GLAUSER, A., *Victor Hugo et la poésie pure*, Geneva 1957.

GRANT, E. M., *The career of Victor Hugo*, Cambridge (Mass) 1946.

GREGH, F., *Victor Hugo, sa vie, son oeuvre*, 1954.

GUILLEMIN, H., *Victor Hugo par lui-même*, 1951.

JOURNET, R. and ROBERT, G., *Notes sur les Contemplations*, 1958.

LEVAILLANT, M., *La crise mystique de Victor Hugo*, 1954.

MAUROIS, A., *Olympio, ou la vie de Victor Hugo*, 1954. Tr. G. Hopkins, *Victor Hugo*, London 1956.

PY, A., *Les mythes grecs dans la poésie de Victor Hugo*, Geneva 1963.

VENZAC, G., *Les premiers maîtres de Victor Hugo, 1809–1818*, 1955.

HUYSMANS, Joris-Karl 1848–1907

CARLO, B., *Bibliografia huysmansiana*, Milan 1938.

CEVASCO, G. A., *J.-K. Huysman in England and America: a bibliographical study*, Charlottesville (Va) 1961.

See also DEFFOUX below.

Oeuvres complètes, ed. L. Descaves and C. Grolleau, 23 vols, 1928–34.

Tr. S. Putnam, *Downstream and other works*, Chicago (Ill) 1927.

Le drageoir aux épices, 1874; 1916.
Marthe, Brussels 1876; ed. P. Lambert, Paris 1955. Tr. Putnam above; tr. R. Baldick, *Marthe*, London 1948.
Les soeurs Vatard, 1879.
Sac au dos, 1880 (in collective work *Les soirées de Médan*).
Croquis parisiens, 1880. Tr. R. Griffiths, *Parisian sketches*, London 1962.
En ménage, 1881.
A vau l'eau, Brussels 1882. Tr. Putnam above, *Downstream*; tr. R. Baldick, London 1956.
L'art moderne, 1883.
A rebours, 1884; 1903 (with *Préface de l'auteur*). Tr. J. Howard, *Against the grain*, New York 1922; tr. R. Baldick, *Against nature*, Harmondsworth 1959.
Certains, 1889.
Là-bas, 1891. Tr. K. Wallis, *Down there*, New York 1924.
  En route, 1895; 1897. Tr. C. K. Paul, London 1896.
    Là-haut (early version of *En route*), ed. P. Cogny, A. Artinian and P. Lambert, 1965.
La cathédrale, 1898. Tr. C. Bell, *The cathedral*, London 1898.
La Bièvre et Saint Séverin, 1898 (*La Bièvre* first pbd in *De Nieuwe Gids*, Amsterdam, Aug. 1886).
L'oblat, 1903. Tr. E. Perceval, *The oblate*, London and New York 1924.
Trois primitifs, 1905.

Lettres inédites à Emile Zola, ed. P. Lambert, 1953.
Lettres à Camille Lemonnier, ed. C. Vanwelkynhuyzen, Geneva 1957.

BALDICK, R., *The life of Joris-Karl Huysmans*, Oxford 1955. Tr. M. Thomas, *La vie de J. K. Huysmans*, 1958.
BILLY, A., *Huysmans et Cie*, 1962.
BRANDRETH, H. R. T., *Huysmans*, London and New York 1963.
COGNY, P., *Huysmans à la recherche de l'unité*, 1953.
CRESSOT, M., *La phrase et le vocabulaire de J. K. Huysmans*, 1938.
DEFFOUX, L., *J. K. Huysmans sous divers aspects*, 1927; Brussels 1942 (incl. bibl. of works).
SEILLÈRE, E., *Joris-Karl Huysmans and the symbolist movement*, 1931.

JARRY, Alfred 1873–1907

Bibl. See LEVESQUE below.

Oeuvres complètes, ed. R. Massat, 8 vols, Monaco 1948; ed. M. Arrivé, 1972 onwards (1 vol pbd).
Oeuvres poétiques complètes, ed. H. Parisot and A. Frédérique, 1945.

Tr. S. W. Taylor and C. Connolly, ed. R. Shattuck and S. W. Taylor, *Selected works*, London 1965.

Les minutes du sable mémorial, 1894.

Ubu, Paris and Geneva 1896–1944; ed. M. Saillet, 1962 (*Tout Ubu*). Tr. B. Keith and G. Legman, *King Turd*, New York 1953; tr. C. Connolly and S. W. Taylor, *The Ubu plays*, London 1968. Comprising:
    Ubu roi, 1896 (earlier version, entitled *César Antéchrist*, pbd 1895).
    Ubu enchaîné, 1900 (with *Ubu roi*).
    Ubu cocu, Geneva 1944.

Messaline, 1901. Tr. L. Coleman, *The garden of Priapus*, New York, 1936.

Le surmâle, 1902. Tr. B. Wright, *The supermale*, London 1968.

Gestes et opinions du docteur Faustroll, pataphysicien, 1911.

La revanche de la nuit (poems), ed. M. Saillet, 1949.

ESSLIN, M., in his *The theatre of the absurd*, New York 1961; 1968. Tr. M. Buchet et al., *Le théâtre de l'absurde*, Paris 1963.

LEBOIS, A., *Alfred Jarry, l'irremplaçable*, 1950.

LEVESQUE, J. H., *Alfred Jarry, une étude*, 1951 (incl. bibl. of works).

LOT, F., *Alfred Jarry, son oeuvre*, 1934.

PERCHE, L., *Alfred Jarry*, 1965.

RACHILDE, *Alfred Jarry, ou le surmâle des lettres*, 1928.

SHATTUCK, R., in his *The banquet years: the arts in France 1885–1918*, London 1959; 1969.

LABICHE, Eugène   1815–1888

Bibl. See SOUPAULT below.

Théâtre complet, ed. E. Augier, 10 vols, 1878–9 (cntg about a third of plays); 5 vols, 1949–50 (selection).

Oeuvres complètes, 8 vols, 1966–8.

La fille bien gardée (in collab. with Marc-Michel), 1850.

Le chapeau de paille d'Italie (in collab. with Marc-Michel), 1851. Tr. C. V. Chesley, *A Leghorn hat*, Boston 1917; tr. T. Walton, *An Italian straw-hat*, London 1956; tr. F. Davies, New York 1967.

Edgar et sa bonne (in collab. with Marc-Michel), 1852.

L'affaire de la rue de Lourcine (in collab. with Albert Monnier), 1857.

Le voyage de Monsieur Perrichon (in collab. with Marc-Michel), 1860. Tr. M. Ivey, *The journey of Mr Perrichon*, New York 1924; tr. R. H. Ward, *A trip abroad*, New York 1958 (in *Let's get a divorce and other plays*); tr. and adapt. K. Cartledge, *Mr Perrichon's holiday*, 1965.

Les vivacités du capitaine Tic (in collab. with Edouard Martin), 1861.

La poudre aux yeux (in collab. with Edouard Martin), 1861; ed. E. Fromageat, Berne 1941 (abr.). Tr. M. J. Jagose, *Throwing dust in people's eyes*, London 1930?.

169

La station Champbaudet (in collab. with Marc-Michel), 1862.

Célimare le bien-aimé (in collab. with A. Delacour), 1863. Tr. L. and T. Hoffmann, *Celimare*, London 1959.

La cagnotte (in collab. with A. Delacour), 1864.

Les trente millions de Gladiator (in collab. with Philippe Gille), 1875.

SOUPAULT, P., *Eugène Labiche, sa vie et son oeuvre*, 1945; 1955 (incl. list of dates of plays).

LAFORGUE, Jules   1860–1887

GIOVINE, E. de, in her *Bibliographie de Corbière, Lautréamont et Laforgue*, 1962; Florence 1969.

See also Durry ed. of *Choix de poèmes* below.

Oeuvres complètes, 3 vols, 1902–3; ed. G. Jean-Aubry, 6 vols, 1922–30.

Poésies complètes, ed. P. Pia, 1970.

Choix de poèmes, ed. M. J. Durry, 1952 (incl. bibl. of works).

Tr. W. J. Smith, *Selected writings*, New York 1956.

Tr. P. Terry, *Poems*, Berkeley (Calif) 1958.

Les complaintes, 1885. Tr. Smith above, *The complaints* (selection).

L'imitation de Notre-Dame de Lune, 1886. Tr. Smith above, *The imitation of Our Lady of the Moon*.

Moralités légendaires, 1887. Tr. F. Newman, *Six moral tales*, New York 1928.

Les derniers vers, ed. E. Dujardin and F. Fénéon, 1890 (incl. *Fleurs de bonne volonté*, extracts of which were first pbd in earlier version as *Le concile féerique*, 1886); ed. M. Collie and J. M. L'Heureux, Toronto 1965. Tr. Smith above, *Last poems* and *Flowers of goodwill* (selection).

Berlin, la cour et la ville, 1922. Tr. Smith above, *Berlin, the city and the court*.

Mélanges posthumes, 1923.

Stéphane Vassiliew, ed. F. Ruchon, Lausanne 1946.

Lettres à un ami, 1880–1886, ed. G. Jean-Aubry, 1941 (other correspondence pbd 1925, in *Oeuvres complètes* above). Tr. Smith above (selection).

COLLIE, M., *Laforgue*, Edinburgh and London 1963.

DEBAUVE, J. L., *Laforgue en son temps*, Neuchâtel 1972.

DURRY, M. J., *Jules Laforgue*, 1952.

GUICHARD, L., *Jules Laforgue et ses poésies*, 1950.

RAMSEY, W., (ed.), *Jules Laforgue, essays on a poet's life and work*, Carbondale (Ill) 1969.

RAMSEY, W., *Jules Laforgue and the ironic inheritance*, New York 1953.

REBOUL, P., *Laforgue*, 1960.

RUCHON, F., *Jules Laforgue, sa vie, son oeuvre*, Geneva 1924.

SELUJA CECÍN, A., *El Montevideano Jules Laforgue, su vida y su obra*, Montevideo 1964.

LAMARTINE, Alphonse de   1790–1869

BAILLON, J. and HARRIS, E., *Etat présent des études lamartiniennes*, 1933.
GUYARD, M. F., *Etat présent des études lamartiniennes*, 1961 (in *L'Information Littéraire*, May–June).

Oeuvres complètes, 4 vols, 1834 (poetry); 41 vols, 1860–66; 22 vols, 1900–7.
Oeuvres poétiques complètes, ed. M. F. Guyard, 1963.

Méditations poétiques, 1820; 1823 (enl.); ed. G. Lanson, 2 vols, 1915; ed.
   F. Letessier, 1968. Tr. H. Christmas, *The poetical meditations*, London
   1839.
      Nouvelles méditations poétiques, 1823.
La mort de Socrate, 1823. Tr. H. Cope, *The death of Socrates*, London 1829.
Le dernier chant du pélerinage d'Harold, 1825. Tr. anon., *The last canto of
   Childe Harold's pilgrimage*, London 1827.
Harmonies poétiques et religieuses, 1830 (incl. *Novissima verba, Eternité de
   la Nature* and *Premier regret*).
A Némésis, 1831.
Sur la politique rationnelle, 1831. Tr. anon. *The polity of reason*, London 1848.
Des destinées à la poésie, 1834 (as preface to *Oeuvres complètes* above).
Souvenirs, impressions, pensées et paysages pendant un voyage en Orient, 4
   vols, 1835 (incl. *Gethsémani*, tr. J. H. Urquhart, *Gethsemane*, London
   1838); ed. L. Fam, 1959. Tr. anon., *Travels in the East*, London 1835;
   tr. anon., *A pilgrimage to the Holy Land*, 3 vols, 1937.
Jocelyn, 2 vols, 1836; 1841; ed. J. des Cognets, 1925; ed. M. F. Guyard, 1967.
   Tr. F. H. Jobert, 1837; tr. R. Anstruther, London 1844; tr. H. P. Stuart,
   New York 1954.
La chute d'un ange, 2 vols, 1838; ed. M. F. Guyard, Geneva and Lille 1954
   (*Fragment du livre primitif*).
Receuillements poétiques, 1839; 1850 (enl.); ed. J. des Cognets, 1925.
Histoire des Girondins, 8 vols, 1847. Tr. H. T. Ryde, *History of the Girond-
   ists*, 3 vols, London 1847–8.
Raphaël, pages de la vingtième année, 1849. Tr. anon., *Raphael, or pages of
   the book of life*, New York 1849.
Les confidences, 1849. Tr. E. Plunkett, *Confidential disclosures*, New York
   1849.
Graziella, 1849 (in *Les confidences* above); ed. G. Roth, 1925; ed. G. Charlier,
   1926. Tr. W. C. Urquhart, London 1871; tr. R. Wright, 1929.
Histoire de la révolution de 1848, 2 vols, 1849. Tr. anon., *History of the French*

revolution of 1848, London 1849; tr. F. A. Durivage and W. S. Chase, 2 vols, Boston (Mass) 1849.

Toussaint Louverture, 1850; ed. G. Raffalovitch, New York and London 1931.

Geneviève, 1850. Tr. M. Howitt, London 1847; tr. A. R. Scoble, London 1850.

Le tailleur de pierres de Saint-Point, 1851. Tr. anon., *The stonemason of Saint-Point*, London and New York 1851.

Nouvelles confidences, 1851.

Les visions, 1851 (in *Nouvelles confidences* above); ed. H. Guillemin, 1936.

Histoire de la Restauration, 8 vols, 1851–2. Tr. the author and Captain Rafter, *The history of the restoration of monarchy in France*, 4 vols, London 1851–3; 1882–91.

Histoire des constituants, 4 vols, 1855. Tr. anon., *History of the constituent assembly*, London 1858.

Vie des grands hommes, 5 vols, 1855–6. Tr. anon., *Biographies and portraits of some celebrated people*, 2 vols, London 1866.

Cours familier de littérature, 28 vols, 1856–69 (pbd in monthly instalments); 3 vols, 1871–2 (selection, as *Souvenirs et portraits*); ed. J. des Cognets, 2 vols, 1926 (selection).

La vigne et la maison, 1856 (in *Cours familier de littérature*, *entretien 15* above).

Mémoires politiques, 4 vols, 1863 (in *Oeuvres complètes*, vols 37–40 above).

La France parlementaire, *1834–1851*, *oeuvres oratoires et écrits politiques*, 6 vols, 1864–5.

Poésies inédites, 1873.

Saül, 1879; ed. J. des Cognets, 1918.

Correspondance, 6 vols, 1873–5; ed. M. Levaillant, 2 vols, Paris, Geneva and Lille 1943–8 (covering 1830–6).

Lettres inédites, ed. H. Guillemin, Porrentruy 1944.

BOENIGER, Y., *Lamartine et le sentiment de la nature*, 1934.

BOUCHARD, M., *Lamartine, ou le sens de l'amour*, 1940.

DÉRIEUX, H., *Lamartine raconté par ceux qui l'ont vu*, 1938.

DUMONT, F. and GITAN, J., *De quoi vivait Lamartine*, 1952.

FRÉJAVILLE, G., *Les Méditations de Lamartine*, 1931.

GRILLET, C., *La Bible dans Lamartine*, Lyon and Paris 1938.

GUILLEMIN, H., *Lamartine, l'homme et l'oeuvre*, 1940.

   Connaissance de Lamartine, Fribourg 1942.

   Lamartine et la question sociale, 1946.

GUYARD, M. F., *Alphonse de Lamartine*, Brussels 1956.

HAZARD, P., *Lamartine*, 1925.

LUPPÉ, A. M. P. de, *Les travaux et les jours d'Alphonse de Lamartine*, 1942; 1948.

VERDIER, A., *Les amours italiennes de Lamartine, Graziella et Lena*, 1963.

LAUTRÉAMONT, Comte de 1846–1870
(pseudonym of Isidore Ducasse)

GIOVINE, E. de, in her *Bibliographie de Corbière, Lautréamont et Laforgue*, 1962; Florence 1969.

HAES, F. de, *Images de L. Isidore Ducasse*, 1970 (critical survey and bibl.). See also SOULIER below.

Oeuvres complètes, ed. P. Soupault, 1927; ed. E. Jaloux, 1938; ed. R. Caillois, 1946; introd. A. Breton et al., 1953; ed. M. Bonnet, 1969; ed. H. Juin, 1970.

Les chants de Maldoror, 1868 (canto 1); Paris and Brussels 1874 (cantos 1–6; ptd 1869 but unpbd). Tr. J. Rodker, *Lay of Maldoror*, London 1924; tr. G. Wernhaus, *Maldoror*, New York 1943.

Poésies, 2 vols, 1870.

FAURISSON, R., *A-t-on lu Lautréamont ?*, 1972.

JEAN, M. and MAZEI, A., *Maldoror, essai sur Lautréamont et son oeuvre*, 1947.

LEFRANÇOIS, R., *L'énigme de Maldoror*, Montreal 1969.

PIERRE-QUINT, L., *Lautréamont et Dieu*, 1930; 1967.

PLEYNET, M., *Lautréamont par lui-même*, 1967.

SOULIER, J. P., *Lautréamont, génie ou maladie mentale*, Geneva 1964 (incl. bibl.).

SOUPAULT, P., *Lautréamont*, 1953.

LECONTE DE LISLE, Charles-Marie-René 1818–1894

LAFONTAINE, R. C., *Essai de bibliographie des poèmes*, 1906.

DiORIO, D. M., *A hundred and twenty years of criticism (1850–1970)*, University (Miss.) 1972.

Poésies complètes, 4 vols, 1927–8.
Poésies choisis, ed. E. Eggli, Manchester 1943.

Translated in anthologies.

Poèmes antiques, 1852; 1874 (enl.).
Poèmes et poésies, 1855; 1857 (incl. *Chemin de la croix*, later renamed *La Passion*).
Poésies barbares, 1862; 1878 (enl.).
Catéchisme populaire républicain (based partly on notes compiled by Ernest Courbet and Louis Xavier de Ricard), 1870.
Histoire populaire du christianisme, 1871.
Histoire populaire de la Révolution française, 1871.
Les Erinnyes, 1873.
Poèmes tragiques, 1884 (incl. *Les Erinnyes* above); 1886 (enl.).
Derniers poèmes, 1895.
Premières poésies et lettres intimes, ed. B. Guinaudeau, 1902.

Contes en prose et impressions de jeunesse, 1911.

BROWN, I., *Leconte de Lisle, a study of the man and his poetry,* New York 1924.

ESTÈVE, E., *Leconte de Lisle, l'homme et l'oeuvre,* 1903; 1923.

FLOTTES, P., *Le poète Leconte de Lisle,* 1929.
  Leconte de Lisle, l'homme et l'oeuvre, 1954.

FAIRLIE, A., *Leconte de Lisle's poems on the barbarian races,* Cambridge 1947.

JOBIT, P., *Leconte de Lisle et le mirage de l'île natale,* 1951.

PUTTER, I., *The pessimism of Leconte de Lisle,* 2 vols, Berkeley (Calif) 1954–61.

VALENTINI, R.C., *Un poète presque oublié: Leconte de Lisle,* Vimodrome (Italy) 1958.

VIANEY, J., *Les Poèmes barbares de Leconte de Lisle,* 1933.

LOTI, Pierre   1850–1923
(pseudonym of Louis-Marie-Julien Viaud)

Bibl. See BORGEAUD below; also SERBAN below

Oeuvres complètes, 11 vols, 1893–1911.

Aziyadé, Stamboul 1876–1877, 1879.

Rarahu, 1879; 1880 (renamed *Le mariage de Loti*). Tr. C. Bell, *Rarahu, or the marriage of Loti,* New York 1892; tr. G. F. Monkshood, *The marriage of Loti,* London 1908.

Le roman d'un Spahi, 1881. Tr. M. L. Watkins, *The romance of a Spahi,* Chicago and New York 1890; tr. G. F. Monkshood and E. Tristan, London 1902; tr. anon., *Love in the desert,* 1928.

Mon frère Yves, 1883. Tr. M. P. Fletcher, *My brother Yves,* London 1887; tr. W. P. Baines, *A tale of Brittany,* 1923.

Pêcheur d'Islande, 1886; ed. P. O. Codebo, Turin 1949. Tr. C. Cadiot, *An Iceland fisherman,* London 1888; tr. W. P. Baines, London 1924; tr. G. Endore, New York 1946.

Madame Chrysanthème, 1887. Tr. L. Ensor, Paris and London 1889.

Le livre de la pitié et de la mort, 1891. Tr. T. P. O'Connor, *The book of pity and death,* London 1892.

Le roman d'un enfant, 1890. Tr. C. Bell, *A child's romance,* New York 1891.
  Prime jeunesse, 1919.

Fantôme d'Orient, 1891. Tr. J. E. Gordon, *A phantom from the East,* London 1892.

Ramuntcho, 1897; ed. N. Scarlyn Wilson, London 1961. Tr. W. P. Baines, *A tale of the Pyrenees,* London 1923.

L'Inde (sans les Anglais), 1903. Tr. G. A. F. Inman, *India,* London 1906.

Les désenchantées, 1906. Tr. C. Bell, *Disenchanted,* London 1906.

Un jeune officier pauvre, 1923. Tr. R. E. Stein, *Notes of my youth,* London 1924.

Journal intime, 2 vols, 1925–31.

BORGEAUD, H., *Pierre Loti*, Caen 1950 (incl. bibl. of works and critical bibl.).

EKSTRÖM, P. G., *Evasions et désespérances de Pierre Loti*, 1953.

LEFÈVRE, R., *La vie inquiète de Pierre Loti*, 1934.

LE TARGAT, F., *A la recherche de Pierre Loti*, 1974.

MILLWARD, K. G., *L'oeuvre de Pierre Loti et l'esprit fin de siècle*, 1955.

SERBAN, N., *Pierre Loti, sa vie et son oeuvre*, 1924 (incl. bibl.).

TRAZ, R. de, *Pierre Loti*, 1948.

MAETERLINCK, Maurice   1862–1949

LECAT, M., *Bibliographie*, Brussels 1939.
See also HAUSE and VIVIER below.

Théâtre, 3 vols, Brussels 1901–2.
Théâtre inédit, 1959.
Poésies complètes, ed. J. Hanse, Brussels 1966.

Tr. R. Hovey, *The plays*, 2 vols, Chicago (Ill) 1894–6.
Tr. B. Miall, *Poems*, London and New York 1915.

Serres chaudes, Ghent 1889; ed. L. Piérard, Paris and Brussels 1947. Tr. Miall above, *Hot houses*.
La princesse Maleine, Ghent 1889; Paris 1918. Tr. G. Harry, *The Princess Maleine*, London 1892; tr. Hovey above, vol 1.
L'intruse, Ghent 1890. Tr. M. Vielé, *The intruder*, Washington 1891; tr. W. Wilson, London 1892; tr. Hovey above, vol 1; tr. H. M. Block, New York 1962 (in *Masters of modern drama*).
Les aveugles, Brussels 1890 (with *L'intruse* above). Tr. M. Vielé, *The blind*, Washington 1891 (with *The intruder* above); tr. L. A. Tadema, *The sightless*, London 1895; tr. Hovey above, vol 1, *The blind*.
Pelléas et Mélisande, Brussels 1892. Tr. C. Porter and H. A. Clarke, *Pelléas and Melisande*, Boston (Mass) 1894; tr. E. Winslow, New York 1894; tr. L. A. Tadema, London 1895; tr. Hovey above, vol 2.
Alladines et Palomides, 3 actes; Intérieur, 1 acte, et La mort de Tintagiles, 4 actes, Brussels 1894. Tr. C. Porter and H. A. Clarke, *Alladine and Palomides*, Boston (Mass) 1895; tr. A. Sutro and W. Archer, *Alladines and Palomides, Interior*, and *The death of Tintagiles*, London 1899 (as *Three little dramas for marionettes*); tr. Hovey above, vol 2, *Alladine and Palomides, Home* and *The death of Tintagiles*.
Le trésor des humbles, 1895. Tr. A. Sutro, *The treasure of the humble*, London and New York 1897.
Douze chansons, 1896; 1900 (*Quinze chansons*). Tr. Miall above, *Fifteen songs*.
La sagesse et la destinée, 1898. Tr. A. Sutro, *Wisdom and destiny*, London and New York 1898.

La vie des abeilles, 1901. Tr. A. Sutro, *The life of the bee*, London and New York 1901.

    La vie des termites, 1926. Tr. A. Sutro, *The life of the white ant*, London and New York 1927.

    La vie des fourmis, 1930. Tr. B. Miall, *The life of the ant*, London and New York 1930.

Le temple enseveli, 1902; 1925. Tr. A. Sutro, *The buried temple*, London and New York 1902.

Monna Vanna, 1902. Tr. A. I. D. Coleman, New York 1903; tr. A. Sutro, London 1904.

L'intelligence des fleurs, 1907. Tr. A. Teixera de Mattos, *Life and flowers*, London 1907.

L'oiseau bleu, 1909; 1911. Tr. A. Teixera de Mattos, *The blue bird*, London and New York 1909; London 1910 (with 6th act).

La mort, 1913. Tr. A. Teixera de Mattos, *Death*, London 1911 (abr.); 1913 (complete, as *Our eternity*).

Avant le grand silence, 1934. Tr. B. Miall, *Before the great silence*, London 1935.

ANDRIEV, J. M., *Maurice Maeterlinck*, 1962.

BITHELL, J., *Life and writings of Maurice Maeterlinck*, London 1913.

COMPÈRE, G., *Le théâtre de Maurice Maeterlinck*, Brussels 1955.

GUARDINO, A., *Le théâtre de Maeterlinck*, 1934.

HALLS, W. D., *Maurice Maeterlinck, a study of his life and thought*, Oxford 1960.

    Maurice Maeterlinck 1862–1892, Brussels 1962.

HARRY, G., *Maurice Maeterlinck*, Brussels 1909.

HAUSE, J. and VIVIER, R., *Maurice Maeterlinck, 1862–1962*, 1962 (incl. bibl.).

LEBLANC, G., *Souvenirs 1895–1918*, 1931.

THOMAS, E., *Maurice Maeterlinck*, New York 1911.

MALLARMÉ, Stéphane   1842–1898

MONDA, M. and MONTEL, F., *Bibliographie des poètes maudits: Stéphane Mallarmé*, 1927.
See also Mondor-Jean-Aubry ed. of *Oeuvres complètes* below.

Poésies, 1913; ed. P. Beausire, Lausanne 1945; ed. Y. Le Dantec, Paris 1948.
Oeuvres complètes, ed. H. Mondor and G. Jean-Aubry, 1945; 1951 (incl. bibl.).

Tr. R. Fry, *Poems*, London 1936.
Tr. A. Elis, *Stéphane Mallarmé in English verse*, London 1937.
Tr. B. Cook, *Selected prose poems, essays and letters*, Baltimore (Md) 1956.
Tr. C. F. McIntyre, *Selected poems*, Berkeley (Calif) 1957.

Tr. A. Hartley, *Mallarmé*, Harmondsworth 1965 (selection).

L'après midi d'un faune, 1876; 1882. Tr. A. Huxley, London 1956.
 Improvisation d'un faune (first version, refused for pbn in *Le Parnasse contemporain*), 1948.
Les dieux antiques (based on English work by G. W. Cox), 1880.
Les poésies, 1887 (incl. *L'Après-midi d'un faune* above).
Album de vers et de prose, Brussels and Paris 1887.
Les poëmes d'Edgar Poe (tr.), Brussels 1888.
Pages, Brussels 1891.
Divagations (incl. poems first pbd in *Pages* above), 1897.
Un coup de dés jamais n'abolira le hasard, 1914 (first pbd in *Cosmopolis*, May 1897); ed. C. Roulet, Neuchâtel 1949. Tr. B. Coffey, *Dice thrown never will annul chance*, Dublin 1965.
Pour un tombeau d'Anatole, ed. J. P. Richard, 1961.

Correspondance, ed. H. Mondor, J. P. Richard and L. J. Austin, 1959 onwards (4 vols pbd).
Correspondance Mallarmé—Whistler, ed. C. P. Barbier, 1964.

CHADWICK, C., *Mallarmé, sa pensée dans sa poésie*, 1962.
CHISHOLM, A. R., *Mallarmé's Grand oeuvre*, Manchester 1962.
DAVIES, G., *Les Tombeaux de Mallarmé*, 1950.
FOWLIE, W., *Mallarmé*, Chicago (Ill) and London 1953.
MICHAUD, G., *Mallarmé, l'homme et l'oeuvre*, 1953. Tr. M. Collins and B. Humez, *Mallarmé*, New York 1965.
MONDOR, H., *Vie de Mallarmé*, 2 vols, 1941–2.
NOULET, E., *L'oeuvre poétique de Stéphane Mallarmé*, 1940.
RICHARD, J. P., *L'univers imaginaire de Mallarmé*, 1961.
SCHÉRER, J., *Le Livre de Mallarmé*, 1957.
THIBAUDET, A., *La poésie de Stéphane Mallarmé*, 1912.
WALZER, P. O., *Essai sur Stéphane Mallarmé*, 1963.
WOOLLEY, G., *Stéphane Mallarmé, 1842–98*, New York 1942.

MAUPASSANT, Guy de   1850–1893

ARTINIAN, A., *Maupassant criticism in France, 1880–1940*, New York 1941.
SPAZIANI, M., *Bibliographie de Maupassant en Italie*, Florence 1957.
Index to the stories, Boston (Mass) 1960.
See also Dumesnil–Loize ed. of *Oeuvres complètes* below; also DELAISEMENT below.

Oeuvres complètes, 29 vols, 1899–1904; ed. P. Neveux, 29 vols, 1907–10; ed. R. Dumesnil and J. Loize, 15 vols, 1934–8 (incl. bibl.); ed. A. M. Schmidt and G. Delaisement, 3 vols, 1956–9.

Tr. anon., *The life and work*, 17 vols, London and New York 1903.
Tr. M. Laurie, *The works*, 10 vols, London 1923–9.
Tr. anon., *The novels and tales*, 18 vols, 1928.
Tr. G. Hopkins, *Short stories*, 1959.

Histoire du vieux temps, 1879.
Boule de suif, 1880 (in collective work *Les soirées de Médan*). Tr. anon.,
    London 1899; tr. H. N. P. Sloman, in *Boule de suif and other stories*, Har-
    mondsworth 1946; tr. A. R. McAndrew, New York 1964.
Des vers, 1880.
La Maison Tellier, 1881; 1891 (enl.). Tr. D. Flower, *The Tellier house*,
    London 1964.
Mlle Fifi, 1882; 1883. Tr. anon., *Mademoiselle Fifi and twelve other stories*,
    New York 1917.
Une vie, 1883. Tr. anon., *A woman's life*, London 1888; tr. A. White, 1949;
    tr. H. N. P. Sloman, Harmondsworth 1965.
Contes de la bécasse, 1883.
Clair de lune, 1884.
Au soleil, 1884.
Les soeurs Rondoli, 1884.
Miss Harriet, 1884. Tr. H. N. P. Sloman, *Miss Harriet and other stories*,
    Harmondsworth 1951.
Toine, 1885.
Yvette, 1885. Tr. A. Galsworthy, *Yvette and other stories*, London 1905; tr.
    H. K. Hayes, 1913.
Bel-Ami, 1885; ed. G. Delaisement, 1957. Tr. anon., Chicago (Ill) 1889;
    tr. E. Sutton, London 1948; tr. H. N. P. Sloman, Harmondsworth 1961.
Contes de jour et de la nuit, 1885.
Monsieur Parent, 1886.
Le petite roque, 1886.
Mont-Oriol, 1887. Tr. anon., New York 1891; tr. M. Laurie, London 1949.
Le horla, 1887; ed. P. Cogny, 1959. Tr. J. Sturges, *The horla*, London 1890.
Pierre et Jean, 1888. Tr. C. Bell, *Pierre and Jean*, London 1890; tr. H. Craig,
    1923; tr. M. Turnell, 1962.
Le rosier de Mme Husson, 1888; 1888 (enl.).
Sur l'eau, 1888. Tr. L. Ensor, *Afloat*, London 1889.
Fort comme la mort, 1889. Tr. T. E. Comba, *Strong as death*, London and
    Philadelphia (Pa) 1899; tr. M. Laurie, *The master passion*, Edinburgh 1949.
La main gauche, 1889.
La vie errante, 1890.
Notre coeur, 1890; ed. P. Cogny, 1962. Tr. A. L. Donovan, *The human
    heart*, Chicago (Ill) 1890.
L'inutile beauté, 1890.
La paix du ménage, 1893.

Correspondance inédite, ed. A. Artinian, 1951.

BESNARD-COURSODON, M., *Étude thématique et structurale de l'oeuvre de Maupassant 'Le Piège'*, 1973.

DELAISEMENT, G., *Maupassant journaliste et chroniqueur*, 1956 (incl. bibl. of works).

DUMESNIL, R., *Guy de Maupassant*, 1947.

JAMES, H., *The house of fiction*, London 1957.

LANOUX, A., *Maupassant le Bel-ami*, 1967.

LEMOINE, F., *Guy de Maupassant*, 1957.

MAYNIAL, E., *La vie et l'oeuvre de Maupassant*, 1907.

SCHMIDT, A. M., *Maupassant par lui-même*, 1960.

STEEGMULLER, F., *Maupassant, a lion in the path*, New York 1949.

SULLIVAN, E. D., *Maupassant, the novelist*, Princeton (NJ) 1954.
Maupassant, the short stories, London 1962.

TURNELL, M., in his *The art of French fiction*, London 1959.

VIAL, A., *Guy de Maupassant et l'art du roman*, 1954.

MÉRIMÉE, Prosper   1803–1870

TRAHARD, P. and JOSSERAND, P., *Bibliographie des oeuvres*, 1929.

Oeuvres, ed. P. Trahard and E. Champion, 12 vols, 1927–33.
Romans, contes et nouvelles, ed. H. Martineau, 1934; ed. M. Parturier, 2 vols, 1967

Tr. various, *The writings*, 8 vols, New York 1905.
Tr. anon., *Stories*, London and Edinburgh 1908.
Tr. E. M. Waller et al., *Golden tales*, London and New York 1929.
Tr. anon., ed. A. Zaidenburg, *Tales of love and death*, Emmaus (Pa) 1948.

Théâtre de Clara Gazul, 1825; 1830 (incl. *L'occasion* and *Le Carrosse du Saint Sacrement*); 1842 (enl.); ed. P. Trahard, 1927; ed. P. Martino, 1929.
Tr. anon., *The plays of Clara Gazul*, London 1825.
La Guzla, ou choix de poésies illyriques, 1827.
Chronique du temps de Charles IX, 1829; 1842; ed. G. Dulong, 1933; ed. M. Rat, 1949; ed. R. J. B. Clark, 1969. Tr. anon., *1572, a chronicle of the times of Charles the Ninth*, New York 1830; tr. A. R. Scoble, *A chronicle of the reign of Charles IX*, London 1853; tr. G. Saintsbury, London and New York 1890; tr. D. Parmée, *A slight misunderstanding*, 1959.
Mosaïque, 1833 (incl. *Mateo Falcone* and *Tamango*); ed. M. Levaillant, 1927.
Les âmes du Purgatoire, 1837 (in collective work *Dodecaton, ou le livre des douze*, with stories by MUSSET, SAND, STENDHAL, etc).
Notes d'un voyage en Corse, 1840.
Carmen, 1845; 1852 (in *Nouvelles*, with *Arsène Guillot* and *L'abbé Aubain*); ed. A. Dupouy, 1930; ed. M. Revon, 1954 (with *Mateo Falcone* and

Tamango above). Tr. T. J. Diven, Chicago (Ill) 1878; tr. anon., London 1881 (in *Popular French novels*); tr. E. Sutton, 1949; tr. A. Brown, in *Carmen and other stories*, 1960; tr. E. Marielle, Harmondsworth 1965; tr. G. Chapman, London 1966.

Colomba, Brussels 1841 (pirate ed.); Paris 1841 (with *Les âmes du Purgatoire* above and *La Vénus d'Ille*); ed. C. Francisi, Turin 1933. Tr. A. R. Scoble, London 1853; tr. anon., 1881 (in *Popular French novels*, with *Carmen* above); tr. E. Sutton, London 1949 (with *Carmen* above); tr. E. Marielle, Harmondsworth 1965 (with *Carmen* above).

Histoire de Don Pèdre 1er, 1848; ed. G. Laplane, 1961. Tr. anon., *The history of Peter the Cruel*, 2 vols, London 1849.

Dernières nouvelles, 1873 (incl. *Lokis* and *La chambre bleue*); ed. L. Lemonnier, 1929.

Lettres à une inconnue, 1874. Tr. H. P. du Bois, *Letters to an unknown*, New York and Chicago (Ill) 1897; tr. E. A. S. Watt, *The love letters of a genius*, London 1905.

Correspondance générale, 1822–1865, ed. M. Parturier et al., 16 vols, 1941–61.

BASCHET, R., *Du romantisme au Second Empire: Mérimée*, 1959.
BILLY, A., *Mérimée*, 1959.
BOWMAN, F. P., *Mérimée: heroism, pessimism, irony*, Berkeley (Calif) 1962.
FILON, A., *Mérimée et ses amis*, 1894.
LÉON, P., *Mérimée et son temps*, 1962.
PATER, W. H., *Prosper Mérimée*, London 1895 (in *Miscellaneous Studies*).
TRAHARD, P., *La jeunesse de Prosper Mérimée, 1803–1834*, 2 vols, 1924.
    Prosper Mérimée de 1834 à 1853, 1928.
    La vieillesse de Prosper Mérimée, 1854–1870, 1930.

MICHELET, Jules   1798–1874

Oeuvres complètes, 40 vols, 1893–8; ed. H. Chabot, 6 vols, 1930; ed. P. Viallaneix, 1971 onwards (3 vols pbd).
Ecrits de jeunesse, ed. P. Viallaneix, 1959.

Introduction à l'histoire universelle, 1831; 1834.
Histoire romaine, 2 vols, 1831. Tr. W. Hazlitt, *History of the Roman Republic*, London 1847.
Histoire de France, 17 vols, 1833–67; 17 vols, 1871–4; 1875 (extracts, as *Tableau de la France*; ed. L. Refort, 1934). Tr. W. K. Kelly, *The history of France*, 2 vols, London 1844–6 (vols 1–6, to Renaissance); tr. G. H. Smith, 2 vols, 1844–7 (part tr.).
Du prêtre; De la femme; De la famille, 1845. Tr. C. Cocks, *Priests, Women and Families*, London 1845; tr. G. H. Smith, 1850.
    La femme, 1860. Tr. J. W. Palmer, *Woman*, New York 1860.

Le peuple, 1846; ed. L. Refort, 1946. Tr. C. Cocks, *The people*, London 1846.
Histoire de la Révolution française, 7 vols, 1847–53; 6 vols, 1868–9 (enl.);
ed. G. Walter, 2 vols, 1939. Tr. C. Cocks, *History of the French Revolution*,
2 vols, London 1847–8 (tr. of vols 1–2).
L'oiseau, 1856. Tr. 'A.E.', *The bird*, London 1868.
    L'insecte, 1857. Tr. W. H. D. Adams, *The insect*, London and New
        York 1875.
L'amour, 1858. Tr. J. W. Palmer, *Love*, New York 1860.
La mer, 1861. Tr. W. H. D. Adams, *The sea*, London 1875.
    La montagne, 1868. Tr. W. H. D. Adams, *The mountain*, London 1872.
La sorcière, 1862; ed. L. Refort, 2 vols, 1956. Tr. L. J. Trotter, *The witch
of the Middle Ages*, London 1863; tr. A. R. Allinson, *Satanism and witch-
craft*, New York 1939.
La Bible de l'humanité, 1864. Tr. V. Calfa, *The bible of humanity*, New York
1877.
Histoire du XIXe siècle, 3 vols, 1872–5.

Ma jeunesse, 1798–1820, ed. Mme Michelet, 1884; ed. G. Monod, 1927
(enl.).
    Mon journal, 1820–1823, ed. Mme Michelet, 1888; ed. G. Monod,
        1904; ed. P. Viallaneix (in *Ecrits de jeunesse* above), 1959.
Journal, ed. P. Viallaneix, 2 vols, 1959–62.

BARTHES, R., *Michelet par lui-même*, 1954.
CARRÉ, J.-M., *Michelet et son temps*, 1926.
FEBVRE, L., *Michelet*, 1946.
GUÉHENNO, J., *L'évangile éternel*, 1927.
HAAC, O., *Les principes inspirateurs de Michelet*, 1951.
HALÉVY, D., *Jules Michelet*, 1928.
MONOD, G., *La vie et la pensée de Jules Michelet, 1798–1852*, 1923.
PUGH, A. R., *Michelet and his ideas on social reform*, New York 1923.
VAN DER ELST, R., *Michelet naturaliste*, 1914.
VIALLANEIX, P., *La voie royale, essai sur le peuple dans l'oeuvre de Michelet*,
1959.

MIRBEAU, Octave   1850–1917

Oeuvres complètes, 10 vols, 1934–6.

Lettres de ma chaumière, 1886.
Le Calvaire (first novel), 1887. Tr. L. Rich, *Calvary*, New York 1922.
Sébastien Roch, 1890.
Les mauvais bergers, 1898.
Le jardin des supplices, 1899. Tr. A. C. Bessie, *The torture garden*, New York
1931; tr. R. Rudorff, *The garden of tortures*, London 1969.

Le journal d'une femme de chambre, 1900. Tr. B. Tucker, *A chambermaid's diary*, New York 1900; tr. anon., London 1934; tr. D. Garman, 1966.
Les affaires sont les affaires, 1903.
La 628-E 8, 1907.
Dingo, 1913.

REVON, M., *Octave Mirbeau, son oeuvre*, 1924.
SCHWARZ, M., *Octave Mirbeau, vie et oeuvre*, The Hague and Paris 1966.

MUSSET, Alfred de   1810–1857

CLOUARD, M., *Bibliographie des oeuvres d'Alfred de Musset et des ouvrages, gravures et vignettes qui s'y rapportent*, 1883.
   Notice bibliographique sur la correspondance, 1898.

Poésies complètes, 1840 (incl. *Les nuits, Contes d'Espagne et d'Italie*, and verse works from *Spectacle dans un fauteuil*, vol 1).
Oeuvres complètes, 10 vols, 1865–6 ('Amis du poète' ed.); 10 vols, 1867; ed. E. Biré, 9 vols, 1907–8; ed. M. Allem, 3 vols, 1933–8; ed. P. van Tieghem, 1963.
Théâtre complet, ed. P. van Tieghem, 1948; ed. G. Sigaux, 4 vols, 1960–1.

Tr. S. S. Gwynn, *Comedies*, London 1890.
Tr. various, *The complete writings*, 10 vols, New York 1905.
Tr. P. Meyer, *Seven plays*, New York 1962.

L'Anglais mangeur d'opium (adapted from De Quincey's *Confessions of an English opium eater*), 1828.
Contes d'Espagne et d'Italie, 1830; ed. M. A. Rees, London 1973.
Un spectacle dans un fauteuil, 3 vols, 1833–4 (vol 1 cntg *La coupe et les lèvres, A quoi rêvent les jeunes filles, Namouna;* vol 2 cntg *Les caprices de Marianne* below and *Lorenzaccio* below; vol 3 cntg *André del Sarto* below, *La nuit vénitienne, Fantasio*, tr. M. Baring, London 1927, and *On ne badine pas avec l'amour*, tr. E. G. Owen, *Love is not to be trifled with*, London 1947).
Les caprices de Marianne, 1834 (in *Spectacle dans un fauteuil*, vol 2 above); ed. G. Michaut, 1908.
Lorenzaccio, 1834 (in *Spectacle dans un fauteuil*, vol 2 above); ed. P. Dimoff, 1936 (in *La genèse de Lorenzaccio*).
André del Sarto, 1834 (in *Spectacle dans un fauteuil*, vol 3 above); ed. P. Gastinel, Rouen 1933.
La confession d'un enfant du siècle, 2 vols, 1836; 1840; ed. H. Bonnier, 1964; ed. M. Allem and M. Cordroc'h, 1968. Tr. K. Warren, *The confession of a child of the century*, Chicago (Ill) 1892; tr. G. F. Monkshood, *A modern man's confession*, London 1908.
Les deux maîtresses, 1840 (with *Emmeline* and *Le fils du Titien*);
   Frédéric et Bernerette, 1840 (with *Croisilles* and *Margot*);

1841 (collected ed., entitled *Nouvelles*). Tr. G. Fosdick, *The two mistresses* [etc.], Philadelphia (Pa) 1900.

Comédies et proverbes, 1840 (incl. prose plays in *Spectacle dans un fauteuil* above, with *La quenouille de Barberine*, *Le chandelier*, *Il ne faut jurer de rien*, and *Un caprice*, tr. A. G. Wirt, *A caprice*, Boston (Mass) 1922; tr. G. Graveley, St Albans 1955, in *A comedy and two proverbs*); 2 vols, 1853 (incl. enl. version of *Barberine*, tr. collectively, Glasgow 1919, and with *Il faut qu'une porte soit ouverte ou fermée*, first pbd 1848, tr. G. Graveley, St Albans 1955, in *A comedy and two proverbs*; tr. J. Barzun, *A door should be either open or shut*, n.p. 1956, *Louison*, first pbd 1849, *On ne saurait penser à tout*, *Carmosine* and *Bettine*); ed. P. and F. Gastinel, 4 vols, 1934–57: ed. B. Dussane, 1970.

Les nuits, 1840 (in *Poésies complètes* above). Tr. W. H. Pollock, in *The poet and the muse*, London 1880 (*Nuits de mai, d'août* and *d'octobre*).

Nouvelles, 1848 (cntg *Pierre et Camille* and *Le secret de Javotte*, with 2 stories by Paul de Musset).

L'habit vert (in collab. with Emile Augier), 1849. Tr. B. H. Clark, *The green coat*, New York 1914.

Poésies nouvelles, 1850; ed. E. Bouvet, 1961.

Contes, 1854 (cntg *Pierre et Camille* and *Le secret de Javotte* from *Nouvelles* above, with 3 other stories, and *Lettres sur la littérature*, later known as *Lettres de Dupuis et Cotonet*).

Oeuvres posthumes, 1860.

ALLEM, M., *Alfred de Musset*, Grenoble 1948.

GASTINEL, F., *Le romantisme d'Alfred de Musset*, 1933.

HENRIOT, E., *L'enfant du siècle, Alfred de Musset*, 1953.

MUSSET, P. de, *Biographie d'Alfred de Musset*, 1877.

SOUPAULT, P., *Alfred de Musset*, 1957.

VAN TIEGHEM, P., *Alfred de Musset, l'homme et l'oeuvre*, 1944; 1969.

NERVAL, Gérard de   1808–1855
(pseudonym of Gérard Labrunie)

MARIE, A., *Bibliographie des oeuvres*, 1926 (as vol 1 of *Oeuvres complètes* below).

SENELIER, J., *Essai de bibliographie*, 1959.
    Bibliographie nervalienne, 1960–1967, 1968.

VILLAS, J., *A critical biography, 1900–1967*, Columbia (Mo) 1968.

Oeuvres complètes, 6 vols, 1867–77; ed. A. Marie et al., 7 vols, 1926–32; ed. H. Clouard, 10 vols, 1927–8; ed. H. Bachelin, 10 vols, 1927–30; ed. A. Béguin and J. Richer, 2 vols, 1952–6; ed. H. Lemaître, 2 vols, 1958; ed. M. Cornand, 7 vols, 1959–61.

Oeuvres complémentaires, ed. J. Richer, 1955 onwards (6 vols pbd).

Tr. R. Aldington, *Aurelia*, London 1932 (with other works).
Tr. and ed. G. Wagner, *Selected writings*, New York 1957.
Tr. B. Hill, *Fortune's fool, selected poems*, London 1959.

Napoléon et la France guerrière, 1826.
Faust, tragédie de Goethe, 1828; 1840 (*Faust*, [. . .] *suivi du second Faust*);
    ed. F. Baldensperger, 1932.
Léo Burckart, 1839.
Scènes de la vie orientale, 2 vols, 1848–50; 2 vols, 1851 (renamed *Voyage en
    Orient*); ed. F. Herbault, 2 vols, 1964. Tr. Aldington above (extracts).
    Comprising:
1   *Les femmes du Caire*, 1848; 1851. Tr. C. Elphinstone, *The women of
    Cairo: scenes of life in the Orient*, 2 vols, 1929.
2   *Les femmes du Liban*, 1850; 1851.
Contes et facéties, 1852 (incl. *La main enchantée, La reine des poissons, Le
    monstre vert* and *Le prince des sots*).
Les illuminés, ou les précurseurs de socialisme, 1852 (incl. *Le diable rouge*);
    ed. A. Marie, 1929. Tr. Aldington above (extracts).
Petits châteaux de Bohême, 1852.
Les filles du feu, 1854 (cntg *Sylvie, Angélique, Jenny, Octavie, Isis, Corilla,
    Emilie* and *Les chimères*); ed. N. I. Popa, 2 vols, 1931. Tr. J. Whitall,
    Daughters of fire, New York 1922 (*Sylvie, Emilie, Octave*); tr. Aldington
    above (*Sylvie*); tr. Wagner above (*Emilie* and *Sylvie*).
Les chimères, 1854 (with *Filles du feu* above; sonnets, incl. *El desdichado,
    Delfica* and *Le Christ aux Oliviers*); ed. J. Guillaume, Brussels 1966; ed.
    N. Rinsler, 1973. Tr. anon., *Three sonnets of Chimères*, New York 1960
    (in *The poem itself*).
Le rêve et la vie, 1855. Tr. V. Holland, *Dreams and life*, 1933.
Aurélia, 1855 (in *Le rêve et la vie* above); ed. J. Richer, 1965. Tr. Aldington
    above; tr. Wagner above.
La Bohême galante, 1855 (incl. stories first pbd in *Contes et facéties* and *Petits
    châteaux de Bohême* above, *Nuits d'octobre* and *Promenades et souvenirs*).
    Tr. Aldington above (extracts).

Lettres à Franz Liszt, ed. J. Guillaume and C. Pichois, Namur 1972.

ALBÉRÈS, R. M., *Gérard de Nerval*, 1955.
BÉGUIN, A., *Gérard de Nerval*, 1936.
CELLIER, L., *Gérard de Nerval, l'homme et l'oeuvre*, 1956.
CHAMBERS, R., *Gérard de Nerval et la poétique du voyage*, 1969.
DURRY, M. J., *Gérard de Nerval et le mythe*, 1956.
MARIE, A., *Gérard de Nerval, l'homme, le poète*, 1955.
PEYROUZET, E., *Gérard de Nerval inconnu*, 1965.
RHODES, S. A., *Gérard de Nerval, poet, traveler and dreamer*, New York 1951.

RICHER, J., *Gérard de Nerval et les doctrines ésotériques*, 1947.
  Nerval, expérience et création, 1963.
SCHURER, K., *Thématique de Nerval*, 1968.

NODIER, Charles   1780–1844

LARAT, J., *Bibliographie critique des oeuvres*, 1924.
BENDER, E. J., *Bibliographie*, Bloomington (Ind) 1969.
BELL, S. F., *Charles Nodier, his life and works, a critical bibliography, 1923–1967*, Chapel Hill (NC) 1971.

Oeuvres complètes, 13 vols, 1832–7.
Contes fantastiques, ed. A. Cazes, 1914.
Contes choisis, ed. R. N. Raimbault, Angers 1941.
Contes, ed. P. G. Castex, 1961.

Poems translated in anthologies.

La Napoleone, 1802; 1827 (in *Poésies diverses* below).
La peintre de Salzbourg, 1802; 1820.
Essais d'un jeune barde, 1804.
Les tristes, ou mélange tiré des tablettes d'un suicide, 1806.
Jean Sbogar, 2 vols, 1818; 1832 (in *Oeuvres complètes* above).
Le vampire (in collab. with Carmouche and Jouffroy), 1820.
Smarra, ou les démons de la nuit, 1821.
Trilby, ou le lutin d'Argail, 1822.
Poésies diverses, 1827 (incl. *La Napoleone* above).
La fée aux miettes, 1832 (in *Oeuvres complètes* above); ed. A. Viatte, Rome 1962.

Also pbd works of lexicography, bibliography, criticism and natural history.

HAMENACHEM, M. S., *Charles Nodier: essai sur l'imagination mythique*, 1972.
HENRY-ROSIER, M., *La vie de Charles Nodier*, 1931.
JUIN, H., *Charles Nodier*, 1970.
LARAT, J., *La tradition et l'exotisme dans l'oeuvre de Charles Nodier*, 1923.
MAIXNER, R., *Charles Nodier et l'Illyrie*, 1960.
MÖNCH, W., *Charles Nodier und die deutsche und englische Literatur*, Berlin 1931.
NELSON, H., *Charles Nodier*, New York 1972.
OLIVER, A. R., *Charles Nodier: pilot of romanticism*, Syracuse (NY) 1964.

PROUDHON, Pierre-Joseph   1809–1865

Oeuvres complètes, 33 vols, 1868–76; ed. C. Bouglé and H. Moysset, 12 vols, 1923–35.

Tr. B. R. Tucker, *The works*, Princeton (NJ) 1876.

Tr. E. Fraser, ed. S. Edwards, *Selected writings*, London 1970.

Qu'est-ce que la propriété?, 1840. Tr. B. R. Tucker, *What is property?*, 2 vols, London 1898–1902.

Système des contradictions économiques, ou philosophie de la misère, 1846.

Correspondance, ed. C. Proudhon and J. A. Langlois, 14 vols, 1875.

Lettres de Proudhon à sa femme, 1950.

DESJARDINS, A., *Pierre-Joseph Proudhon, sa vie, ses oeuvres, sa doctrine*, 2 vols, 1896.

GURVITCH, G., *Proudhon, sa vie, son oeuvre, avec un exposé de sa philosophie*, 1965.

HALÉVY, D., *La vie de Proudhon*, 1948.

 Le mariage de Proudhon, 1955.

SAINTE-BEUVE, C. A. de, *Proudhon, sa vie et sa correspondance 1838–1848*, 1872; ed. D. Halévy, 1948.

WOODCOCK, G., *Pierre-Joseph Proudhon, a biography*, New York 1956.

RENAN, Ernest   1823–1892

GIRARD, H. and MONCEL, H., *Bibliographie des oeuvres*, 1923.

Oeuvres complètes, ed. H. Psichari, 10 vols, 1947–61.

Sagesse de Renan, ed. H. Peyre, 1968 (selection).

Averroès et l'averroïsme, 1852.

Etudes d'histoire religieuse, 1857. Tr. O. B. Frothingham, *Studies of religious history and criticism*, New York 1864; tr. H. F. Gibbons, London 1893.

 Nouvelles études d'histoire religieuse, 1884. Tr. anon., *Studies in religious history, second series*, London 1886; tr. W. M. Thomson, 1895.

Essais de morale et de critique, 1859 (incl. *De la poésie des races celtiques*, tr. and ed. W. G. Hutchison, in *The poetry of the Celtic races and other studies*, London 1896).

Henriette Renan, 1862; 1898 (as *Ma soeur Henriette*, with *Lettres intimes*). Tr. L. Teller, *My sister Henriette*, Chicago (Ill) 1895; tr. L. Page, Portland (Me) 1900.

Histoire des origines du christianisme, 8 vols, 1863–83. Tr. anon., *History of the origins of Christianity*, 7 vols, London 1888–90.

Vie de Jésus, 1863 (as vol 1 of *Histoire des origines du christianisme* above); 1867. Tr. C. E. Wilbour, *Life of Jesus*, New York and Paris 1864; tr. W. G. Hutchison, London 1897; tr. anon., 1904.

La réforme intellectuelle et morale, 1871.

Caliban, suite de La tempête, 1878. Tr. E. G. Vickery, *Caliban*, New York and London 1896.

 L'eau de Jouvence, 1881.

Souvenirs d'enfance et de jeunesse, 1883; ed. G. Guisan, Lausanne 1961. Tr. C. B. Pitman, *Recollections of my youth*, London 1883; tr. J. L. May, *The memoirs*, 1935.

Le broyeur de lin, 1883 (as pt 1 of *Souvenirs* above); ed. C. Duckworth, London 1963.

Histoire du peuple d'Israël, 5 vols, 1887–93. Tr. J. H. Allen and E. W. Latimer, *History of the people of Israel*, 5 vols, Boston (Mass) 1888–96; tr. C. B. Pitman and D. V. Bingham, 3 vols, London 1888–91.

L'avenir de la science, pensées de 1848, 1890. Tr. A. D. Vandam and C. B. Pitman, *The future of science, ideas of 1848*, London and Boston (Mass) 1891.

Correspondance, ed. H. Psichari, 2 vols, 1960–1 (in *Oeuvres complètes*, vols 9–10 above).

Cahiers Renaniens, 1971 onwards.

CHADBOURNE, R. M., *Ernest Renan as an essayist*, Ithaca (NY) 1957.

CRESSON, A., *Ernest Renan, sa vie, son oeuvre, avec un exposé de sa philosophie*, 1949.

DUSSAUD, R., *L'oeuvre scientifique d'Ernest Renan*, 1951.

MOTT, L. F., *Ernest Renan*, New York and London 1921.

POMMIER, J., *Renan d'après des documents inédits*, 1923.

    La pensée religieuse de Renan, 1925.

    La jeunesse cléricale d'Ernest Renan, 1933.

PSICHARI, H., *Renan d'après lui-même*, 1937.

WARDMAN, H. W., *Ernest Renan, a critical biography*, London 1964.

RENARD, Jules   1864–1910

Bibl. See GUICHARD below.

Oeuvres complètes, 17 vols, 1925–7; ed. L. Guichard, 2 vols, 1970 (fiction). *Théâtre complet*, 1911; ed. L. Pauwels, 1957.

L'écornifleur, 1892. Tr. E. Hyams, *The sponger*, London 1957.

    Monsieur Vernet (dramatized version of *L'écornifleur*), 1903.

Poil de carotte, 1894; ed. L. Guichard 1965. Tr. A. Sutro, *Carrots*, London 1904; tr. G. W. Stonier, 1946.

    Poil de carotte (dramatized version), 1900.

La vigneron dans sa vigne, 1894; 1900.

Histoires naturelles, 1896; 1904 (enl.); ed. L. Guichard, 1967. Tr. T. W. Earp and G. W. Stonier, *Hunting with the fox*, Oxford 1948; tr. R. Howard, *Natural histories*, New York 1966.

Bucoliques, 1898.

Le plaisir de rompre, 1898.

Le pain de ménage, 1899.

Ragotte, 1908.
La bigote, 1909.
L'oeil clair, 1913.

Journal intime, 1935; ed. L. Guichard and G. Sigaux, 1960. Tr. L. Bogan and E. Roget, *Journal*, New York 1964.
Lettres inédites, 1883–1910, ed. L. Guichard, 1957.

COULTER, H. B., *The prose work and technique of Jules Renard*, Washington (DC) 1935.
GUICHARD, L., *Les oeuvres et l'âme de Jules Renard*, 1936.
    Jules Renard, 1961 (incl. bibl.).
POLLITZER, M., *Jules Renard, sa vie, son oeuvre*, 1956.
SCHNEIDER, P., *Jules Renard par lui-même*, 1956.

RIMBAUD, Arthur   1854–1891

MONDA, M. and MONTEL, F., *Bibliographie des poètes maudites: Arthur Rimbaud*, 1927.
See also ETIEMBLE below.

Poésies, ed. R. Darzens, 1891 (as *Reliquaire*); ed. Vanier, 1895; ed. H. de Bouillane de Lacoste, 1939; ed. S. Bernard, 1960.
Oeuvres, ed. P. Berrichon, 1912; ed. P. Pia, Maastricht, 1931; ed. F. Ruchon, Geneva 1944; ed. R. de Renéville and J. Mouquet, Paris 1946.

Tr. N. Cameron, *Selected verse poems*, London 1942.
Tr. B. Belitt, *Four poems*, London 1948 (*Les poètes de sept ans, Les premières communions, Le bateau ivre, Mémoire*).
Tr. B. Hill, *A drunken boat*, London 1952 (with other poems).
Tr. J. Leclercq, *Poems of the damned*, New York 1960.
Tr. O. Bernard, *Rimbaud, selected verse*, Harmondsworth 1962.
Tr. and ed. W. Fowlie, *Complete works, selected letters*, Chicago (Ill) and London 1966.

Une saison en enfer, Brussels 1873; ed. H. de Bouillane de Lacoste, Paris 1941. Tr. G. F. Lees, *A season in hell*, London 1932; tr. L. Varèse, New York 1945; tr. N. Cameron, London 1949.
Les illuminations, 1886 (incl. revised versions of poems first pbd in *Saison en enfer* above); ed. H. de Bouillane de Lacoste, 1949; ed. M. Matucci, Florence 1952; ed. A. Py, Paris 1967. Tr. H. Rootham, *Prose poems from Les illuminations*, London 1932; tr. L. Varèse, New York 1946; tr. W. Fowlie, London 1953.

Lettres, 1899.
Correspondance inédite, 1870–1875, ed. R. G. Lecomte, 1929; ed. J. M. Carré, 1931 (enl., as *Lettres de la vie littéraire*).

Correspondance, 1888–91 (Rimbaud and Alfred Ilg), ed. J. Vollemy, 1965.

CARRÉ, J. M., *La vie aventureuse de Rimbaud*, 1926. Tr. H. and M. Josephson, *A season in hell*, New York 1931.

CHADWICK, C., *Etudes sur Rimbaud*, 1960.

ETIEMBLE, R., *Le mythe de Rimbaud*, 5 vols, 1952–67; 5 vols, 1961–70 (incl. bibl.).

FROHOCK, W. M., *Rimbaud's poetic practice*, Cambridge (Mass) 1963.

FOWLIE, W., *Rimbaud*, Chicago (Ill) 1965.

GRAFF, D. A. de, *Arthur Rimbaud, sa vie, son oeuvre*, Assen (Netherlands) 1961.

HACKETT, C. A., *Rimbaud*, London 1957.

MATARASSO, H. and PETITFILS, P., *Vie d'Arthur Rimbaud*, 1962.

PETITFILS, P., *L'oeuvre et le visage d'Arthur Rimbaud*, 1949.

STARKIE, E., *Rimbaud*, London and New York 1947; London 1961.

RODENBACH, Georges   1855–1898

Bibl. See MAES below.

Oeuvres, 2 vols, 1923–5.

Translated in anthologies, incl. *The romantic period*, ed. J. Payne, 2 vols, London 1906.

Tristesses, 1879.
La jeunesse blanche, 1886.
Bruges-la-morte, 1892. Tr. T. Duncan, London 1903.
Les vies encloses, 1896.
Le carillonneur, 1897.
Le rouet des brumes, 1901.

BODSON-THOMAS, A., *L'esthétique de Rodenbach*, Liège 1942.

MAES, P., *Georges Rodenbach*, Gembloux 1952 (incl. bibl.).

RUCHON, F., *L'amitié de Stéphane Mallarmé et de Georges Rodenbach*, Geneva 1949.

SAINTE-BEUVE, Charles Augustin de   1804–1869

BONNEROT, J., *Bibliographie de l'oeuvre;* 4 vols, 1937–52.
   Un demi-siècle d'études sur Sainte-Beuve, 1904–54, 1957.

PIERRET, C., *Table générale et analytique des Causeries du lundi, des Portraits de femmes et Portraits littéraires*, 1881.

GIRAUD, V., *Table alphabétique et analytique des Premiers lundis, Nouveaux lundis et Portraits contemporains*, 1904.

See also *Premiers lundis* below.

Poésies complètes, 1840; 1869 (enl.); 1910 (enl.).

Les grands écrivains français, ed. M. Allem, 23 vols, 1926–32 (selection from *Lundis* and *Portraits* below).

Premiers lundis, Portraits littéraires, Portraits de jeunes ed. M. Leroy, 2 vols, 1949–50.

Aperçus de l'oeuvre critique, ed. G. Corbière-Gille, 1973 (extracts).

Tr. W. Sharp, *The essays*, 3 vols, London and Philadelphia (Pa) 1901.

Tr. K. P. Wormeley and G. B. Ives, *Portraits of the seventeenth [eighteenth] century, historic and literary*, 4 vols, London 1904–5 (selection from *Causeries du lundi, Portraits de femmes* and *Portraits littéraires* below).

Tr. and ed. F. Steegmuller and N. Guterman, *Selected essays*, New York 1963.

Tableau historique et critique de la poésie française et du théâtre français au 16e siècle, 2 vols, 1828; 1843 (enl.); ed. J. Troubat, 2 vols, 1876.

Vie, poésies et pensées de Joseph Delorme, 1829; 1830 (enl.); ed. G. Antoine, 1957.

Les consolations, 1830.

Critiques et portraits littéraires, 1832; 5 vols, 1836–9 (revd and enl.).

> *Portraits littéraires*, 2 vols, 1844 (incl. revd articles from 1836–9 ed. of *Critiques et portraits littéraires* above); 3 vols, 1862–4.

> *Portraits de femmes*, 1844 (most articles first pbd in *Critiques et portraits littéraires*, 1836–9 above); 1870. Tr. H. W. Preston, *Portraits of celebrated women*, Boston (Mass) 1868.

> *Portraits contemporains*, 3 vols, 1846 (incl. articles from 1836–9 ed. of *Critiques et portraits littéraires* above); 5 vols, 1869–71 (enl.).

> *Derniers portraits littéraires*, 1852; 1864 (as vol 3 of *Portraits littéraires* above).

Volupté, 2 vols, 1834; 1869; ed. P. Poux, 2 vols, 1927; ed. O. Centlivres, 2 vols, Lausanne 1964; ed. R. Molho, Paris 1969.

Pensées d'août, 1837.

Port-Royal, 5 vols, 1840–59; 7 vols, 1867–71; 10 vols, 1926–32; ed. M. Leroy, 3 vols, 1953–5.

Le livre d'amour, 1843 (incl. 3 poems first pbd in *Poésies complètes* above); ed. J. Troubat, 1904.

Les causeries du lundi, 15 vols, 1851–62 (collected articles first pbd in *Le Constitutionnel* and *Le Moniteur*); 15 vols, 1857–72. Tr. E. J. Trechmann, 8 vols, London and New York 1909–11.

> *Nouveaux lundis*, 13 vols, 1863–70 (collected articles first pbd in *Le Constitutionnel, Le Moniteur* and *Le Temps*).

> *Premiers lundis*, 3 vols, 1874–5 (collected articles pbd from 1824; incl. *Table générale des oeuvres*, by C. Berthoud).

Chateaubriand et son groupe littéraire sous l'Empire, 2 vols, 1860; 1873 (enl.); ed. M. Allem, 2 vols, 1948.

Les cahiers, ed. J. Troubat, 1876.
Mes poisons, ed. V. Giraud, 1926.
Cahiers intimes, ed. V. Giraud, 1933; ed. R. Molho, 1973 onwards (1 vol pbd).
Correspondance générale, ed. J. and A. Bonnerot, 16 vols, Paris and Toulouse 1935–70.

ALLEM, M., *Portrait de Sainte-Beuve*, 1954.
BILLY, A., *Sainte-Beuve: sa vie et son temps*, 2 vols, 1952.
FAYOLLE, R., *Sainte-Beuve et le 18e siècle*, 1972.
GIESE, W. F., *Sainte-Beuve, a literary portait*, Madison (Wis) 1931.
LEHMANN, A. G., *Sainte-Beuve, a portrait of the critic, 1804–42*, Oxford 1962.
LEROY, M., *La pensée de Sainte-Beuve*, 1940.
MICHAUT, G., *Sainte-Beuve avant les Lundis*, 1903.
MOTT, L. F., *Sainte-Beuve*, 1921.
    Sainte-Beuve, New York and London 1925.
NICOLSON, H., *Sainte-Beuve*, London 1957.
REGARD, M., *Sainte-Beuve, l'homme et l'oeuvre*, 1960.

SAMAIN, Albert   1858–1900

BONNEAU, G., *Essai de bibliographie*, 1925.

Oeuvres complètes, 4 vols, 1911–12; 3 vols, 1924.

Translated in anthologies, incl. *French lyrics in English verse*, tr. W. F. Giese, Madison (Wis) 1946.

Au jardin de l'Infante, 1893.
Aux flancs du vase, 1898.
Le chariot d'or, 1901.
Contes, 1902.
Polyphème, 1906.

Carnets inédits, 1939.
Des lettres, 1887–1900, 1933.

BOCQUET, L., *Albert Samain, sa vie et son oeuvre*, 1903.
    Autour d'Albert Samain, 1933.
BONNEAU, G., *Albert Samain, poète symboliste*, 1925.
GRAVEREAU, G., *Albert Samain, poète de l'automne et de l'amour*, 1948.

SAND, George   1804–1876
(pseudonym of Amandine-Aurore Dupin, baronne Dudevant)

SPOELBERCH DE LOVENJOUL, C. de, *Etude bibliographique sur les oeuvres*, Brussels 1868.

191

COLIN, G., *Bibliographie des premières publications des romans*, Brussels 1965.
CORDROC'H, M., *Répertoire des lettres publiées*, 1962.
See also KARENINE below.

Oeuvres complètes, 24 vols, 1836–40; 16 vols, 1842–4; 9 vols, 1851–6; 115 vols, 1857–1926.
Oeuvres choisies, ed. S. Rocheblave, 1937.

Tr. M. M. Hays et al., *The works*, 6 vols, London 1847.
Tr. G. B. Ives, *The masterpieces*, 20 vols, Philadelphia (Pa) 1900–02.

Most novels were first pbd in serial form in periodicals, and there were many pirate editions. Dates below are for the first authorized edition.

Rose et Blanche (in collab. with Jules Sandeau), 5 vols, 1831.
Indiana, 2 vols, 1832; ed. P. Salomon, 1962 (revd 1969). Tr. anon., Philadelphia (Pa) 1881.
Valentine, 2 vols, 1832.
Lélia, 2 vols, 1833; 3 vols, 1839; ed. A. Maurois, 1958.
Le secrétaire intime, 1834.
Jacques, 2 vols, 1834. Tr. A. Blackwell, 2 vols, New York 1947.
Mauprat, 2 vols, 1837; ed. C. Sicard, 1969. Tr. V. Vaughan, Boston (Mass) 1870; tr. S. Young, London 1901.
Spiridion, 1839 (in *Oeuvres* above). Tr. anon., London 1842.
Le compagnon du tour de France, 2 vols, 1841. Tr. F. G. Shaw, *The journeyman joiner*, New York, 1847.
Un hiver à Majorque, 2 vols, 1842. Tr. and ed. R. Graves, *Winter in Majorca*, London 1956.
Consuelo, 8 vols, 1842–3. Tr. F. G. Shaw, 2 vols, Boston (Mass) 1846; tr. F. Robinson, New York 1951;
　　La comtesse de Rudolstadt, 5 vols, 1844–5. Tr. F. G. Shaw, *The Countess of Rudolstadt*, 2 vols, Boston 1847; tr. F. Robinson, Philadelphia (Pa) 1870;
　　ed. L. Cellier and L. Guichard, 3 vols, 1959.
Le meunier d'Angibault, 3 vols, 1845. Tr. anon., *The miller of Angibault*, London 1847; tr. M. E. Dewey, Boston (Mass) 1871.
La mare au diable, 2 vols, 1846; ed. P. Salomon and J. Mallion, 1956 (revd 1966). Tr. F. G. Shaw, *The enchanted lake*, London 1850; tr. H. Miles, *The devil's pool*, 1929; tr. A. Cowan 1966.
Le péché de M. Antoine, 6 vols, 1846–7.
La petite Fadette, 2 vols, 1848; ed. P. Salomon and J. Mallion, 1958 (revd 1969); ed. G. van den Bugaert, 1967. Tr. anon., *Little Fadette*, London 1850; tr. J. M. Sedgewick, New York 1893; tr. H. Miles, London 1928; tr. E. Figes, 1967.
François le Champi, 2 vols, 1850; ed. P. Salomon and J. Mallion, 1956 (with

La mare au diable above; revd 1966). Tr. G. Masson *Francis the waif*, London and New York 1889; tr. E. Collis, *The country waif*, London 1930.

Les maîtres sonneurs, 1852; ed. P. Salomon and J. Mallion, 1958 (revd 1968). Tr. K. P. Wormeley, *The bagpipers*, Boston (Mass) 1890.

Histoire de ma vie, 20 vols, 1854–5; ed. G. Lubin, 2 vols, 1970–1.

Les beaux messieurs de Bois doré, 5 vols, 1858. Tr. S. Clovis, *The gallant lords of Bois-Doré*, 2 vols, New York 1890.

Elle et lui, 1859.

Jean de la roche, 1860.

Le marquis de Villemer, 1861. Tr. R. Keeler, *The Marquis de Villemer*, Boston (Mass) 1871.

Mlle de la Quintinie, 1863.

Mlle de Merquem, 1868. Tr. anon., New York 1868.

Souvenirs et idées, 1904.

Journal intime, ed. A. Sand, 1926. Tr. and ed. M. J. Howe, *The intimate journal*, London and New York 1929.

Lettres d'un voyageur, 2 vols, 1837 (in *Oeuvres* above). Tr. E. A. Ashurst, *Letters of a traveller*, London 1847.

   Nouvelles lettres, 1877.

Correspondance, ed. M. Sand, 6 vols, 1881–6; ed. G. Lubin, 1964 onwards (10 vols pbd). Tr. R. L. de Beaufort, *Letters*, 3 vols, London 1886; tr. V. Lucas, Boston, New York and London 1930 (selection).

Correspondance entre George Sand et Gustave Flaubert, ed. H. Amic, 1904. Tr. A. L. McKenzie, *The George Sand—Gustave Flaubert letters*, New York 1921.

Lettres à Musset et Sainte-Beuve, ed. S. Rocheblave, 1897.

Correspondance, journal intime (George Sand and Alfred de Musset), ed. L. Evrard, Monaco 1956.

KARENINE, V., *George Sand, sa vie et ses oeuvres*, 4 vols, 1899–1926 (incl. bibl. in vol 4).

MARIX-SPIRE, T., *Les romantiques et la musique: le cas George Sand, 1804–1838*, 1954.

MAUROIS, A., *Lélia, ou la vie de George Sand*, 1952. Tr. G. Hopkins, *Lelia, the life of George Sand*, London and New York 1953.

PAILLERON, M. L., *George Sand*, 3 vols, 1938–53.

POLI, A. R., *L'Italie dans la vie et dans l'oeuvre de George Sand*, 1960.

ROUGET, M. T., *Essai sur l'évolution psychologique et littéraire de George Sand*, Lyon 1939.

SALOMON, P., *George Sand*, 1953; 1958.

SEILLIÈRE, E., *George Sand, mystique de la passion, de la politique, et de l'art*, 1920.

SÉNANCOUR, Étienne de   1770–1846

MERLANT, J., *Bibliographie des oeuvres*, 1905.
See also LE GALL below; also SENELIER below.

Rêveries sur la primitive de l'homme, 1799; 1833; ed. J. Merlant, 2 vols, 1939–40.
Oberman, 2 vols, 1804; 1833 (enl.); introd. G. Sand, 1840; ed. G. Michaut, 2 vols, 1912–13; ed. A. Monglond, 3 vols, 1948 (with *Journal intime*); ed. G. Borgeaud, Paris 1965. Tr. J. P. Frothingham, 2 vols, Cambridge (Mass) 1901 (selection); tr. and ed. J. A. Barnes, 2 vols, London 1910–15.
De l'amour, 1806.
Observations critiques sur Le génie du christianisme, 1816.

LE GALL, B., *L'imaginaire chez Sénancour*, 2 vols, 1966 (incl. bibl. in vol 2).
MERLANT, J., *Sénancour*, 1907.
RAYMOND, M., *Sénancour, sensations et révélations*, 1965.
SENELIER, J., *Hommage à Sénancour; textes et lettres inédits; bibliographie des oeuvres*, 1971.

STAËL, Madame de   1766–1817
(Germaine Necker)

SCHAZMANN, P. E., *Bibliographie des oeuvres*, Paris and Neuchâtel 1938.
LONCHAMP, F. C., *L'oeuvre imprimée de Germaine de Staël; description biblio-graphique raisonnée et annotée de tous les ouvrages publiés par ses soins ou ceux de ses héritiers, 1768–1821*, Geneva 1949.
TOURTEBATTE, B. W., *Répertoire chronologique de la correspondance de Madame de Staël, 1799–1817*, Chicago (Ill) 1949.

Oeuvres complètes, ed. A. de Staël, 17 vols, 1820–1.

Lettres sur les ouvrages et le caractère de J.-J. Rousseau, Geneva (or Paris) 1788. Tr. anon., *Letters on the works and character of J.-J. Rousseau*, London 1789.
De la littérature considérée dans les rapports avec les institutions sociales, n.p. 1800; ed. P. Van Tieghem, Geneva and Paris 1959. Tr. anon., *The influence of literature upon society*, London 1812.
Delphine, 4 vols, Geneva 1802; 6 vols, 1818. Tr. anon., 3 vols, London 1803; tr. anon., 3 vols, Philadelphia (Pa) 1836.
Corinne, ou l'Italie, 2 vols, 1807; 3 vols, 1817. Tr. D. Lawler, *Corinna, or Italy*, 5 vols, London 1807; tr. I. Hill, *Corinne*, 1833; tr. E. Baldwin and P. Driver, 1883.
De l'Allemagne, 3 vols, 1810; 3 vols, London 1813; ed. J. de Pange and S. Balayé, 5 vols, Paris 1958–9. Tr. anon., *Germany*, 3 vols, London 1813; tr. O. W. Wight, 2 vols, New York 1859.

Dix années d'exile, 1821 (in *Oeuvres complètes* above); ed. P. Gautier 1904.
Tr. anon., *Ten years' exile*, London and New York 1821.

Correspondance générale, ed. B. Jasinski, 1962 onwards (4 vols pbd).
Lettres [. . .] *conservées en Bohême*, ed. M. Ullrichova, Prague, 1959.
Lettres à Narbonne, ed. J. de Pange and G. Solovieff, 1960.
Lettres [. . .] *au Comte de Ribbing*, ed. J. de Pange and S. Balayé, 1960.
Madame de Staël et le duc de Wellington, ed. V. de Pange, 1962. Tr. H. Kurtz,
    The unpublished correspondence of Mme de Staël and the Duke of Wellington,
    London 1965.
Tr. anon., *Mme de Staël and the Grand Duchess Louise, a selection from the
    unpublished letters*, London 1862.
Tr. C. Harwood, *Mme de Staël and Benjamin Constant, unpublished letters*,
    New York and London 1907.
Tr. and ed. M. Berger, *Madame de Staël on politics, literature and national
    character*, London and New York 1964.

ANDREWS, W., *Germaine, a portrait of Mme de Staël*, London and New York
    1964.
ESCARPIT, R., *L'Angleterre dans l'oeuvre de Mme de Staël*, 1954.
GAUTIER, P., *Mme de Staël et Napoléon*, 1903.
HAUSSONVILLE, O. d', *Mme de Staël et M. Necker*, 1925.
    Mme de Staël et l'Allemagne, 1928.
HEROLD, J. C., *Mistress to an age*, New York 1959.
WHITFORD, R. C., *Mme de Staël's literary reputation in England*, Urbana (Ill)
    1918.

STENDHAL   1783–1842
(pseudonym of Henri Beyle)

PAUPE, A., *Histoire des oeuvres*, 1903.
CORDIER, H., *Bibliographie stendhalienne*, 1914.
ROYER, L. and DEL LITTO, V., *Bibliographie stendhalienne*, Grenoble and
    Lausanne 1930 onwards (7 vols pbd, covering 1928–64).
Table de tous les articles parus sur Stendhal, 1950.

Oeuvres complètes, ed. E. Champion et al., 34 vols, 1913–40; ed. H. Martineau,
    79 vols, 1927–37; ed. V. Del Litto and E. Abravanel, 18 vols, Lausanne
    1961-2.
Romans et nouvelles, ed. H. Martineau, 2 vols, 1947.
Oeuvres intimes, ed. H. Martineau, 1955.
Romans, ed. S. de Sacy, 1959.

Tr. C. K. Scott-Moncrieff, *The works*, 6 vols, New York 1925-8; 7 vols,
    London 1926-8 (with *On love*, tr. V. Holland).
Selected journalism, ed. G. Strickland, London 1959 (from English reviews,

with trs of other critical writings).

Lettres écrites de Vienne en Autriche, sur le célèbre compositeur Jh. Haydn, suivies d'une vie de Mozart, et de considérations sur Métastase et l'état présent de la musique en France et en Italie (plagiarized from Carpani's *Le Haydine*), 1814; 1817 (renamed *Vies de Haydn, de Mozart et de Métastase*). Tr. C. Berry, *The lives of Haydn and Mozart, with observations on Metastase*, London 1817; tr. and ed. R. N. Coe, 1972.

Histoire de la peinture en Italie, 2 vols, 1817. Tr. D. Wakefield, in *Stendhal and the arts*, London 1973 (extracts).

Rome, Naples et Florence en 1817, 1817; 1826 (enl.); ed. R. Beyer, 1964; ed. V. del Litto, 1973. Tr. anon., *Rome, Naples and Florence, in 1817*, London 1818; tr. R. N. Coe, 1959.

De l'amour, 2 vols, 1822. Tr. anon., *Maxims of love*, London 1906; tr. V. Holland, *On love*, 1928 (in *Works* above); tr. G. and S. Sale, *Love*, 1957; tr. B. Rhys, 1959.

Racine et Shakespeare, 2 vols, 1823–5. Tr. G. Daniels, *Racine and Shakespeare*, New York 1962.

Vie de Rossini, 2 vols, 1824. Tr. anon., *Memoirs of Rossini*, London 1824; tr. R. N. Coe, *Life of Rossini*, 1956.

Armance, 1827. Tr. C. K. Scott-Moncrieff, London and New York 1928; tr. G. and S. Sale, London 1960.

Promenades dans Rome, 2 vols, 1829; ed. V. del Litto, 1973 (in *Voyages en Italie*). Tr. and ed. H. Chevalier, *A Roman journal*, London 1959.

Le rouge et le noir, 2 vols, 1831; ed. P. G. Castex, 1973. Tr. E. P. Robins, *Red and black*, London 1898; tr. C. K. Scott-Moncrieff, *The red and the black*, New York 1926 (London 1927 as *Scarlet and black*); tr. M. R. B. Shaw, London 1953; tr. L. Bair, *The red and the black*, New York 1958; tr. R. M. Adams, 1969; tr. L. C. Parks, 1971.

Mémoires d'un touriste, 2 vols, 1838. Tr. A. Seager, *Memoirs of a tourist*, Evanston (Ill) 1962 (abr.).

La Chartreuse de Parme, 2 vols, 1839; ed. A. Adam, 1973. Tr. E. P. Robins, *The Charterhouse of Parma*, 3 vols, New York 1895; tr. C. K. Scott-Moncrieff, 1925; tr. M. R. B. Shaw, Harmondsworth 1958; tr. L. Bair, New York 1960.

L'abbesse de Castro, 1839; 1855 (renamed *Chroniques italiennes*, with 5 new stories). Tr. C. K. Scott-Moncrieff, *The Abbess of Castro and other stories*, New York and London 1926.

Romans et nouvelles, 1854 (incl. *Armance* above); ed. H. Martineau, 1928.

Voyage dans le Midi de la France, 1854; ed. H. Martineau, 1930. Tr. E. Abbott, *Travels in the south of France*, London 1971.

Nouvelles inédites, 1855 (incl. *Féder*, tr. H. L. R. Edwards, London 1960).

Lucien Leuwen, 1855 (as *Le chasseur vert*, in *Nouvelles inédites* above); 1901; ed. H. Martineau, 1962. Tr. L. Varèse, New York 1950; tr. H. L. R. Edwards, London 1951.

Vie de Napoléon—fragments, 1876; ed. H. Martineau, 1962. Tr. R. N. Coe, *Life of Napoleon*, London 1956.

Lamiel, 1889. Tr. J. Leclercq, New York 1929; tr. T. W. Earp, London 1951.

Vie de Henry Brulard, 1890 (incomplete); 2 vols, 1913; ed. M. Crouzet and H. Martineau, 1964. Tr. C. A. Phillips, *The life of Henry Brulard*, London 1925; tr. J. Stewart and B. C. J. G. Knight, London and New York 1958.

Souvenirs d'égotisme, 1892; ed. H. Martineau, 1950. Tr. H. and M. Joseph-son, *Memoirs of egotism*, New York 1949; tr. T. W. Earp, *Memoirs of an egotist*, London 1949.

Journal, ed. H. Martineau, 5 vols, 1937. Tr. and ed. R. Sage, *The private diaries of Stendhal*, London 1955 (selection).

Correspondance, ed. H. Martineau, 10 vols, 1933–4; ed. H. Martineau and V. Del Litto, 3 vols, 1963–8. Tr. N. Cameron, ed. E. Boudot-Lamotte, *To the happy few*, London and New York 1952 (selection).

ALBÉRÈS, R. M., *Le naturel chez Stendhal*, 1956.

BALZAC, H. de, *Étude sur M. Beyle*, Geneva 1943 (rpt of article in *Revue Parisienne*, 1840).

BARDÈCHE, M., *Stendhal romancier*, 1947.

BILLY, A., *Ce cher Stendhal*, 1958.

BLIN, G., *Stendhal et les problèmes du roman*, 1953.
    Stendhal et les problèmes de la personnalité, 1958.

BROMBERT, V., *Stendhal et la voie oblique*, New Haven (Conn) 1954.

CARACCIO, A., *Stendhal, l'homme et l'oeuvre*, 1951; 1963. Tr. D. Bagley, *Stendhal*, New York 1965.

DÉDÉYAN, C., *L'Italie dans l'oeuvre romanesque de Stendhal*, 1963.

DEL LITTO, V., *La vie intellectuelle de Stendhal, 1802–1821*, 1958.

DURAND, G., *Le décor mythique de La Chartreuse de Parme*, 1961.

GREEN, F. C., *Stendhal*, New York and Cambridge 1939.

HAZARD, P., *Stendhal*, 1927. Tr. E. Hand, New York 1929.

HEMMINGS, F. W. J., *Stendhal, a study of his novels*, Oxford 1964.

LEVIN, H., *Toward Stendhal*, New York 1945.

MARTINEAU, H., *L'oeuvre de Stendhal*, 1945; 1951.
    Le coeur de Stendhal, 2 vols, 1952–3.

MICHEL, F., *Études stendhaliennes*, 1958.

MOUILLAUD, G., *Le rouge et le noir de Stendhal: le roman possible*, 1973.

PRÉVOST, J., *La création chez Stendhal*, Marseilles 1942; Paris 1951.

Stendhal-Club, ed. V. Del Litto, 1958 onwards.

TILLETT, M., *Stendhal, the background to the novels*, London 1971.

WOOD, M., *Stendhal*, London 1971.

SUE, Eugène   1804–1857

Oeuvres complètes, 199 vols, 1904–7.

Plik et Plok, 1831.

Les mystères de Paris, 10 vols, 1842–3. Tr. H. L. Williams, *The mysteries of Paris*, London 1896.

Le Juif errant, 10 vols, 1844–5. Tr. H. L. Williams, *The wandering Jew*, London 1868.

Les sept péchés capitaux, 16 vols, 1848–9.

Les mystères du peuple (unfinished), 16 vols, 1849–57. Tr. M. L. Booth, *Mysteries of the people*, New York 1867.

ATKINSON, N., *Eugène Sue et le roman feuilleton*, 1930.

BORY, J. L., *Eugène Sue, le roi du roman populaire*, 1962.

MOODY, J., *Les idées sociales d'Eugène Sue*, 1938.

TAINE, Hippolyte Adolphe   1828–1893

GIRAUD, V., *Taine*, 1902 (bibl.).

Voyage aux eaux des Pyrénées, 1855; 1860. Tr. J. S. Fiske, *A tour through the Pyrenees*, New York 1874.

Les philosophes français du XIXe siècle en France, 1857; 1868.

Histoire de la littérature anglaise, 4 vols, 1863–4; 5 vols, 1892. Tr. H. van Laun, *History of English literature*, 2 vols, Edinburgh and New York 1871.

Philosophie de l'art (collected art lectures), 1865; 2 vols, 1882 (enl.; with *De l'idéal dans l'art*); ed. J. F. Revel, 1964. Tr. J. Durand, *Lectures on art*, 2 vols, New York 1889 (incl. *The ideal in art*, first pbd separately 1870).

Voyage en Italie (collected articles), 2 vols, 1866. Tr. J. Durand, *Italy*, 2 vols, New York 1869.

De l'intelligence, 2 vols, 1870; 2 vols, 1883. Tr. T. O. Haye, *On intelligence*, 2 vols, London 1871.

Notes sur l'Angleterre (collected articles), 1872. Tr. W. F. Rae, *Notes on England*, London and New York 1872; tr. E. Hyams, London 1957.

Origines de la France contemporaine, 6 vols, 1876–93. Tr. J. Durand, *The origins of contemporary France*, 4 vols, London 1876–85 (tr. of vols 1–4); 6 vols, New York 1876–94 (complete tr.).

Derniers essais de critique et d'histoire, 1894.

Correspondance, 4 vols, 1902–7 (as *Sa vie et sa correspondance*, with unpbd material). Tr. R. L. Devonshire, *Life and letters*, 3 vols, London 1902–8.

AULARD, A., *Taine, historien de la Révolution française*, 1907.

CHEVRILLON, A., *Taine, formation de sa pensée*, 1932.

CRESSON, A., *Hippolyte Taine, sa vie, son oeuvre, sa philosophie*, 1951.

GIRAUD, V., *Essai sur Taine, son oeuvre et son influence*, Fribourg 1901.

KAHN, S. J., *Science and aesthetic judgement: a study of Taine's critical method*, New York 1953.

ROE, F. C., *Taine et l'Angleterre*, 1923.

WEINSTEIN, L., *Hippolyte Taine*, New York 1972.

THIERRY, Augustin   1795–1856

Oeuvres complètes, 10 vols, 1858–60; 9 vols, 1883.

Histoire de la conquête de l'Angleterre par les Normands, 3 vols, 1825; 4 vols, 1845. Tr. C. C. Hamilton, *History of the conquest of England by the Normans*, 3 vols, London 1825; tr. W. Hazlitt, 2 vols, 1856.

Récits des temps mérovingiens, 2 vols, 1840; ed. H. Peyre, 1948. Tr. anon., *Narratives of the Merovingian era*, Philadelphia (Pa) 1845 (in *The historical essays*).

Essai sur l'histoire de la formation et des progrès du tiers état, 1853. Tr. F. B. Wells, *The formation and progress of the Tiers Etat*, 2 vols, London 1855.

DUPRONT, A., *Augustin Thierry*, 1935.

THIERRY, A. A., *Augustin Thierry d'après la correspondance et ses papiers de famille*, ed. G. Hanotaux, 1922.

TOCQUEVILLE, Alexis de   1805–1859

Oeuvres complètes, 9 vols, 1860–5; ed. J. P. Mayer et al, 1951 onwards (11 vols pbd).

Scritti politici, ed. N. Matteucci, 2 vols, Turin 1968–9.

De la démocratie en Amérique, 4 vols, 1835–40. Tr. H. Reeve, *Democracy in America*, 4 vols, London 1835–40 (ed. F. Bowen, 2 vols, Cambridge 1862; revd P. Bradley, 2 vols, New York 1945).

L'Ancien Régime et la Révolution française, 1856. Tr. H. Reeve, *On the state of society in France before the revolution of 1789*, London 1856; tr. M. W. Patterson, *Ancien Régime*, Oxford 1933; tr. S. Gilbert, *The old regime and the French revolution*, New York 1955.

Voyages en Angleterre, Irlande, ed. J. P. Mayer and A. Jardin, 1958 (as vol 5, part 2 of *Oeuvres complètes* above). Tr. G. Lawrence and K. P. Mayer, ed. J. P. Mayer, *Journeys to England and Ireland*, London and New Haven (Conn) 1958.

Souvenirs, 2 vols, 1893; ed. L. Monnier, 1964 (as vol 12 of *Oeuvres complètes* above). Tr. A. Teixera de Mattos, *The recollections*, London 1896; tr. G. Lawrence, London 1970.

Correspondance d'Alexis de Tocqueville et d'Arthur de Gobineau, ed. L. Schemann, 1909; ed. M. Degros, 1959 (as vol 9 of *Oeuvres complètes* above). Tr. and ed. J. Lukacs, *Correspondence with Gobineau*, New York 1959 (with *The European Revolution*).

BROGAN, H., *Tocqueville*, London 1973.

DRESCHER, S., *Tocqueville and England*, Cambridge (Mass) 1964.
  Dilemmas of democracy: Tocqueville and modernization, Pittsburg (Pa) 1968.
LIVELY, J., *The social and political thought of Tocqueville*, Oxford 1962.
MAYER, J. P., *A prophet of the mass age: a study of Alexis de Tocqueville*, London 1939 (tr. M. M. Bozman and C. Hahn); New York 1940 (enl.; renamed *A. de Tocqueville, a biographical essay in political science*).

VALLÈS, Jules   1832–1885

GILLE, G., *Sources, bibliographie et iconographie vallésiennes*, 1941.

Oeuvres, ed. L. Scheler et al., 8 vols, 1950–7; ed. G. Gille, 1968 (selected works).

Les réfractaires, 1866.
La rue, 1866.
Les enfants du peuple, 1879.
Jacques Vingtras, 1879–86. Comprising:
    L'enfant, 1879.
    Le bachelier, 1881.
    L'insurgé, 1886.
Les chroniques de l'homme masqué, 1882.
La rue à Londres (collected articles), 1884.
Mazas, 1894.
Les blouses, 1919 (first pbd in serial form 1880).
Souvenirs d'un étudiant pauvre, 1930.
Le tableau de Paris, ed. B. Lecache, 1932.
Un gentilhomme, 1932 (first pbd in serial form 1869)
Le cri du peuple, ed. L. Scheler, 1953 (collected articles first pbd 1848–71).

Le proscrit (correspondence with A. Arnould), 1950 (in *Oeuvres*, vol 4 above).

GILLE, G., *Jules Vallès*, 2 vols, 1941.
HIRSCH, M. L., *Jules Vallès l'insurgé*, 1949.

VERHAEREN, Émile   1855–1916

CULOT, J. M., *Bibliographie*, Gembloux and Brussels 1955.

Oeuvres, 9 vols, 1912–33.
Meilleures pages, ed. L. Christophe, Brussels 1955.

Tr. various, *The plays*, London and Boston (Mass) 1916.
Tr. A. Strettell, *Poems*, London and New York 1899 (selection).
Tr. F. S. Flint, *The love poems*, London 1916.
Tr. K. Wallis, *Five tales*, New York 1924.

Les Flamandes, Brussels 1883.

Les moines, 1886.

Les soirs, Brussels 1888.

Les débâcles, Brussels 1888.

Les flambeaux noirs, Brussels 1891.

Les campagnes hallucinées, Brussels 1893.

Les heures claires, Brussels 1896. Tr. C. R. Murphy, *The sunlit hours,* New York 1916.

Les heures d'après-midi, Brussels 1905. Tr. C. R. Murphy, *Afternoon,* New York and London 1917.

Les heures du soir, Leipzig 1911. Tr. C. R. Murphy, *The evening hours,* New York 1918.

Le cloître, Brussels 1899. Tr. O. Edwards, *The cloister,* London 1915.

Les forces tumultueuses, 1902.

Toute la Flandre, 5 vols, 1904–11.

La multiple splendeur, 1906.

Les rythmes souverains, 1910.

Hélène de Sparte, 1912. Tr. J. Bithell, *Helen of Sparta,* London and Boston 1916 (in *The plays* above).

La Belgique sanglante, Brussels 1915. Tr. M. Sadler, *Belgium's agony,* London 1915.

Les ailes rouges de la guerre, Brussels 1916.

Impressions, 3 vols, 1926–8.

BAUDOUIN, C., *Le symbole chez Verhaeren,* Geneva 1924. Tr. E. and C. Paul, *Psychoanalysis and aesthetics,* London and New York 1924.

HELLENS, F., *Émile Verhaeren,* 1955.

MANSELL-JONES, P., *Émile Verhaeren, a study in the development of his art and ideas,* Cardiff and London 1926.

STARKIE, E., *Émile Verhaeren: sa vie et son oeuvre; les sources du lyrisme,* 1927.

VERLAINE, Paul   1844–1896

TOURNOUX, G. A., *Bibliographie verlainïenne,* Leipzig 1912.

MONTEL, F., *Bibliographie,* 1924.

VAN BEVER, A., and MONDA, M., *Bibliographie et iconographie,* 1926.

CUÉNOT, C., *Etat présent des études verlainiennes,* 1938.

Oeuvres complètes, ed. C. Morice, 5 vols, 1899–1900; ed. idem, 5 vols, 1911; ed. A. Fontainas, 8 vols, 1931–2; ed. Y. Le Dantec, 5 vols, 1946–53; ed. J. Borel and H. de Bouillane de Lacoste, 2 vols, 1959–60.

Oeuvres poétiques complètes, ed. Y. Le Dantec, 1938; ed. J. Robichez, 1969.

Oeuvres en prose complètes, ed. J. Borel, 1972.

Poésies choisies, ed. A. Fongano, Rome 1954 (revd 1959).

Tr. G. Hall, *Selections,* Chicago (Ill) 1895.

Tr. A. Wingate, *Poems,* London 1904 (selection).

Tr. R. Grant and C. Apcher, *Forty poems*, London 1948.

Tr. C. F. MacIntyre, *Selected poems*, Berkeley (Calif) 1948.

Tr. B. Hill, *The sky above the roof*, London 1957 (selection).

Poèmes saturniens, 1866; ed. J. H. Bornecque, 1967.

Fêtes galantes, 1869. Tr. A. C. Kennedy, Nice 1912.

La bonne chanson, 1870.

Romances sans paroles, Sens 1874; 1887; ed. A. Van Bever, Paris 1924.

Sagesse, 1881; 1889; ed. A. Van Bever, 1911; ed. L. Morice, 1964.

Les poètes maudits: Tristan Corbière, Arthur Rimbaud, Stéphane Mallarmé, 1884; 1884 (enl., with chapters on Marceline Desbordes-Valmore, Villiers de L'Isle Adam, and 'Pauvre Lélian', anagram of Paul Verlaine).

Jadis et naguère, 1884 (incl. *Art poétique*); 1891; ed. A. Van Bever, 1921.

Les mémoires d'un veuf, 1886.

Amour, 1888; 1892; ed. A. Van Bever, 1921.

Parallèlement, 1889; 1894 (enl.).

Bonheur, 1891; ed. H. de Bouillane de Lacoste, 1949.

Chansons pour elle, 1891. Tr. A. C. Kennedy, Harrogate 1926.

Mes hôpitaux, 1891.

Liturgies intimes, 1892; 1893 (enl.).

Mes prisons, 1893; ed. C. Cuénot, 1973.

Quinze jours en Hollande, 1893.

Confessions, notes autobiographiques, 1895. Tr. J. Richardson, *Confessions of a poet*, London 1950.

Chair (dernières poésies), 1896.

Invectives, 1896.

Oeuvres posthumes, ed. G. Kahn, 1903; 3 vols, 1911–29.

Oeuvres oubliées, ed. M. Monda, 2 vols, 1926–9.

Correspondance, ed. A. Van Bever, 3 vols, 1922–9.

Lettres inédites, ed. G. Zayed, 2 vols, Geneva and Paris 1957–64.

ADAM, A., *Verlaine, l'homme et l'oeuvre*, 1953; 1966.

BORNECQUE, J. H., *Verlaine par lui-même*, 1966.

COULON, M., *Verlaine, poète saturnien*, 1929. Tr. E. Rickword, *Poet under Saturn*, London 1932.

CUÉNOT, C., *Le style de Verlaine*, 1963.

NADAL, O., *Paul Verlaine*, 1961.

UNDERWOOD, V. P., *Verlaine et l'Angleterre*, 1956.

VERLAINE, Mme Paul, *Mémoires de ma vie*, 1936.

ZAYED, G., *La formation littéraire de Verlaine*, Geneva 1962.

VERNE, Jules   1828–1905

Bibl. See Evans ed. of *Master of science fiction* below.

Voyages extraordinaires, 10 vols, 1962–6.
Les oeuvres, ed. G. Sigaux and C. N. Martin, 23 vols, Lausanne 1966–7.

Tr. anon., *The best novels*, New York 1905.
Tr. anon., ed. I. O. Evans, *Master of science fiction*, London 1956 (extracts; incl. bibl.).

Paille rompue, comédie, 1850.
Cinq semaines en ballon, 1863 (in Hetzel's *Magasin d'éducation et de récréation*). Tr. anon., *Five weeks in a balloon*, New York 1876.
Voyage au centre de la terre, 1864. Tr. anon., *Journey to the centre of the Earth*, New York 1874; tr. W. T. Bradley, London 1960.
De la terre à la lune, 1865. Tr. L. Mercier and E. C. King, *From the Earth to the Moon, in 97 hours, 20 minutes*, London 1873.
Voyages et aventures du Capitaine Hatteras, 2 vols, 1866. Tr. anon., *Adventures of Captain Hatteras*, New York 1875.
Les enfants du capitaine Grant, 3 vols, 1867–8. Tr. anon., *A voyage round the world*, New York and London 1876–7.
Vingt mille lieues sous les mers, 1870. Tr. anon., *Twenty thousand leagues under the sea*, Boston (Mass) and New York 1874; tr. W. J. Miller and J. A. Tisch, New York 1965.
Le tour du monde en quatre-vingts jours, 1873. Tr. anon., *The tour of the world in eighty days*, Boston 1873; tr. I. O. Evans, *Around the world in eighty days*, London 1967.
L'île mystérieuse, 3 vols, 1874. Tr. W. H. G. Kingston, *The mysterious island*, 3 vols, London 1875.
Michel Strogoff, 2 vols, 1876. Tr. W. H. G. Kingston, *Michael Strogoff*, London 1877.
Mathias Sandorff, 3 vols, 1885. Tr. anon., 2 vols, London 1886.
L'île à hélices, 2 vols, 1895. Tr. W. J. Gordon, *Floating island*, London and Edinburgh 1896; tr. I. O. Evans, *Propeller island*, London 1965.
Le phare du bout du monde, 1905. Tr. anon., *The lighthouse at the end of the world*, London 1923.

ALLOTT, K., *Jules Verne*, London 1940.
ALLOTTE DE LA FUŸE, M., *Jules Verne, sa vie, son oeuvre*, 1928.
CHESNAUX, J., *Une lecture politique de Jules Verne*, 1971.
DIESBACH, G. de, *Le tour de Jules Verne en 80 livres*, 1969.
EVANS, I. O., *Jules Verne and his work*, London 1965.
JULES-VERNE, J., *Jules Verne*, 1973.
MORE, M., *Le très curieux Jules Verne*, 1960.
    Nouvelles explorations de Jules Verne, 1963.
VIERNE, S., *Jules Verne et le roman initiatique*, 1973.

VIGNY, Alfred de   1797–1863

CURZON, H. de, *Bibliographie des ouvrages relatifs à Alfred de Vigny*, Besançon 1897.

LANGLAIS, J., *Essai de bibliographie*, 1905.

Oeuvres complètes, 7 vols, 1837–9; ed. E. Tréfen, 9 vols, 1903–13; ed. F. Baldensperger, 8 vols, 1914–35; ed. idem, 2 vols, 1948; ed. P. Viallaneix, 1965.

Poèmes antiques et modernes, Les destinées, ed. A. Jarry, 1973.

Translated in anthologies.

Poèmes, 1822 (incl. *Héléna*, ed. E. Estève, 1907, and *La fille de Jephté*).

Eloa, ou la soeur des anges, 1824.

Poèmes antiques et modernes, 1826 (incl. *Le déluge, Moïse, Le cor*); 1837 (enl.); ed. E. Estève, 1914.

Cinq-mars, 2 vols, 1826. Tr. W. Hazlitt, London 1847; tr. M. Pemberton, *The spider and the fly*, London and Philadelphia (Pa) 1925.

La maréchale d'Ancre, 1831.

Les consultations du docteur Noir: Stello, 1832; ed. M. Revon, 1937. Tr. I. Massey, *Stello; a session with Doctor Noir*, Montreal 1963;
   Un roman inédit, Daphné, ed. F. Gregh, 1912;
   ed. F. Germain, 1970.

Chatterton, 1832 (as episode in *Stello* above).
   Chatterton (dramatized version), 1835; ed. E. Lauvrière, Oxford 1908; ed. L. Petroni, Bologna 1962.

Servitude et grandeur militaire, 1835; ed. F. Germain, 1965. Tr. F. W. Huard, *Military servitude and grandeur*, New York 1919; tr. H. Hare, *The military necessity*, New York and London 1953; tr. M. Barnett, *The military condition*, 1964.

Les destinées, poèmes philosophiques, ed. L. Ratisbonne, 1864 (incl. *La mort du loup, Le mont des Oliviers, La maison du berger*); ed. E. Estève, 1924; ed. V. L. Saulnier, 1947; ed. P. G. Castex, Paris 1964.

Journal d'un poète, ed. L. Ratisbonne, 1867.

Mémoires inédits, fragments et projets, ed. J. Sangnier, 1958.

Correspondance 1816–1863, ed. E. Sakellaridès, 1905.

Correspondance 1822–1863, ed. L. Séché, 2 vols, 1914? (in his ed. of *Oeuvres complètes*).

BONNEFOY, G., *La pensée religieuse et morale d'Alfred de Vigny*, 1944.

CASTEX, P. G., *Vigny, l'homme et l'oeuvre*, 1952.

ESTÈVE, E., *Alfred de Vigny; sa pensée et son art*, 1923.

FLOTTES, P., *La pensée politique et sociale d'Alfred de Vigny*, 1927.
   Vigny et sa fortune littéraire, Bordeaux 1970.

GERMAIN F., *L'imagination d'Alfred de Vigny*, 1961.

GUILLEMIN, H., *Monsieur de Vigny, homme d'ordre et poète*, 1955.

LA SALLE, B. de, *Alfred de Vigny*, 1963.

LAUVRIÈRE, E., *Alfred de Vigny, sa vie et son oeuvre*, 2 vols, 1910; 2 vols, 1946.

VIALLANEIX, P., *Vigny par lui-même*, 1964.

WHITRIDGE, A., *Alfred de Vigny*, London and New York 1933.

VILLIERS DE L'ISLE-ADAM, Auguste de   1838–1889

BOLLÉRY, J., *Biblio-iconographie*, 1939.

RAITT, A. W., *Etat présent des études sur Villiers de l'Isle-Adam*, 1956 (in *L'Information littéraire*, Jan.–Feb.).

Oeuvres complètes, ed. M. Longuet, 11 vols, 1914–31; ed. J. H. Bornecque, 1957.

Premières poésies, 1856–1858, Lyon 1859.

Isis, 1862.

Elën, drame, 1865; Saint Brieuc 1866 (with poem *Elën*).

Morgane, Saint Brieuc, 1866.

La révolte, 1870. Tr. T. Barclay, *The revolt and the escape*, London 1901.

Le nouveau monde, 1880.

Contes cruels, 1883 (incl. poem *Elën* above, renamed *Au bord de la mer*); 1889; ed. J. Bolléry and P. G. Castex, 2 vols, 1954–6. Tr. H. Miles, *Sardonic tales*, New York and London 1927; tr. R. Baldick, *Cruel Tales*, Oxford 1963.

   Nouveaux contes cruels, 1889.

L'Eve future, 1886; ed. J. Bolléry and P. G. Castex, 1957.

L'amour suprême, 1886; 1888 (renamed *Le secret de l'échafaud*).

Tribulat Bonhomet, 1887; ed. P. G. Castex and J. M. Bellefroid, 1967.

Axël, 1890; ed. P. Mariel, 1960. Tr. H. P. R. Finberg, London 1925.

Reliques, ed. P. G. Castex, 1954.

   Nouvelles reliques, ed. P. G. Castex and J. M. Bellefroid, 1968.

Correspondance générale, ed. J. Bolléry, 2 vols, 1962.

DAIREAUX, M., *Villiers de l'Isle-Adam, l'homme et l'oeuvre*, 1936.

DOYON, R. L., *Le Bestiaire de Villiers de l'Isle-Adam*, 1957.

RAITT, A. W., *Villiers de l'Isle-Adam et le mouvement symboliste*, 1965.

ZOLA, Émile   1840–1902

MITTERAND, H. et al., *Emile Zola journaliste, bibliographie chronologique et analytique*, 2 vols, 1968–72.

See also HEMMINGS below; also LAPORTE below.

Oeuvres, ed. M. Le Blond, 50 vols, 1927–9; ed. H. Mitterand, 16 vols, 1967–70.

Contes à Ninon, 1864. Tr. E. A. Vizetelly, *Stories for Ninon*, London 1895.
    Nouveaux contes à Ninon, 1874.

La confession de Claude, 1865. Tr. G. D. Cox, *Claude's confession*, London 1882.

Mes haines, 1866.
    Mon salon, 1866; ed. A. Ehrard, 1970.
    Edouard Manet, 1867; ed. A. Ehrard, 1970 (with *Mon salon* above).

Thérèse Raquin, 1867; ed. H. Mitterand, 1970. Tr. J. Stirling, Philadelphia
    (Pa) 1881; tr. L. W. Tancock, Harmondsworth 1962.

Les mystères de Marseille, 3 vols, 1867–8. Tr. M. A. Cooney, *The mysteries
    of Marseilles*, New York 1885; tr. E. A. Vizetelly, London 1895.

Madeline Férat, 1868. Tr. J. Stirling, Philadelphia (Pa) 1880; tr. A. Brown,
    London 1957; tr. L. Marcourt, *Shame*, New York 1954.

*Les Rougon-Macquart, histoire naturelle et sociale d'une famille sous le second
    Empire*, 1871–93; ed. H. Guillemin, 20 vols, Lausanne 1959–61; ed. A.
    Lanoux and H. Mitterand, Paris 1960–7; ed. P. Cogny, 6 vols, 1969–70.
    Tr. E. A. Vizetelly et al., *The Rougon-Macquart novels*, London 1885–
    1907. Comprising:

1 *La fortune des Rougon*, 1871; ed. R. Ricatte, 1969. Tr. J. Stirling, *The
    Rougon-Macquart family*, Philadelphia (Pa) 1879; tr. anon., *The fortune
    of the Rougons*, London 1886.

2 *La curée*, 1872; ed. C. Duchet, 1970. Tr. A. Teixeira de Mattos, *The
    kill*, London 1895.

3 *Le ventre de Paris*, 1873; ed. M. Baroli, 1969. Tr. J. Stirling, *The
    markets of Paris*, Philadelphia (Pa) 1879; tr. D. Hughes and M. J.
    Mason, *Savage Paris*, London 1958.

4 *La conquête de Plassans*, 1874. Tr. J. Stirling, *The conquest of Plassans*,
    Philadelphia (Pa) 1870; tr. B. Rhys, *A priest in the house*, London 1957.

5 *La faute de l'abbé Mouret*, 1875. Tr. J. Stirling, *Albine, or the abbé's
    temptation*, Philadelphia (Pa) 1882; tr. A. Brown, *The sinful priest*,
    London 1957.

6 *Son Excellence Eugène Rougon*, 1876; ed. E. Carassus, 1973. Tr. anon.,
    His Excellency, London 1897; tr. A. Brown, 1958.

7 *L'assommoir*, 1877; ed. J. Dubois, 1969. Tr. J. Stirling, Philadelphia
    (Pa) 1879 (New York 1950 as *Nana's mother*); tr. A. Symons,
    Drunkard, London 1928; tr. G. Hopkins, *The dram-shop*, 1951; tr.
    A. H. Townsend, *L'assommoir*, New York 1962.

8 *Une page d'amour*, 1878; ed. C. Becker, 1973. Tr. M. N. Sherwood,
    Hélène, a love episode, Philadelphia (Pa) 1878; tr. J. Stewart, *A love
    affair*, London 1957.

9 *Nana*, 1880. Tr. J. Stirling, Philadelphia (Pa) 1880; tr. L. Bair, New
    York 1964.

10 *Pot-bouille*, 1882; ed. C. Becker, 1969. Tr. P. Pinkerton, *Piping hot*,
    New York 1924 (London and New York 1953 as *Restless house*).

11 *Au bonheur des dames*, 1882. Tr. J. Stirling, *The bonheur des dames, or

the shopgirls of Paris, Philadelphia (Pa) 1883; tr. A. Fitzlyon, *Ladies' delight*, London 1957.

12 *La joie de vivre*, 1884. Tr. K. Philip, *Life's joys*, New York 1884; tr. J. Stewart, *Zest for life*, London 1955.

13 *Germinal*, 1885. Tr. Carlynne, Chicago and New York 1885; tr. Havelock Ellis, London 1895; tr. L. W. Tancock, Harmondsworth 1954; tr. W. R. Trask, New York 1962.

14 *L'oeuvre*, 1886. Tr. K. Woods, *The masterpiece*, New York 1946; tr. T. Walton, London and New York 1950.

15 *La terre*, 1887. Tr. anon., *The soil*, Chicago (Ill) 1888; tr. A. Lindsay, *Earth*, London and New York 1954; tr. M. C. Crosland, London 1962.

16 *Le rêve*, 1888. Tr. anon., *The dream*, Chicago (Ill) and New York 1888; tr. E. E. Chase, London 1893.

17 *La bête humaine*, 1890. Tr. E. de V. Vermont, *Human brutes*, Chicago (Ill) 1890; tr. A. Brown, *The beast in man*, London 1956.

18 *L'argent*, 1891. Tr. B. R. Tucker, *Money*, Boston (Mass) 1891; tr. E. A. Vizetelly, London 1894.

19 *La débâcle*, 1892. Tr. E. A. Vizetelly, *The downfall*, London 1892; tr. W. M. Sloane, New York 1902; tr. J. Hands, *The debacle*, London 1968.

20 *Le docteur Pascal*, 1893. Tr. M. J. Serrano, *Doctor Pascal*, New York 1893; tr. V. Kean, London 1957.

Le roman expérimental, 1880. Tr. B. M. Sherman, *The experimental novel and other essays*, New York 1893.

Une campagne, 1880–1881, 1882.

Le naturalisme au théâtre, 1881.

Nos auteurs dramatiques, 1881.

Les romanciers naturalistes, 1881.

Naïs Micoulin, 1884.

Les trois villes, 1894–8. Tr. E. A. Vizetelly, *The three cities*, London 1894–8. Comprising:

  Lourdes, 1894. Tr., London 1894.

  Rome, 1896. Tr., London 1896.

  Paris, 1898. Tr., London 1898.

La verité en marche, 1901 (incl. *Lettre à M. Felix Faure*, known as '*J'accuse*', first pbd in *L'Aurore*, 13 Jan. 1898). Tr. L. F. Austin, *The Dreyfus case: four letters to France*, London and New York 1898 (extracts).

Les quatre Evangiles (unfinished), 1899–1903. Tr. E. A. Vizetelly, London and New York 1900–3. Comprising:

  Fécondité, 1899. Tr., *Fruitfulness*, London and New York 1900.

  Travail, 1901. Tr., *Work*, London and New York 1901.

  Vérité, 1903. Tr., *Truth*, London and New York 1903.

Correspondance, 2 vols, 1907–8.

BARBUSSE, H., *Zola*, 1932.

DEZALAY, A., *Lectures de Zola*, 1973.

GUILLEMIN, H., *Zola, légende ou vérité*, 1960.
   Présentation des Rougon-Macquart, 1964.

HEMMINGS, F. W. J., *Emile Zola*, Oxford 1953; 1966 (incl. bibl.).

JOSEPHSON, M., *Zola and his time*, New York 1928.

LAPORTE, A., *Le naturalisme ou l'immortalité littéraire; Emile Zola: l'homme et l'oeuvre suivi de la bibliographie de ses ouvrages et de la liste des écrivains qui ont écrit pour ou contre lui*, 1894.

MATTHEWS, J. H., *Les deux Zola, science et personnalité dans l'expression*, Geneva 1957.

ROBERT, G., *Emile Zola, principes et caractères géneraux de son oeuvre*, 1952.

TERNOIS, R., *Zola et son temps*, Dijon 1961.

TURNELL, M., in his *The art of French fiction*, London 1951; 1959.

WILSON, A., *Emile Zola, an introductory study*, London 1952.

6
The Twentieth Century

ADAMOV, Arthur   1908–1970

Bibl. See GAUDY below.

Théâtre, 3 vols, 1953–66.

L'invasion, 1950.
La parodie, 1950 (with *L'invasion* above).
La grande et la petite manoeuvre, 1953 (in *Théâtre*, vol 1 above).
Tous contre tous, 1953 (in *Théâtre*, vol 1 above).
Le professeur Taranne, 1953 (in *Théâtre*, vol 1 above). Tr. A. Bermel, *Professor Taranne*, New York 1960 (in *Four modern French comedies*); tr. P. Meyer, London 1962 (in *Two plays*).
Le sens de la marche, 1955 (in *Théâtre*, vol 2 above).
Le ping-pong, 1955 (in *Théâtre*, vol 2 above). Tr. R. Howard, *Ping pong*, New York 1959; tr. D. Prouse, London 1962 (in *Two plays*, with *Professor Taranne* above).
Les retrouvailles, 1955 (in *Théâtre*, vol 2 above).
Théâtre de société (in collab. with Guy Demoy and Maurice Regnault), 1958.
Printemps 71, 1961.
Ici et maintenant, 1964.
Paolo Paoli, 1966 (in *Théâtre*, vol 3 above). Tr. G. Brereton, London 1960.
Sainte Europe, 1966 (in *Théâtre*, vol 3 above).
La politique des restes, 1966 (in *Théâtre*, vol 3 above).
Je . . . ils, 1969.
Off limits, 1969.
Si l'été revenait, 1970.

ESSLIN, M., in his *The theatre of the absurd*, New York 1961; 1968. Tr. M. Buchet et al., *Le théâtre de l'absurde*, Paris 1963.
GAUDY, R., *Arthur Adamov*, 1971 (incl. bibl.).
WELLWARTH, G. E., in his *The theater of protest and paradox*, New York 1964.

ALAIN   1868–1951
(pseudonym of Émile Chartier)

DEWITT, S., *Essai de bibliographie, 1893–June 1961*, Brussels 1962.

[*Oeuvres*], 1956–60, comprising:
    Propos, ed. M. Savin, 1956 (selection).
    Les arts et les dieux [etc], ed. G. Bénézé, 1958.
    Les passions et la sagesse, ed. G. Bénézé, 1960.

Les cent-un propos, 5 vols, Rouen and Paris 1908–28 (collected articles first
    pbd in *La Dépêche de Rouen* and *Nouvelle Revue Française*).
Quatre-vingt-un chapitres sur l'esprit et les passions, 1917.
Système des beaux-arts, 1920; 1926.
Mars, ou la guerre jugée, 1921. Tr. D. Mudie and E. Hill, *Mars, or the truth
    about war*, London and Toronto 1930.
Le citoyen contre les pouvoirs, 1926.
Idées, 1932; 1939 (enl.).
Les dieux, 1934.
Histoire de mes pensées, 1936.
Cahiers de Lorient, 2 vols, 1964.

BÉNÉZÉ, G., *Généreux Alain*, 1962.
BRIDOUX, A., *Alain, sa vie, son oeuvre*, 1965.
HALDA, B., *Alain*, 1965.
Hommage à Alain, 1952 (in *Nouvelle Revue Française*).
MAUROIS, A., *Alain*, 1950.
PASCAL, G., *Pour connaître la pensée d'Alain*, 1946; 1957.

ALAIN-FOURNIER   1886–1914
(pseudonym of Henri-Alban Fournier)

Bibl. See LEONARD below; also LOIZÉ below.

Le grand Meaulnes, 1913; ed. I. Rivière, Lausanne 1938. Tr. F. Delisle, *The
    Wanderer*, Boston 1928; tr. F. Davison, *Lost domain*, Oxford 1959; tr.
    S. Morris, London 1966.
Miracles, 1924 (incl. fragment of *Colombe Blanchet*).

Correspondance, 1905–1914 (with Jacques Rivière), ed. I. Rivière, 4 vols,
    1926–8; 2 vols, 1948 (enl.).
Lettres au petit B., 1930.
Lettres [. . .] à sa famille, 1905–1914, 1930; 1950 (1898–1914).

BORGAL, C., *Alain-Fournier*, 1955; 1963 (enl.).
GUIOMAR, M., *Inconscient et imaginaire dans Le grand Meaulnes*, 1964.
Hommage à Alain-Fournier, Orleans 1930; Paris 1930.
JÖHR, W., *Alain-Fournier, le paysage d'une âme*, Neuchâtel 1945.
LÉONARD. A., *Alain-Fournier et Le grand Meaulnes*, 1943 (incl. bibl.).

LOIZÉ, J., *Alain-Fournier: sa vie et Le grand Meaulnes*, 1968 (incl. bibl.).
PILON, E., *Alain-Fournier*, 1920.
RIVIÈRE, I., *Vie et passion d'Alain-Fournier*, Monaco 1963.
RIVIÈRE, J., Introduction to *Miracles* above.

ANOUILH, Jean   1910–

KELLY, K. W., *An annotated bibliography*, Metuchen (NJ) 1973.
See also JOLIVET below.

Tr. various, *The collected plays*, 2 vols, London 1966–7.
Tr. various, *Jean Anouilh*, 3 vols, New York 1958–67 (collected plays).

Le voyageur sans bagages, 1937. Tr. J. Whiting, *Traveller without luggage*, London and New York 1959; tr. L. Hill, New York 1967 (in *Jean Anouilh*, vol 3 above).
La sauvage, 1938. Tr. L. Hill, *Restless Heart*, London 1958.
Le bal des voleurs, 1938. Tr. L. Hill, *Thieves' carnival*, London 1952.
Pièces noires, 1942.
Eurydice, 1942 (in *Pièces noires* above). Tr. K. Black, *Point of Departure*, London 1951 (New York 1952, as *Legend of lovers*); tr. L. Small, *Eurydice*, London 1951 (with *Antigone* below, tr. L. Galantière).
L'hermine, 1942 (in *Pièces noires* above). Tr. M. John, *The ermine*, London 1955 (in *Plays of the year*, vol 13).
Pièces roses, 1942; 1958 (with *Humulus le muet*, first pbd Grenoble 1945).
Le rendez-vous de Senlis, 1942 (in *Pièces roses* above). Tr. E. O. Marsh, *Dinner with the family*, London 1958.
Léocadia, 1942 (in *Pièces roses* above). Tr. P. Moyes, *Time remembered*, London 1955.
Antigone, 1946. Tr. L. Galantière, New York 1946.
Nouvelles pièces noires, 1946.
Médée, 1946 (in *Nouvelles pièces noires* above). Tr. L. Small, *Medea*, London 1956 (in *Plays of the year*, vol 15); tr. L. and A. Klein, New York 1957 (in *The modern theater*, vol 5).
Roméo et Jeannette, 1946 (in *Nouvelles pièces noires* above). Tr. M. John?, *Romeo and Jeannette*, New York 1958 (in *Jean Anouilh*, vol 1 above).
L'invitation, au château, 1948. Tr. C. Fry, *Ring round the moon*, New York and London 1950.
Ardèle, ou la marguerite, 1949. Tr. L. Hill, *Ardèle*, London 1951.
La répétition, ou l'amour puni, Paris and Geneva 1950. Tr. P. Hansford-Johnson and K. Black, *The rehearsal*, London 1961.
Pièces brillantes, 1951.
Colombe, 1951 (in *Pièces brillantes* above). Tr. D. Cannan, London 1952; tr. L. Kronenberger, New York 1954.
Cécile, ou l'école des pères, 1951 (in *Pièces brillantes* above). Tr. L. and A.

Klein, *Cecile, or the school for fathers*, Bloomington (Ind) 1956.

La valse des toréadors, 1952. Tr. L. Hill, *The waltz of the toreadors*, London 1953 (in *Plays of the year*, vol 8); 1956.

L'alouette, 1953. Tr. C. Fry, *The lark*, London 1955; tr. L. Hill, New York 1959 (in *Jean Anouilh*, vol 2 above).

Ornifle, ou le courant d'air, 1955.

Pièces grinçantes, 1956.

Pauvre Bitos, 1956 (in *Pièces grinçantes* above). Tr. L. Hill, *Poor Bitos*, London and New York 1964.

L'Hurluberlu, 1959. Tr. L. Hill, *The fighting cock*, New York 1960.

Becket, ou l'honneur de Dieu, 1959. Tr. L. Hill, *Becket, or the honour of God*, New York 1960.

Pièces costumées, 1960.

La foire d'empoigne, 1960 (in *Pièces costumées* above). Tr. L. Hill, *Catch as catch can*, New York 1967 (in *Jean Anouilh*, vol 3 above).

La grotte, 1961. Tr. L. Hill, *The cavern*, New York 1966.

La boulanger, la boulangère et le petit mitron, 1969.

Cher Antoine, ou l'amour raté, 1969. Tr. L. Hill, *Dear Antoine, or the love that failed*, New York 1971.

Les poissons rouges, 1970.

Ne réveillez pas Madame, 1970.

Le directeur de l'Opéra, 1972. Tr. L. Hill, *The director of the Opera*, London 1973.

HARVEY, J., *Anouilh, A study in theatrics*, New Haven (Conn) 1964.

JOLIVET, P., *Le théâtre de Jean Anouilh*, 1963 (incl. bibl.).

LUPPÉ, R. de, *Jean Anouilh*, 1959.

PRONKO, L. C., *The world of Jean Anouilh*, Berkeley (Calif) and London 1961.

THODY, P., *Anouilh*, Edinburgh 1968.

VANDROMME, P., *Jean Anouilh, un auteur et ses personnages*, 1965 (incl. criticism by Anouilh).

APOLLINAIRE, Guillaume   1880–1918
(pseudonym of Wilhelm Apollinaris de Kostrowitzky)

ADÉMA, M., *Bibliographie générale de l'oeuvre*, 1949.
See also his *Guillaume Apollinaire* below.

Oeuvres complètes, ed. M. Décaudin, 4 vols, 1963.
Oeuvres poétiques [. . .] *Théâtre*, ed. M. Adéma and M. Décaudin, 1956.

Tr. R. Shattuck, *Selected writings*, London 1950; Norfolk (Conn) 1971.
Tr. O. Bernard, *Selected poems*, Harmondsworth 1965.
Also translated in anthologies, incl. *An anthology of French poetry from Nerval to Valéry*, ed. A. Flores, New York 1958.

L'enchanteur pourrissant, 1909; ed. J. Burgos, 1972.

L'hérésiarque et Cie, 1910; ed. P. Pia, 1954. Tr. R. I. Hall, *The Heresiarch and Co.*, New York 1965 (London 1967, as *The wandering Jew and other stories*).

Les peintres cubistes, 1913. Tr. L. Abel, *Cubist painters*, New York 1944; 1962.

Alcools, 1913; ed. R. Lefèvre, 1965. Tr. A. H. Greet, Berkeley (Calif) and London 1965; tr. W. Meredith, New York 1965.

Le poète assassiné, 1913; ed. M. Décaudin, 1959. Tr. R. Padgett, *The poet assassinated*, London and New York 1968.

Les mamelles de Tirésias, 1918. Tr. L. Simpson, *The breasts of Tiresias*, New York 1964 (in *Modern French theater*).

Calligrammes, 1918.

La femme assise, 1920.

Il y a, 1925.

Anecdotiques, 1926; ed. M. Adéma, 1955.

Ombre de mon amour, recueil posthume, Geneva 1948.

Les diables amoureux, ed. M. Décaudin, 1964.

Lettres à sa marraine, 1915–1918, 1948; ed. M. Adéma, 1951.

Tendre comme le souvenir (letters), 1952.

Lettres à Lou, ed. M. Décaudin, 1969.

ADÉMA, M., *Guillaume Apollinaire le mal-aimé*, 1952. Tr. D. Folliot, *Apollinaire*, London 1954.
　　Guillaume Apollinaire, 1968 (incl. bibl.).

BATES, S., *Guillaume Apollinaire*, New York 1967.

BONNEFOY, C., *Apollinaire*, 1969.

CARMODY, F. J., *The evolution of Apollinaire's poetics, 1901–1914*, Berkeley (Calif) 1963.

DAVIES, M., *Apollinaire*, London and New York 1964.

DURRY, M. J., *Guillaume Apollinaire, Alcools*, 3 vols, 1956–65.

PIA, P., *Apollinaire par lui-même*, 1954.

ROUVEYRE, A., *Apollinaire*, 1945.

SHATTUCK, R., *The banquet years: the arts in France 1885–1918*, London 1959; 1969.

STEEGMULLER, F., *Apollinaire, poet among the painters*, New York and London 1964.

ARAGON, Louis 1897–

Lui Aragon, bio-bibliografichesky ukazatel', Moscow 1956.
See also GINDINE below.

Poésies, anthologie 1917–1960, 1960.

Oeuvres romanesques croisées, 1964 onwards (38 vols pbd; novels of Aragon and Elsa Triolet pbd jointly).

L'oeuvre poétique, ed. J. Ristat, 12 vols, 1974.

Tr. S. Spender, R. Humphries, et al., ed. H. Josephson and M. Cowley, *Aragon, poet of the French Resistance*, New York 1945 (selection; London 1946, as *Aragon, poet of resurgent France*).

Feu de joie, 1920.

Le paysan de Paris, 1926. Tr. S. W. Taylor, *Paris peasant*, London 1971.

Le mouvement perpétuel, 1926.

Le traité du style, 1928.

La grande gaîté, 1929.

Persécuté persécuteur, 1931 (incl. *Front rouge*, tr. E. E. Cummings, *Red Front*, Chapel Hill (NC) 1933).

Le monde réel, 1934–51. Comprising:

> *Les cloches de Bâle*, 1934. Tr. H. M. Chevalier, *The bells of Basel*, New York 1936.
>
> *Les beaux quartiers*, 1936. Tr. H. M. Chevalier, *Residential quarter*, New York 1938.
>
> *Les voyageurs de l'impériale*, 1942. Tr. H. Josephson, *The century was young*, New York 1941; tr. H. M. Chevalier, *Passengers of destiny*, New York 1961.
>
> *Aurélien*, 1944. Tr. E. Wilkins, 2 vols, New York 1947.
>
> *Les communistes*, 6 vols, 1949–51; 4 vols, 1966–7 (in *Oeuvres romanesques croisées*, vols 23–6 above).

Hourra l'Oural, 1934.

Le crève-coeur, 1941.

Les yeux d'Elsa, 1942.

Le musée Grévin, Saint Flour 1943 (pbd clandestinely).

La Diane française, 1945.

Le nouveau crève-coeur, 1948.

La lumière de Stendhal, 1954.

Les yeux et la mémoire, 1954.

Littératures soviétiques, 1955.

Le roman inachevé, 1956.

La semaine sainte, 1958. Tr. H. M. Chevalier, *Holy Week*, New York and London 1961.

Elsa, 1959.

Les poètes, 1960.

Histoire de l'URSS 1917–1960, 2 vols, 1962 (in *Histoire parallèle*, with MAUROIS' *Histoire des Etats Unis*). Tr. P. O'Brian, *A history of the USSR from Lenin to Krushchev*, New York 1964.

Le fou d'Elsa, 1963.

La mise à mort, 1965.

Blanche, ou l'oubli, 1967.

Théâtre/roman, 1974.

ARBAN, D., *Aragon parle*, 1969.
L'Arc, no. 53, 1973.
BIBROWSKA, S., *Une mise à mort, l'itinéraire romanesque d'Aragon*, 1972.
GINDINE, Y., *Aragon prosateur surréaliste*, Geneva 1966 (incl. bibl.).
GARAUDY, R., *Du surréalisme au monde réel, l'itinéraire d'Aragon*, 1961.
GAVILLET, A., *La littérature au défi: Aragon surréaliste*, Neuchâtel 1958.
JUIN, H., *Aragon*, 1960.
ROY, C., *Aragon*, 1945.
SADOUL, G., *Aragon*, 1967.
SUR, J., *Aragon, le réalisme de l'amour*, 1966.

ARTAUD, Antonin   1896–1948

Oeuvres complètes, 1956 onwards (13 vols pbd).
L'ombilic des limbes, précédé de Correspondance avec Jacques Rivière et suivi de Le Pèse-nerfs, Fragments d'un journal d'Enfer, l'Art et la mort, Textes de la période surréaliste, introd. A. Jouffroy, 1968.

Tr. B. Frechtman et al., ed. J. Hirschman, *Artaud anthology*, San Francisco 1965.
Tr. P. Zweig, *Black poet and other texts*, 1966.
Tr. V. Corti and A. Hamilton, *Collected works*, London 1968 onwards (4 vols pbd).

L'ombilic des limbes, 1925. Tr. Corti, *Umbilical limbo*, in *Collected works*, vol 1 above.
Le pèse-nerfs, 1925. Tr. Corti, *Nerve scales*, in *Collected works*, vol 1 above.
Héliogabale ou l'anarchiste couronné, 1934.
Le théâtre et son double, 1938 (collected essays). Tr. M. C. Richards, *The theatre and its double*, New York 1958; tr. Corti, in *Collected works*, vol 4 above.
Artaud le Mômo, 1947.
Van Gogh, le suicidé de la société, 1947.
Les Cenci, 1964 (in *Oeuvres complètes*, vol 4 above). Tr. S. W. Taylor, *The Cenci*, London 1969; tr. Corti, in *Collected works*, vol 4 above.

ARMAN-LAROCHE, J. L., *Antonin Artaud et son double*, Périgueux and Paris 1964.
BONNETON, A., *Le naufrage prophétique d'Antonin Artaud*, 1962.
BRAU, J. L., *Antonin Artaud*, 1971.
CHARBONNIER, G., *Essai sur Antonin Artaud*, 1959.
HORT, J., *Antonin Artaud*, Geneva 1960.
SELLIN, E., *The dramatic concepts of Antonin Artaud*, Chicago (Ill) and London 1968.

BEAUVOIR, Simone de 1908–

Bibl. See WASMUND below.

BERGHE, C. L. van den, *Dictionnaire des idées dans l'oeuvre de Simone de Beauvoir*, 1966.

L'invitée, 1943. Tr. R. Senhouse and Y. Moyse, *She came to stay*, London 1949.
Pyrrhus et Cineas, 1944.
Les bouches inutiles, 1945.
Le sang des autres, 1945; ed. J. F. Davis, London 1973. Tr. R. Senhouse and Y. Moyse, *The blood of others*, London and New York 1948.
Tous les hommes sont mortels, 1946. Tr. L. Friedman, *All men are mortal*, Cleveland (Ohio) 1956.
Pour une morale de l'ambiguité, 1947. Tr. B. Frechtman, *The ethics of ambiguity*, New York 1948.
L'Amérique au jour le jour, 1948. Tr. P. Dudley, *America day by day*, London 1952.
Le deuxième sexe, 2 vols, 1950. Tr. H. M. Parshley, *The second sex*, London and New York 1953.
Les mandarins, 1954. Tr. L. Friedman, *The mandarins*, Cleveland (Ohio) 1956.
Privilèges, 1955 (incl. *Faut-il brûler Sade?*, tr. A. Michelson, *Must we burn De Sade?*, London and New York 1953, rptd in *The Marquis de Sade, with selections from his writings*, New York 1953).
La longue marche, essai sur la Chine, 1957. Tr. A. Wainhouse, *The long march*, London and Cleveland (Ohio) 1958.
Mémoires d'une jeune fille rangée, 1959. Tr. J. Kirkup, *Memoirs of a dutiful daughter*, London and Cleveland (Ohio) 1959.
  La force de l'âge, 1960. Tr. P. Green, *The prime of life*, London and Cleveland (Ohio) 1962.
  La force des choses, 1963. Tr. R. Howard, *The force of circumstance*, London and New York 1965.
  Tout compte fait, 1972. Tr. P. O'Brian, *All said and done*, New York 1974.
Une mort très douce, 1964. Tr. P. O'Brian, *A very easy death*, London and New York 1966.
Les belles images, 1966. Tr. P. O'Brian, London and New York 1968.
La femme rompue. L'âge de discrétion. Monologue, 1967. Tr. P. O'Brian, *The woman destroyed*, New York 1969.
La vieillesse, 1970. Tr. P. O'Brian, *The coming of age*, New York 1972 (and London, as *Old age*).

HOURDIN, G., *Simone de Beauvoir et la liberté*, 1962.

JEANSON, F., *Simone de Beauvoir ou l'entreprise de vivre*, 1966.

JULIENNE-CAFFIÉ, J., *Simone de Beauvoir*, 1966.

MARKS, E., *Simone de Beauvoir: encounters with death*, New Brunswick (NJ) 1973.

WASMUND, D., *Der Skandal der Simone de Beauvoir: Probleme des Selbstverwirklichung im Existentialismus*, Munich 1963 (incl. bibl.).

BECKETT, Samuel 1906–

FEDERMAN, R. and FLETCHER, J., *Samuel Beckett: His works and his critics: an essay in bibliography*, Berkeley (Calif) and London 1970.

DAVIS, R. J., BRYER, J. R., FRIEDMAN, M. J. and HOY, P. C., *Oeuvres et critique franco-anglaise*, 1972 (bibl. of works 1929–66 and criticism 1929–70).

Unless otherwise indicated, translations are by the author.

Proust, critical study, London 1931.

More pricks than kicks, London 1934.

Murphy, London 1938. French tr., Paris 1947.

Molloy, 1951. English tr. in collab. with P. Bowles, Paris and New York 1955.

    Malone meurt, 1951. English tr., *Malone dies, a novel*, New York 1956.

    L'innommable, 1953. English tr., *The unnamable*, New York 1958.

En attendant Godot, 1952. English tr., *Waiting for Godot*, New York 1954.

Watt, 1953. French tr. in collab. with L. and A. Janvier, 1968.

Nouvelles et textes pour rien, 1955. English tr., *Stories and texts for nothing*, New York 1967.

All that fall, New York and London 1957. French tr. in collab. with R. Pinget, *Tous ceux qui tombent*, Paris 1957.

Fin de partie, suivie de Acte sans paroles, 1957. English tr., *Endgame* [. . .] *followed by Act without words*, New York and London 1958.

From an abandoned work, London 1958. French tr. in collab. with L. and A. Janvier, *D'un ouvrage abandonné*, Paris 1957.

Krapp's last tape, and Embers, London 1959. French tr. in collab. with P. Leyris, *La dernière bande*, and, in collab. with R. Pinget, *Cendres*, Paris 1960.

Comment c'est, 1961. English tr., *How it is*, New York and London 1964.

Happy days, New York 1961. French tr., *Oh ! les beaux jours*, Paris 1963.

Cascando, Frankfurt-am-Main 1963 (with English tr., in *Dramatische Dichtungen*, vol 1).

Play, and two short pieces for radio, London 1964 (incl. *Words and music*). French tr., *Comédie et actes divers*, Paris 1966 (incl. *Paroles et musique; Comédie* first pbd Frankfurt-am-Main 1964, in *Dramatische Dichtungen*, vol 2).

Imagination morte imaginez, 1965. English tr., *Imagination dead imagine*, London 1965.

Gedichte, Frankfurt-am-Main 1966 (collected poetry in French).

Assez, 1966. English tr., *Enough*, London 1967 (in *No's knife*).

Bing, 1966. English tr., *Ping*, London 1967 (in *No's knife*).

Têtes-mortes, 1967.

Acte sans paroles 2, 1966 (in *Comédie et actes divers* above). English tr., *Act without words 2*, London 1967 (with *Eh Joe* below).

Eh Joe and other writings, London 1967. French tr. (*Eh Joe* only), *Dis Joe*, Paris 1966 (in *Comédie et actes divers* above).

Film, London 1967 (with *Eh Joe* above). French tr., Frankfurt-am-Main 1968 (in *Film, He Joe, in drei Sprachen*).

Come and go, London 1967. French tr., *Va et vient*, Paris 1966 (in *Comédie et actes divers* above).

Sans, 1969. English tr., *Lessness*, London 1970.

Le dépeupleur, 1970. Tr., *The lost ones*, London 1972.

Mercier et Camier, 1970.

Premier amour, 1970.

Breath and other shorts, 1971 (with *Come and go, Act without words 1 and 2*, and *From an abandoned work* above).

COE, R. N., *Samuel Beckett*, New York, Edinburgh and London 1964.

COHN, R., *Samuel Beckett: the comic gamut*, New Brunswick (NJ) 1962.

ESSLIN, M., ed., *Samuel Beckett: a collection of critical essays*, Englewood Cliffs (NJ) 1965.

FEDERMAN, R., *Journey to chaos: Samuel Beckett's early fiction*, Berkeley (Calif) and Cambridge 1965.

FLETCHER, J., *The novels of Samuel Beckett*, London and New York 1964; 1970.

    Samuel Beckett's art, New York and London 1967.

GROSSVOGEL, D. I., in his *Four playwrights and a postscript*, Ithaca (NY) 1962.

GUICHARNAUD, J., in his *Modern French theatre*, New Haven (Conn) 1961.

HOFFMAN, F. J., *Samuel Beckett: the language of self*, Carbondale (Ill) 1962.

JACOBSEN, J. and MUELLER, W. R., *The testament of Beckett*, New York 1964.

JANVIER, L., *Pour Samuel Beckett*, 1966.

    Samuel Beckett par lui-même, 1969.

KENNER, H., *Samuel Beckett*, New York 1962; Berkeley (Calif) 1968.

MÉLÈSE, P., *Beckett, théâtre de tous les temps*, 1966.

ROBINSON, M., *The long sonata of the dead*, London and New York 1969.

BERGSON, Henri   1859–1941

Bibl. See ARBOUR below.

Oeuvres, 7 vols, Geneva 1945; ed. A. Robinet, 1959.

Ecrits et paroles, ed. R. M. Mossé-Bastide, 3 vols, 1957–60.

Essai sur les données immédiates de la conscience, 1889. Tr. F. L. Pogson, *Time and free will*, London and New York 1910.

Matière et mémoire, 1896. Tr. N. M. Paul and W. Scott Palmer, *Matter and memory*, London and New York 1911.

Le rire, 1900. Tr. C. Brereton and F. Rothwell, *Laughter*, London and New York 1911.

L'évolution créatrice, 1907. Tr. A. Mitchell, *Creative evolution*, London and New York 1911.

L'énergie spirituelle, 1919. Tr. H. W. Carr, *Mind-energy*, London and New York 1920.

L'intuition philosophique, 1927 (first pbd in *Revue de Métaphysique et de Morale*, Apr. 1911).

Les deux sources de la morale et de la religion, 1932. Tr. R. Ashley Andra and C. Brereton, *The two sources of morality and religion*, London and New York 1935.

La pensée et le mouvant, 1934. Tr. M. L. Andison, *The creative mind*, New York 1946.

ALEXANDER, I. W., *Bergson: philosopher of reflection*, London 1957.

ARBOUR, R., *Henri Bergson et les lettres françaises*, 1955 (incl. bibl.).

DELEUZE, G., *Le bergsonisme*, 1966.

Etudes bergsoniennes, 1948 onwards.

GOUHIER, H., *Bergson et le Christ des évangiles*, 1962.

JANKELEVITCH, V., *Henri Bergson*, 1959.

LINDSAY, A. D., *The philosophy of Bergson*, London 1911.

THIBAUDET, A., *Le bergsonisme*, 1924.

BERNANOS, Georges   1888–1948

JURT, J., *Essai de bibliographie des études en langue française*, 2 vols, 1972–3 (covering 1926–71).

See also BRIDEL below; also Estève ed. of *Sous le soleil de Satan* below.

Oeuvres, 6 vols, Geneva 1947.

Oeuvres romanesques, suivies de Dialogues des Carmélites, ed. M. Estève, 1961.

Essais et écrits de combat, ed. M. Estève et al., 1971 onwards (1 vol pbd; incl. *La grande peur*, *Les grandes cimetières*, *Nous autres Français* and *Les enfants humiliés*).

Sous le soleil de Satan, 1926; ed. M. Estève, 1973 (extracts; incl. bibl.). Tr. V. Lucas, *The star of Satan*, London 1927; tr. P. Morris, New York and London 1940; tr. H. L. Binsse, *Under the sun of Satan*, New York 1949.

L'imposture, 1927.

La joie, 1929. Tr. L. Varèse, *Joy*, London 1948.

La grande peur des bien-pensants, 1931.

Un crime, 1935. Tr. A. Green, *The crime*, London 1936 (New York 1936, as *A crime*).

Journal d'un curé de campagne, 1936. Tr. P. Morris, *The diary of a country priest*, London and New York 1937.

Nouvelle histoire de Mouchette, 1937. Tr. J. C. Whitehouse, *Mouchette*, London and New York 1966.

Les grands cimetières sous la lune, 1938. Tr. P. Morris, *A diary of my times*, London and New York 1938.

Nous autres Français, 1939.

Lettres aux Anglais, Rio de Janeiro 1942 (first pbd in *Fontaine*, Paris, and *Cahiers libres*, Geneva 1942). Tr. H. L. Binsse, *Plea for liberty*, New York 1944; New York and London 1945 (with R. Bethell).

Monsieur Ouine, Rio de Janeiro 1943; Paris 1946. Tr. G. Dunlap, *The open mind*, London 1945.

Le chemin de la Croix-des-âmes, 2 vols, Rio de Janeiro, 1942.

La France contre les robots, 1947. Tr. anon., *Tradition of freedom*, London 1950.

Dialogues des Carmélites, Neuchâtel and Paris 1949. Tr. M. Legat, *The fearless heart*, London 1952; tr. G. Hopkins, *The Carmelites*, 1961.

Un mauvais rêve, 1951. Tr. W. J. Strachan, *Night is darkest*, London 1953.

Les enfants humiliés, journal 1939–1940, 1949. Tr. anon., *Tradition of Freedom*, London 1950.

BÉGUIN, A., *Bernanos par lui-même*, 1956.

BLUMENTHAL, G. R., *The poetic imagination of Georges Bernanos*, Baltimore (Md) and London 1966.

BRIDEL, Y., *L'esprit d'enfance dans l'oeuvre romanesque de Georges Bernanos*, 1966 (incl. bibl.).

Bulletin de la Société des amis de Georges Bernanos, 60 issues, 1949–69.
   Courrier Georges Bernanos, 1969 onwards.

DAUDET, L., *Révélation d'un grand romancier*, 1926 (in *Action Française*, 7 April).

ESTANG, L., *Présence de Bernanos*, 1947.

GILLESPIE, M. J., *Le tragique dans l'oeuvre de Bernanos*, 1960.

MILNER, M., *Georges Bernanos*, 1967.

PICON, G., *Georges Bernanos*, 1948.

SPEAIGHT, R., *Georges Bernanos, a study of the man and the writer*, London 1973.

URS VON BALTHAZAR, H., *Le chrétien Bernanos*, 1965 (tr. from German M. de Gandillac).

BRETON, André   1896–1966

SHERINGHAM, M., *A bibliography*, London 1972.
See also Bédouin ed. of *Oeuvres choisies* below.

Poèmes, 1948.
Oeuvres choisies, ed. J. L. Bédouin, 1950 (incl. bibl.).

Poésie et autre, ed. G. Legrand, 1960 (selection).

Tr. K. White, *Selected poems,* London 1969.

Les champs magnétiques (in collab. with Philippe Soupault), 1920.
Les pas perdus, 1924.
Manifeste du surréalisme. Poisson soluble, 1924; 1929;
    Second manifeste du surréalisme, 1930;
    1946 (*Les manifestes du surréalisme suivis de Prolégomènes à un troisième manifeste du surréalisme ou non*); 1962. Tr. R. Seaver and H. R. Lane, *Manifestos of surrealism,* Ann Arbor (Mich) 1969.
Le surréalisme et la peinture, 1928; 1965.
Nadja, 1928; 1963. Tr. R. Howard, New York and London 1960.
Les vases communicants, 1932.
Qu'est-ce que le surréalisme?, Brussels 1934. Tr. D. Gascoyne, *What is surrealism?,* London 1936.
Point du jour, 1934.
L'amour fou, 1937.
Fata morgana, Marseilles 1941 (banned by censorship); Buenos Aires 1942.
    Tr. C. Mills, Chicago 1969 (first pbd in *New Directions,* Norfolk (Conn) 1941).
Arcane 17, New York 1945.
Jeunes cerisiers garantis contre les lièvres, New York 1946 (with tr. by E. Roditi, *Young cherry trees secured against hares*).
La clé des champs, 1953.

AUDOIN, P., *Breton,* 1970.
BROWDER, C., *André Breton, arbiter of surrealism,* Geneva 1967.
CARROUGES, M., *André Breton et les données fondamentales du surréalisme,* 1950.
GRACQ, J., *André Breton: quelques aspects de l'écrivain,* 1948.
MAURIAC, C., *André Breton: essai,* 1949.
SARANE, A., *André Breton par lui-même,* 1971.

CAMUS, Albert   1913–1960

CRÉPIN, S., *Essai de bibliographie,* Brussels 1960.
FITCH, B. T., *Essai de bibliographie des études en langue française consacrées à Albert Camus, 1937–1962,* 1965; 1972 (to 1970; in collab. with P. C. Hoy).
ROEMING, R. F., *A bibliography,* Madison (Wis) and London 1968.
HOY, P. C., *Camus in English,* Melton Mowbray 1968; Paris 1971 (contributions to periodicals 1945–68).

Oeuvres complètes, ed. A. Sauret, 6 vols, 1962; ed. R. Quilliot, 2 vols, 1962–5.

Tr. S. Gilbert and J. O'Brien, *The complete fiction,* London 1960; *Collected plays,* London 1965 (without *State of siege*).
L'envers et l'endroit, Algiers 1937.

Noces, Algiers 1939 (incl. *L'été à Algiers*, tr. J. O'Brien, *Summer in Algiers*, London and New York 1955, in *The myth of Sisyphus and other essays*).

L'étranger, 1942. Tr. S. Gilbert, *The outsider*, London 1946 (New York 1946, as *The stranger*).

Le mythe de Sisyphe, 1942. Tr. J. O'Brien, in *The myth of Sisyphus and other essays*, London and New York 1955.

Le malentendu [. . .] *suivie de Caligula*, 1944; ed. P. Thody, London 1973 (*Caligula*). Tr. S. Gilbert, *Caligula and Cross purpose*, London 1947.

Lettres à un ami allemand, 1945. Tr. J. O'Brien, *Letters to a German friend*, London and New York 1961 (in *Resistance, rebellion and death*).

La peste, 1947; ed. W. J. Strachan, London 1962. Tr. S. Gilbert, *The plague*, London and New York 1948.

L'état de siège, 1948. Tr. S. Gilbert, *State of siege*, New York 1958 (in *Caligula and three other plays*).

Les justes, 1950; ed. E. O. Marsh, London 1960. Tr. S. Gilbert, *The just assassins*, New York 1958 (in *Caligula and three other plays*).

Actuelles, 3 vols, 1950–8 (collected political writings). Tr. J. O'Brien, New York 1961 (parts, in *Resistance, rebellion and death*). Comprising:
> *Chroniques 1944–1948*, 1950.
> *Chroniques 1948–1953*, 1953.
> *Chronique algérienne, 1939–1958*, 1958.

L'homme révolté, 1951. Tr. A. Bower, *The rebel*, London 1953.

L'été, 1954 (incl. *L'exil d'Hélène, Le minotaure ou la halte d'Oran*, and *Retour à Tipasa*, tr. J. O'Brien, *Helen's exile, The minotaur or the stop in Oran*, and *Return to Tipasa*, London and New York 1955, in *The myth of Sisyphus and other essays*).

La chute, 1956. Tr. J. O'Brien, *The fall*, London and New York 1957.

L'exil et le royaume, 1957. Tr. J. O'Brien, *Exile and the kingdom*, London and New York 1958.

Carnets: mai 1935–février 1942, 1962. Tr. P. Thody, *Carnets 1935–1942*, London 1963 (New York 1963, as *Notebooks*).
> *Carnets: janvier 1942–mars 1951*, 1964. Tr. P. Thody, *Notebooks 1942–1951*, New York 1963.

BRÉE, G., *Camus*, New Brunswick 1958.

CRUICKSHANK, J., *Albert Camus and the literature of revolt*, New York 1960.

KING, A., *Camus*, Edinburgh and London 1964.

LEBESQUE, M., *Camus par lui-même*, 1964.

LUPPÉ, R. de, *Albert Camus*, 1951. Tr. J. Cumming and J. Hargreaves, London 1967.

O'BRIEN, C. C., *Camus*, London 1970.

QUILLIOT, R., *La mer et les prisons*, 1956.

SARTRE, J. P., in his *Situations I*, 1947.

SCOTT, N. A., *Albert Camus*, New York and London 1962; 1969.

THODY, P., *Albert Camus, a study of his work*, New York and London 1957.
Albert Camus 1913–1960, London 1961.

CÉLINE, Louis Ferdinand   1894–1961
(pseudonym of Louis-Ferdinand Destouches)

Bibl. See OSTROVSKY below; also ROUX, *Cahier L.-F. Céline* below.

Oeuvres, ed. J. A. Ducourneau, 1966 onwards (4 vols pbd).

Voyage au bout de la nuit, 1932; 1962. Tr. J. P. Marks, *Journey to the end of the night*, London and Boston (Mass) 1934.
L'église, 1933.
Mea culpa suivi de La vie et l'oeuvre de Semmelweiss, 1936. Tr. R. A. Parker, *Mea culpa, with The life and work of Semmelweiss*, London and New York 1937.
Mort à crédit, 1936; 1962 (with *Voyage au bout de la nuit* above). Tr. J. P. Marks, *Death on the instalment plan*, London and Boston (Mass) 1938; tr. R. Manheim, New York 1966.
Bagatelles pour un massacre, 1937.
L'école des cadavres, 1938.
Les beaux draps, 1941.
Guignol's band, 1944. Tr. B. Frechtman and J. T. Nile, Norfolk (Conn) and London 1954.
    Le pont de Londres, 1964.
Le casse-pipe, 1949.
Féerie pour une autre fois, 1952.
    Normance, 1954.
Entretiens avec le professeur Y, 1955.
D'un château l'autre, 1957. Tr. R. Manheim, *Castle to castle*, New York 1968.
Ballets sans personne, sans musique, sans rien, 1959.
Nord, 1960. Tr. R. Manheim, *North*, New York and London 1972.
Rigodon, 1969. Tr. R. Manheim, *Rigadoon*, New York 1974.

DEBRIE-PANEL, N., *Louis-Ferdinand Céline*, Lyon 1961.
OSTROVSKY, E., *Céline and his vision*, New York 1967 (incl. bibl.).
POULET, R., *Entretiens familiers avec Louis-Ferdinand Céline*, 1958; 1971.
RICHARD, J. P., *Nausée de Céline*, 1973.
ROUX, D. de, *La mort de Louis-Ferdinand Céline*, 1966.
    (ed.), *Cahier Louis-Ferdinand Céline*, 1973 (first pbd as *L'Herne*, nos 3 and 5, 1963–5).
THIHER, A., *Céline: the novel as delirium*, New Brunswick (NJ) 1972.
VANDROMME, P., *Louis-Ferdinand Céline*, 1962.

CENDRARS, Blaise 1887–1961
(pseudonym of Frédéric Sauser)

Bibl. See *Oeuvres complètes* below; also LEVESQUE below.

Oeuvres complètes, 8 vols, 1960–5 (incl. bibl. by H. Richard in vol 8); ed.
N. Franck, 15 vols, 1968–71.
Poésies complètes, 1944; 2 vols, 1967–8.

Tr. various, ed. W. Albert, *Selected writings*, New York 1966.

Les Pâques, poèmes, 1912 (later renamed *Les Pâques à New York*).
La prose du Transsibérien et de la petite Jehanne de France, poème, 1913. Tr.
J. Dos Passos, New York and London 1931 (with *Panama* below).
Le Panama, ou les aventures de mes sept oncles, poème, 1918. Tr. J. Dos Passos,
Panama, or the adventures of my seven uncles, New York and London 1931
(with other poems).
L'or; la merveilleuse histoire du général Johann August Suter, 1925. Tr.
H. L. Stuart, *Sutter's gold*, New York and London, 1926.
Moravagine, 1926. Tr. A. Brown, London 1968.
Dan Yack, 1927–9. Comprising:
1 *Le plan de l'aiguille*, 1927. Tr. anon., *Antarctic fugue*, London 1948.
2 *Les confessions de Dan Yack*, 1929.
Rhum, l'aventure de Jean Galmot, 1930.
Histoires vraies, 1937.
La vie dangereuse, 1938.
L'homme foudroyé, 1945. Tr. N. Rootes, *The astonished man*, London, 1970.
La main coupée, 1946. Tr. N. Rootes, *Lice*, London 1973 (abr.).
Bourlinguer, 1948. Tr. N. Rootes, *Planus*, London 1972.
Le lotissement du ciel, 1949.
Emmène-moi au bout du monde, 1956. Tr. A. Brown, *To the end of the world*,
London 1967.

BUHLER, J., *Blaise Cendrars, l'homme et l'oeuvre*, 1962.
LEVESQUE, J. H., *Blaise Cendrars; avec une anthologie*, 1946 (incl. bibl.).
LOVEY, J. C., *Situation de Blaise Cendrars*, Neuchâtel 1965.
PARROT, L., *Blaise Cendrars*, 1948; 1953.
T'SERSTEVENS, A., *L'homme que fut Blaise Cendrars, souvenirs*, 1972 (incl.
letters).

CÉSAIRE, Aimé 1913–

CASE, F. I., *Bibliographie*, Toronto 1973.

Aimé Césaire, ed. L. Kesteloot, 1962 (selection).

Cahier d'un retour au pays natal, 1947 (extracts first pbd in *Volonté*, no. 20, Aug. 1939); 1956. Tr. L. Abel and Y. Goll, *Memo on my Martinique*, New York 1947; tr. E. Snyders, *Return to my native land*, Paris 1968; tr. J. Berger and A. Bostock, Harmondsworth 1969.

Les armes miraculeuses, 1946; 1970.

Et les chiens se taisaient, 1946 (with *Les armes miraculeuses* above); 1956 (enl.).

Discours sur le colonialisme, 1951; 1955. Tr. J. Pinkham, *Discourse on colonialism*, New York and London 1972.

Lettre à Maurice Thorez, 1957. Tr. anon., *Letter to Maurice Thorez*, New York 1972.

Ferrements, 1960.

Cadastre, 1961 (cntg *Soleil cou coupé*, first pbd 1948, and *Corps perdu*, first pbd 1950). Tr. E. Snyders and S. Upson, New York 1973 (cntg *Beheaded sun* and *Disembodied*).

Toussaint-Louverture, 1961; 1962.

La tragédie du roi Christophe, 1963; 1970. Tr. R. Manheim, *Tragedy of King Christophe*, New York 1970.

Une saison au Congo, 1966; 1967. Tr. R. Manheim, *A season in the Congo*, New York 1969.

Une tempête (based on Shakespeare's *Tempest*), 1969. Tr. R. Manheim, *The tempest*, New York 1974.

BRETON, A., *Un grand poète noir*, New York 1943 (in *Hémisphères*, nos 3–4).

HARRIS, R. E., *L'humanisme dans le théâtre d'Aimé Césaire*, Ottawa 1973.

JUIN, H., *Aimé Césaire, poète noir*, 1956.

CHAR, René   1907–

BENOÎT, P. A., *Bibliographie des oeuvres de René Char de 1928 à 1963*, Ribaute-les-Tavernes (Gard) 1964.

See also BERGER below.

Poèmes et prose choisis, 1957.

Commune présence, 1964 (selected poems).

Poèmes, anthologie 1934–1969, 1970.

Translated in anthologies, incl. *French poetry from Baudelaire to the present*, tr. E. Marks, New York 1962; *Contemporary French poetry*, ed. A. Aspel and D. Justice, Ann Arbor (Mich) 1965.

Le marteau sans maître, 1934.

Seuls demeurent, 1945.

Feuillets d'Hypnos, 1946. Tr. J. Mathews, W. C. Williams et al., *Hypnos waking*, New York 1956.

Fureur et mystère, 1948.
Le soleil des eaux, 1949.
Lettera amorosa, 1953.
Recherche de la base et du sommet, suivi de Pauvreté et privilège, 1955.
La communication poétique, 1969.
Le nu perdu, 1971.

BERGER, P., *René Char*, 1956 (incl. bibl.).
GUERRE, P., *René Char*, 1961.
MOUNIN, G., *Avez-vous lu Char ?*, 1946.
RAU, G., *René Char, ou la poésie accrue*, 1957.

CLAUDEL, Paul   1868–1955

BENOIST-MÉCHIN, J. and BLAIZOT, G., *Bibliographie des oeuvres de Paul Claudel*, 1931.
LABRIOLLE, J. de, *Claudel and the English-speaking world*, London 1973 (ed. and tr. R. Little).
PETIT, J. et al., *Bibliographie des oeuvres de Paul Claudel*, 1973.
See also LESORT below; also WATERS below.

Théâtre, ed. J. Madaule, 2 vols, 1947–8; ed. J. Madaule and J. Petit, 2 vols, 1965–7 (enl.).
Oeuvres complètes, ed. R. Mallet, 26 vols, 1950–67.
Oeuvre poétique, ed. J. Petit, 1957.
Oeuvres en prose, ed. J. Petit and C. Galpérine, 1965.
Poésies, 1970 (selection).
Je crois en Dieu, ed. A. Du Sarment, 1961. Tr. H. Weaver, New York and London 1965.

Tr. J. Heard, *Three plays*, Boston 1945.

Tête d'or, 1890; 1901. Tr. J. S. Newberry, London and New Haven (Conn) 1919.
La ville, 1893; 1901; ed. J. Petit, 1967. Tr. J. S. Newberry, *The city*, London and New Haven (Conn) 1920.
Connaissance de l'Est, 1900; ed. G. Gadoffre, 1973. Tr. T. Frances and R. Benét, *The East I know*, London and New Haven (Conn) 1914.
L'arbre, 1901.
La jeune fille Violaine, 1901 (with *L'arbre* above).
  L'annonce faite à Marie, mystère, 1917. Tr. L. M. Sill, *The tidings brought to Mary*, London and New Haven (Conn) 1916; tr. W. Fowlie, Chicago (Ill) 1960.
Partage de midi, 1906. Tr. W. Fowlie, *Break of noon*, Chicago (Ill) 1960 (with *The tidings brought to Mary* above).

Art poétique, 1907. Tr. R. Spodheim, *Poetic art*, New York 1958.

Cinq grandes odes, 1910; 1913 (enl.). Tr. E. Lucie-Smith, *Five great odes*, London 1967.

L'otage, drame, 1911. Tr. F. Smith et al., *The hostage*, London and New Haven (Conn) 1917; tr. Heard above.

Cette heure qui est entre le printemps et l'été, cantate à trois voix, 1913.

Protée, drame, 1914 (in *Deux poèmes d'été*, with *Cantate à trois voix* above); 1927. Tr. J. S. Newberry, *Proteus*, Rome 1921.

Corona benignitatis anni Dei, 1915. Tr. M. David, *Coronal*, New York 1943.

Trois poèmes de guerre, 1915. Tr. E. J. O'Brien, *Three poems of the war*, London and New Haven (Conn) 1919.

Le pain dur, drame, 1918. Tr. Heard above.

L'ours et la lune, farce pour un théâtre de marionnettes, 1919.

Le père humilié, 1920. Tr. Heard above, *The humiliation of the father*.

Poèmes de guerre, 1914–1916, 1922.

Feuilles de saints, 1925.

Le soulier de satin ou le pire n'est pas toujours sûr, 4 vols, 1928–9. Tr. J. O'Connor and the author, *The satin slipper; or the worst is not the surest*, London and New Haven (Conn) 1931.

Positions et propositions, 2 vols, 1928–34. Tr. J. O'Connor, *Ways and Cross-ways*, New York 1933 (tr. of vol 1).

Le livre de Christophe Colomb, 1933. Tr. the author, A. Meyer et al., *The book of Christopher Columbus*, London and New Haven (Conn) 1930.

Jeanne d'Arc au bûcher, 1939. Tr. D. Arundell, Paris and New York 1939; 1947.

L'histoire de Tobie et de Sara, 1942; 1953. Tr. A. Fiske, *Tobias and Sara*, New York 1962 (in *Port-Royal and other plays*).

Poèmes et paroles pendant la Guerre de Trente Ans, 1945.

Journal, ed. F. Varillon and J. Petit, 2 vols, 1968–9.

Mémoires improvisés, quarante et un entretiens avec Jean Amrouche (text of broadcast interviews), ed. L. Fournier, 1969.

Paul Claudel et André Gide, correspondance 1899–1926, ed. R. Mallet, 1949. Tr. J. Russell, *The correspondence, 1899–1926, between Paul Claudel and André Gide*, London and New York 1952.

BARJON, L., *Paul Claudel*, 1953.

BASTIEN, J., *L'oeuvre dramatique de Paul Claudel*, Rheims 1957.

BEAUMONT, E., *The theme of Beatrice in the plays of Claudel*, London 1954. Tr. H. Foster, *Le sens de l'amour dans le théâtre de Claudel*, East Lansing (Mich) 1966.

Bulletin de la Société Paul Claudel, 1958 onwards.

Cahiers Paul Claudel, 1959 onwards.

CHAIGNE, L., *Vie de Paul Claudel et genèse de son oeuvre*, 1961; 1962.

CHIARI, J., *The poetic drama of Paul Claudel*, New York and London 1954.
CHONEZ, C., *Introduction à Paul Claudel*, 1947.
GADOFFRE, G., *Claudel et l'univers chinois*, 1969.
GUILLEMIN, H., *Claudel et son art d'écrire*, 1955.
LESORT, P. A., *Paul Claudel par lui-même*, 1963 (incl. bibl.).
MADAULE, J., *Le génie de Paul Claudel*, 1933.
   Le drame de Paul Claudel, 1935; 1964.
MERCIER-CAMPICHE, M., *Le théâtre de Claudel*, 1969.
PERCHE, L., *Paul Claudel, une étude*, 1952.
WATERS, H. A., *Paul Claudel*, New York 1970 (incl. bibl.).

COCTEAU, Jean   1889–1963

Bibl. See CROSLAND below; also KIHM below.

Oeuvres complètes, 11 vols, Lausanne 1946–51.
Théâtre complet, 2 vols, 1957.

Tr. various, *Five plays*, New York 1961.
Tr. various, *The infernal machine and other plays*, Norfolk (Conn) 1964.
Tr. M. Crosland et al., *Cocteau's world*, London 1972 (selection).

La lampe d'Aladin, 1909.
Le Cap de Bonne Espérance, 1919.
Le Potomak, 1913–1914, 1919; 1924 (with *Prospectus 1916*).
   La fin du Potomak, 1939.
Plain-chant, poèmes, 1923.
Thomas l'Imposteur, histoire, 1923. Tr. L. Galantière, *Thomas the Impostor*,
   New York and London 1925; tr. D. Williams, *The impostor*, London 1947.
Le grand écart, roman, 1923. Tr. L. Galantière, *The grand écart*, New York
   and London 1925; tr. D. Williams, *The miscreant*, London 1958.
Les mariés de la Tour Eiffel, 1924. Tr. D. Fitts, *The wedding on the Eiffel
   Tower*, New York 1937 (in *New Direction*); tr. M. Benedikt, 1964 (in
   Modern French theater).
Roméo et Juliette (based on Shakespeare), 1926.
Orphée, tragédie, 1927. Tr. C. Wildman, London 1933; tr. J. Savacool,
   Orpheus, in *The infernal machine and other plays* above.
Antigone, 1927 (with *Les mariés* above). Tr. C. Wildman, in *Five plays* above.
Opera, oeuvres poétiques 1925–1927, 1927.
Oedipe-roi, 1928 (with *Roméo et Juliette* above). Tr. C. Wildman, *Oedipus
   Rex*, London 1962; tr. E. E. Cummings, in *The infernal machine and
   other plays* above.
Les enfants terribles, roman, 1929; ed. R. K. Totten, London 1972. Tr. S.
   Putnam, *Enfants terribles*, New York 1930; tr. R. Lehmann, *Children of
   the game*, London 1955 (New York 1957, as *The holy terrors*).

Opium, 1930. Tr. E. Boyd, London 1932; tr. M. Crosland and S. Road, 1961.

La voix humaine, pièce, 1930. Tr. C. Wildman, *The human voice*, London 1951.

La machine infernale, pièce, 1934; ed. W. M. Landers, London 1957. Tr. C. Wildman, *The infernal machine*, London 1936; tr. A. Bermel, in *The infernal machine and other plays* above.

Portraits-souvenir, 1900–1914. Tr. M. Crosland, *Paris-album*, London 1956.

Les Chevaliers de la Table Ronde, pièce, 1937.

Les parents terribles, pièce, 1938; ed. R. K. Totten, London 1972. Tr. C. Franck, *Intimate relations*, London 1956 (in *From the modern repertoire*).

Les monstres sacrés, 1940. Tr. E. O. Marsh, *The holy terrors*, in *Five plays* above.

La machine à écrire, 1941. Tr. R. Duncan, *The typewriter*, London 1948.

Renaud et Armide, 1943.

Léone, 1944 (in *La Table Ronde*).

L'aigle à deux têtes, 1946. Tr. R. Duncan, *The eagle has two heads*, London 1948; tr. C. Wildman, *The eagle with two heads*, 1962.

La belle et la bête: journal d'un film, 1946. Tr. R. Duncan, *Diary of a film*, London and New York 1950.

Anna la bonne, Lausanne 1949 (in *Oeuvres complètes*, vol 8 above).

Bacchus, 1952. Tr. M. Hoeck, in *The infernal machine and other plays*, above.

Journal d'un inconnu, 1953. Tr. A. Brown, *The hand of a stranger*, London 1956.

Clair-obscur, poèmes, Monaco 1954.

Le cordon ombilical, 1962.

BROSSE, J., *Jean Cocteau*, 1970.

BROWN, F., *An impersonation of angels: a biography of Jean Cocteau*, London and Harlow 1969.

CROSLAND, M., *Jean Cocteau*, London and New York 1955 (incl. bibl. of works).

FOWLIE, W., *Jean Cocteau, the history of a poet's age*, Bloomington (Ind) 1966.

KIHM, J. J., *Cocteau*, 1960 (incl. bibl.).

MOURGUE, S., *Cocteau*, 1965.

OXENHANDLER, N., *Scandal and parade: the theatre of Jean Cocteau*, New Brunswick (NJ) 1957.

STEEGMULLER, F., *Cocteau*, London 1970.

SPRIGGE, E. and KIHM, J. J., *Jean Cocteau, the man and the mirror*, London and New York 1968.

COLETTE   1873–1954
(Sidonie-Gabrielle Colette)

Bibl. See Goudeket ed. of *Oeuvres complètes* below; also HARRIS below.

Oeuvres complètes, ed. M. Goudeket, 15 vols, 1948–50 (incl. bibl. in vol 15).

Tr. various, *The works*, 17 vols, London 1951–64.

Tr. various, ed. R. Phelps, *Earthly Paradise: an autobiography drawn from the lifetime writings*, London and New York 1966.

Les Claudine, 1900–3 (pbd under husband Willy's name). Comprising:
   Claudine à l'école, 1900. Tr. anon., *Claudine at school*, New York 1930; tr. A. White, London 1956.
   Claudine à Paris, 1901. Tr. J. Whitall, *Claudine in Paris*, London 1931 (and New York as *Young lady of Paris*); tr. A. White, New York 1958.
   Claudine en ménage, 1902. Tr. F. A. Blossom, *The indulgent husband*, New York 1935; tr. A. White, *Claudine married*, New York 1960.
   Claudine s'en va, 1903. Tr. A. White, *Claudine and Annie*, London 1962.
La retraite sentimentale, 1907.
Les vrilles de la vigne, 1908.
L'ingénue libertine, 1909. Tr. 'R.C.B.', *The gentle libertine*, London 1931.
La vagabonde, 1911. Tr. C. Remfry-Kidd, *Renée la vagabonde*, London and New York 1931; tr. E. McLeod, *The vagabond*, London 1954.
L'envers du music-hall, 1913. Tr. A. M. Callimachi, *Music-hall sidelights*, London 1957.
L'entrave, 1913. Tr. V. G. Garvin, *Recaptured*, London 1931; tr. A. White, *The shackle*, 1963.
Mitsou, ou comment l'esprit vient aux jeunes filles, 1919. Tr. J. Terry, *Mitsou, or how girls grow wise*, New York and London 1930; tr. R. Postgate, *Mitsou, or the education of young women*, London 1957.
Chéri, 1920. Tr. J. Flanner, New York 1929; tr. R. Senhouse, London 1951.
   La fin de Chéri, 1926. Tr. V. G. Garvin, *The last of Chéri*, London 1933; tr. R. Senhouse, 1951 (with *Chéri*).
La maison de Claudine, 1922. Tr. C. King, *The mother of Claudine*, London 1937; tr. E. McLeod and U. V. Troubridge, *My mother's house*, 1953.
Le blé en herbe, 1923. Tr. P. Mégroz, *The ripening corn*, London 1931; tr. R. Senhouse, *Ripening seed*, London 1955.
L'enfant et les sortilèges, 1925. Tr. C. Fry, *The boy and the magic*, London and New York 1964.
Sido, 1929. Tr. E. McLeod, London and New York 1953.
La naissance du jour, 1932. Tr. R. Benét, *A Lesson in love*, New York 1932 (and London, as *Morning glory*); tr. E. McLeod, *Break of Day*, London and New York 1961.
Ces plaisirs, 1932; 1941 (renamed *Le pur et l'impur*). Tr. E. Daly, *The pure and the impure*, New York 1933; tr. anon., *These pleasures*, London 1934; tr. H. Briffault, London 1968.
Duo, 1934. Tr. M. Laurie, *The married lover*, London 1935; tr. F. A. Blossom, New York 1935.
   Le Toutounier, 1939.

Mes apprentissages, 1936. Tr. H. Beauclerk, *My apprenticeships*, London 1957; tr. A. M. Callimachi, London 1957 (with *Music-hall sidelights* above).

De ma fenêtre, 1942.

Gigi, Lausanne 1944. Tr. R. Senhouse, New York 1952.

L'étoile vesper, Geneva 1946.

La fanal bleu, 1949. Tr. R. Senhouse, *The blue lantern*, London and New York 1963.

Contes des mille et un matins, 1970. Tr. M. Crosland and D. Le Vay, *The thousand and one mornings*, London 1973.

Lettres, ed. C. Pichois and R. Forbin, 1958 onwards (4 vols pbd). Comprising:
> *Lettres à Helène Picard*, 1958.
> *Lettres de la vagabonde*, 1961.
> *Lettres au petit corsaire*, 1963.
> *Lettres à ses pairs*, 1973.

CHAUVIÈRE, C., *Colette*, 1931.

CROSLAND, M., *Madame Colette*, London 1953.

GOUDEKET, M., *Près de Colette*, 1956. Tr. E. McLeod, *Close to Colette*, London 1957.

HARRIS, E., *L'approfondissement de la sensualité dans l'oeuvre romanesque de Colette*, 1973.

LARNAC, J., *Colette, sa vie, son oeuvre*, 1927.

MARKS, E., *Colette*, New Brunswick (NJ) 1960.

WILLY, *Indiscrétions et commentaires sur les Claudine*, 1963.

CROMMELYNCK, Fernand   1888–1970

CULOT, J. M., in his *Bibliographie des écrivains français de Belgique*, vol 1, Brussels 1958.

Théâtre complet, 1957.

Nous n'irons plus au bois, Brussels 1906.

Le sculpteur de masques, Brussels 1908 (1-act verse play); 1918 (3-act play in prose).

Les amants puérils, 1921.

Le cocu magnifique, 1921.

Carine, ou la jeune fille folle de son âme; Tripes d'Or, 1930.

Une femme qu'a le coeur trop petit, 1934.

Chaud et froid, ou l'idée de Monsieur Dom, 1941.

BERGER, A., *A la rencontre de Fernand Crommelynck*, 1947.

GROSSVOGEL, D. I., in his *Twentieth century French drama*, New York 1961.

LILAR, S., in her *Soixante ans de théâtre belge*, Brussels 1952. Tr. anon., *The Belgian theater since 1890*, New York 1950.

MALLINSON, V., in his *Modern Belgian literature, 1830–1960*, London 1966.

SURER, P., in his *Le théâtre français contemporain*, 1964.

DRIEU LA ROCHELLE, Pierre   1893–1945

Bibl. See GROVER below; also VANDROMME below.

Interrogation, 1917.
Fond de cantine, 1920.
Etat civil, 1921.
Mesure de la France, 1922.
Plainte contre inconnu, 1924.
L'homme couvert de femmes, 1925.
Le jeune Européen, 1927.
Blèche, 1928 (first pbd in *Revue de France* as *Boucles*).
Genève ou Moscou, 1928.
Une femme à sa fenêtre, 1930. Tr. P. Kirwan, *Hotel Acropolis*, London 1931.
Le feu follet, 1931. Tr. R. Howard, *The fire within*, New York 1965; tr. M. Robinson, *Will o' the wisp*, London 1966.
L'Europe contre les patries, 1931.
La comédie de Charleroi, 1934. Tr. D. Gallagher, *The comedy of Charleroi*, Cambridge 1973.
Journal d'un homme trompé, 1934.
Socialisme fasciste, 1934.
Rêveuse bourgeoisie, 1937; 1960.
Gilles, 1939 (censored ed.); 1942 (complete).
Notes pour comprendre le siècle, 1941.
Chronique politique, 1934–1942, 1943.
Le Français d'Europe, 1944 (banned).
Les chiens de paille, 1944 (banned); 1964.
Récit secret, 1951 (privately ptd).
Exorde, 1961 (with *Journal 1944–1945*, and *Récit secret* above). Tr. A. Hamilton, *Secret Journal and other writings*, Cambridge 1970.
Histoires déplaisantes, 1963.
Sur les écrivains, ed. F. Grover, 1964 (collected criticism).
Mémoires de Dirk Raspe, 1966.

ANDREU, P., *Drieu témoin et visionnaire*, 1952.

GROVER, F. G., *Drieu la Rochelle and the fiction of testimony*, Berkeley (Calif) and London 1958; 1962 (incl. bibl.).

VANDROMME, P., *Drieu la Rochelle*, 1958 (incl. bibl.).

DUHAMEL, Georges   1884–1966

SAURIN, M., *Les écrits de Georges Duhamel*, 1951 (covering 1907–50).
ZÉPHIR, J. J., *Bibliographie duhamé lienne*, 1972 (covering 1907–70).

Les oeuvres complètes, 28 vols, 1948–54 (selected works).

Des légendes, des batailles, 1907.
La lumière, pièce, 1911. Tr. S. Best, *The light*, Boston (Mass) 1914.
Compagnons, poèmes, 1912.
Le combat, pièce, 1913. Tr. S. Best, *The combat*, Boston (Mass) 1915.
Civilisation, 1914–1917, 1918. Tr. E. S. Brooks, *Civilisation, 1914–1917*, New York 1919; tr. T. P. Conwil-Evans, *Civilisation, 1914–1918*, London 1919.
Vie des martyrs, 1914–1916, 1917; 1929. Tr. F. Simmonds, *The new book of martyrs*, London and New York 1918.
Lapointe et Ropiteau, comédie, Geneva 1919.
L'oeuvre des athlètes, comédie, 1920 (with *Lapointe et Ropiteau* above).
Elégies, 1920.
Les hommes abandonnés, 1921.
Vie et aventures de Salavin, 5 vols, 1923–32. Tr. G. Billings, *Salavin*, London 1936. Comprising:
1 *Confession de minuit*, 1923. Tr., *Confession at midnight*.
2 *Deux hommes*, 1924. Not translated.
3 *Journal de Salavin*, 1927. Tr., *Salavin's journal*.
4 *Le club des Lyonnais*, 1929. Tr., *The Lyonnais club*.
5 *Tel qu'en lui-même*, 1932. Tr., *End of illusion*.
Le prince Jaffar, 1924.
Le voyage de Moscou, 1927.
Scènes de la vie future, 1930. Tr. C. M. Thompson, *America the menace*, London 1931.
Géographie cordiale de l'Europe, 1931.
Chronique des Pasquier, 10 vols, 1933–41. Tr. B. de Holthoir, *The Pasquier chronicles*, London 1937 (tr. of vols 1–5), *Cécile among the Pasquiers*, 1940 (tr. of vols 6–8), and *Suzanne and Joseph Pasquier* (tr. of vols 9–10). Comprising:
1 *Le notaire du Havre*, 1933. Tr., *News from Havre* (first pbd 1934).
2 *Le jardin des bêtes sauvages*, 1934. Tr., *Caged beasts* (first pbd 1935, as *Young Pasquier*).
3 *Vue de la terre promise*, 1934. Tr., *In sight of the promised land* (first pbd 1935).
4 *La nuit de la Saint-Jean*, 1935. Tr., *St John's Eve*.
5 *Le désert de Bièvres*, 1937. Tr., *The house in the desert*.
6 *Les maîtres*, 1937. Tr., *Pastors and masters*.
7 *Cécile parmi nous*, 1938. Tr., *Cécile*.
8 *Le combat contre les ombres*, 1939. Tr., *The fight against the shadows*.
9 *Suzanne et les jeunes hommes*, 1941. Tr., *Suzanne*.

10 *La passion de Joseph Pasquier*, Montreal 1944. Tr., *Joseph Pasquier*.

Lumières sur ma vie, 5 vols, 1945–53. Tr. B. Collier, *Light on my days*, London 1948 (tr. of vols 1–2). Comprising:

1 *Inventaire de l'abîme, 1884–1901*, 1944.
2 *Biographie de mes fantômes, 1901–1906*, 1945.
3 *Le temps de la recherche*, 1947.
4 *La pesée des âmes, 1914–1919*, 1949.
5 *Les espoirs et les épreuves, 1919–1928*, 1953.

Les voyageurs de l'Espérance, 1953.

FALLS, W. F., *Le message humain de Georges Duhamel*, 1948.

KEATING, L. C., *Critic of civilisation*, Lexington (Ky) 1965.

KNAPP, B. L., *Georges Duhamel*, New York 1972.

SANTELLI, C., *Georges Duhamel, l'homme, l'oeuvre*, 1947.

SIMON, P. H., *Georges Duhamel*, 1947.

TERRISSE, A., *Georges Duhamel éducateur*, 1951.

THÉRIVE, A., *Georges Duhamel, ou l'intelligence du coeur*, 1926.

DURAS, Marguerite 1914–
(pseudonym of Marguerite Donnadieu)

Théâtre, 2 vols, 1965–8.

Tr. S. Pitt-Rivers, et al., *Four novels*, New York 1965.
Tr. B. Bray and S. Orwell, *Three plays*, London 1967.

La vie tranquille, roman, 1944.

Un barrage contre le Pacifique, roman, 1950. Tr. A. White, *A sea of troubles*, London 1953; tr. H. Briffaut, *The sea wall*, New York 1953.

Le marin de Gibraltar, roman, 1952. Tr. B. Bray, *The sailor from Gibraltar*, London 1966.

Les petits chevaux de Tarquinia, roman, 1953. Tr. P. DuBerg, *The little horses of Tarquinia*, London 1960.

Des journées entières dans les arbres, 1954. Tr. Bray and Orwell above, *Days in the trees*.

Le square, roman, 1955. Tr. S. Pitt-Rivers and I. Morduch, *The square*, London 1959.

  Le square, 1965 (in *Théâtre*, vol 1 above). Tr. Bray and Orwell above, *The square*.

Moderato cantabile, 1958. Tr. R. Seaver, New York 1960.

Dix heures du soir en été, roman, 1960. Tr. A. Borchardt, *Ten-thirty on a summer night*, London 1962.

Hiroshima mon amour, scénario et dialogues, 1960. Tr. R. Seaver, London 1966.

Les viaducs de Seine-et-Oise, 1960. Tr. Bray and Orwell, *The viaducts of Seine-et-Oise*.

234

Une aussi longue absence, scénario et dialogues, 1961. Tr. B. Wright, London 1966 (with *Hiroshima mon amour,* tr. Seaver above).

L'après-midi de M. Andesmas, 1962. Tr. A. Borchardt, *The afternoon of Monsieur Andesmas,* London 1964.

Le ravissement de Lol V. Stein, 1964. Tr. R. Seaver, *The ravishing of Lol Stein,* New York 1966; tr. E. Ellenbogen, *The rapture of Lol V. Stein,* London 1967.

Les eaux et forêts, 1965 (in *Théâtre,* vol 1 above). Tr. B. Bray, *The rivers and forests,* London 1964 (with *The afternoon of Monsieur Andesmas* above).

La musica, 1965 (in *Théâtre,* vol 1 above).

Le vice-consul, Tr. E. Ellenbogen, *The vice-consul,* London 1968.

L'amante anglaise, 1967. Tr. B. Bray, London and New York 1968.

Suzanna Andler, 1968 (in *Théâtre,* vol 2 above).

Abahn, Sabana, David, 1970.

L'amour, 1971.

Détruire, dit-elle, 1972.

Nathalie Granger, suivi de La femme du Gange, 1973.

Les parleuses (in collab. with Xavière Gauthier), 1974.

BERGER, Y., *Marguerite Duras,* 1960.

Cahiers Renaud-Barrault, no. 52, 1965.

HALL, H., *L'univers romanesque de Marguerite Duras,* 1965.

VIRCONDELET, A., *Marguerite Duras: une étude, une biographie,* 1972.

ÉLUARD, Paul 1895–1952
(pseudonym of Eugène Grindel)

Bibl. See Dumas-Scheler ed. of *Oeuvres complètes* below; also JUCKER-WEHRLI below.

Oeuvres complètes, ed. M. Dumas and L. Scheler, 2 vols, 1968 (incl. bibl. in vol 2).

Poèmes pour tous; choix de poèmes 1917–52, 1963.

La jarre peut-elle être plus belle que l'eau?, 1951 (cntg *La vie immédiate, La rose publique, Les yeux fertiles, Cours naturel*).

Tr. S. Beckett et al., ed. G. Reavey, *Thorns of thunder: selected poems,* London 1936.

Tr. L. Alexander, *Selected writings,* Norfolk (Conn) 1951.

Mourir de ne pas mourir, 1924.

Capitale de la douleur, poésie, 1926 (incorporating *Mourir de ne pas mourir* above).

L'amour, la poésie, 1929.

L'immaculée conception (in collab. with André BRETON), 1930.

La vie immédiate, poèmes, 1932.

La rose publique, 1934.

Les yeux fertiles, 1936.

Donner à voir, 1939.

Poésie et vérité, Algiers 1942; Neuchâtel 1942 (enl.). Tr. R. Penrose and E. L. T. Mesens, *Poetry and truth*, London 1944.

Au rendez-vous allemand, 1944.

Poésie ininterrompue, 2 vols, 1946–53.

Une leçon de morale, poèmes, 1949.

Le dur désir de durer, 1946. Tr. S. Spender and F. Cornford, London and New York 1950.

Le livre ouvert I (1938–1940), 1940;
   Le livre ouvert II (1939–41), 1942;
1947 (1939–1944).

CAWS, M. A., in her *The poetry of Dada and Surrealism*, Princeton (NJ) 1970.

DECAUNES, L., *Paul Eluard*, 1965.

JUCKER-WEHRLI, U., *La poésie de Paul Eluard et le thème de la pureté*, Zurich 1965 (incl. bibl. of works).

PARROT, L. and MARCENAC, J., *Paul Eluard*, 1953.

PERCHE, L., *Paul Eluard*, 1964.

FARGUE, Léon-Paul   1876–1947

Bibl. See CHONEZ below.

Poésies, 1963.

Nocturnes, 1905.

Tancrède, 1892–1894, 1911; 1943.

Poèmes (premier cahier), 1911.

Pour la musique, 1914.

Suite familière, 1928.

Espaces, 1929 (with *Vulturne*, first pbd 1928, and *Epaisseurs*, first pbd 1929).

Sous la lampe, 1930 (with *Suite familière* above, and *Banalité*, first pbd 1928).

D'après Paris, 1932.

Ludions, 1933; 1943 (with *Tancrède* above).

Le piéton de Paris, 1939.

Haute solitude, 1941.

Lanterne magique, 1944. Tr. G. Micholet-Coté, *The magic lantern*, London 1946.

Méandres, Geneva 1946.

BEUCLER, A., *Dimanche avec Léon-Paul Fargue*, 1947.
   Vingt ans avec Léon-Paul Fargue, 1952. Tr. G. Sainsbury, *The last of the Bohemians*, New York 1954 (London 1955 as *Poet of Paris: Twenty years with Léon-Paul Fargue*).

CHONEZ, C., *Léon-Paul Fargue*, 1950; 1959 (incl. bibl.).
LA ROCHEFOUCAULD, E. de, *Léon-Paul Fargue*, 1959.

FORT, Paul   1872–1960

Translated in anthologies, incl. *Contemporary French poetry*, tr. J. Bithell, London 1912.

La petite bête, 1890.
Ballades françaises, 40 vols, 1897–1951; 17 vols, 1922–58; 1963 (selection).
   Tr. J. S. Newberry, *Selected poems and ballads*, New York 1921.
Chroniques de France, 1923–7. Comprising:
   Les compères du roi Louis, 1923.
   Ysabeau, 1924.
   Le camp du drap d'or, 1926.
   L'or, 1927 (with *Ruggieri*).
Mes mémoires, 1944.

BÉARN, P., *Paul Fort*, 1960.
CLAUZEL, R., *Paul Fort, ou l'arbre à poèmes*, 1925.
DONNAY, M. T., *Le Paul Fort que j'ai connu*, 1960.
MASSON, G. A., *Paul Fort*, 1922.

GENET, Jean   1910–

Bibl. See COE below; also MAGNAN below.

Poèmes, Lyon 1948; 1962.
Oeuvres complètes, 1951 onwards (4 vols pbd).

Tr. R. Seaver, *Reflections on the theatre, and other writings*, London 1972.

Le condamné à mort, Fresnes septembre 1942, n.p.n.d.; Décines (Isère) 1966 (with other poems). Tr. various, *The man condemned to death*, New York 1965 (pirate ed.).
Notre Dame des Fleurs, Monaco 1944. Tr. B. Frechtman, *Our Lady of the Flowers*, Paris 1949.
Miracle de la rose, Lyon 1946. Tr. B. Frechtman, *Miracle of the rose*, New York and London 1966.
Pompes funèbres, n.p. (given as Bikini) 1947. Tr. B. Frechtman, New York 1969.
Querelle de Brest, n.p. 1947. Tr. G. Streatham, *Querelle of Brest*, London 1966.
Journal du voleur, 1949. Tr. B. Frechtman, *Thief's journal*, Paris 1954.
Haute surveillance, 1949; 1970. Tr. B. Frechtman, *Deathwatch*, New York 1954.

Les bonnes, Sceaux 1954. Tr. B. Frechtman, *The maids*, New York 1954.

Le balcon, Décines (Isère) 1956. Tr. B. Frechtman, *The balcony*, New York and London 1958.

Les nègres, Décines (Isère) 1958. Tr. B. Frechtman, *The blacks*, New York and London 1960.

Les paravents, Décines (Isère) 1961. Tr. B. Frechtman, *The screens*, New York 1962.

Lettres à Roger Blin, 1966. Tr. R. Seaver, *Letters to Roger Blin: Reflections on the theatre*, New York 1969; London 1972 (with other texts).

COE, R. N., *The vision of Jean Genet*, London 1968.

ESSLIN, M., in his *Theatre of the absurd*, New York 1961; 1968. Tr. M. Buchet et al., *Le théâtre de l'absurde*, Paris 1963.

DRIVER, T. F., *Jean Genet*, New York and London 1966.

GROSSVOGEL, D. I., in his *Twentieth century French drama*, New York 1961.

MACMAHON, J. H., *The imagination of Jean Genet*, New Haven (Conn) 1963.

MAGNAN, J. M., *Essai sur Jean Genet*, 1966 (incl. bibl.).

SARTRE, J. P., *Saint Genet, comédien et martyr*, 1952 (as *Oeuvres complètes*, vol 1 above). Tr. B. Frechtman, *Saint Genet, comedian and martyr*, New York 1963.

SONTAG, S., in her *Against interpretation*, New York 1967.

THODY, P., *Jean Genet, a study of his novels and plays*, London 1968.

WELLWARTH, G. E., in his *The theater of protest and paradox*, New York 1964.

GHELDERODE, Michel de   1898–1962
(pseudonym of Adhémar-Adolphe-Louis Martens)

CULOT, J. M., BRUCHER, R. et al., in their *Bibliographie des écrivains français de Belgique*, vol 2, Brussels 1966.

See also VANDROMME below.

Théâtre complet, 3 vols, Brussels 1942–3; 5 vols, Paris 1950–7.

Tr. G. Hauger and G. Hopkins, *Seven plays*, New York 1960.

Tr. G. Hauger, *Seven plays II*, New York 1964.

L'histoire comique de Keizer Karel, Louvain 1922.

Ixelles, mes amours; poèmes 1924–1927, Ostend 1928.

Escurial, Brussels 1928 (in *Théâtre*, vol 2). Tr. L. Abel, New York 1957 (in *The modern theatre*, vol 5).

Barabbas, Brussels and Paris 1932. Tr. Hauger, in *Seven plays* above.

Pantagleize, Brussels and Paris 1934. Tr. Hauger, in *Seven plays* above.

Les femmes au tombeau, tragédie pour marionnettes, Brussels 1934. Tr. Hauger, *The women at the tomb*, in *Seven plays* above.

Sire Halewyn, Brussels 1934. Tr. Hopkins, *Lord Halewyn*, in *Seven plays* above.

Hop Signor !, Brussels 1938. Tr. Hauger, in *Seven plays II* above.

Sortilèges, Brussels and Paris 1941; Liège and Paris 1947; Verviers and Brussels 1962 (enl., as *Sortilèges et autres contes crépusculaires*).

Mademoiselle Jaïre, Brussels 1942 (in *Théâtre complet*, vol 1 above). Tr. Hauger, *Miss Jaïrus*, in *Seven plays II* above.

L'Ecole des bouffons, Brussels 1942 (in *Théâtre complet*, vol 2 above). Tr. K. S. White, *School for buffoons*, San Francisco (Calif) 1968.

Fastes d'enfer, Brussels 1943 (in *Théâtre complet*, vol 3 above). Tr. Hauger, *Chronicles of Hell*, in *Seven plays* above.

La Flandre est un songe, Brussels 1953.

Les entretiens d'Ostende recueillis par Roger Iglesis et Alain Trutat, 1956 (text of broadcast interviews). Tr. Hauger, *Selections from the Ostend interviews*, in *Seven plays* above.

DECOCK, J., *Le théâtre de Michel de Ghelderode*, 1969.

FRANCIS, J., *Michel de Ghelderode, dramaturge des pays de par deça*, Brussels 1949.

LILAR, S., in her *Soixante ans de théâtre belge*, Brussels 1952. Tr. anon., *The Belgian theater since 1890*, New York 1950.

VANDROMME, P., *Ghelderode*, 1963 (incl. bibl.).

WEISS, A., *Le monde théâtral de Michel de Ghelderode*, 1966.

GIDE, André   1869–1951

NAVILLE, A., *Bibliographie des écrits*, 1949; 1962 (revd J. Naville; completed to 1952).

FONGARO, A., *Bibliographie d'André Gide en Italie*, Florence 1966.

COTNAM, J., *Essai de bibliographie chronologique des écrits*, 1971 (first pbd in *Bulletin du Bibliophile*).

MARTIN, C., *Répertoire chronologique des lettres publiées*, 1971.

Oeuvres complètes, ed. L. Martin-Chauffier, 15 vols, 1932–9.
Théâtre complet, 8 vols, 1947–9.
Romans, récits et soties, oeuvres lyriques, 1958.

Tr. J. Mathews, *My theatre; five plays and an essay*, New York and Toronto 1952.
Les cahiers d'André Walter, 1891; 1930 (with *Les poésies d'André Walter*). Tr. W. Baskin, *The white notebook*, New York 1965 (part tr.); *The notebooks of André Walter*, New York 1968.
Le traité du Narcisse, 1891.
Le voyage d'Urien, 1893. Tr. W. Baskin, *Urien's voyage*, London and New York 1964.

Paludes, 1895. Tr. G. D. Painter, *Marshlands*, Norfolk (Conn) 1953.

Les nourritures terrestres, 1897; 1927.

  Les nouvelles nourritures, 1935.

  Tr. D. Bussy, *Fruits of the earth*, London and New York 1949.

Le Prométhée mal enchaîné, 1899. Tr. L. Rothermere, *Prometheus illbound*, London 1919; tr. G. D. Painter, *Prometheus misbound*, Norfolk (Conn) 1953 (with *Marshlands* above).

Le roi Candaule, 1901. Tr. Mathews, *King Candaulus*, in *My theatre* above.

L'immoraliste, 1902. Tr. D. Bussy, *The immoralist*, New York and London 1930; tr. R. Howard, New York 1970.

Prétextes, 1903. Tr. A. P. Bertocci et al., ed. J. O'Brien, *Pretexts*, London 1960 (selection).

  Nouveaux prétextes, 1911.

La porte étroite, 1909. Tr. D. Bussy, *Strait is the gate*, London and New York 1924.

Isabelle, 1911. Tr. D. Bussy, London and New York 1931 (in *Two symphonies*).

Souvenirs de la cour d'assises, 1913. Tr. P. A. Wilkins, *Recollections of the assize court*, London and Melbourne 1941.

Les caves du Vatican, 1914. Tr. D. Bussy, *The Vatican swindle*, New York 1925 (London and New York 1928, as *Lafcadio's adventures*; London 1952 as *The Vatican cellars*).

La symphonie pastorale, 1919. Tr. D. Bussy, London 1931 (in *Two symphonies*, with *Isabelle* above).

Dostoïevsky (incl. *Dostoïevsky d'après sa correspondance*, first pbd 1908), 1923. Tr. anon., *Dostoyevsky*, London 1925.

Corydon, 1924. Tr. H. Gibb, New York 1950.

Si le grain ne meurt, 3 vols, 1924. Tr. D. Bussy, *If it die . . .*, New York 1935.

Les faux-monnayeurs, 1925. Tr. D. Bussy, *The counterfeiters*, London 1928; 1950 (as *The coiners*).

Le journal des faux-monnayeurs, 1926. Tr. J. O'Brien, *Journal of the counterfeiters*, New York 1951 (with *The counterfeiters*, tr. Bussy above; London 1952, as *Logbook of the coiners*).

Voyage au Congo, 1927; 1927 (enl.). Tr. D. Bussy, *Travels in the Congo*, New York 1927; New York and London 1929 (enl.).

Le retour du Tchad, 1928. Tr. D. Bussy, in *Travels in the Congo* above, New York and London 1929.

L'école des femmes, 1929. Tr. D. Bussy, *The school for wives*, New York 1929.

  Robert, 1930. Tr. D. Bussy, London 1953 (with *The school for wives*).

  Geneviève, 1936. Tr. D. Bussy, London 1953 (with *The school for wives*).

L'affaire Redureau, 1930.

La séquestrée de Poitiers, 1930.

Retour de l'U.R.S.S., 1936. Tr. D. Bussy, *Back from the U.S.S.R.*, London 1937 (and New York, as *Return from the U.S.S.R.*).

Retouches à mon retour de l'U.R.S.S., 1937. Tr. D. Bussy, *Afterthoughts*, London 1938.

Thésée, New York 1946. Tr. J. Russell, *Theseus*, London 1948.

Et nunc manet in te, Neuchâtel 1947. Tr. J. O'Brien, London 1952 (and New York, as *Madeleine*).

Journal, 1939–50 (for the years 1889–1949); 1954 (1939–49, with *Souvenirs*). Tr. J. O'Brien, *The journals* [. . .] *1889–1949*, 4 vols, New York and London 1947–51; 2 vols, New York 1956 (abr.). Comprising:

Journal, 1889–1939, 1939.

Journal, 1939–1942, 1946 (parts first pbd New York 1944 and Algiers 1944).

Journal, 1942–1949, 1950.

Correspondance, ed. R. Mallet, 1948–55. Comprising:

Francis-Jammes—André Gide, 1948.

Paul Claudel—André Gide, 1949.

Paul Valéry—André Gide, 1955. Tr. J. Guicharnaud, *Self-portraits*, Chicago 1966 (abr.).

Correspondance André Gide—Arnold Bennett, ed. L. Brugmans, Geneva and Paris 1964.

Correspondance André Gide—Roger Martin du Gard, ed. J. Delay, 2 vols, 1968.

AMES, V. M., *André Gide*, New York 1947.

BOISDEFFRE, P. de, *Vie d'André Gide*, 1970 onwards (1 vol pbd).

BRÉE, G., *André Gide, l'insaisissable Protée*, 1954. Tr. and revd the author, *Gide*, New Brunswick (NJ) 1964.

DELAY, J., *La jeunesse d'André Gide*, 2 vols, 1956–8. Tr. J. Guicharnaud, *The youth of André Gide*, London and Chicago, 1963 (abr.).

GUÉRARD, A. J., *André Gide*, Cambridge (Mass) and Oxford 1951; 1969.

HYTIER, J., *André Gide*, Algiers 1938. Tr. R. Howard, London and New York 1963.

IRELAND, G. W., *Gide, a study of his creative writings*, Edinburgh, London and New York 1963; 1970.

LAFILLE, P., *André Gide, romancier*, 1954.

LAMBERT, J., *Gide familier*, 1958.

MARTIN DU GARD, R., *Notes sur André Gide, 1913–1951*, 1951. Tr. J. Russell, *Notes on André Gide*, London 1953 (and New York, as *Recollections of André Gide*).

MAURIAC, C., *Conversations avec André Gide*, 1952.

O'BRIEN, J., *Portrait of André Gide, a critical biography*, London and New York 1953.

PAINTER, G. D., *André Gide, a critical and biographical study*, London 1951; 1968 (revd and enl.). French tr. J. R. Major, *André Gide*, Paris 1968.

PIERRE-QUINT, L., *André Gide, sa vie, son oeuvre*, 1932; 1953. Tr. D. M. Richardson, *André Gide*, New York and London 1934.

SCHLUMBERGER, J., *Madeleine et André Gide*, 1956.

STARKIE, E., *André Gide*, New Haven (Conn) and London 1954.

THOMAS, D. L., *André Gide: the ethic of the artist*, New York and London 1950.

GIONO, Jean   1895–1970

Bibl. see BOISDEFFRE below; also REDFERN below.

Oeuvres, 5 vols, 1965–6.

Oeuvres romanesques complètes, ed. R. Ricatte, P. Citron and L. Ricatte, 1972 onwards (3 vols pbd).

Accompagnés de la flûte, 1924.

Trilogie Pan, 3 vols, 1929–30. Comprising:
> *Colline*, 1929. Tr. J. Leclercq, *Hill of Destiny*, New York 1929.
> *Un des Baumugues*, 1929. Tr. J. Leclercq, *Lovers are never losers*, London and New York 1931.
> *Regain*, 1930. Tr. H. Fluchère and G. Myers, *Harvest*, London, New York and Toronto 1939.

Naissance de l'Odyssée, 1930.

Le grand troupeau, 1931. Tr. N. Glass, *To the slaughterhouse*, London 1969.

Le chant du monde, 1934. Tr. H. Fluchère and G. Myers, *The song of the world*, New York 1937.

Que ma joie demeure, 1935. Tr. K. A. Clarke, *Joy of man's desiring*, New York 1940.

Les vraies richesses, 1936.

Refus d'obéissance, 1937.

Théâtre, 1943 (cntg *Le bout de la route*, *Lanceurs de graines*, *La femme du boulanger*).

L'eau vive, 1943.

Un roi sans divertissement, 1947.

Noé, 1947.

Les âmes fortes, 1949.

Les grands chemins, roman, 1951.

Le hussard sur le toit, 1951. Tr. J. Griffin, *The hussar on the roof*, London 1953.

Le moulin de Pologne, 1952. Tr. P. de Mendelssohn, *The malediction*, London 1955.

Le bonheur fou, 1957. Tr. P. Johnson, *The straw man*, New York 1959.

Angelo, 1958. Tr. A. E. Murch, London 1960.

Deux cavaliers de l'orage, 1965. Tr. A. Brown, *Two riders of the storm*, London 1967.

Le déserteur, 1966.

Ennemonde et autres caractères, 1968. Tr. D. Le Vay, *Ennemonde*, London 1970.

L'iris de Suse, 1970.
Le récits de la demi-brigade, 1972.

ANTONIETTO, F., *Le mythe de la Provence dans les premiers romans de Jean Giono*, Aix-en-Provence 1961.
BOISDEFFRE, P. de, *Giono*, 1965 (incl. bibl.).
CHONEZ, C., *Giono par lui-même*, 1956; 1961.
PUGNET, J., *Jean Giono*, 1955.
REDFERN, W. D., *The private world of Jean Giono*, Durham (NC) and Oxford 1967 (incl. bibl.).
SMITH, M. A., *Jean Giono*, New York 1966.
VILLENEUVE, R. de, *Giono ce solitaire*, 1955.

GIRAUDOUX, Jean   1882–1944

LE SAGE, L., *L'oeuvre de Jean Giraudoux: essai de bibliographie chronologique*, University Park (Pa) and Paris 1956.
    L'oeuvre de Jean Giraudoux 2, University Park (Pa) 1958 (critical bibl.).
See also ALBÉRÈS below; also RAYMOND below.

Théâtre complet, 16 vols, Neuchâtel and Paris 1945–53.
De pleins pouvoirs à sans pouvoirs, 1950 (late political essays).
Oeuvre romanesque, 2 vols, 1955 (novels and selected stories).
Oeuvres littéraires diverses, 1958 (most literary essays).

Tr. P. La Farge and P. H. Judd, *Three plays*, New York 1964.

Provinciales, nouvelles, 1909; 1927 (with *Premier rêve signé* and *Echo*).
L'école des indifférents, nouvelles, 1911; 1934.
Lectures pour une ombre, 1917.
Simon le pathétique, roman, 1918; 1926.
Elpénor, 1919; 1926 (enl.). Tr. R. Howard and R. Bruce, New York, 1958.
Amica America, 1919; 1938.
Adorable Clio, 1920.
Suzanne et le Pacifique, 1921. Tr. B. R. Redman, *Suzanne and the Pacific*, London and New York 1923.
Siegfried et le Limousin, roman, 1922. Tr. L. C. Wilxoc, *My friend from Limousin*, New York and London 1923.
    Siegfried, pièce, 1928. Tr. P. Carr, New York 1930; tr. La Farge and Judd, in *Three plays* above.
La prière sur la Tour Eiffel, 1923.
Juliette au pays des hommes, 1924 (with *La prière sur la Tour Eiffel* above).
Bella, 1926. Tr. J. F. Scanlan, London 1927.
Eglantine, roman, 1927.
Amphitryon 38, 1929. Tr. S. N. Behrman, New York and London 1930; tr. La Farge and Judd in *Three plays* above.

Les aventures de Jérôme Bardini, 1930.

Judith, 1931. Tr. J. Savacool, New York 1955 (in *From the modern theatre*, vol 3); tr. C. Fry, New York 1963 (in *Plays*).

La France sentimentale, 1932 (incl. *Visite chez le prince*, first pbd 1924).

Intermezzo, 1933. Tr. M. Valency, *The enchanted*, New York 1950.

Combat avec l'ange, 1934.

La guerre de Troie n'aura pas lieu, 1935. Tr. C. Fry, *Tiger at the gates*, London 1955.

Supplément au voyage de Cook, 1937. Tr. M. Valency, *The virtuous island*, New York 1956.

L'impromptu de Paris, 1937.

Electre, 1937. Tr. W. Smith, Bloomington (Ind) 1952 (in *From the modern repertoire*); tr. La Farge and Judd, in *Three plays* above.

La cantique des cantiques, 1938 (with *L'impromptu de Paris* above). Tr. H. Briffault, *Song of songs*, New York 1961 (in *The makers of the modern theater*); tr. J. Raikes, 1961 (in *The genius of the French theatre*).

Les cinq tentations de La Fontaine, 1938 (lectures).

Choix des élues, roman, 1938.

Ondine, 1939. Tr. M. Valency, New York 1954.

Pleins pouvoirs, 1939.

Littérature, 1941.

Sodome et Gomorrhe, 1943. Tr. H. Briffault, *Sodom and Gomorrha*, New York 1961 (in *The makers of the modern theater*).

Le film de Béthanie, texte de Les Anges du péché, 1944.

Armistice à Bordeaux, Monaco, Neuchâtel and Paris 1945.

Sans pouvoirs (unfinished), Monaco 1946.

L'Apollon de Bellac, Neuchâtel 1946. Tr. M. Valency, *The Apollo of Bellac*, New York 1954.

La folle de Chaillot, Neuchâtel and Paris 1946; ed. D. J. Conlan, Cambridge 1964. Tr. M. Valency, *The madwoman of Chaillot*, New York 1947.

Les contes d'un matin, 1952.

Pour Lucrèce, 1953. Tr. C. Fry, *Duel of angels*, New York 1959.

La menteuse, ed. R. M. Albérès and J. Bour, 1958. Tr. R. Howard, *Lying woman*, London 1972.

Les Gracques, ed. R. M. Albérès and J. Bour, 1958 (with *La menteuse* above).

ALBÉRÈS, R. M., *Esthétique et morale chez Jean Giraudoux*, 1957; 1962 (incl. bibl. by R. M. Albérès and L. Le Sage).

CELLER, M. M., *Giraudoux et la métaphore*, The Hague and Paris 1974.

COHEN, R., *Giraudoux: the three faces of destiny*, Chicago (Ill) and London 1968.

DEBIDOUR, V. H., *Jean Giraudoux*, 1963.

HOULET, J., *Le théâtre de Giraudoux*, 1945.

INSKIP, D., *Jean Giraudoux: the making of a dramatist*, London 1958.

LE SAGE, L., *Jean Giraudoux: his life and works,* University Park (Pa) 1959.
MARKER, C., *Giraudoux par lui-même,* 1952; 1959.
RAYMOND, A. G., *Giraudoux devant la victoire et la défaite,* 1963 (incl. critical bibl.).
SARTRE, J. P., in his *Situations I,* 1947.

GRACQ, Julien 1910–
(pseudonym of Louis Poirier)

HOY, P. C., *Essai de bibliographie, 1938–1972,* London 1973.

Au château d'Argol, 1938. Tr. L. Varèse, *The castle of Argol,* London and Norfolk (Conn) 1951.
Un beau ténébreux, 1945. Tr. W. J. Strachan, *A dark stranger,* Norfolk (Conn) 1951.
Liberté grande, 1946; 1958.
André Breton, 1947.
Essai, 1947 (preface to ed. of Lautréamont's *Chants de Maldoror*).
Le roi pêcheur, 1948.
La littérature à l'estomac, 1950. Tr. in *Transition,* no. 6, London 1950.
Le rivage des Syrtes, 1951.
Penthesilée (tr. from Heinrich von Kleist), 1954.
Un balcon en forêt, 1958. Tr. R. Howard, *Balcony in the forest,* London 1960.
Préférences, 1961; 1969 (enl.).
Lettrines, 2 vols, 1967–74.
La presq'île, 1970.

LEUTRAT, J. L., *Julien Gracq,* 1967.
MOURGUE, G., in his *Dieu dans la littérature d'aujourd'hui,* 1961.
PICON, G., in his *L'usage de la lecture,* vol 2, 1961.

GREEN, Julien 1900–

HOY, P. C., *Essai de bibliographie des études en langue française consacrées à Julien Green, 1923–1967,* 1970.
See also ALONSO below; also BURNE below.

Oeuvres complètes, 10 vols, 1954–65; ed. J. Petit, 3 vols, 1972–3.

Mont Cinère, 1926. Tr. W. J. Strachan, *Avarice House,* Norfolk (Conn) 1950.
Suite anglaise, 1927.
Adrienne Mesurat, 1927. Tr. H. L. Stuart, *The closed garden,* New York and London 1928.
Les clefs de la mort, 1929.
Léviathan, 1929 (with *Christine*). Tr. V. Holland, *The dark journey,* London 1928.

Epaves, 1932. Tr. V. Holland, *The strange river*, New York 1932.

Le visionnaire, 1934. Tr. V. Holland, *The dreamer*, London and New York 1934.

Minuit, 1936. Tr. V. Holland, *Midnight*, London, New York and Toronto 1936.

Memories of happy days, New York 1942 (in English).

Moïra, n.p. 1950. Tr. D. Folliot, London and New York 1951.

Sud, pièce, 1953. Tr. the author?, *South*, London 1956 (in *Plays of the year*, vol 12).

L'ennemi, 1954.

L'ombre, pièce, 1956.

Chaque homme dans sa nuit, roman, 1960. Tr. A. Green, *Each in his darkness*, London and New York 1961.

L'autre, roman, 1971. Tr. B. Wall, *The other one*, London 1973.

Jeunesse, 1974.

Journal, 9 vols, 1938–72. Tr. J. Godefroi, *Personal record, 1928–1939*, New York 1939; tr. A. Green, *Diary 1928–1957*, 1962 (selection). Comprising:

1 *Les années faciles, 1928–1934*, 1938; 1970.
2 *Derniers beaux jours, 1935–1939*, 1939.
3 *Devant la porte sombre, 1940–1943*, 1946.
4 *L'oeil de l'ouragan, 1943–1945*, 1949.
5 *Le revenant, 1946–1950*, 1951.
6 *Le miroir intérieur, 1950–1954*, 1955.
7 *Le bel aujourd'hui, 1955–1958*, 1958.
8 *Vers l'invisible, 1958–1967*, 1967.
9 *Ce qui reste de jour, 1967–1972*, 1972.

ALONSO, J. L., *La obra de Julien Green*, Burgos 1962 (incl. bibl.).

BRODIN, P., *Julien Green*, 1957.

BURNE, G. S., *Julien Green*, New York 1972 (incl. bibl.).

EIGELDINGER, M., *Julien Green et la tentation de l'irréel*, 1947.

FONGARO, A., *L'existence dans les romans de Julien Green*, Rome 1954.

GORKINE, M., *Julien Green*, 1956.

PETIT, J., *Julien Green*, 1969.

PRÉVOST, J. L., *Julien Green, ou l'âme engagée*, Lyons 1960.

SAINT-JEAN, R. de, *Julien Green par lui-même*, 1967.

SEMOLUÉ, J., *Julien Green, ou l'obsession du mal*, 1964.

STOKES, S., *Julien Green and the thorn of puritanism*, New York 1955.

HÉMON, Louis   1880–1913

Maria Chapdelaine, Montreal and Quebec 1916. Tr. A. Macphail, Montreal and Toronto 1921; tr. W. H. Blake, New York and London 1921.

La belle que voilà, 1923. Tr. W. A. Bradley, *My fair lady*, New York 1923.

Colin-Maillard, 1924. Tr. H. Richmond, *Blind man's buff*, London 1924.

Battling Malone, pugiliste, 1925. Tr. W. A. Bradley, *Battling Malone and other stories*, London 1925 (with *My fair lady* above).

Monsieur Ripois et la Nemesis, 1926. Tr. W. A. Bradley, *Monsieur Ripois and Nemesis*, New York and London 1925.

The journal, New York 1924 (tr. W. A. Bradley).

MACANDREW, A., *Louis Hémon, sa vie et son oeuvre*, 1936.

POTVIN, D., *Le roman d'un roman*, 1950.

IONESCO, Eugène   1912–

Bibl. See BENMUSSA below; also COE below; also VERNOIS below.

Théâtre, 4 vols, 1954–66.

Tr. D. Watson (vols 1–3 and 5–9) and D. Prouse (vol 4), *Plays*, 9 vols, London 1958–73.

La cantatrice chauve, 1954 (in *Théâtre* above, vol 1). Tr., *The bald prima-donna*, London 1958 (in *Plays* above, vol 1).

La leçon, 1954 (in *Théâtre* above, vol 1). Tr. *The lesson*, London 1958 (in *Plays* above, vol 1).

Jacques, ou la soumission, 1954 (in *Théâtre* above, vol 1). Tr., *Jacques or obedience*, London 1958 (in *Plays* above, vol 1).

Les chaises, 1954 (in *Théâtre* above, vol 1). Tr., *The chairs*, London 1958 (in *Plays* above, vol 1).

Victimes du devoir, 1954 (in *Théâtre* above, vol 1). Tr., *Victims of duty*, London 1958 (in *Plays* above, vol 2).

Amédée, ou comment s'en débarrasser, 1954 (in *Théâtre* above, vol 1). Tr., *Amédée, or how to get rid of it*, London 1958 (in *Plays* above, vol 2).

Tueur sans gages, 1958 (in *Théâtre* above, vol 2). Tr., *Killer*, London 1960 (in *Plays* above, vol 3).

Le nouveau locataire, 1958 (in *Théâtre* above, vol 2). Tr., *The new tenant*, London 1958 (in *Plays* above, vol 2).

L'avenir est dans les oeufs, 1958 (in *Théâtre* above, vol 2). Tr., *The future is in eggs*, London 1960 (in *Plays* above, vol 4).

Rhinocéros, 1959; ed. C. Abastado, 1970. Tr. D. Prouse, London 1960 (in *Plays* above, vol 4); tr. D. Watson 1962.

Notes et contre-notes, 1962 (collected articles). Tr. D. Watson, *Notes and counter-notes*, London 1964.

Le roi se meurt, 1963; ed. C. Audry, 1969. Tr. D. Watson, *Exit the king*, London 1964.

Le piéton de l'air, 1963 (in *Théâtre* above, vol 3). Tr., *A stroll in the air*, London 1965 (in *Plays* above, vol 6).

Délire à deux, 1963 (in *Théâtre* above, vol 3). Tr., *Frenzy for two*, London 1965 (in *Plays* above, vol 6).

La soif et la faim, 1966 (in *Théâtre* above, vol 4). Tr., *Hunger and thirst*, London 1968 (in *Plays* above, vol 7).

Présent passé, passé présent, 1968. Tr. H. R. Lane, *Present past, past present*, New York 1971.

Découvertes, Geneva 1969.

Jeux de massacre, 1970. Tr., *Here comes a chopper*, London 1971 (in *Plays* above, vol 8).

Macbett, 1972. Tr., London 1973 (in *Plays* above, vol 9).

Le solitaire, roman, 1973.

Journal en miettes, 1967. Tr. J. Stewart, *Fragments of a journal*, 1968.

ABASTADO, C., *Eugène Ionesco*, Paris and Montreal 1971.

BENMUSSA, S., *Ionesco*, 1966 (incl. bibl.).

COE, R. N., *Ionesco*, New York 1961 (incl. bibl.).

BONNEFOY, C., *Entretiens avec Ionesco*, 1970.

DONNARD, J. H., *Ionesco dramaturge*, 1966.

ESSLIN, M., in his *The theatre of the absurd*, New York 1961; 1968. Tr. M. Buchet et al., *Le théâtre de l'absurde*, Paris 1963.

GROSSVOGEL, D. I., in his *Four playwrights and a postscript*, Ithaca (NY) 1962.

GUICHARNAUD, J., in his *Modern French theatre*, New Haven (Conn) 1961; 1967

LAUBREAUX, R. (ed.), *Les critiques de notre temps et Ionesco*, 1973.

PRONKO, L. C., *Eugène Ionesco*, New York and London 1965.

SERREAU, G., in her *Histoire du nouveau théâtre*, 1966.

SONTAG, S., in her *Against interpretation*, New York 1966.

VERNOIS, P., *Le dynamique théâtrale d'Eugène Ionesco*, 1972 (incl. bibl.).

WELLWARTH, G. E., in his *The theater of protest and paradox*, New York 1964.

JACOB, Max   1876–1944

Bibl. See Auric ed. of *Nouvelles inédites* below.

Tr. and ed. S. J. Collier, *Drawings and poems*, Hull 1951 (selection). Also translated in anthologies.

Saint Matorel, 1911; 1936 (with *Oeuvres mystiques et burlesques de Frère Matorel*).

La côte, 1911.

Le cornet à dés, poèmes en prose, 1917; 1923 (enl.).

La défense de Tartuffe, 1919; 1964.

La laboratoire central, 1921.

Les pénitents en maillot rose, 1925.

Ballades, 1938.

Derniers poèmes en vers et en prose, 1945; 1961 (enl.).

Conseils à un jeune poète, 1945.

Nouvelles inédites, ed. G. Auric, Mesnil 1949 (cntg *Mendiante professionnelle* and *Jalousie*; incl. bibl. of works).

ANDREU, P., *Max Jacob*, 1962.
BILLY, A., *Max Jacob*, 1945.
CADOU, R. G., *Esthétique de Max Jacob*, 1955.
EMIE, L., *Dialogues avec Max Jacob*, 1954.

JAMMES, Francis 1868–1938

Bibl. See MALLET below.

Oeuvres, 5 vols, 1913–26.

Tr. J. Hausmann, *Homer had a dog: selections*, Prairie City (Ill) 1946.

De l'angélus de l'aube à l'angélus du soir, 1898 (incl. *La naissance du poète*, first ptd privately 1897).
Clara d'Ellébeuse, 1899.
Le deuil des primevères, 1901 (incl. *Quatorze prières*, first ptd privately 1898, and *Le poète et l'oiseau*, first pbd 1899).
Le triomphe de la vie, poèmes, 1902.
Le roman du lièvre, 1903 (incl. poems pbd earlier). Tr. G. Edgerton, *Romance of the rabbit*, New York 1925.
Clairières dans le ciel, 1906 (incl. poems pbd earlier).
Les Géorgiques chrétiennes, Chants 1–7, 2 vols, 1911–2.
Le premier livre des quatrains, 1923.
    Le deuxième livre, 1923.
    Le troisième livre, 1924.
    Le quatrième livre, 1925.
Cloches pour deux mariages, 1923.
Ma France poétique, 1926.
De tout temps à jamais, 1935.
Sources, 1936.

MALLET, R., *Francis Jammes, sa vie, son oeuvre*, 1950; 1961.
    Une étude, 1956 (incl. bibl.).
    Jammes et le jammisme, 1961.

JOUHANDEAU, Marcel 1888–

Bibl. See CABANIS below.

Tr. M. Turnell, *Marcel and Elise*, New York 1953 (incl. extracts from *Monsieur Godeau marié*, *Chroniques maritales*, *Nouvelles chroniques maritales*, *Chronique d'une passion*, *Ménagerie domestique*, *L'imposteur*).

La jeunesse de Théophile, 1921.

Les Pincengrains, 1924.
Monsieur Godeau intime, 1926.
Monsieur Godeau marié, 1933.
Elise, 1933.
Binche Anna, 1933.
Chaminadour, 2 vols, 1934–6.
    Descente aux enfers, 1963.
Le jardin de Cordoue, 1938.
Chroniques maritales, 1938.
    Nouvelles chroniques maritales, 1943.
De l'abjection, 1939.
Chronique d'une passion, 1944.
Essai sur moi-même, Lausanne 1946.
Mémorial, 7 vols, 1948–72.
Scènes de la vie conjugale. 1, Ménagerie domestique, 1948.
La faute plutôt que le scandale, 1949.
L'imposteur, 1950.
Du pur amour, 1955; 1969 (enl.).
L'école des filles, 1960.
    Une adolescence, 1971.

Journaliers, 17 vols, 1961–72.

CABANIS, J., *Jouhandeau,* 1959 (incl. bibl.).
CURTIS, J. L., *Haute école,* 1950.
GAULNIER, J., *L'univers de Jouhandeau,* 1960.
MAURIAC, C., *Introduction à une mystique de l'Enfer,* 1938.

KATEB Yacine   1929–

Bibl. See BONN below.

Soliloques, Bône 1946.
Nedjma, roman, 1956.
Le cercle des représailles, 1959 (with *Le cadavre encerclé, La poudre d'intelli-gence, Les ancêtres redoublent de férocité, Le vautour*).
Le polygone étoilé, 1966. Tr. L. Ortzen, London 1970 (extracts, in *North African writing*).
L' homme aux sandales de caoutchouc, 1970.

BONN, C., in his *La littérature algérienne de langue française et ses lectures,* Ottawa 1974 (incl. bibl.).

LÉAUTAUD, Paul   1872–1956

Bibl. See DORMOY, *Léautaud* below.

Bestiaire, 1959 (extracts about animals).

Le petit ami, 1903.
　Amour, 1934; 1939.
　In memoriam, 1956 (with *Le petit ami* and *Amour* above).
　Tr. H. Hare, *The child of Montmartre*, London 1959.
Théâtre de Maurice Boissard, 1907–1923, 1926 (collected dramatic criticism
　first pbd in *Mercure de France, Nouvelle Revue Française* and *Nouvelles
　Littéraires*); 1943 (with supplement for 1939–41).
Madame Cantili, 1925; 1947 (with *Mademoiselle Barbette* and *Ménagerie
　intime*).

Journal littéraire, 19 vols, 1954–66 (parts first pbd Paris 1926 and Brussels
　1942). Tr. G. Sainsbury, *Journal of a man of letters 1898–1907*, London
　1960 (abr.).
Entretiens avec Robert Mallet, 1951 (conversations recorded for radio).

DORMOY, M., *Léautaud*, 1958 (incl. bibl.).
　Visages de Léautaud, 1969.
　La vie secrète de Paul Léautaud, 1972.
HARDING, J., *Lost illusions, Paul Léautaud and his world*, London 1974.
Mercure de France, May 1957 (special issue).
SUARÈS, A., *Portrait de Léautaud*, 1951.

MALRAUX, André 1901–

LANGLOIS, W. G., *Essai de bibliographie des études en langue anglaise, 1924–
1970*, 1972.
See also HOFFMANN below; also VANDEGANS below.

Oeuvres complètes, 7 vols, Geneva 1945; 4 vols, Paris 1970.

Lunes en papier, 1921.
La tentation de l'Occident, 1926.
Les conquérants, 1928; 1949. Tr. W. S. Whale, *The conquerors*, London
　and New York 1929.
Les puissances du désert, 1: La voie royale, 1930. Tr. S. Gilbert, *The royal
　way*, London and New York 1935.
La condition humaine, 1933; 1946. Tr. A. MacDonald, *Storm in Shanghai*,
　London 1934; 1948 (as *Man's estate*).
Le temps du mépris, 1935. Tr. H. M. Chevalier, *Days of contempt*, London
　1936 (and New York, as *Days of wrath*).
L'espoir, 1937. Tr. S. Gilbert and A. MacDonald, *Days of hope*, London
　1938 (and New York, as *Man's hope*).
La lutte avec l'ange, 1: Les noyers de l'Altenburg, Lausanne 1943. Tr. A. W.
　Fielding, *The walnut trees of Altenburg*, London 1952.

La psychologie de l'art, 3 vols, Geneva and Paris 1947–50; Paris 1951 (renamed *Les voix du silence*; enl., with *Les métamorphoses d'Apollon*). Tr. S. Gilbert, *The psychology of art*, 3 vols, London and New York 1949–50; London 1954 (enl., as *The voices of silence*). Comprising:

   Le musée imaginaire, Geneva 1947. Tr., *Museum without walls*, London 1949.

   La création artistique, Geneva 1948. Tr., *The creative act*, London 1949.

   La monnaie de l'absolu, Geneva and Paris 1950. Tr., *The twilight of the absolute*, New York 1950.

Saturne, essai sur Goya, 1950. Tr. C. W. Chilton, *Saturn, an essay on Goya*, London 1957.

La métamorphose des dieux, 1958. Tr. S. Gilbert, *The metamorphosis of the gods*, London and New York 1960.

   L'irréel, 1974.

Antimémoires, 1967; 1972 (enl.). Tr. T. Kilmartin, *Antimemoirs*, London and New York 1968.

Oraisons funèbres, 1971 (collected speeches 1958–65).

Les chênes qu'on abat, 1971.

Lazare, 1974.

BLEND, C. D., *André Malraux, tragic humanist*, Columbus (Ohio) 1962.

BOAK, D., *André Malraux*, Oxford 1968.

FROHOCK, W. M., *André Malraux and the tragic imagination*, Stanford (Calif) 1952.

GAILLARD, P., *André Malraux*, 1970.

GOLDBERGER, A., *Visions of a new hero*, 1965.

HOFFMANN, J., *L'humanisme de Malraux*, 1963 (incl. bibl.).

LEWIS, R. W. B., *Malraux: a collection of critical essays*, Englewood Cliffs (NJ) 1964.

MALRAUX, C., *Le bruit de nos pas*, 3 vols, 1965–9. Tr. P. O'Brian, *Memoirs*, New York and London 1967 (abr.).

PICON, G., *Malraux par lui-même*, 1953.

RICHTER, W., *The rhetorical hero*, London 1964.

VANDEGANS, A., *La jeunesse littéraire d'André Malraux*, 1964 (incl. bibl.).

MARTIN DU GARD, Roger   1881–1958

PAEVSKOI, A. V. and EISCHISKINA, N. M., *Rozhe Marten dyu Gar: bio-bibliografichesky ukazatel'*, Moscow 1958.

See also SCHALK below; also SCHLOBACH below.

Oeuvres complètes, 2 vols, 1955; 2 vols, 1972.

Devenir !, 1908.

Jean Barois, 1913. Tr. S. Gilbert, New York 1949.

Le testament du Père Leleu, 1920.

Les Thibault, 11 vols, 1922–40. Tr. M. Boyd, *The world of the Thibaults*, 2 vols, New York 1926 (tr. of vols 1–4); tr. S. Haden-Guest (tr. of vols 1–2) and S. Gilbert (tr. of vols 3–5). *The Thibaults*, 2 vols, London 1933–4; tr. S. Gilbert, London and New York 1939 (tr. of vols 1–7); tr. S. Gilbert, *Summer 1914*, 2 vols, London 1939–40 (tr. of vols 8–11). Comprising:

1 *Le cahier gris*, 1922.
2 *Le pénitencier*, 1922.
3–4 *La belle saison*, 1923.
5 *La consultation*, 1928.
6 *La Sorellina*, 1928.
7 *La mort du père*, 1929.
8–10 *L'été 1914*, 1936.
11 *Epilogue*, 1940.

La gonfle, 1928.
Confidence africaine, 1931.
Un taciturne, pièce en trois actes, 1932.
Vieille France, 1933. Tr. J. Russell, *The postman*, London 1954.
Notes sur André Gide, 1913–1951, 1951. Tr. J. Russell, *Notes on André Gide*, London 1953 (and New York, as *Recollections of André Gide*).
Souvenirs autobiographiques et littéraires, 1955 (in *Oeuvres complètes* above).

BOAK, D., *Roger Martin du Gard*, Oxford 1963.
CAMUS, A., *Roger Martin du Gard*, 1955 (as preface to *Oeuvres complètes* above).
GIBSON, R. *Roger Martin du Gard*, New York and London 1961.
LALOU, R., *Roger Martin du Gard*, 1937.
ROBIDOUX, R., *Roger Martin du Gard et la religion*, 1964.
SCHALK, D. C., *Roger Martin du Gard, the novelist and history*, Ithaca (NY) 1967 (incl. bibl.).
SCHLOBACH, J., *Geschichte und Fiktion in L'Été 1914*, Munich 1965 (incl. bibl.).

MAURIAC, François 1885–1970

GOESCH, K., *Essai de bibliographie chronologique, 1908–1960*, 1965. See also CORMEAU below.

Oeuvres complètes, 12 vols, 1950–6.

Les mains jointes, 1909; 1927.
L'enfant chargé de chaînes, 1913. Tr. G. Hopkins, *Young man in chains*, London 1961.
La robe prétexte, 1914. Tr. G. Hopkins, *The stuff of youth*, London 1960.
De quelques coeurs inquiets, 1920.

La chair et le sang, 1920. Tr. G. Hopkins, *Flesh and blood,* London 1954.

Préséances, 1921. Tr. G. Hopkins, *Questions of precedence,* London 1958.

Le baiser au lépreux, 1922. Tr. J. Whitall, *The kiss to the leper,* London 1923; tr. G. Hopkins, *A kiss for the leper,* London 1950.

Génitrix, 1923. Tr. G. Hopkins, London 1950 (with *A kiss for the leper* above).

Le désert de l'amour, 1925. Tr. S. Putnam, *The desert of love,* New York 1929; tr. G. Hopkins, London 1949 (with *The enemy,* tr. of *Le Mal,* pbd Paris 1942).

Orages, 1925.

Proust, 1926.

Thérèse Desqueyroux, 1927. Tr. E. Sutton, *Thérèse,* London and New York 1928; tr. G. Hopkins, London 1947.

  La fin de la nuit, 1935. Tr. G. Hopkins, London 1947 (with *Thérèse* above).

Destins, 1928. Tr. E. Sutton, *Destinies,* London and New York 1929; tr. G. Hopkins, *Lines of life,* London and New York 1957.

La vie de Jean Racine, 1928.

Dieu et Mammon, 1929. Tr. B. and B. Wall, *God and Mammon,* London and Toronto 1936.

Trois récits, 1929 (cntg *Coups de couteau, Le démon de la connaissance, Un homme de lettres*).

Ce qui était perdu, 1930. Tr. H. F. Kynaston-Snell, *Suspicion,* London 1931; tr. J. H. F. McEwen, *That which was lost,* London 1951.

Souffrances et bonheur du Chrétien, 1931. Tr. H. Evans, *Anguish and joy of the Christian life,* Wilkes-Barre (Pa) 1964.

Blaise Pascal et sa soeur Jacqueline, 1931.

Le noeud de vipères, 1932. Tr. W. B. Wells, *Vipers' tangle,* London and New York 1933; tr. G. Hopkins, *The knot of vipers,* London 1951.

Le mystère Frontenac, 1933. Tr. G. Hopkins, *The Frontenac mystery,* London 1952.

Le romancier et ses personnages, 1933.

Les anges noirs, 1936. Tr. G. Hopkins, *The dark angels,* London 1951 (with *That which was lost,* tr. McEwen above).

Vie de Jésus, 1936. Tr. J. Kernan, *Life of Jesus,* New York 1937.

Asmodée, 1938. Tr. B. Bartlett, London 1939; tr. B. Thurman, London 1957.

Les chemins de la mer, 1939. Tr. G. Hopkins, *The unknown sea,* London and New York 1948.

La Pharisienne, 1941. Tr. G. Hopkins, *A woman of the Pharisees,* London and New York 1946.

Le cahier noir, 1943 (pbd clandestinely). Tr. anon., *The black notebook,* London 1944.

Les mal aimés, 1945.

Du côté de chez Proust, 1947. Tr. E. Pell, *Proust's way,* New York 1950.

Passage du Malin, 1948.
Le sagouin, Paris and Geneva 1951. Tr. G. Hopkins, *The little misery*, London 1952 (and New York, as *The weakling*).
Le feu sur la terre, 1951.
Galigaï, 1952. Tr. G. Hopkins, *The loved and the unloved*, New York 1952.
L'agneau, 1954. Tr. G. Hopkins, *The lamb*, London and New York 1955.
Le pain vivant, 1955.
Mémoires intérieurs, 1959. Tr. G. Hopkins, London 1960.
 Nouveaux mémoires intérieurs, 1965.
Ce que je crois, 1962. Tr. W. Fowlie, *What I believe*, New York 1963.
De Gaulle, 1964. Tr. R. Howard, London and New York 1966.
Mémoires politiques, 1967.
Un adolescent d'autrefois, 1969; ed. J. E. Flower, London 1972. Tr. J. Stewart, *Maltaverne*, New York 1970.
 Maltaverne, 1972.

Journal, 4 vols, 1934–50.
Journal d'un homme de trente ans (extracts from diary 1914–23), 1948.
Bloc-notes, 1952–1957, 1958.
 Le nouveau bloc-notes, 1958–1960, 1961.

ALYN, M., *François Mauriac*, 1960.
CORMEAU, N., *L'art de François Mauriac*, 1951 (incl. bibl. to 1947).
DU BOS, C., *François Mauriac et le problème du romancier catholique*, 1933.
FLOWER, J. E., *Intention and achievement: an essay on the novels of François Mauriac*, Oxford 1969.
JENKINS, C., *Mauriac*, Edinburgh and London 1965.
SARTRE, J.-P., in his *Situations I*, 1947. Tr. A. Michelson, London 1955 (in *Literary and philosophical essays*).

MAUROIS, André 1885–1967
(pseudonym of Emile Herzog)

Oeuvres complètes, 16 vols, 1950–5; 1965 onwards (5 vols pbd).
Romans, 1961.

Tr. A. Foulke, *The collected stories*, New York 1967.

Les silences du colonel Bramble, 1918; 1947. Tr. T. Wake, *The silence of Colonel Bramble*, London and New York 1920; London 1940 (with verses tr. W. Jackson).
 Les discours du docteur O'Grady, 1922; 1947 (with *Colonel Bramble* above).
 Nouveaux discours du docteur O'Grady, 1950. Tr. G. Hopkins, *The return of Doctor O'Grady*, London 1951.
Ariel, ou la vie de Shelley, 1923. Tr. E. D'Arcy, *Ariel, a Shelley romance*, London 1924 (and New York, as *Ariel: the life of Shelley*).

Dialogues sur le commandement, 1924. Tr. J. L. May, *Captains and kings, three dialogues on leadership*, London 1925.

Bernard Quesnay, 1926. Tr. B. W. Downs, London and New York 1927.

La vie de Disraëli, 1927. Tr. H. Miles, *Disraeli, a picture of the Victorian age*, London and New York 1928.

Climats, 1928. Tr. J. Collins, *Whatever gods may be*, London 1929 (and New York, as *Atmospheres of love*), tr. V. Schiff and E. Cook, *The climates of love*, London 1957.

Byron, 2 vols, 1930; 1952 (renamed *Don Juan, ou la vie de Byron*). Tr. H. Miles, London and New York 1930.

Lyautey, 1931. Tr. H. Miles, *Marshal Lyautey*, London 1931 (and New York, as *Lyautey*).

Voltaire, London 1932. Tr. H. Miles, London and New York 1932.

Le cercle de famille, 1932. Tr. H. Miles, *The family circle*, London and New York 1932.

Edouard VII et son temps, 1933. Tr. H. Miles, *King Edward and his times*, London 1933 (and New York, as *The Edwardian era*).

L'instinct du bonheur, 1934. Tr. E. Johannsen, *A time for happiness*, London and New York 1942.

Magiciens et logiciens, 1935 (essays on Kipling, Wells, Conrad, D. H. Lawrence, etc). Tr. H. Miles, *Prophets and poets*, New York 1935; 1968 (as *Points of view*, with 2 essays tr. M. Ilford).

Histoire d'Angleterre, 1937. Tr. H. Miles, *A history of England*, London and New York 1937.

Chateaubriand, 1938. Tr. V. Fraser, *Chateaubriand, poet, statesman, lover*, London and New York 1938.

Un art de vivre, 1939. Tr. J. Whitall, *The art of living*, London and New York 1940.

Histoire des Etats Unis 1492–1946, 1947; 1954 (with supplement to 1954).
  Histoire des Etats Unis de 1917 à 1961, 1962 (in *Histoire parallèle*, with ARAGON's *Histoire de l'URSS*). Tr. P. O'Brian, *A history of the USA from Wilson to Kennedy*, London 1964.

A la recherche de Marcel Proust, 1949. Tr. G. Hopkins, *Proust: portrait of a genius*, New York 1950 (and London, as *The quest for Proust*).

Lélia, ou la vie de George Sand, 1952. Tr. G. Hopkins, *Lélia, the life of George Sand*. London and New York 1953.

Le poème de Versailles (text of *son et lumière* spectacle), 1954. Tr. A. S. Alexander, *A vision of Versailles*, Brionne 1955.

Olympio, ou la vie de Victor Hugo, 1954. Tr. G. Hopkins, *Victor Hugo*, London 1956 (and New York, as *Olympio, the life of Victor Hugo*).

Aux innocents les mains pleines, 1955.

Les trois Dumas, 1957. Tr. G. Hopkins, *Three musketeers, a study of the Dumas family*, London 1957 (and New York, as *The Titans: a three-generation biography of the Dumas*).

Portrait d'un ami qui s'appelait moi, Paris and Namur 1959.

La vie de Sir Alexander Fleming, 1959. Tr. G. Hopkins, *The life of Sir Alexander Fleming*, London and New York 1959.

Prométhée, ou la vie de Balzac, 1965. Tr. N. Denny, *Prometheus, the life of Balzac*, London and New York 1965.

Mémoires, 2 vols, New York 1941–4; 1970 (enl.). Tr. D. and J. Lindley, *I remember, I remember*, New York 1942 (and London 1943, as *Call no man happy*; revd and enl. D. Lindley, London 1970).

DROIT, M., *André Maurois*, 1953.

FILLON, A., *André Maurois romancier*, 1937.

GUÉRY, S., *La pensée d'André Maurois*, 1951.

LEMAÎTRE, G., *André Maurois*, Stanford (Calif) and London 1939; New York 1968.

SUFFEL, J., *André Maurois*, 1963.

MAURRAS, Charles 1868–1952

FORGES, J. and JOSEPH, R., *Biblio-iconographie générale*, 2 vols, Roanne 1954. See also FORGES and JOSEPH below.

Oeuvres capitales, 4 vols, 1954 (collected works).

Le chemin de Paradis, 1895.

Les amants de Venise, 1902; 1926.

L'avenir de l'intelligence, 1905.

Enquête sur la monarchie, 1900–1909, 1909 (incl. *Chez nos exilés* and *Enquête sur la monarchie*, 2 pts, first pbd separately by *Gazette de France*, 1900); 1924 (enl.).

Anthinéa, 1901; 1912.

L'étang de Berre, 1915.

Les conditions de la victoire, 4 vols, 1916–1918.

Tombeaux, 1921.

L'allée des philosophes, 1923.

La musique intérieure, 1925.

Dictionnaire politique et critique, ed. P. Chardon, 5 vols, 1931–4 (consisting of 25 separate booklets).

Lettres de prison, 1958.

BARKO, I. P., *L'ésthétique littéraire de Charles Maurras*, Geneva and Paris 1961.

DAUDET, L., *Charles Maurras et son temps*, 1928.

FORGES, J. and JOSEPH, R., *Le poète Charles Maurras*, 1962 (incl. bibl. of poetical works).

HAVARD DE LA MONTAGNE, R., in his *Histoire de l'Action Française*, 1949.

MASSIS, H., *Maurras et notre temps*, 2 vols, Paris and Geneva 1951; 2 vols, Paris 1960.

MAURRAS, H., *Souvenirs des prisons de Charles Maurras*, 1965.

THIBAUDET, A., *Les idées de Charles Maurras*, 1920 (in *Trente ans de vie française*, vol 1).

MICHAUX, Henri 1899–

L'espace du dedans, 1945 (selected works). Tr. R. Ellmann, *Selected writings*, New York 1951.

Qui je fus, 1927.

Ecuador, journal de voyage, 1929.

Mes propriétés, 1929.

La nuit remue, 1931 (incl. *Mes propriétés* above).

Un barbare en Asie, 1933. Tr. S. Beach, *Barbarian in Asia*, New York 1949.

Plume, précédé de Lointain intérieur, 1938; 1963.

Arbres des tropiques, 1942.

Epreuves, exorcismes, 1940–1944, 1945.

Apparitions, 1946.

Ailleurs, 1948.

Passages, 1937–1950 (collected articles), 1950; 1963 (enl.).

Mouvements, 1952.

Misérable miracle, la mescaline, Monaco 1956; Paris 1972. Tr. L. Varèse, *Miserable miracle, mescaline*, San Francisco 1963.

L'infini turbulent, 1957; 1964 (enl.).

Connaissance par les gouffres, 1961. Tr. H. M. Chevalier, *Light through darkness*, New York 1963.

Vents et poussières, 1955–1962, 1962.

Moments, 1973.

BELLOUR, R., *Henri Michaux, ou une mesure de l'être*, 1965.

BERTELÉ, R., *Henri Michaux*, 1953; 1965.

BRECHON, R., *Michaux*, 1959.

COULON, P. de, *Henri Michaux poète de notre société*, Neuchâtel 1950.

GIDE, A., *Découvrons Henri Michaux*, 1941.

MONTHERLANT, Henry de 1896–1972

Bibl. See BATCHELOR below; also CRUICKSHANK below.

Romans et oeuvres de fiction non théâtrales, 1959; 8 vols, 1963–4.

Théâtre, 1954; 1958 (enl.); 5 vols, 1965–6; 1968.

Essais, 1963. Tr. J. Weightman, ed. P. Quennell, *Selected essays*, London 1960.

Tr. J. Griffin, *The Master of Santiago, and four other plays*, New York and London 1951.

La relève du matin, 1920; 1933.

Le songe, 1922. Tr. T. Kilmartin, *The dream*, London 1962.

Les olympiques, 1924–9. Comprising:
    Le paradis à l'ombre des épees, 1924.
    Les onze devant la porte dorée, 1924.
    Earinus, 1929.

Chant funèbre pour les morts de Verdun, 1924.

Les bestiaires, 1926. Tr. E. G. Rich, *The bullfighters*, New York 1927. Tr. P. Wiles, *The matador*, London 1957.

Les célibataires, 1934. Tr. T. McGreevy, *Lament for the death of an upper class*, London 1935 (New York 1936, as *Perish in their pride*); tr. T. Kilmartin, *The bachelors*, 1960.

Service inutile, 1935.

Les jeunes filles, 1936. Tr. T. McGreevy, *Young girls*, London 1937.
    Pitié pour les femmes, 1936. Tr. J. Rodker, *Pity for women*, London 1937.
    Le démon du bien, 1937. Tr. J. Rodker, *The demon of good*, London 1940.
    Les lépreuses, 1939. Tr. J. Rodker, *The lepers*, London 1940.

Le solstice de juin, 1941.

Fils de personne, 1944. Tr. Griffin above, *No man's son*.

Le maître de Santiago, 1947. Tr. Griffin above.

Malatesta, 1948. Tr. Grffin above.

Celles qu'on prend dans ses bras, 1950.

Notes sur mon théâtre, 1950.

La reine morte, 1951; 1971. Tr. Griffin above, *Queen after death*.

La ville dont le prince est un enfant, trois actes, 1951; 1959.

Le fichier parisien, Geneva 1952; 1974 (enl.).

Histoire d'amour de La rose de sable, 1954 (2 chs first pbd 1946). Tr. A. Brown, *Desert love*, London 1957.
    La rose de sable, 1968 (complete text).

Port-Royal, 1955.

Le cardinal d'Espagne, 1960.

Le chaos et la nuit, 1963. Tr. T. Kilmartin, *Chaos and night*, London and New York 1964.

La guerre civile, 1964. Tr. J. Griffin, *Civil war*, Harmondsworth 1967 (in *Theatre at war*).

Les garçons, 1969. Tr. T. Kilmartin, *The boys*, London 1974.

Un assassin est mon maître, 1971.

Mais aimons-nous ceux que nous aimons ?, 1973.

Carnets XXIX à XXXV, 1947 (for 1935–8).
    Carnets XLII et XLIII, 1948 (for 1942–3).
    Carnets XXII à XXVIII, 1955 (for 1932–4).
    Carnets XIX à XXI, 1956 (for 1930–2).
    Va jouer avec cette poussière, carnets 1958–1964, 1966.
    La marée du soir, carnets 1968–1971, 1972.

BATCHELOR, J. W., *Existence and imagination: the theatre of Henry de Montherlant*, Brisbane 1967 (incl. bibl.).

BEER, J. de, *Montherlant, ou l'homme encombré de Dieu*, 1963.

BORDONOVE, G., *Henry de Montherlant*, 1954; 1960.

CRUICKSHANK, J., *Montherlant*, Edinburgh and London 1964 (incl. bibl.).

DEBRIE-PAVEL, N., *Montherlant: l'art et l'amour*, Lyons 1960.

LAPRADE, J. de, *Le théâtre de Montherlant*, 1950.

MARISSEL, A., *Montherlant*, 1966.

SIPRIOT, P., *Montherlant par lui-même*, 1953.

La Table Ronde, nos. 148 and 155, 1960.

PÉGUY, Charles   1873–1914

Bibl. See DELAPORTE below.

Oeuvres complètes, 20 vols, 1917–55.
Oeuvres, 3 vols, 1948–59.
Oeuvres poétiques complètes, ed. F. Porché, 1941.
Oeuvres en prose, ed. M. Péguy, 2 vols, 1957–9.

Tr. J. and A. Green, *Basic verities*, New York 1943.

Many works first published in *Cahiers de la Quinzaine*.

Jeanne d'Arc, drame en 3 pièces (in collab. with Marcel and Pierre Baudouin), Suresnes 1897.
Le mystère de la charité de Jeanne d'Arc, 2 vols, 1910–26. Tr. J. Green, *The mystery of the charity of Joan of Arc*, London 1950.
    Le porche du mystère de la deuxième vertu, 1912.
      Le mystère des Saints Innocents, 1912. Tr. P. Pakenham, in *Mystery of the holy innocents and other poems*, New York, London and Toronto 1956.
Notre jeunesse, 1910. Tr. A. Dru, in *Temporal and eternal*, London and New York 1958 (selection).
Victor-Marie, Comte Hugo, 1911.
La tapisserie de sainte Geneviève et de Jeanne d'Arc, 1913.
    La tapisserie de Notre Dame, 1913.
    Eve, 1913.
Note sur M. Bergson et la philosophie bergsonienne, 1914.
    Note conjointe sur M. Descartes et la philosophie cartésienne, 1924.
Clio, 1917 (in *Oeuvres complètes*, vol 9 above). Tr. A. Dru, in *Temporal and eternal*, London and New York 1958 (selection).

DELAPORTE, J., *Connaissance de Péguy*, 2 vols, 1944; 2 vols, 1959 (incl. bibl. in vol 2).

DRU, A., *Péguy*, New York and London 1957.

FRAISSE, S., *Péguy et le monde antique*, 1973.
(ed.), *Les critiques de notre temps et Péguy*, 1973.
GRIFFITHS, R., in his *The reactionary revolution: the Catholic revival in French literature, 1870–1914*, London 1966.
GUYON, B., *Péguy, l'homme et l'oeuvre*, 1960.
JUSSEM-WILSON, N., *Charles Péguy*, New York 1965.
ROLLAND, R., *Péguy*, 2 vols, 1944.
VILLIERS, M., *Charles Péguy, a study in integrity*, London and New York 1965.

PRÉVERT, Jacques   1900–

Bibl. See QUÉVAL below.

Tr. L. Ferlinghetti, *Jacques Prévert*, Harmondsworth 1966 (selection).

Paroles, 1945 (incl. *Tentative de description d'une dîner de têtes à Paris-France*); 1951 (enl.). Tr. L. Ferlinghetti, *Selections from Paroles*, San Francisco (Calif) 1958.
Histoires, 1946 (with poems by André Verdet).
    Histoires, et d'autres histoires, 1963.
Les visiteurs du soir (film script, in collab. with Pierre Laroche), 1947.
Spectacle, 1951.
Grand bal du printemps, Lausanne 1951.
La pluie et le beau temps, 1955.
Fatras, 1966.
Imaginaires, Geneva 1970.
Chose et autres, 1972.

BERGER, P., *Jacques Prévert*, 1958 (in *Présences contemporaines*).
GREET, A. H., *Jacques Prévert's word-games*, Berkeley (Calif) 1969.
POZNER, A., *Hebdromadaires*, La Chapelle-sur-Loire 1972.
QUÉVAL, J., *Jacques Prévert*, 1955 (incl. bibl.).
    Jacques Prévert, Lyon 1961.

PROUST, Marcel   1871–1922

SILVA RAMOS, G. de, *Bibliographie proustienne*, 1932 (in *Cahiers Marcel Proust*, no. 6).
ALDEN, D. W., *Marcel Proust and his French critics*, Los Angeles (Calif) 1940.
TADIE, J. Y., *Lectures de Proust*, 1971.
KOLB, P., *La correspondance de Marcel Proust*, Urbana (Ill) 1949.
See also Kolb–Price ed. of *Textes retrouvés* below; also BONNET, *Le progrès spirituel* and *Proust de 1907 à 1914* below; also CHANTAL below.
SPALDING, P. A., *A reader's handbook to Proust: an index guide to Remembrance of Things Past*, London 1952.

Oeuvres complètes, 17 vols, 1929–35; ed. P. Clarac, A. Ferré and Y. Sandre, 5 vols, 1954–71.

Tr. G. Hopkins, *A selection*, London 1948.
Tr. and ed. J. O'Brien, *The maxims*, New York 1948.
Tr. L. Varèse, G. Hopkins and B. Dupee, *Pleasures and days and other writings*, New York 1957.

Les plaisirs et le jours, 1896. Tr. L. Varèse, *Pleasures and regrets*, New York 1948.
La Bible d'Amiens (tr. of Ruskin's *Bible of Amiens*), 1904.
> *Sésame et les lys* (tr. of Ruskin's *Sesame and lilies*), 1906.
A la recherche du temps perdu, 11 vols, 1913–27; ed. P. Clarac and A. Ferré, 3 vols, 1954 (in *Oeuvres complètes* above). Tr. C. K. Scott Moncrieff and S. Hudson, *Remembrance of things past*, 11 vols, London and New York 1922–31 (only *Le temps retrouvé* tr. Hudson). Comprising:
> *Du côté de chez Swann*, 1913. Tr., *Swann's way*, 2 vols, London 1922.
> *A l'ombre des jeunes filles en fleurs*, 1919. Tr., *Within a budding grove*, 2 vols, New York 1924.
> *Le côté de Guermantes, I*, 1920.
> *Le côté de Guermantes, II—Sodome et Gomorrhe, I*, 1921. Tr., *The Guermantes way*, 2 vols, New York 1925.
> *Sodome et Gomorrhe, II*, 1922.
> *Sodome et Gomorrhe, III—La prisonnière*, 2 vols, 1923. Tr., *Cities of the plain*, 2 vols, New York 1927; *The captive*, London and New York 1929.
> *Albertine disparue*, 1925. Tr., *The sweet cheat gone*, London and New York 1930.
> *Le temps retrouvé*, 2 vols, 1927. Tr., *Time regained*, London 1931; also tr. A. Mayor, *Past recaptured*, New York 1970.
Pastiches et mélanges, 1919; ed. J. Milly, 1970 (*Pastiches* only). Tr. Hopkins, in *A selection* above (*Mélanges* only).
Chroniques, 1927.
Jean Santeuil, ed. B. de Fallois, 3 vols, 1952. Tr. G. Hopkins, London 1955.
Contre Sainte-Beuve, 1954; 1971 (in *Oeuvres complètes* above). Tr. S. Townsend Warner, *By way of Sainte Beuve*, London 1958; New York 1958 (enl., as *On art and literature, 1869–1919*).
Textes retrouvés, ed. P. Kolb and L. B. Price, Chicago (Ill) and London 1968 (incl. bibl. of works).

Correspondance générale, ed. R. Proust and P. Brach, 6 vols, 1930–6; ed. P. Kolb, 1970 onwards (1 vol pbd). Tr. M. Curtiss, *Letters*, New York 1949 (selection).
Correspondance avec sa mère, ed. P. Kolb, 1953. Tr. G. D. Painter, *Letters to his mother*, London 1956.

Marcel Proust et Jacques Rivière, correspondance 1914–1922, ed. P. Kolb, 1955.

Lettres à Reynaldo Hahn, ed. P. Kolb, 1956.

Choix de lettres, ed. P. Kolb, 1965.

BARDÈCHE, M., *Marcel Proust romancier*, 2 vols, 1973.

BECKETT, S., *Proust*, London 1931.

BONNET, H., *Le progrès spirituel de Proust*, 2 vols, 1946–9 (incl. bibl.).
Marcel Proust de 1907 à 1914, 1959 (incl. supplementary bibl.).

BIBESCO, M., *Au bal avec Marcel Proust*, 1928 (in *Cahiers Marcel Proust*, no. 4).

BRÉE, G., *Du temps perdu au temps retrouvé*, 1950.
Marcel Proust and deliverance from time, New Brunswick (NJ) and London 1955 (tr. C. J. Richards and A. D. Truitt).

CATTAUI, G., *Marcel Proust*, 1952; 1958. Tr. R. Hall, London 1967.

CHANTAL, R. de, *Marcel Proust critique littéraire*, Montreal 1967 (incl. bibl.).

DANDIEU, A., *Marcel Proust, sa révélation psychologique*, 1930.

GREEN, F. C., *The mind of Proust*, Cambridge 1949.

GUICHARD, L., *Sept études sur Marcel Proust*, Cairo 1942; Paris 1959 (renamed *Introduction à la lecture de Proust*).

Hommage à Marcel Proust, 1927 (*Cahiers Marcel Proust*, no 1).

LARCHER, P. L., *Le parfum de Combray*, 1945.

MAURIAC, F., *Du coté de chez Proust*, 1947. Tr. E. Pell, *Proust's way*, New York 1950.

MAUROIS, A., *A la recherche de Marcel Proust*, 1949. Tr. G. Hopkins, *Proust, portrait of a genius*, New York 1950 (and London, as *The quest for Proust*).

MOSS, H., *The magic lantern of Marcel Proust*, New York 1962.

MOUTON, J., *Le style de Marcel Proust*, 1948.

PAINTER, G. D., *Marcel Proust*, 2 vols, 1959–65.

PIERRE-QUINT, L., *Marcel Proust, sa vie, son oeuvre*, 1928.

PRICE, L. B. (ed.), *Marcel Proust*, Urbana (Ill) and London 1973.

SHATTUCK, R., *Proust*, London 1974.

STRAUSS, W. A., *Proust and literature, the novelist as critic*, Cambridge (Mass) 1957.

RADIGUET, Raymond   1903–1923

Bibl. See GOESCH below.

Le diable au corps, 1923. Tr. K. Boyle, *The devil in the flesh*, Paris and New York 1932; tr. A. M. Sheridan Smith, London 1968.

Le bal du comte d'Orgel, 1924. Tr. M. Cowley, *The Count's ball*, New York 1929; tr. V. Schiff, *Count d'Orgel opens the ball*, London 1952 (New York 1953, as *Count d'Orgel*).

Les joues en feu, 1925.

GOESCH, K., *Raymond Radiguet*, Geneva 1955 (incl. bibl.).

MASSIS, H., *Raymond Radiguet*, 1929.

RAMUZ, Charles-Ferdinand   1878–1947

BRINGOLF, T., *Bibliographie de l'oeuvre*, Lausanne 1942.
Notes bibliographiques sur l'oeuvre, 1967.

Oeuvres complètes, 23 vols, Lausanne 1940–54.

Tr. G. Paulding, *What is Man?*, New York 1948 (extracts).

Alive, 1905.
Les circonstances de la vie, 1907.
Jean-Luc persécuté, et deux autres histoires de la montagne, 1909.
Aimé Pache, peintre vaudois, 1911.
Vie de Samuel Belet, 1913. Tr. M. Savill, *The life of Samuel Belet*, London 1951.
Raison d'être, Lausanne 1914.
La guerre dans le haut pays, Lausanne 1915.
Le règne de l'esprit malin, Lausanne 1917. Tr. J. Whitall, *The reign of the evil one*, New York 1922.
La guérison des maladies, Lausanne 1917.
Les signes parmi nous, Lausanne 1919.
Histoire du soldat, 1920. Tr. R. Newmarch, *The soldier's tale*, London 1924; tr. M. Flanders and K. Black, 1955.
Terre du ciel, Geneva 1921.
Présence de la mort, Geneva 1922. Tr. A. R. McDougall and A. Comfort, *The end of all men*, New York 1944 (London 1946, as *The triumph of death*).
Passage du poète, Lausanne 1923.
La séparation des races, 1923.
L'amour du monde, 1925.
La grande peur dans la montagne, 1926. Tr. M. Stansbury, *Terror on the mountain*, London 1967.
La beauté sur la Terre, Lausanne 1927. Tr. anon., *Beauty on Earth*, London and New York 1929.
Salutations paysannes et autres morceaux, Geneva 1921.
Adam et Eve, Lausanne 1932.
Taille de l'homme, Lausanne 1933.
Derborence, Lausanne 1934. Tr. S. F. Scott, *When the mountain fell*, New York and London 1949.
Le garçon savoyard, Lausanne 1936.
Si le soleil ne revenait pas, Lausanne 1937.
Besoin de grandeur, Lausanne 1937. Tr. G. Paulding, *What is man?*, New York 1948.

Paris, notes d'un Vaudois, Lausanne 1938.
Découverte du monde, Lausanne 1939.
La guerre aux papiers, Lausanne 1942.
Pays de Vaud, Lausanne 1943.
Vues sur le Valais, Basle 1943.
Nouvelles, Lausanne 1944.
Les servants et autres nouvelles, Lausanne 1946.
Histoires: L'homme, La vieille Rosine, Le petit enterrement, Neuchâtel 1946.
La Mont du Grand Favre, et autres nouvelles, 1970.

Journal, 1896–1942, Lausanne 1943.
    Journal, dernières pages, 1942–1947, Lausanne 1949.
Lettres, 2 vols, 1956–9.
Ses amis et son temps (correspondence), ed. G. Guisan, 1967 onwards (6 vols pbd).

CINGRIA, H., *Ramuz, notre parrain*, Bienne 1956.
DUNOYER, J. M., *Ramuz, peintre vaudois*, Lausanne 1959.
GUISAN, G., *Charles-Ferdinand Ramuz, ou le génie de la patience*, Lausanne 1958.
    Charles-Ferdinand Ramuz, 1966.
HAGGIS, D. R., *Charles-Ferdinand Ramuz, ouvrier du langage*, 1968.
NICOD, M., *Du réalisme à la réalité: evolution artistique et itinéraire spirituel de Ramuz*, Geneva 1966.
PARSONS, C. R., *Vision plastique de Charles-Ferdinand Ramuz*, Quebec 1964.

ROBBE-GRILLET, Alain   1922–

FRAIZER, D. W., *An annotated bibliography of critical studies, 1953–1972*, Metuchen (NJ) 1973.
See also STOLTZFUS below.

Les gommes, 1953. Tr. R. Howard, *The erasers*, New York 1964.
Le voyeur, 1955. Tr. R. Howard, *The voyeur*, New York 1958.
La jalousie, 1957. Tr. R. Howard, *Jealousy*, New York and London 1959.
Dans le labyrinthe, 1959. Tr. R. Howard, *In the labyrinth*, New York 1960; tr. C. Brooke-Rose, London 1967.
L'année dernière à Marienbad, 1961. Tr. R. Howard, *Last year at Marienbad*, London 1962.
Instantanés, 1962. Tr. B. Wright, *Snapshots*, London 1965; tr. B. Morrisette, New York 1968.
L'immortelle, cine-roman, 1963. Tr. A. M. Sheridan-Smith, *The immortal one*, London 1971.
Pour un nouveau roman, 1963 (collected articles). Tr. B. Wright, *Towards a new novel*. London 1965 (with *Snapshots* above); tr. R. Howard, *For a new novel: essays on fiction*, New York 1965.

La maison de rendez-vous, 1965. Tr. R. Howard, New York 1966.
Projet pour une révolution à New York, 1970. Tr. R. Howard, *Project for a revolution in New York*, New York 1972.

BERNAL, O., *Alain Robbe-Grillet, un roman de l'absence*, 1964.
GARDIES, A., *Alain Robbe-Grillet*, 1972.
MIESCH, J., *Robbe-Grillet*, 1965.
MORRISSETTE, B., *Les romans de Robbe-Grillet*, 1963; 1971 (enl.).
STOLTZFUS, B. F., *Alain Robbe-Grillet and the new French novel*, Carbondale (Ill) 1964 (incl. bibl.).

ROLLAND, Romain   1866–1944

STARR, W. T., *A critical bibliography of the published writings*, Evanston (Ill) 1950.
VAKSMAKHER, N. M., PAÏEVSKAYA, A. V. and GALPERINA, E. L., *Romen Rollan, bio-bibliographichesky ukazatel'*, Moscow 1959.
See also BONNEROT below.

Textes politiques, sociaux et philosophiques choisis, ed. J. Albertini, 1970.

Les origines du théâtre lyrique moderne: histoire de l'opéra en Europe avant Lully et Scarlatti, 1895.
Théâtre de la Révolution, 1898–1939. Comprising:
  Les loups, 1898. Tr. B. H. Clark, *The wolves*, New York 1937; tr. J. Holmstrom, *The hungry wolves*, London 1966.
  Danton, 1900. Tr. B. H. Clark, New York 1918.
  Le quatorze juillet, 1902. Tr. B. H. Clark, *The fourteenth of July*, New York 1918 (with *Danton* above).
  Robespierre, 1939.
Le théâtre du peuple, 1903; 1913. Tr. B. H. Clark, *The people's theatre*, New York 1918.
Jean-Christophe, 10 vols, 1905–12; 1950. Tr. G. Cannan, *John Christopher*, 4 vols, London 1910–3.
Vie de Michel-Ange, 1907. Tr. F. Lees, *The life of Michael Angelo*, London 1912.
Vie de Beethoven, 1907. Tr. F. Rothwell, *Beethoven*, London 1907; tr. B. C. Hull, London and New York 1917.
Musiciens d'autrefois, 1908. Tr. M. Blaiklock, *Some musicians of former days*, London and New York 1915.
Musiciens d'aujourd'hui, 1908. Tr. M. Blaiklock, *Musicians of today*, London 1915 (in *The musician's bookshelf*).
Vie de Tolstoï, 1911. Tr. B. Miall, *Tolstoy*, London and New York 1911.
Les tragédies de la foi, 1913 (cntg *Saint Louis*, first pbd in *Revue de Paris*, 1897, *Aërt*, first pbd 1898, *Le triomphe de la raison*, first pbd 1899).

Au-dessus de la mêlée, 1915. Tr. C. K. Ogden, *Above the battlefield*, London and Chicago (Ill) 1916.

Colas Breugnon, 1919; 1930.

Liluli, Geneva 1919. Tr. anon., New York 1920.

Voyage musical au pays du passé, 1920. Tr. B. Miall, *A musical tour through the land of the past*, London and New York 1922.

Pierre et Luce, Geneva 1920. Tr. C. De Kay, *Pierre and Luce*, London 1922·

Clérambault, 1920. Tr. anon. *Clerambault, or one against all*, Edinburgh 1933.

L'âme enchantée, 7 vols, 1922–33; 4 vols, 1934. Tr. B. R. Redman et al., *The soul enchanted*, 6 vols, New York 1925–1934.

Mahatma Gandhi, 1923; 1926. Tr. C. D. Groth, New York and London 1924.

Beethoven, les grandes époques créatrices, 7 vols, 1928–50. Tr. E. Newman, *Beethoven the creator*, London and New York 1929.

Essai sur la mystique et l'action de l'Inde vivante, 3 vols, 1929–30. Tr. E. F. Malcolm-Smith, *Prophets of the New India*, London and New York 1930. Comprising:

> *La vie de Ramakrishna*, 1929. Tr., *Ramakrishna*.
> *La vie de Vivekananda et l'Evangile universel*, 2 vols, 1930. Tr., *Vivekananda*.

Quinze ans de combat, 1919–34, 1935. Tr. K. S. Shelvankar, *I will not rest*, London 1936.

Par la révolution, la paix, 1935.

Le voyage intérieur, 1942; 1959 (enl.). Tr. E. Pell, *The journey within*, New York 1947.

Péguy, 2 vols, 1944.

Le périple, 1946.

Mémoires et fragments de journal, 1956.

Journal des années de guerre, 1914–1919, ed. M. Rolland, 1952.

Correspondance, 1948–67 (in *Cahiers Romain Rolland*, nos 1–17).

BARRÈRE, J. B., *Romain Rolland par lui-même*, 1955.

BONNEROT, J., *Romain Rolland, sa vie, son oeuvre, bibliographie*, 1921.

CHEVAL, R., *Romain Rolland, l'Allemagne et la guerre*, 1963.

JOUVE, P. J., *Romain Rolland vivant*, 1920.

MARCH, H., *Romain Rolland*, New York 1971.

ROBICHEZ, J., *Romain Rolland*, 1961.

SÉNÉCHAL, C., *Romain Rolland*, 1933.

STARR, W. T., *Romain Rolland and a world at war*, Evanston (Ill) 1956.
> *Romain Rolland*, The Hague and Paris 1971.

ZWEIG, S., *Romain Rolland: The man and his work*, New York 1921 (tr. E. and C. Paul).

ROMAINS, Jules   1885–1972
(pseudonym of Louis Farigoule)

Bibl. See BERRY below.

Théâtre, 7 vols, 1924–35.
Pièces en un acte, 1930.

Le bourg régénéré, 1906; 1920.
La vie unanime, poème, 1908.
Le manuel de déification, 1910.
Mort de quelqu'un, 1911. Tr. D. McCarthy and S. Waterlow, *The death of a nobody*, London 1914.
Puissances de Paris, 1911.
Odes et prières, 1913.
Les copains, 1913. Tr. J. LeClercq, *The boys in the back room*, New York 1937.
Sur les quais de La Villette, 1914; 1923 (renamed *Le vin blanc de La Villette*).
Europe, 1916.
Donogoo-Tonka, 1920.
La vision extra-rétinienne, 1920. Tr. C. K. Ogden, *Eyeless sight*, London and New York 1924.
Psyché, 3 vols, 1922–9. Tr. J. Rodker, *The body's rapture*, London and New York 1933. Comprising:
    Lucienne, 1922. Tr., *Lucienne's story*.
    Le dieu des corps, 1928. Tr., *The body's rapture*.
    Quand le navire, 1929. Tr., *Love's questing*.
M. le Trouhadec saisi par la débauche, 1922.
Knock, ou le triomphe de la médicine, 1924. Tr. H. Granville Barker, *Doctor Knock*, London 1925; tr. J. B. Gidney, *Knock*, New York 1962.
Le dictateur, 1926.
Chants des dix années, 1928.
Volpone (based on Jonson's play; in collab. with Stefan Zweig), 1929.
Les hommes de bonne volonté, 27 vols, 1932–46; 4 vols, 1958. Tr. W. B. Wells (vols 1–3) and G. Hopkins (vols 4–14), *Men of good will*, 14 vols, New York 1934–46.
L'homme blanc, 1937.
Grâce encore pour la Terre!, New York 1941.
Bertrand de Ganges, New York 1944.
L'an mil, 1947.
Pierres levées, 1948.
Le moulin et l'hospice, 1949.
Violation de frontières, 1951. Tr. G. Hopkins, *Tussles with time*, London 1952.
Le fils de Jerphanion, 1956.
Une femme singulière, 1957. Tr. A. Pomerans, *The adventuress*, London 1958.

Mémoires de Madame Chauverel, 2 vols, 1959–60.
Pour raison garder, 2 vols, 1960–3.
Ai-je fait ce que j'ai voulu?, 1964.
Lettre ouverte contre une vaste conspiration, 1966.
Amitiés et rencontres, 1970.

BERRY, M., *Jules Romains, sa vie, son oeuvre*, 1953 (incl. bibl.).
BOURIN, A. and J. R., *Connaissance de Jules Romains*, 1961.
CUISENIER, A., *Jules Romains et Les hommes de bonne volonté*, 1954.
FOWLIE, W., in his *Clowns and angels: studies in modern French literature*, New York 1943.
NORRISH, P. J., *Drama of the group, a study of unanimism in the plays of Jules Romains*, Cambridge 1958.

SAINT-EXUPÉRY, Antoine de   1900–1944

JENSEN, F. S., *Une bibliographie*, Copenhagen 1954.

Les oeuvres complètes, 1950; 1953; 1959.

Tr. L. Galantière and S. Gilbert, *Airman's odyssey*, New York 1943 (cntg *Flight to Arras, Night flight*, and *Wind, sand and stars*).

Courrier Sud, 1929. Tr. S. Gilbert, *Southern mail*, New York 1933.
Vol de nuit, 1931; ed. A. Bottequin, 1970. Tr. S. Gilbert, *Night flight*, Paris, New York and London 1932.
Terre des hommes, 1939. Tr. L. Galantière, *Wind, sand and stars*, London and Toronto 1939.
Pilote de guerre, New York 1942; Lyons 1943 (pbd clandestinely). Tr. L. Galantière, *Flight to Arras*, New York, London and Toronto 1942.
Lettre à un otage, New York 1943. Tr. J. Gerst, *Letter to a hostage*, London 1950.
Le petit prince, New York 1943. Tr. K. Woods, *The little prince*, New York 1943.
Citadelle, 1948; ed. P. Chevrier and L. Wencelius, 1959. Tr. S. Gilbert, *The wisdom of the sands*, New York 1950.
Un sens à la vie, textes inédits, ed. C. Reynal, 1956.

Carnets, ed. M. Quesnel and P. Chevrier, 1953.
Lettres de jeunesse, 1923–1931, ed. R. de Saussine, 1953.
Lettres à sa mère, 1956.

ALBÉRÈS, R. M., *Saint-Exupéry*, 1946; 1961.
CATE, C., *Antoine de Saint-Exupéry: his life and times*, London 1971.
CHEVRIER, P., *Antoine de Saint-Exupéry*, 1971.
MIGEO, M., *Saint-Exupéry*, 1958. Tr. H. Briffault, New York 1960.

ROY, J., *Passion et mort de Saint-Exupéry*, 1964 (*Passion* first pbd 1951).
QUESNEL, M., *Saint-Exupéry, ou la verité de la poésie*, 1965.

SAINT-JOHN PERSE   1887–
(pseudonym of Alexis Saintléger Léger)

LITTLE, J. R., *A bibliography*, London 1971.
See also *Oeuvres complètes* below.
LITTLE, J. R., *Word index of the complete prose and poetry*, Durham 1967.

Oeuvres complètes, 1972 (incl. correspondence and bibl.).
Oeuvre poétique, 1953; 2 vols, 1960; 3 vols, 1967–70.
Choix de textes, ed. A. Bosquet, 1953; 1971.

Tr. various, *Collected poems*, Princeton (NJ) 1971.

Eloges, 1911; 1925 (enl.); 1948 (enl.). Tr. L. Varèse, *Eloges and other poems*, New York 1944; 1956; tr. A. Hartley, *Panegyrics*, Harmondsworth 1959 (in *The Penguin book of French verse*, vol 4).
Anabase, 1924; 1948. Tr. T. S. Eliot, *Anabasis*, London 1930; 1959.
Exil, Buenos Aires 1942; Paris 1946 (with *Pluies*, first pbd Buenos Aires 1944, *Poème à l'étrangère*, and *Snows*); ed. R. Little, London 1970 (*Exil* only). Tr. D. Devlin, *Exile and other poems*, New York 1949 (with *Rains*, first pbd Sewanee (Tenn) 1945, *Poem to a foreign lady*, and *Snows*).
Vents, 1946. Tr. H. Chisholm, *Winds*, New York 1953.
Amers, 1957. Tr. W. Fowlie, *Seamarks*, New York 1958; tr. S. E. Morrison, Boston (Mass) 1964 (extracts, in his *Spring Tides*).
Chronique, 1960. Tr. R. Fitzgerald, New York 1961.
L'ordre des oiseaux, 1962. Tr. W. Fowlie, *Birds*, New York 1963; tr. R. Fitzgerald, 1966; tr. J. R. Little, Durham 1967; tr. E. Lucie-Smith, London 1970 (extracts, in *Anthology of French poetry today*).
Chant pour un équinox, 1972 (in *Oeuvres complètes* above).

BOSQUET, A., *Saint-John Perse*, 1953; 1971 (enl.).
EMMANUEL, P., *Saint-John Perse, praise and presence*, Washington 1971.
GALAND, R. M., *Saint-John Perse*, New York 1972.
KNODEL, A. J., *Saint-John Perse, a study of his poetry*, Edinburgh and Chicago (Ill) 1966.
LITTLE, J. R., *Saint-John Perse*, London 1973.
PAULHAN, J., and OSTER, P. (ed.), *Honneur à Saint-John Perse*, 1965.

SARRAUTE, Nathalie   1900–

Bibl. See CRANAKI and BELAVAL below.

Tropismes, 1938; 1957 (enl.); ed. S. M. Bell, London 1972. Tr. M. Jolas, *Tropisms*, London 1963.

Portrait d'un inconnu, 1948. Tr. M. Jolas, *Portrait of a man unknown*, New York and London 1959.

Martereau, roman, 1953. Tr. M. Jolas, New York 1959.

L'ère du soupçon, essais sur le roman, 1956. Tr. M. Jolas, *The age of suspicion*, London 1963 (with *Tropisms* above).

Le planétarium, roman, 1959. Tr. M. Jolas, *The planetarium*, New York 1960.

Les fruits d'or, 1963. Tr. M. Jolas, *The golden fruits*, New York 1964.

Le silence, suivi de Le mensonge, 1967. Tr. M. Jolas, *Silence and The lie*, London 1969.

Entre la vie et la mort, 1968. Tr. M. Jolas, *Between life and death*, New York 1969.

Isma, 1970 (with *Le silence* and *Le mensonge* above).

Vous les entendez?, 1972.

CRANAKI, M. and BELAVAL, Y., *Nathalie Sarraute*, 1965 (incl. bibl.).

MICHA, R., *Nathalie Sarraute*, 1966.

SONTAG, S., in her *Against interpretation*, New York 1966.

TEMPLE, R. Z., *Sarraute*, New York 1968.

TISON-BRAUN, M., *Nathalie Sarraute, ou la recherche de l'authenticité*, 1971.

SARTRE, Jean-Paul 1905–

CONTAT, M. and RYBALKA, M., *Les écrits de Sartre*, 1970.

See also FELL below; also MCMAHON below; also THODY below.

Théâtre, 1962.

Oeuvre romanesque, 5 vols, 1965.

Tr. various, ed. R. D. Cumming, *The philosophy of Jean-Paul Sartre*, New York 1965 (selection).

L'imagination, 1936. Tr. F. Williams, *Imagination*, Ann Arbor (Mich) 1962.

La nausée, 1938. Tr. L. Alexander, *The diary of Antoine Roquentin*, London 1949 (and Norfolk (Conn) as *Nausea*); tr. R. Baldick, *Nausea*, Harmondsworth 1965.

Le mur, 1939. Tr. L. Alexander, *The wall*, Norfolk (Conn) 1948 (and London 1949, as *Intimacy*).

Esquisse d'une théorie des émotions, 1939. Tr. B. Frechtman, *The emotions*, New York 1948; tr. P. Mairet, *Sketch for a theory of the emotions*, London 1962.

L'imaginaire, 1940. Tr. B. Frechtman, *The psychology of imagination*, New York 1948.

Les mouches, 1942. Tr. S. Gilbert, *The flies*, London 1946.

L'être et le néant, 1943. Tr. H. E. Barnes, *Being and nothingness*, New York 1956.

Huis clos, 1943. Tr. S. Gilbert, *In camera*, London 1946 (with *The flies* above); tr. P. Bowles, *No exit*, New York 1958.

Les chemins de la liberté, 1945–9. Comprising:

1 *L'âge de raison, roman*, 1945. Tr. E. Sutton, *The age of reason*, New York 1947.

2 *Le sursis*, 1945. Tr. E. Sutton, *The reprieve*, London and New York 1947.

3 *La mort dans l'âme*, 1949. Tr. G. Hopkins, *Iron in the soul*, London 1950 (New York 1951, as *Troubled sleep*).

La putain respectueuse, 1946. Tr. K. Black, *The respectful prostitute*, London 1949; tr. L. Abel, New York 1949.

Réflexions sur la question juive, 1946. Tr. E. de Mauny, *Portrait of the anti-Semite*, London 1948; tr. G. J. Becker, *Anti-Semite and Jew*, New York 1948.

Morts sans sépulture, Lausanne 1946. Tr. K. Black, *Men without shadows*, London 1949; tr. L. Abel, *The victors*, New York 1949.

L'existentialisme est un humanisme, 1946. Tr. B. Frechtman, *Existentialism*, New York 1947; tr. P. Mairet, *Existentialism and humanism*, London 1948.

Situations, 9 vols, 1947–72 (collected articles and criticism). Tr. B. Frechtman, *What is literature?*, New York 1949 (tr. of *Qu'est-ce que la littérature*, in *Situations III*); tr. A. Michelson, *Literary and philosophical essays*, London 1955 (selection); tr. B. Eisler, *Situations*, London 1965 (tr. of *Situations IV*).

Baudelaire, 1947; 1963. Tr. M. Turnell, Norfolk (Conn) 1949.

Les jeux sont faits, 1947. Tr. L. Varèse, *The chips are down*, New York 1948.

Les mains sales, 1948. Tr. K. Black, *Crime passionnel*, London 1949; tr. L. Abel, *Dirty hands*, New York 1949.

L'engrenage, 1948. Tr. M. Savill, *In the mesh*, London 1954.

Entretiens sur la politique (in collab. with David Rousset and Gérard Rosenthal), 1949.

Le diable et le bon Dieu, 1951; ed. D. J. Conlon, London 1971. Tr. K. Black, *Lucifer and the Lord*, London 1953.

Saint Genet, comédien et martyr, 1952. Tr. B. Frechtman, *Saint Genet: actor and martyr*, New York 1963.

Kean (adapt. from DUMAS Père), 1954; ed. D. Bradby, London 1973. Tr. K. Black, London 1954; tr. F. Hauser, 1972.

Nekrassov, 1955. Tr. S. and G. Leeson, London 1956.

Les séquestrés d'Altona, 1960. Tr. G. and S. Leeson, *Loser wins*, London 1960 (and New York, as *The condemned of Altona*).

Critique de la raison dialectique, 1960 (with *Question de méthode*, tr. H. E. Barnes, *The problem of method*, London 1963).

Les mots, 1963. Tr. I. Cléphane, *Words*, London 1964; tr. B. Frechtman, New York 1964.

Les Troyennes (adapt. from Euripides), 1965. Tr. R. Duncan, *The Trojan women*, London and New York 1967.
L'idiot de la famille, 3 vols, 1972.

ALBÉRÈS, R. M., *Jean-Paul Sartre*, 1953; 1960.
FELL, J. P., *Emotion in the thought of Sartre*, New York 1965 (incl. bibl.).
GARAUDY, R., *Questions à Jean-Paul Sartre*, 1962.
JEANSON, F., *Le problème moral et la pensée de Sartre*, 1947; 1965 (with *Un quidam nommé Sartre*).
　　Sartre par lui-même, 1955.
KERN, E. G. (ed.), *Sartre, a collection of critical essays*, New York 1962.
LAING, R. D. and COOPER, D. G., *Reason and violence*, London 1964.
MCMAHON, J. H., *Humans being, the world of Jean-Paul Sartre*, Chicago (Ill) 1964 (incl. bibl.).
MASTERS, B., *Sartre, a study*, London and Totowa (NJ) 1974.
MURDOCH, I., *Sartre, romantic rationalist*, Cambridge and New Haven (Conn) 1953.
PAISSAC, H., *Le dieu de Sartre*, 1950.
PATTE, D., *L'athéisme d'un Chrétien*, 1965.
SUHL, B., *Jean-Paul Sartre, the philosopher as literary critic*, New York and London 1970.
THODY, P., *Sartre, a literary and political study*, London and New York 1960 (incl. bibl.).
　　Sartre, London 1971.

SENGHOR, Léopold　1906–

Bibl. See Mercier-Battestini ed. of *Poète sénégalais* below; also MEZU below

Poèmes, 1964 (collected poems).
Poète sénégalais, ed. R. Mercier, M. and S. Battestini, 1964 (selection; incl. bibl.).

Tr. J. Reed and C. Wake, *Selected poems*, Oxford and New York 1964.
Tr. and ed. J. Reed and C. Wake, *Prose and poetry*, Oxford 1965 (selection).

Chants d'ombre, 1945.
Hosties noires, 1948.
Chants pour Naëtt, 1949.
Ethiopiques, 1956.
Nocturnes, 1961 (incorporating *Chants pour Naëtt* above, renamed *Chants pour Signare*). Tr. J. Reed and C. Wake, London 1969.
Nation et voie africaine du socialisme, 1961.
Liberté, 1964–71. Comprising:

1 *Négritude et humanisme*, 1964. Tr. M. Cook, *On African socialism*, New York and London 1964 (pt 1).

2 *Nation et voie africaine du socialisme*, 1971 (first pbd 1961 above).

BÂ, S. W., *The concept of negritude in the poetry of Léopold-Sédar Senghor*, Princeton (NJ) 1973.

MARKOVITZ, I. L., *Senghor and the politics of negritude*, London 1969.

MEZU, S. O., *Léopold-Sédar Senghor et la défense et illustration de la civilisation noire*, 1968 (incl. bibl.).

The poems of Léopold-Sédar Senghor, London 1973.

MILCENT, E. and SORDET, M., *Léopold-Sédar Senghor et la naissance de l'Afrique moderne*, 1969.

MOORE, G. S., in his *Seven African writers*, Oxford 1968.

SUPERVIELLE, Jules   1884–1960

Bibl. See ETIEMBLE below; also ROY below.

Poèmes choisis, Montevideo 1959.
Contes et poèmes, ed. J. Orr, Edinburgh 1950 (selection).

Tr. M. Boulton, *The shell and the ear*, Hull 1951.
Tr. J. Kirkup et al., *Selected writings*, New York 1967 (poems).
Tr. T. Savory, *Poems*, Santa Barbara (Calif) and London 1967.

Poèmes: Voyage en soi; Paysages; Les poèmes de l'humour triste; Le goyavier authentique, 1919.
Débarcadères, 1922.
L'homme de la Pampa, 1923.
Gravitations, 1925; 1932.
Le voleur d'enfants, 1926. Tr. A. Pryce-Jones, *The Colonel's children*, London 1950.
Le survivant, 1929. Tr. J. Russell, *The survivor*, London 1951.
Le forçat innocent, 1930 (incl. *Oloron Sainte Marie*, first pbd 1927).
L'enfant de la haute mer, 1930 (incl. *Le boeuf et l'âne de la crèche*, tr. D. Starke, *The ox and ass at the manger*, London 1932; tr. N. R. Smith, 1945). Tr. D. Japp and N. Nicholls, *Souls of the soulless*, London 1933.
La belle au bois, 1932; 1953.
Les amis inconnus, 1934.
Bolivar, 1936.
L'arche de Noë, 1938.
La fable du monde, 1938.
Poèmes de la France malheureuse, 1939–1941, Buenos Aires 1941.
1939–1945, poèmes, 1945.
Shéhérazade, 1949.
Oublieuse mémoire, 1949.

Premiers pas de l'univers, 1950.
Naissances, poèmes, suivis de: En songeant à un art poétique, 1951.
Robinson, 1953 (with *La belle au bois* above).
Le corps tragique, 1959.

BLAIR, D. S., *Jules Supervielle, a modern fabulist*, Oxford 1960.
ETIEMBLE, R., *Supervielle*, 1960 (incl. bibl.); 1968 (abr.).
HIDDLESTON, J. A., *L'univers de Jules Supervielle*, 1965.
ROY, C., *Jules Supervielle*, 1949 (incl. bibl.); 1970.

TZARA, Tristan   1896–1963
(pseudonym of Samuel Rosenfeld)

Bibliographie des oeuvres, 1916–1950, 1951.

La première aventure céleste de Monsieur Antipyrine, Zurich 1916.
    La deuxième aventure, 1938.
Vingt-cinq poèmes, Zurich 1918.
Sept manifestes dada, 1924; 1963.
Mouchoir de nuages, 1925.
L'homme approximatif, 1931.
Où boivent les loups, 1932.
L'antitête, 1933.
Grains et issues, 1935.
Le coeur à gaz, 1946.
Midis gagnés, poèmes, 1939; 1948 (enl.).
La fuite, poème dramatique, 1947.
Morceaux choisis, 1947.
Le surréalisme et l'après-guerre, 1947.
Le fruit permis, 1956.
Lampisteries, 1963 (collected texts 1917–24, with *Sept manifestes dada* above).

LACÔTE, R. and HALDAS, G., *Tristan Tzara*, 1952; 1960.
SANOUILLET, M., *Dada à Paris*, 1965.

VALÉRY, Paul   1871–1945

DAVIS, R. and SIMONSON, R., *Bibliographie des oeuvres*, 1926.
ARNOLD, A. J., *Paul Valéry and his critics*, Charlottesville (Va) 1970.
See also Hytier ed. of *Oeuvres* below; also LATOUR below.

Oeuvres complètes, 12 vols, 1931–52; ed. J. Hytier, 2 vols, 1957–60 (incl. bibl. in vol 2).

Tr. D. Devlin et al., *Selected writings*, Norfolk (Conn) 1950.
Tr. J. Mathews et al., *Collected works*, New York 1956 onwards (13 vols pbd).

Also translated in anthologies, incl. *Cassell's anthology of French poetry*, tr. A. Conder, London 1950; *An anthology of French poetry from Nerval to Valéry*, ed. A. Flores, Garden City (NY) 1958.

Introduction à la méthode de Léonard de Vinci, 1895. Tr. T. McGreevy, *Introduction to the method of Leonardo da Vinci*, London and New York 1929.

La soirée avec Monsieur Teste, 1896. Tr. R. Davis, *An evening with Monsieur Teste*, Paris 1925; tr. M. Gould, London 1936; tr. J. Mathews, *Monsieur Teste*, New York 1948.

La Jeune Parque, 1917.

Album de vers anciens, 1890–1900, 1921.

Charmes, ou poèmes, 1922 (incl. *Le cimetière marin*, tr. C. Day Lewis, *The graveyard by the sea*, London 1946; tr. G. D. Martin, Edinburgh 1971); ed. C. G. Whiting, London 1973.

L'âme et la danse, 1923. Tr. D. Bussy, *Dance and the soul*, London 1951.

Eupalinos, ou l'architecte, 1923 (with *L'âme et la danse* above). Tr. W. McC. Stewart, *Eupalinos, or the architect*, London and New York 1932.

Variété, 5 vols, 1924–44. Tr. M. Cowley, *Variety*, New York 1927 (tr. of vol 1); tr. W. A. Bradley, *Variety, Second series*, New York 1938 (selection from vols 2 and 3).

Propos sur l'intelligence, 1925.

Regards sur le monde actuel, 1931. Tr. F. Scarfe, *Reflections on the world today*, New York 1948.

L'idée fixe, ou deux hommes à la mer, 1933.

Degas, Danse, Dessin, 1938 (in *Oeuvres complètes* above). Tr. H. Burlin, *Degas, Dance, Drawing*, New York 1948.

Mon Faust, 1941.

Mauvaises pensées et autres, 1941.

Cahiers, 29 vols, 1957–61; ed. J. Robinson, 1973 onwards (1 vol pbd; selection).

Correspondance André Gide-Paul Valéry, 1890–1942, ed. R. Mallet, 1955. Tr. J. Guicharnaud, *Self-portraits: the Gide-Valéry letters*, Chicago (Ill) 1966 (abr.).

BELLEMIN-NOEL, J., (ed.), *Les critiques de notre temps et Valéry*, 1971.

BOURBON-BUSSET, J. de., *Paul Valéry, ou le mystique sans Dieu*, 1964.

CAIN, L. J., *Trois essais sur Paul Valéry*, 1958.

CROW, C. M., *Paul Valéry, consciousness and nature*, Cambridge 1972.

DUCHESNE-GUILLEMIN, J., *Etudes pour un Paul Valéry*, Neuchâtel 1964.

GRUBBS, H. A., *Paul Valéry*, New York 1968.

HYTIER, J., *La poétique de Valéry*, 1953. Tr. R. Howard, *The poetics of Valéry*, Magnolia (Mass) 1967.

INCE, W. N., *The poetic theory of Paul Valéry*, London 1961.
LATOUR, J. de, *Examen de Valéry*, 1935 (incl. bibl. of prose works).
LAWLER, J. R., *Lecture de Valéry: une étude de Charmes*, 1963.
MONDOR, H., *Propos familiers de Paul Valéry*, 1957.
    Précocité de Valéry, 1957.
ROBINSON, J., *L'analyse de l'esprit dans les Cahiers de Valéry*, 1963.
SCARFE, F., *The art of Paul Valéry*, London 1954.
THIBAUDET, A., *Paul Valéry*, 1923.
WALZER, P. O., *La poésie de Valéry*, Geneva 1953.

VIAN, Boris   1920–1959

Bibl. See DUCHÂTEAU below.

Théâtre, 2 vols, 1965–71 (complete except for *Les bâtisseurs d'empire*).
Théâtre, 1965 (cntg *Les bâtisseurs d'empire*, *Equarrissage pour tous* and *Le goûter des généraux*).

J'irai cracher sur vos tombes, 1946.
Vercoquin et le plancton, 1946.
L'automne à Pekin, 1947.
L'écume des jours, 1947. Tr. S. Chapman, *Froth on the daydream*, London 1967; tr. J. Sturrock, *Mood indigo*, New York 1969.
Barnum's digest, 1948.
Les fourmis, 1949.
Equarrissage pour tous, 1950. Tr. M. Estrin, *Knackery for all*, New York 1966; tr. S. W. Taylor, *Knacker's ABC*, New York 1968.
L'herbe rouge, 1950.
Le dernier des métiers, 1950.
Cantilènes en gelée, 1950.
L'arrache-coeur, 1953. Tr. S. Chapman, *Heartsnatcher*, New York and London 1968.
Le chevalier de neige, 1953.
En avant la zizique et par ici les gros sous, 1958.
Je voudrais pas crever, 1959.
Les bâtisseurs d'empire, ou le Schmürz, 1959. Tr. S. W. Taylor, *The empire builders*, London 1962.
Les lurettes fourrées, 1962.
Le goûter des généraux, 1963. Tr. S. W. Taylor, *Generals' tea party*, Harmondsworth 1967.
Trouble dans les Andains, 1966.
Théâtre inédit, ed. N. Arnaud, 1970 (cntg *Tête de Méduse*, *Série blême*, *Le chasseur français*).
Le loup-garou, ed. N. Arnaud, 1970 (with other stories).

ARNAUD, N., *Les vies parallèles de Boris Vian*, 1966.

BAUDIN, H., *Boris Vian, la poursuite de la vie totale*, 1966.
CISMARU, A., *Boris Vian*, New York 1974.
CLOUZET, J., *Boris Vian*, 1966.
DUCHÂTEAU, J., *Boris Vian*, 1969 (incl. bibl.).
NOAKES, W. D., *Boris Vian, témoin d'une époque*, 1964.
RYBALKA, M., *Boris Vian, essai d'interprétation*, 1969.

VITRAC, Roger   1899–1952

Théâtre, 4 vols, 1946–64.
Dés-lyre, poésies complètes, ed. H. Béhar, 1964.

Connaissance de la mort, 1926.
Cruautés de la nuit, Marseilles 1927.
Victor, ou les enfants au pouvoir, 1929.
Le coup de Trafalgar, 1935.
Les demoiselles du large, 1938 (in *Les Oeuvres Libres*, no. 206).
Le camelot, 1946 (in *Théâtre*, vol 1 above).
Les mystères de l'amour, 1948 (in *Théâtre*, vol 2 above). Tr. R. J. Gladstone, *The mysteries of love*, New York 1964.
Le loup-garou, 1948 (in *Théâtre*, vol 2 above).
Le sabre de mon père, 1951.

BÉHAR, H., *Roger Vitrac, un réprouvé du surréalisme*, 1966.

Yacine KATEB

See KATEB Yacine.

Index of Writers